5

THE COLONIAL PERIOD OF AMERICAN HISTORY

THE SETTLEMENTS
III

THE COLONIAL PERIOD

OF

AMERICAN HISTORY

BY

CHARLES M. ANDREWS

With a New Foreword by Leonard W. Labaree

THE SETTLEMENTS

III

NEW HAVEN AND LONDON · YALE UNIVERSITY PRESS

Copyright 1937 by Yale University Press and
© 1964 by Yale University.
Ninth printing, September 1967.
Printed in the United States of America by
The Murray Printing Company,
Forge Village, Massachusetts.

CONTENTS

CONTENTS

FOREWORD

THE four volumes of *The Colonial Period of American History* which Charles McLean Andrews published between 1934 and 1938 were the culmination of a lifetime of thought and study by the man who was generally recognized as the outstanding American colonial historian of his generation. He had produced his first work in the field in 1889, and as his books and articles continued to appear during the years that followed, the special features of his approach and interpretation became increasingly evident. They found their fullest expression in these four volumes, his last major contributions to our understanding of the Colonial Period.

A combination of three characteristics sets this work apart from all other general histories of the American colonies which had gone before or have appeared since Andrews wrote: First, the volumes give strong emphasis to the English background. He viewed the colonies as what they were at the time—parts of the expanding English world—and not as what some of them later became—units of a transatlantic republic. They were the products of a great movement in the British Isles for the occupation and settlement of fruitful areas across the ocean. The men, the circumstances, and the institutions in England responsible for that movement and later the policies developed in Great Britain for the exploitation and development of these "plantations" all receive major attention. Second, Andrews wrote not only of the colonies which declared their independence in 1776, but also of those which did not: Bermuda, the West Indies, Nova Scotia, and Newfoundland. In the seventeenth century and most of the eighteenth the English colonial world was a single indivisible whole; to understand that world as it actually was, it became necessary in Andrews' judgment to understand all its interrelated parts. No other work on a comparable scale has treated all these seventeenth-century settlements as equally significant parts of the general history of English colonization in the New World. Third, in common with many scholars of his generation, Andrews adopted a largely institutional approach. While earlier writers usually followed a narrative "political" thread for the most part, and many more recent scholars have been chiefly interested in social, economic, or intellectual developments, Andrews believed that a people's institutions—chiefly though by no means exclusively their political institutions—offered the best clues to that people's character and development.

The first three volumes, subtitled *The Settlements,* deal with the English background of the colonizing movement and with the establishment of communities of Englishmen along the Atlantic coast of North America and on nearby islands. Each such community is treated separately. The first two volumes are concerned with those projected before 1650, the third with those settled in the second half of the seventeenth century. In each instance the author carries the narrative down to the date (which differs from one colony to another) at which it can be said to be firmly established, when its institutions are well rooted and the direction of its further development can be clearly discerned. The fourth volume, called *England's Commercial and Colonial Policy,* describes the gradual development in the mother country of a program through which these overseas possessions could be brought into an effective and profitable relationship to Britain herself. As the subtitle suggests, this program and the laws and regulations adopted to carry it out were largely economic in emphasis. In the minds of Englishmen of the seventeenth and eighteenth centuries colonies were worth having and worth protecting against foreign enemies only if their trade and commerce could be so channeled and controlled and their economic life so developed that they would benefit the homeland as well as themselves. This volume is still the most thorough and complete treatment in print of the evolution of British colonial policy and of the means adopted to carry out that policy, its successes, and its failures, in the years before 1763.

One day early in December 1937, Andrews said to the writer of this foreword: "This morning I took the finished manuscript of my fourth volume to the Press. I have now done the job I promised the Press and myself that I would do. If I live and am able to complete the other volumes I planned, well and good. But if not, I am satisfied. These four volumes are the ones I just *had* to write." He had indeed planned three more parts of this work, but serious illness intervened while the fourth volume was in page proofs (he had just celebrated his seventy-fifth birthday), and though he lived until September 1943, he never regained sufficient physical strength to resume the heavy burden that writing on this extensive scale required.

The fact that he never completed the other volumes called for by his original plan has led some critics to accuse him of having only a limited and partial approach to the general subject of his *magnum opus*. Recognizing that this might be so, he wrote an extended paper, probably sometime in 1938 or 1939, in which he explained his scheme for the whole work, which he said had been "clearly in mind from the beginning," and his specific intent for the volumes which he never wrote. In accordance with his wishes, this paper remained unpublished until after his death.[1]

Upon the broad base of the first three volumes on colonial settlement, he explained, stood the fourth volume representing the British side of the developing Anglo-American structure. The fifth projected volume was to present the other side; in it "we would take our stand on colonial soil and see what was happening there during the first sixty years of the eighteenth century." Instead of dealing with institutional aspects of colonial history, it would be concerned with the "social, economic, educational, domestic, and religious, and in some respects political," evolution of American life and would reveal "trends and divergencies [from British patterns] indicating a progressive movement and indicative of what may be called an Americanizing process." These developments, as Andrews saw them, fostered change and growth in the political and institutional aspects of colonial society. Volume 6 would therefore be a political, and especially a constitutional, history of eighteenth-century America, which would give particular emphasis to the evolution of the colonial assembly and its slow winning "of a place in each colony analagous to that of the House of Commons in England at the same time." The seventh and last volume would deal with the years after 1763, when the colonies, with "practical self-government" achieved, came into conflict with the British government, which still adhered to its policy of holding the colonies in strict subjection and was even introducing new forms of enforcement. "Thus the colonial situation which was hardly American at all in the seventeenth century, takes on an Anglo-American coloring during the first sixty years of the eighteenth, owing to the formulation for the first time by the mother country of a clear-cut colonial policy, and becomes discordantly Anglo-American during the years 1763-1776, when the issue takes

---

1. "On the Writing of Colonial History," *William and Mary Quarterly*, 3d Series, I (1944), 27–48.

the form of an open conflict between self-government on one side and centralization on the other."

This was the plan on which Andrews would have carried through his project had he been able. We must regret that the final three volumes had to be left unwritten. Yet we can only be grateful for the four he did write during the five years after his retirement from more than four decades as a college and university professor. In this reissue of *The Colonial Period of American History* a new generation of readers will still find not only a great narrative of American beginnings, skillfully told, but a broad view of the characteristics and attitudes of the men and women on both sides of the Atlantic whose faith and optimism made those beginnings possible.

New Haven, Connecticut
February 1964   LEONARD W. LABAREE

BY WAY OF PREFACE

WITH the settlement of New England, the founding of Maryland, and the occupation of the islands in the West Indies, the first period of English colonization in America was brought to an end. There continued to be, as a matter of course, frequent journeyings back and forth across the Atlantic, of Puritans returning to the mother country, of royalists fleeing to Virginia and Barbados, and of new settlers migrating to all the colonies, but between 1634 and 1670 no successful effort was made to plant new settlements on American soil. Except by conquest in Jamaica and New Netherland, nothing was done during these years to widen, in any important particular, the area of English inhabitancy. Englishmen at home had other things to think of, and with the single exception of Virginia, which was taken over by the crown in 1624, they paid very little attention before 1660 to their plantations overseas. During that time there existed a highly decentralized relationship between the colonies and the mother country, a condition which created in the minds of the people already in America a strong feeling of self-sufficiency and which, because of their distance from England and the necessity of trusting in themselves for protection and maintenance, produced among them a lively spirit of local independence.

The second period begins with England's capture of Jamaica in 1655, which ushered in a new era of English and colonial history. The newness is to be discovered, not so much in matters constitutional and political, for the government of Charles II was still structurally medieval and Englishmen of the period still based their legal rights and liberties on "ancientry," as in the intellectual, spiritual, and material life of the times. It appears in the moods of the people, in the changing attitude toward religious beliefs and practices, and in a more pronounced and matter of fact approach to the phenomena of existence. Because of these various and varying shiftings of outlook, the second period bears a gloss of modernity and is farther removed from the days of the first period than the mere difference in time would lead one to suppose. The influence of the civil wars and the Interregnum had been so far-reaching as to change the whole direction of English thought and purpose.

Before 1640 men's minds turned to the past and their actions were governed by habits and traditions still Elizabethan; by the lingering influence of the Reformation and the religious wars; and by the patterns of the literary renaissance, the zest for exploration and discovery, and the abiding hostility for Spain. After 1660 these influences abated. Englishmen, tired of conflicts over creeds, became less emotional in their convictions, more sober and rational. Gradually emancipating themselves from the religious and ethical speculations of the past they came to view the problems of the time with a new understanding. This new attitude toward life in general was exhibited not only by the intellectual leaders and writers on social and economic affairs, but also by those who were engaged in business and in the practical work of government. More than ever before men's interests became worldly and opportunist. More than ever before their imaginations were stirred by the new learning, which declared that nature and man as well as God were worthy objects of study and investigation. This powerful impulse was discernible in the founding of the Royal Society and the awakened interest of its members in scientific knowledge; in the inquiries sent out for all kinds of curious information about England herself and especially about her distant colonies; in the triumphs of Sir Isaac Newton, whose researches, embodied in his famous *Principia,* were first published in 1687; and in the rise to prominence of a remarkable group of men of ability and genius, whose record of achievement has rarely been equalled within so short a period of time.

The heroic age of Puritanism had passed. The divorce between godly discipline as the chief end of human existence and worldly happiness and prosperity as equivalent ends in themselves was already complete. Instead of subordinating man's material welfare to the need of creating a new heaven and a new earth, as the early Puritans had felt called upon to do, the nonconformists of the Restoration saw no harm in cultivating the earth as it was and of finding their duty therein, particularly their duty in business—in the making of cloth, if possible, as that was the godliest of the trades. These Dissenters were the merchants, manufacturers, and middlemen of the period, who in London and the outports and in the textile and clothing towns of the interior were industrially in the ascendant. Always a minority and excluded from high political office, they devoted themselves to a combination of religious radicalism and money-making, finding nothing incongruous in the union.

As time went on, the cloak and sword of the courtier and the somber garb of the Puritan became less conspicuous as the broadcloth of the merchant found its place in the picture, and the courtesy literature of the gallants and the religious polemics of the regenerate were overshadowed by the pamphlets of the mercantilists and the ledgers of the counting house. Like their Puritan predecessors the later Dissenters were devout, but they were not intolerant. They believed that man's religious duty on earth was not impaired by an unfettered play of economic self-interest. They denounced the laws enforcing conformity as not only contrary to the edicts of God but as economically injurious also, just as they denounced the granting of monopolies and the erection of monopolistic corporations as impeding industrial and commercial progress. They favored greater liberty of opinion and greater freedom of trade within the kingdom, even while opposing freedom of trade abroad, an opposition based on the belief held by all orthodox mercantilists that freedom of foreign trade was to England's disadvantage.

Because of these changing views of a new generation, men in office and those who were engaged in private enterprises were ready to promote any policy that would prove financially profitable either on land or on the sea. Hence their willingness to abandon gradually the wasteful open-field system in agriculture and to increase the number of enclosures in the interest of better farming, an increase that was as dear to the heart of the country gentleman as was the breaking of monopolies and the relaxing of the state's control over industry dear to the heart of the man in trade. Hence their demand for the laws of shipping and navigation, as necessary to further the advancement of England's commerce beyond the seas. Hence their shaping of a colonial policy that would render the colonies more valuable assets in England's progress toward commercial and colonial leadership and contributors to her power in competition with her maritime rivals on the continent of Europe.

This interest in material prosperity—one of the outstanding features of the second period of English colonization in America—checked for the time being movements begun under Charles I and continued during the Interregnum for the betterment of the poor and the indigent, the vagabond and the criminal. Not for another century was the welfare of all the people (from a strictly humanitarian point of view) to receive attention. Capitalism was in the saddle and those who lagged behind in the race for employment were rated beyond the pale, as inherently idle, incompetent, and over-indulgent in drink—capitalistic tools for the increase of profits. Hence the enforcement of the unsympathetic poor laws and the inhuman treatment in England of the poor in the cities and the vagrant in the country, and, in the colonies, of the negro and the indentured servant. The criminal always bore the stigma of incorrigibility. Capitalism at this time was a restricted, not a nationalistic, impropriation, and under mercantilism—the influence of which was much more powerful in England and Holland than in France, where, despite the retention of serfdom, behavior toward the poor was less harsh—labor was utilized for the wealth and power of the state and its privileged members. Nationalism and a nationalistic benevolence, as they were beginning to be understood in the late eighteenth and early nineteenth centuries, were beyond the mental range of the men of the Restoration.

It was during these early years of the ascendancy of state and trade in England that the further work of colonizing America was taken up and carried on. They were years of transition, confusion, and striking contrasts. The powers of kingship were at their highest point of legal recognition, despite the fact that Charles II never had enough money wherewith to run either court or kingdom, that the court itself was at loose ends both officially and morally, and that James II was able in three short years to destroy the foundations of the divine plan upon which the system rested. The members of the nobility at Whitehall and elsewhere, though still powerful in decay and protected by the privilege of peers, were, with some noteworthy exceptions, possessed of little moral stamina and were looked upon by those who lived in the cities and the provinces, Anglicans and Dissenters alike, as debauched, spendthrift, and corrupt. Undoubtedly most of them were all of these things; in any case they were not representative of England's best people, those of the countryside, where higher standards of comfort, decency, and right living prevailed, where men were possessed of a larger measure of sobriety and sanity, and where the country gentleman, though not free from the vices of his time, was often an astute business man as well as a squire and a farmer. The hysteria of the period, the fears of Roman Catholic domination, the plots and counterplots, the suspicions of the government and its use of spies and informers, the scandals of a royal entourage largely under French influence, and the self-seeking lives of the hangers-on wherever that entourage might be—all these conditions were but little more than the conspicuous and important but temporary events of a great era. An age that possessed such men as Robert Boyle, who more than anyone else appreciated the importance of the experimental method, Petty, Evelyn, Pepys, Hobbes, Penn, Locke, and Sir Christopher Wren—to mention only a few of its most distinguished men; that was breaking loose from tradition in a spirit of free inquiry; that was exhibiting a widespread desire among all thinking classes for toleration, compromise, and a cessation of conflict; and that was witnessing the slow expansion of the English kingdom into a colonial empire, such an age cannot be denominated either corrupt or degenerate. Its outstanding significance lies in the fact that whereas the first period of colonization took its cues from the past, this, the second period, was preparing the cues for the future.

It was not until the Revolution of 1689, when toleration was established by law and the nonconformists came into their own as an estate of the realm which no government could afford to ignore, that this remarkable period of preparation and achievement reached its climax. Then it was that with colonization practically complete and revolution successful, England renewed her earlier experimental efforts to lay down a consistent maritime, commercial, and colonial programme. How far her experiences with the colonies up to this time contributed to the formation of such a programme and how far progress in the colonies themselves prepared the way for the great struggle of the eighteenth century and the gradual transformation of that which was English into something we can begin to call American the following chapters are intended to show.

THE COLONIAL PERIOD OF AMERICAN HISTORY

CHAPTER I

ROUGH SHAPING A POLICY: I. THE WESTERN DESIGN AND JAMAICA

WITH the oncoming of the civil wars in England and the establishment of the Commonwealth the most diversified and picturesque period of English settlement in America came to an end. It had been marked by many divergencies of origin and varieties of motives and had presented many characteristics that were the inevitable accompaniment of the beginnings of all great colonizing movements in the world's history. Coincident with a troubled time in England, when the commercial, political, religious, and social conditions of the English people were in a state of effervescence, working sometimes in harmony but more often at cross purposes with each other, the settlement of the colonies reproduced to a larger extent than ever was to be the case afterward the complex activities of a confused and changing era. Tracing their earliest manifestations to the adolescent years of Elizabethan expansion, the many early attempts at colonization had pursued a course of failure and success for more than half a century, until by 1650 there were in America and the West Indies thirteen separate communities of people—in Virginia, Bermuda, New Plymouth, Massachusetts Bay, Barbados, St. Christopher, Antigua, Nevis, Montserrat, Connecticut, Rhode Island, New Haven, and Maryland—all busy centers of human existence. The circumstances of their founding, wrapped up as they were with the events of a formative time in England's advance to national stature, are of absorbing interest. They bring into strong relief deeds of adventure and heroism, acts of courage and ordeals of suffering, and they give birth to individuals of remarkable powers, both physical and mental. They put before us experiences that were new, the outcome of which was uncertain, and they show a continuous process of adaptation of English ways and institutions to an unfamiliar environment. Consequently these early years have something of romance in their history, and are glowing and illuminating in that they throw light on the efforts of many men of many minds to carry out their purposes and ideals in a remote quarter of the earth, extending from the bleak climate of Newfoundland and Maine to the tropical heat of Barbados and Guiana. No two of these efforts are alike, even within the same meridian, for all bear the marks of their origins, as private and independent undertakings, and each has a history and a personality of its own. So different are they, in motives, moods, and characteristics, in tendencies, objectives, and results, that any attempt at a synthetic or synoptic treatment of them in this early period of our history is clearly impossible.

But by the middle of the century many of the influences operative at the beginning of the colonizing movement were losing their force and passing away. The proprietary element, which had been conspicuous since the days of Gilbert and Raleigh, was for the moment almost entirely eliminated. Many of the nobility had been drawn into the wars on the side of the king and for the time being had lost not only all interest in colonization but also all opportunity to colonize. Charles I, after 1642, was in no position to issue proprietary charters, even if there had been, as there were not, men of rank who desired him to do so, and Charles II in exile, could do little to provide rewards for those who were aiding him from England or were personally associated with him in his distress. After the issue of the Gorges patent of 1639, no proprietary charters covering both government and soil came out of the English chancery until after the king had returned from his wanderings and was firmly seated on the English throne. Then it was that a new era of colonization began, different in many ways from that which had gone before, the impulses of which sprang not so much from individual initiative as from the desires and demands of men who were in close and intimate connection with Whitehall and the king. For this reason the second period of colonization is proprietary in character, the patents issued differing, in many ways, both in content and effects from those that had gone before.

The times were changing. The Puritan impetus was losing its momentum, and religious influences, despite the continued ascendancy of the Puritan minority during the Protectorate, were losing their hold on the minds of men. However strong these influences continued to be in shaping the faith and conduct of individuals, they were playing a steadily decreasing part in determining matters of state policy, retreating into the background as the demands of trade and commerce and the difficult task of balancing a budget were pressing for recognition and settlement. The Puritan opposition in England was becoming year by year less dangerous as one after another of the leaders was executed and many of the lesser men were imprisoned or driven from the country. On the political side, the Leveller movement and on the social and economic sides the curious Digger agitation were both dying out, and though the Millenarists and Fifth Monarchy men were still active, the dreams and utopias of radicals and idealists were finding fewer followers as the mood of the people at large fluctuated in the desire for a more stable and permanent order.[1] The influential classes in England were becoming more rational and less religious, more prosaic and less romantic, more worldly and less contemplative, and though there was to be agitation enough, both political and religious, during the thirty-eight years following the fall of the Protectorate, the issues at stake were less complex than had been those of thirty years before.

The forces that brought trade and commerce into the foreground were not created by either Cromwell or the Puritans. Cromwell was never commercially minded. By ancestry and experience he was rather the country gentleman, interested, outside of politics, in religion and the army, in land, farming, and property, and his thoughts, always of a deeply religious trend, were shaped much more by the Elizabethan tradition of hostility to Spain, of piratical seizures, and of sea-dog activities, than by the more peaceful but humdrum pursuit of foreign trade. He was more familiar with the battlefield than with the counting-house, and there is nothing in his career to show any special concern for mercantile enterprise or for the accumulation of wealth. But he was regardful of all that had to do with national finance and of any projects whatever that would enable the Puritan administration to pay its debts. The Protectorate faced many a financial crisis, because its yearly expenditures, particularly for the army and navy, were considerably larger than any expenditure had been under Charles I, and the financial methods in vogue, though

1. Pease, *The Leveller Movement* (1916); Behrens, *The Digger Movement* (1906); L. F. Brown, *The Political Activities of the Baptists and Fifth Monarchy Men during the Interregnum* (1912).

conducive to the eventual breaking down of the medieval system of raising money, were never effective in the important task of increasing the available income accruing to the Puritan exchequer. Cromwell's mode of taxation by monthly assessments and extraordinary levies was well conceived and executed, but his government was never able to evolve any satisfactory way of borrowing money, whereby to create anything analogous to a national debt, such as the ministers of Charles II brought into existence after the Stop of the Exchequer in 1672 and those of William in 1694 with the founding of the Bank of England.[1] This failure to borrow money on definite security and at short term rates, brought it about that on the accession of Richard Cromwell in 1658, a deficit existed of some £2,000,-000, so large as to be in part responsible for the depression which after five years of falling prices and overproduction, as well as of shortage of money, reached its height in 1659.[2] It caused distress and suffering among those who had made loans on the forms of security provided by various acts of parliament[3] or had been obliged to accept public faith bills or exchequer tallies (treasury orders), payable whenever there were funds available to meet them.

The merchants, of whom there were some two thousand or more in London and the outports, were demanding of the government that it consider the needs of foreign trade. They worked rather individually than as a class, for those engaged in trade had as yet comparatively little influence upon affairs of state. There were few of them in parliament, none at all in the governing councils or in the

---

1. Shaw in *The Owens College Historical Essays*, "The Beginnings of the National Debt." For Cromwell's financial difficulties, Firth, *The Last Years of the Protectorate*, II, 257–269.

2. Ashley, *Financial and Commercial Policy under the Cromwellian Protectorate*, chs. I–IX, p. 176. The "unspeakable scarcity of money," the refusal of the City of London, where Cromwell was unpopular, to make a loan, and the mounting costs of military and naval preparations, which kept the Protectorate always in a pressing need of funds, are constantly referred to in the despatches of the Venetian resident in England. *Calendar Venetian Papers*, 1653–1654, pp. 144, 174, 182, 185–186; 1655–1656, pp. 28, 224, 230, 233, 241, 253, 282, 286, 292, 306; 1657–1659, pp. 1, 85, 174–175; 1659–1661, pp. 94, 113, 127, 157, 176. He says that the peace of 1654 with the Dutch was due in large part to the excessive charges of the war and that Cromwell decided on the Western Design "to justify the heavy taxes which constitute an almost excessive burden on the people" (1655–1656, pp. 133, 224). Cromwell's inability to pay his soldiers, upon whom the continuance of the Protectorate rested, he thought had much to do with the eventual downfall of the Puritan government (1659–1661, pp. 6–8).

3. Firth and Rait, *Acts and Ordinances*, III, 85–86.

higher offices of administration, and only a small number were on the great committee of trade of 1655. Cromwell made occasional use of them on special committees of advice and deferred to them, both as members of committees and as individuals, when matters of business came up that were connected with the colonies, and he placed individual merchants and contractors in administrative posts, listening with sympathy and understanding to their opinions and to those of others possessing mercantile reputations.[1] Those thus selected, as well as others "behind the curtain," were up to a certain point influential in their suggestions as to policy, perhaps in minor rather than in major matters, but the merchants as a whole were far from always in accord among themselves as to the best course to pursue. Some favored war, others opposed it; some wished trade to be free and loose and ports free and open, while others adhered to the old practice of monopoly and to embargoes on the export of food and raw materials, munitions, and gold and silver, the last named representing the "bullionist" phase of mercantilist thought.[2] Hence at no time during the Protectorate do we find any well defined or clear cut programme for the management either of trade or of the colonies.

Cromwell himself never conceived or formulated such a programme. He never rose to any statesmanlike understanding of the importance of foreign trade or appreciated the necessity of a large and comprehensive plan of colonial administration and control. The times were hardly ripe for conceptions of this kind and the translating of visions into realities is always a slow process, in which hidden

1. Andrews, British Committees, 1622–1675, ch. II; Ashley, pp. 8–11.

2. Though there is nothing to show that Cromwell was influenced by "bullionist" opinion, he may have been in favor of reserves of precious metals and a favorable balance of trade as one way to obtain money wherewith to balance his budget. The chief writers of the period are Sir Ralph Maddison, England Looking In and Out (1640), reprinted in 1655 as Great Britains Remembrancer, Looking in and out . . . presented to his Highness the Lord Protector and to the High Court of Parliament now assembled, dealing with the balance of trade, free ports, and the bullion question; Henry Robinson, England's Safety in Trades Increase (1641, reprinted in W. A. Shaw, Writers on English Monetary History, 1628–1730, 2d printing, 1935) and Lewes Roberts, The Merchant's Mappe of Commerce (first ed. folio, London, 1638, 2d ed., 1671, corrected and enlarged, 3d ed., 1677, 4th ed., 1700), and Treasure of Traffike (1641). Gerald Malynes, an old Dutch merchant, had already written The Maintenance of Free Trade (1622) and Consuetudo, vel Lex Mercatoria, and Thomas Mun had written in 1621 A Discourse of Trade, in which he had defended the trade of the East India Company, rather against the bullionists than for them, thus preparing the way for his own version of 1630 (1664) and other versions of mercantilism.

forces are often working toward ends that are unforeseen. But many of Cromwell's expedients show that he had an inkling of the presence of these powerful commercial and mercantile factors that were preparing the way for a final ascendancy of trade interests, and for the leadership of men possessed of initiative, energy, and wealth, who were eager to take advantage of such opportunities as might offer for the enlargement of their business and the widening of their influence.

Their opportunity finally came with the despatch of the secret and semi-piratical expedition which Cromwell and his ministers contrived in 1654 against Spain, a power with which at the moment England was at peace. The object of the expedition was to drive out the Spaniards from the colonies which Spain possessed in the Caribbean and upon the Spanish Main, for the purpose of converting as many of them as possible into English dependencies. This, the famous "Western Design" of the Protectorate, was an attempt at the unification of England's colonial possessions for religious and financial purposes into one homogeneous whole, and marked the first beginnings of a changing colonial policy.[1] It was at first hardly favored even by the merchants themselves, who eventually were to profit by its results, and it cannot be claimed for Cromwell as an act of honorable statecraft on his part, efficiently and wisely executed.[2] It shows him possessed of an irrational but seemingly inspired ambition to plant a Protestant power on the ruins of Spanish towns and cities that would check Spanish influence in the New World and overthrow the ascendancy of Catholicism and the papacy. It accomplished little in that direction, but it opened a new era of settlement, turned the thoughts of colonially minded men toward the need of a more reliable method of colonial administration, and awakened, almost for the first time, a realization of the importance of the American and West Indian world as an asset in the enlargement of

1. Watts, *Les Colonies anglaises aux Antilles,* pp. 87, 101.

2. The fact that Cromwell did not declare war before sending his expedition to the West Indies aroused great indignation and bitterness among the Spaniards, who charged the English with conduct which placed them in the class of pirates and robbers and beyond the pale of the accepted rules of civilized nations. Juan Francisco de Montemaior de Cuenca, president of the royal audiencia of Santo Domingo (for whose work see below, p. 13, note 3), declared that because of this high-handed and illegal procedure all Englishmen taken in battle would be treated as the property, that is, as the slaves of their captors and not be allowed the privileges of prisoners of war.

English territory and the extension of English commerce. Until this time settlement had been almost entirely a matter of private initiative; from now on, with Jamaica a conquered territory and with trade and profit dominant factors, settlement became more a matter of business and to a greater extent than ever before an interest of the crown as well as of the individual. Though still handing over the actual work of colonization to private proprietors, the English government from this time forward began to give shape to a colonial purpose and policy destined to grow steadily in stature and to become more unified and consistent as the years passed. Though immediately after the Western Design had accomplished its work the governmental programme became chiefly maritime and commercial, toward the end of the century it began to assume a distinctively colonial character.

The causes of the expedition of 1654 are not far to seek. In its Elizabethan aspect it was analogous to the freebooting activities of Drake, Grenville, Raleigh, and Cumberland, and their seventeenth century successors, Shirley, Newport, Warwick, and Jackson, all of whom had preyed, almost with impunity, on Spain's colonial possessions. Cromwell denied the validity of the papal line of demarcation,[1] and in his commission of December 9, 1654, declared that England held herself in all justice obliged to take revenge upon Spain for the cruelties, wrongs, and injuries inflicted upon English peoples by the Spaniards in those parts.[2] He had in mind the continuous efforts made by the latter during those years to drive out the English inhabiting "upon the king of Spain's land" and trading in the king of Spain's waters, and especially three definite acts of inhumanity, which must have affected him deeply, because they concerned in part the attempts of his fellow Puritans of the Providence Company to populate the West Indies.[3] These were the attack on the

---

1. *The Narrative of General Venables* (Camden Society, 1900), p. 109. See also Cromwell's speech of September 17, 1656, delivered to parliament in the Painted Chamber (*Letters and Speeches,* Lomas ed. II, 510–526), and Thurloe, *State Papers,* I, 759–763. That the Spanish claim was still based on the papal act appears from the reply of the "sargento mayor" to Venables, when he asserted that Philip IV possessed the island partly by continuous possession and partly by the "concession and authority of the Holy Apostolic See and of His Holiness Pope Alexander, extended to the Catholic Monarchs and their successors." "English Conquest of Jamaica," *Camden Miscellany,* XIII, 1924, p. 6.

2. *Venables Narrative,* p. 109.

3. *Ibid.,* p. 164. Professor Newton in his *Colonizing Activities of the English Puritans,* pp. 322–324, has laid stress upon the Puritan losses as having provoked Crom-

English in the island of Tortugas or Association in 1635, the capture
of the island of Santa Caterina or Old Providence in 1641, and the
murder of Englishmen on the island of Santa Cruz in 1637 and the
final seizure of the island in 1651 or 1654. In the last named instance
the English there (according to the version current in England)
were "most barbarously" slain by the Spaniards.[1]

Closely identified with this idea of vengeance upon Spain was the
religious conviction, strongly intrenched in the minds of the Puritans, that they were doing God's work in driving out the papists
from the western world and establishing there the true faith, to the
glory of God. "Who knows," wrote Major General Fortescue,
"whether God has not sent us before to make way for the Gospel"[2]

well to undertake the expedition. He notes the fact that William Jessop, formerly
secretary of the Providence Company and at this time one of the clerks of the Council
of State, was in daily contact with Milton, who was the Latin secretary to the council
and had the ear of the Protector. Newton implies that Jessop influenced Milton and
Milton Cromwell. Though Professor Firth thinks that Cromwell's famous manifesto
was drawn up by Lord Saye and Sele, it is commonly ascribed to Milton, who wrote
it in Latin in 1655, the translation by Birch appearing in 1728. The Latin version may
be found in Milton, *Prose Works* (1834), pp. 822–829; the translation, pp. 638–646.

1. Thurloe, *State Papers*, III, 505. Cromwell probably knew of these attacks because two of them were bound up with the history of the Providence Company.
These two are expressly cited in the manifesto mentioned above. For the Tortugas
incident see Newton, *Colonizing Activities*, index. Details regarding the murderous onslaught upon Santa Cruz, by three Spanish frigates from Porto Rico, manned with
negroes and mulattoes, in the course of which forty Englishmen were killed and nine
taken prisoners, can be obtained from certain depositions before the High Court of
Admiralty in 1637–1638 (High Court of Admiralty 13:53; abstracts in *High Court
of Admiralty Examinations, 1637–1638*, Anglo-American Records Foundation, II,
nos. 446, 548, 551, 571). The depositions before the High Court are full of valuable
information regarding this early period of English colonization. The final capture of
Santa Cruz is mentioned in *Calendar State Papers, Colonial*, 1661–1668, §894, pp.
218, 437, 534. Williamson gives the date in one place 1651, in another 1654. It is an
interesting fact that the reoccupation of the island in 1646 should have been the
work of James Ley, Earl of Marlborough, who as a lad had visited Boston in 1637,
coming over to see the country in the same ship with the Davenport company.

Winslow puts the Cromwellian and Puritan point of view in characteristic fashion—
to execute God's "determined vengeance upon that tyrannous, idolatrous and bloudy
nation" that "hath inflicted so many cruelties upon the nations of the earth, in their
distressed members, and not the least upon ours" (Thurloe, *State Papers*, III, 252).
It was this sort of loose and revengeful talk that so angered the Spaniards who,
however much they may have resisted English encroachment, were anxious at this
time to preserve the peace.

2. *Ibid.*, 252, 650; *Venables Narrative*, pp. 5, 6, 19, 24, 41, 56, 129, 130, 136;
Historical Manuscripts Commission, *Seventh Report*, p. 572.
The Puritan responsibility for the inception of the expedition and the policy adopted
in promoting it are everywhere manifest. Many of those intimately connected with it
had been in one way or another identified with the colonies, chiefly in New England.

as well as to perform a service to the commonwealth. Edward Winslow, the erstwhile Pilgrim father, who was one of the leading men on the expedition, expressed very reverently the hope that many Protestant settlements might be founded on the ruins of the Spanish habitations and that each new settlement might have its Congregational church and minister established within it. Vice Admiral Goodson in 1655 sent out a call for godly ministers who would come with sufficient money for their maintenance.[1] The instructions of October 10, 1655, to Fortescue, Goodson, Sedgwick, Searle, and Stokes, commissioners, "to endeavor the promulgation of the Gospel of the Lord Jesus Christ and the power of true religion and holiness and the suppression of idolatry, popery, superstition and prophaneness" seem but an effort—as indeed the whole expedition was but an effort—to bolster up a Puritanism that was already entering upon its decline. The desire to spread Puritan influence underlay Cromwell's unsuccessful attempt to persuade New Englanders from Boston and New Haven to migrate to Jamaica, that they might populate the lands, which he confidently expected to conquer, with a people of the right sort, religiously minded, hardy, and well tested as to their

Major General John Desborough, who had charge of the victualling and equipping of the fleet (though as Venables said, "General Desbrow was no victualler"), was Cromwell's brother-in-law and a brother of Samuel Desborough at one time of Guilford in the New Haven Colony. Edward Winslow ("Honest Mr. Winslow") (as we have already seen, above, Vol. II, 255, note 3) was the most important of the commissioners on board the fleet. He took part in the ill-fated attack on Hispaniola, April 15–May 3, 1655, accompanying the troops under Venables, and survived only to die, May 8, 1655, and be buried at sea just before the fleet reached Jamaica (*Venables Narrative*, pp. 161–162; *Memorials of Sir William Penn*, II, 99, 112; Thurloe, *State Papers*, III, 249–252, 505). He told Penn that the Hispaniola failure broke his heart. Francis Barrington, on board with his family, was of the Essex Barringtons, who befriended Roger Williams. Samuel Eaton, brother of Theophilus, who had lived for a time in New Haven, was an intimate friend of General Venables and visited him in the Tower, whither Venables had been sent by the Protector after his return. Later, Samuel acted as a kind of intermediary on Venables' behalf. Richard Morris and Lewis Morris, both planters, who aided in raising a regiment in Barbados but refused to accompany the expedition, afterward removed to New York, where Richard founded Morrisania and died in 1672. Colonel Richard Holdip (son of James, above, Vol. II, 249), a Barbadian Puritan planter, who is said to have been the first to plant sugar in Barbados, played an important part on the expedition. General Sedgwick, who commanded the fleet sent later to the relief of Jamaica, was the one who had been expected to lead the New Englanders in their war against the Dutch in 1653. He died in Jamaica, May 24, 1656. Strong, in "The Cause of Cromwell's West India Expedition" (*American Historical Review*, IV, 238–242), discusses the part played by other New Englanders in helping Cromwell make up his mind.

1. *Calendar State Papers, Colonial*, 1675–1676, p. 105.

orthodoxy.[1] The purposes of God were constantly on the lips of those who were among the leaders of the undertaking, and such purposes animated even members of the rank and file. Once, in Hispaniola, the soldiers, who can hardly be charged with any surfeit of Puritanism, "wasted a good store of Popish trumperie" that they found in one of the Spanish chapels, and at another time they "pelted to death with oranges" a large statue of the Virgin Mary, "well accoutered." By more than one writer the failure of the design was imputed to the wrath of God falling upon the promoters for their unjust and unrighteous dealings,[2] and well might the Spaniards have echoed this imputation.

But behind the religious motives were others that were more of the world worldly. Though the Cromwellian government was not primarily interested in trade and commerce and was often unfriendly toward the mercantile ambitions of the City of London, it was always in need of money and never backward in promoting any venture that would increase the national wealth. Even if the venture involved the dishonorable seizure of ships and bullion belonging to a nation with which England was ostensibly at peace, Cromwell believed that the expedition of 1654 would not only pay its way by tapping the stream of silver that was flowing along West India routes into Spanish coffers, but would help also to meet the financial situation which from the beginning of the Protectorate was steadily growing worse.[3] He counted on the good fortune that had attended all his past enterprises to reap success in this, but by 1657 it was evident that he wished to be well rid of it, as only making matters infinitely more difficult because of the heavy debt which the costly and wasteful expedition was imposing on the country—a

1. Strong, "A Forgotten Danger to the New England Colonies," *Report*, American Historical Association, 1898, p. 85.

2. The repulse at Hispaniola was ascribed by the Puritans to "God's handiwork for the Sins of the Nation as also for our Sins who were very unfit Instruments for such a work," and for their overconfidence "which much distressed our gratious God" (Thurloe, *State Papers*, III, 505; *Venables Narrative*, pp. 136, 161; *Memorials of Sir William Penn*, II, 93; Historical Manuscripts Commission, *Seventh Report*, pp. 572, 575). On September 6, 1655, Sedgwick wrote to the navy commissioners, "I hope God hath brought down our confident spirits to fill us for some more noble work. When flesh begins to glory, it is mercy if God will stain the glory of it." He hoped that "God has yet a blessing for them and that this design is His and that He will own it." *Calendar State Papers, Colonial,* 1675–1676, §221.

3. Ashley, *Financial and Commercial Policy*, pp. 44, 84–85, 107. See above, p. 4, note 2.

debt which the Protectorate was never able to repay.[1] "The great want is money," wrote Thurloe in that year, "which puts us to the wall in all our business,"[2] and two years later the Venetian resident wrote of "the unspeakable scarcity of money" and of the government's not knowing "which way to turn to get together any amount of it."[3]

That the need of money weighed heavily with the leaders is seen in the policy adopted in 1655–1656, at the instance of Winslow,[4] of forbidding plundering by the soldiers, in order that all returns from prizes might be turned into the government's exchequer. These returns, however, were meager in the extreme and probably nothing of moment was ever obtained to offset the enormously heavy expenses involved. After the declaration setting forth the justness of the war against Spain in October, 1655, parliament appropriated special sums as a war chest, but in any case these sums would have proved insufficient even if they had been all collected, as they were not.

Though the merchants as a whole opposed the war because it blocked and dislocated trade, led to retaliatory acts by the power whose vessels had been seized, made it difficult to get foreign built vessels at all, brought misery upon many flourishing families, and cut down the customs revenue, nevertheless there were individuals among them who saw many advantages accruing to themselves in the prosecution of the war. There were a few who had unpaid claims against the Spanish king and hoped to recoup themselves by

1. The government's financial troubles were increasing toward the end of the year 1657 and its inability to send out an expeditionary force sufficiently large and powerful to occupy Jamaica and at the same time to carry on an offensive campaign against the Spanish possessions in the New World explains in part why the struggle was so prolonged during the years from 1657 to 1660. The *Calendar of State Papers, Domestic*, 1654–1660, is full of details regarding the government's difficulties in financing the expedition and the conquest, while the despatches of the Venetian residents show how little was known about it, where it was going, and what were its objects. As one of them wrote, "The secrets of this government are impenetrable," and it is probable that Cromwell intended that they should be. Spain, apparently, did not know the destination of the fleet until March, 1655, and was greatly concerned for the safety of her galleons. Cromwell's design dwindled in the end (1660) to an attempt on the part of the English to protect Jamaica against Spanish aggression. Watts estimates the actual losses at more than a million pounds sterling (*Les Colonies anglaises*, pp. 338, 360). In 1659 Rumbold wrote to Hyde, "They will hardly ever conquer the debt lying upon them since the Protector's American expedition," *Calendar, Clarendon Papers*, IV, 492.

2. Thurloe, *State Papers*, VII, 4.

3. *Calendar Venetian Papers*, 1659–1661, pp. 94–95.

4. *Venables Narrative*, p. 150.

obtaining letters of marque allowing them to prey on Spanish vessels. Of these the best known is Sir Paul Rycaut, who before his death in 1657 sought to obtain satisfaction from the Spanish government for money loaned, and brought pressure to bear on Cromwell to undertake the Western Design with his claim in part as a pretext.[1] There were others who welcomed the opportunity which the outfitting offered to obtain contracts for victualling and equipment, who anticipated with pleasure the acquisition of new lands, wherefrom to carve additional plantations for the raising of sugar, tobacco, and other tropical and subtropical products, thus swelling the volume of West India trade. The most important member of the latter group was Martin Noell, who made money out of contracts, received grants of land in Jamaica, and shipped servants and supplies to that island on his own account. He had interests in Barbados also, where his brother Thomas acted as his agent and at the expense of his own popularity labored to protect his brother's property there. Noell's letters show the disappointment that he felt because of the failure of the expedition at Hispaniola. Next to Noell was Thomas Povey, frequently mentioned as a friend by Pepys in his diary, a man who rose to prominence during these years and played an important part both in shaping England's policy and in winning for the merchants a more centralized colonial administration. Povey had brothers in the West Indies, who went over with the fleet in 1654 and, through some political wire-pulling, at which both Noell and Povey were adept, were appointed to offices which they filled with varying degrees of credit. Other merchants interested were Maurice Thompson, Thomas Vyner, James and William Drax, Nicholas Crispe, Robert Wilding, Andrew Riccard, and William Berkeley.[2]

The expedition, with Admiral Penn at the head of the fleet and General Venables in command of the troops on board, set sail secretly from the Isle of Wight, December 19, 1654, passed Spithead on the 26th, and after "a happy voyage," "a very comfortable and speedy passage," "a gallant passage" of six weeks, reached Carlisle Bay, Barbados, on January 29, 1655. There the commissioners—Penn, Venables, Winslow, Searle, and Butler—dallied for ten weeks,

1. *Calendar State Papers, Domestic*, 1655, pp. 32–33; *Venetian Papers*, 1655–1656, pp. 34, 51, 96.
2. *Calendar State Papers, Colonial*, 1574–1660, pp. 345, 348, 350–351, etc. Probably a majority of the London merchants were Puritans or Puritan sympathizers. Maurice Thompson was of an almost fanatical Puritan family.

waiting for the supply ships which failed to arrive; there they spent their time collecting horses, provisions, and ammunition and drafting such men as could be obtained to supplement the wholly inadequate force on board.[1] To the 2500 men brought from England they were able to add 3500 from Barbados, and later eight or nine hundred from St. Christopher, eighty from Montserrat, and three hundred from Nevis, the whole totaling more than 7000, without counting the sea-regiment of "1200 proper stout seamen"; but by forcing artisans and servants out of their labor to the distress of employers and masters,[2] they aroused much ill will in Barbados. The ships left that island on March 31, sailing northward and touching at some of the smaller islands. Having decided to make Hispaniola their first point of attack, they headed directly for that island, reaching there, on the southern side, April 13.[3] From April 14 to May 4 they conducted a campaign by sea and land against the city of Santo Domingo—though the ill-managed affair hardly deserves the name of campaign and the share of the fleet was not only inconspicuous but cowardly—and failed miserably to accomplish anything whatever. The failure was due in part to poor generalship, excessive timidity, and want of coöperation between the fleet and the army, the former

1. Barrington wrote just before the fleet started from England, "We ship very thin at present" (Historical Manuscripts Commission, *Seventh Report*, p. 571). For the place of Francis in the Barrington family, Essex Archaeological Society, *Transactions*, II, 24.

2. Barrington's account, p. 572.

3. The Spanish narrative says that the first object of the expedition was the capture of Hispaniola, "to besiege which this fleet had come especially from England, in order, from there [that is, from Hispaniola] to conquer all these islands and the continent." *Camden Miscellany*, XIII, 11.

Montemaior de Cuenca, president at the time of the royal audiencia of Santo Domingo, exaggerates the strength of the English when he says that the fleet consisted of fifty vessels, bearing 9000 men and 200 horses, just as he exaggerates the English losses, placing them at 3000 men. He does not make it clear whether or not the authorities at Santo Domingo had warning beforehand of the attack, but he lays stress upon the desperate efforts which he made as governor about two weeks before the English arrived to get the towns in shape for defense, by repairing fortifications, gathering arms and munitions of war, and exercising the militia (p. 21). For his success in repelling the attack he was thanked in a royal decree (pp. 22-23), and himself thanked God for the rejoicing among the Catholics and for Spain's indebtedness to the Almighty (*Calendar Venetian Papers*, 1655-1656, p. 116), who to his mind was on the side of Spain just as to the Cromwellians the same God was on their side, acting as their inspiration and guide. *Discurso politico historico juridico del derecho, y repartimiento de presas y despojos apprehendidos en justa guerra* (1658). I am indebted to Mr. Philip Ainsworth Means for calling my attention to this rare book, to Mr. Lawrence C. Wroth of the John Carter Browr Library for photostats of parts of it, and to Professor Bemis for a translation.

doing nothing when an active shelling of the town from the water-side might have turned defeat into victory. The soldiers, on the whole, a poor untrained conglomeration of men, insubordinate even before they left England, were suffering from physical exhaustion brought on by the heat, by lack of food and water, and by fatigue incident to marching for some forty and more miles through a damp and unhealthy country covered with an unbroken growth of tall trees. The advance troops got within a cannon shot of the city, but were halted by the defenses of the enemy and by their own help-lessness due to weariness and a totally inadequate supply of field pieces, pikes, and corselets. Though they outnumbered the enemy, at first ten and later six to one, they were always at a disadvantage, and the losses were not less than a thousand, a fifth of the force that actually landed.[1] The story of this offensive is a tale of suffering

1. The fleet divided before the city, one part under Captain Butler, plying back and forth before the shallow harbor, "to amuse the enemy," but without attempting a bombardment; the other, bearing Venables and the troops, misled by the report which proved to be false that a chain-boom had been stretched across the harbor-opening (though in fact two large vessels had been sunk across the entrance), went forty miles to the westward before landing. There at Nisao (Pointe de Niazo) they were put ashore with the idea of approaching the city from the west. After a long march over rough hilly roads the wearied soldiers, when within a few miles of the city, found themselves blocked, first by the River Niazo and then by the River Jayna or Jaina (Hayna, Hyne, Hine), beyond which was a small fort, defending the cross-ing (maps in Watts, in Wright, "Spanish Narratives," Camden Miscellany, XIV, and in Bryan Edwards, "History of St. Domingo," History of the West Indies, 1901, III, 128–129). To avoid this crossing they were forced to march inland for seven or eight miles to find a ford. The officers had no guide and many of the soldiers lost their way. The river Jayna having finally been forded and Venables' force having been augmented by sea troops under Butler and Holdip, two attacks were made, one on April 17, which though successful ended in a retreat because the men were dying of thirst, and the second on April 25 which was thwarted in part by the cowardice of Adjutant General Jackson (for which he was later cashiered), by ambuscades of the enemy (Camden Miscellany, XIV, 10–11), which cost many lives, for the Span-ish "cowkillers" with their machetes gave no quarter, and by the discouragement and physical weakness of the soldiers. Accounts of this harrowing tragedy are: Ven-ables Narrative, pp. 25–35, 93–100, 127–136; Historical Manuscripts Commission, Seventh Report, pp. 572–573; Clarke Papers (Camden Society), III, 54–60, 203–208; Memorials of Sir William Penn, II, 81–99; Thurloe, State Papers, III, 504–508, 545–547; two Venables letters in Carte, Original Letters, II, 46–52. For a criticism of the expedition and the way it was conducted see Harleian Miscellany, III, 487–500, "A Brief and Perfect Journal of the late Proceedings and Success of the Eng-lish army in the West Indies . . . Together with some Queries inserted and an-swered, by I. S., an Eye Witness. To June, 1655." This journal was originally printed as a separate pamphlet in 1655 and passed through at least two separate editions.

Miss Irene A. Wright in Camden Miscellany, XIV, i–xiii, 1–80, has printed "Span-ish Narratives of the English Attack on Santo Domingo, 1655," transcribed and

seldom experienced on so large a scale—a tale of the slaughter of officers and men, and of death by hunger, thirst, and complete prostration, and the reports that came back to England must have created sensations of horror. As one tale puts it, "Most of the slaughter was done by those uncivilized men who hacked at them fiercely with a clumsy weapon in the shape of a half moon, which they are accustomed to use also to wound wild beasts in the country."[1] Bearing a disillusioned and demoralized company the fleet on May 4 sailed for Jamaica.

The reasons for the failure can be succinctly stated. From whatever sources Cromwell obtained his knowledge of Spanish settlements in the Caribbean, it is quite certain that he vastly underrated their strength and the dangers of a war in the tropics.[2] Probably he put his trust, Puritan fashion, in the God of Hosts. The expedition was hastily prepared and manned, and set out amidst great confusion. Officers found themselves separated from their men and from their private belongings, some of which they never recovered. The supplies, insufficient to start with, were never available when most

translated from original documents in the General Archives of the Indies, Seville, with an admirable introduction. The first of the documents, the relation of Captain Manuel Gonzalez Pallano, of the cavalry, one of the participants, "on all occasions," on the Spanish side, especially in the ambuscades, was printed contemporaneously. Miss Wright tells me that she has since seen a copy of this early pamphlet, of which she was not aware when she made her translation from the original. For the information furnished by Don Juan Francisco de Montemaior de Cuenca, see previous note.

1. *Calendar Venetian Papers,* 1655–1656, p. 108.

2. Cromwell's sources of information are usually considered to have been, first, Thomas Gage, a Dominican priest, turned first Anglican then Puritan, who had shortly before written the first authentic account of the provinces of New Spain (Thomas Gage, *The English American or a New Survey of the West Indies,* London, 1648, reprinted, Newton, ed. 1928, Broadway Travellers Series); and secondly, Captain William Jackson, who under the protection of the Earl of Warwick had engaged in a daring raid of reprisal against Spain during the years 1642–1645 ("The Voyages of Captain William Jackson, 1642–1645," Harlow ed., *Camden Miscellany,* XIII, v–xxvi, 1–29). Gage wrote to Cromwell, probably in 1654, presenting "Some briefe and true Observations" (Thurloe, *State Papers,* III, 59–61), and either before or after had a secret interview with him, during which he must have told the Protector that the time was ripe for aggressive action. He went with the expedition, serving as chaplain and interpreter, and died in Jamaica. There is an unmistakable likeness between Jackson's capture of Jamaica in 1643 and that of Venables in 1655.

There is reason to think that Modyford also was influential with Cromwell and that it was his plan which was followed by the fleet (Thurloe, *State Papers,* III, 62–63). It is doubtful, however, if Cromwell was influenced by these men only. Winslow and others among the Puritan laymen and divines probably had something to say also. We read of one William Cooper, who was consulted because he had been in those parts (*ibid.,* II, 250).

wanted and at times were so foul as to be unusable. There was always great scarcity of bread, meal, rice, pease, and particularly of brandy, barrels of which were destroyed by fire on the voyage, and the rest, though supplemented by a reserve from Barbados, was stored in the ships and so inaccessible that soldiers on shore had often but a spoonful a day. No canteens (black Jacks) were provided and water for the men on the march was so scarce that many of them died of thirst. Medicines were always falling short and the surgeons were greatly hampered in caring for the sick and wounded. The soldiers, whether brought from England or obtained in the West Indies, were untrained and averse to discipline, and in such poor physical condition that they were unfit at the start to stand up against the heat of the climate and the hardships of the marching through woods airless and swelteringly hot.[1] Matters were made only worse by the lack of gunpowder, and by the fact that the pikes, and other weapons of attack, many of them obtained in Barbados, were of inferior make.[2] The heavy losses among the officers increased the demoralization of the men, already prevalent because of the rivalries and jealousies in high quarters. Penn and Venables, who were not on good terms, were constantly quarrelling over questions of precedence, charging each other with lack of coöperation and efficiency. The dislike of the commanders for each other communicated itself to the rank and file—the army against the navy and the men against their officers. Barrington wrote "Never was an army so dealt with," and Venables put the matter mildly when he said "Our wants are great and our difficulties many." Professor Firth sums up the situation: "In short," he says, "no worse prepared and equipped expedition ever left the English shores and the consequences of these initial mistakes and negligences were all aggravated by the mistakes and quarrels of those charged with its command."[3]

Many of those, however, who knew the islands of the Caribbean were of the opinion that though the repulse at Hispaniola was a major disaster, the island, if conquered, would have proved far less useful to England than Jamaica was certain to be. Venables thought

1. Montemaior de Cuenca specially mentions the lack of discipline and of guidance and speaks of the advance as carelessly conducted (p. 21).

2. A fine troop of horse was raised in Barbados, but it proved of little use in Hispaniola, and on the departure of the fleet the animals were either killed for food, left for the enemy, or shot because there was no room for them on shipboard.

3. *Venables Narrative*, p. xxxvii.

Jamaica better watered, possessed of a more salubrious climate, more healthful and pleasant to its people, and likely to furnish a superior quality of provisions and livestock at lower prices than would be the case with Hispaniola. Daniel, auditor general, esteemed Jamaica as exceeding all others for fertility and was thankful that "God did us in Espaniola," because Jamaica, though not as big, was a fine provisioning island and lay "in the very heart of the Spaniard to gall him." Modyford thought the same. He was not sorry that the Hispaniola venture had failed, for he considered Jamaica "far more proper for their purposes [as it] hath an excellent harbour and is accounted the most healthful and plentiful of them all," and, he added, "I look on [Jamaica] as much the better place." Sedgwick gave his testimony later, "Many think Jamaica a more considerable island than Hispaniola and may effect more than the other."[1]

Jamaica is an island, one hundred and forty-four miles long and forty-nine miles across at its widest part, the third in size of the Greater Antilles. It is very mountainous, the highest peak rising to 7,360 (7,388) feet and the others ranging from one thousand to something more than six thousand, with an average of nearly thirty-five hundred feet.[2] Its level lands are limited in extent, particularly on the northern side, attaining their widest areas along the southern border from Savannah la Mar to Morant Point, the proportion of level lands standing to the whole in the ratio of about one to six and a half. It was discovered by Columbus on his second voyage, May 3, 1494, and during his third voyage he landed on the northern coast, probably at the mouth of Drax Hall River, near St. Ann's Bay. There he lived, sick and worried, for twelve months in 1503-1504. His son Diego succeeded to his father's titles and inheritance, after the latter's death in 1506 and became Admiral of the Indies and governor in Spain of Jamaica. He appointed one Esquivel as his deputy in 1510, who conquered the island and founded on the north shore near St. Ann's Bay the first towns, Oreston and New Seville, the

1. *Ibid.*, pp. 148–149; *Memorials of Sir William Penn*, II, 124; Thurloe, *State Papers*, III, 505, 510, 565, 622, 650 (Fortescue's opinion, "It's a very fruitful and pleasant land, a fitt receptacle for honnest men," *Calendar State Papers, Colonial*, 1675–1676, §221). Cromwell and his advisers first heard definitely of the capture of Jamaica, from an express sent by Penn in August, 1655, and the news did much "to restore the courage of the Protector, his Council, and the whole nation, with the hope of further conquests in that quarter, including the capture or at least the stopping of the usual gold and silver fleets."

2. 3,468. Cundall, *Jamaica in 1928*, p. 15.

latter the more important of the two. Here he built a fort and set up a sort of municipal government. As the northern side of the island proved unhealthy and the plantable land insufficient, the chief place of residence was removed about 1534 from New Seville to Villa de la Vega,[1] in the southern plain, not far from the coast and along the banks of the Rio Cobre, near the site of a sugar mill established some years before by Esquivel's successor, Francisco de Garay (1515-1522). In 1536 Charles V, as king of Spain, ceded the island and its jurisdiction to Don Luis Colón, son of Diego, confirmed to him the admiral's prerogative, and conferred upon him the title of Duke of Veragua. From this time forward until 1655 the proprietorship of the island, including a considerable amount of civil and criminal jurisdiction, lay in the possession of this family, with the supreme authority remaining in the hands of the crown. Jamaica was construed as appertaining to the marquisate of the dukes of Veragua, in much the same manner as a propriety in English America was construed as a part of the estate of the proprietor in England or, in the case of a royal colony, of the king.

The dukes, who after the death in 1578 of Luis, Diego's son, represented the female line, had the right to appoint the governor and to receive certain revenues, but the profits, estimated at six hundred pesos in 1644,[2] were never large owing to the poverty and tropical indolence of the laboring population. The chief staples during the earlier period were cassava, Indian corn, beef, pork, and bacon and there was always a small export business in hides with the adjoining Spanish islands and mainland and to some extent with Spain. Jamaica was an agricultural colony, growing food for Spanish expeditions to the mainland and supplying Cuba and other Spanish possessions with provisions and stock. The Spanish planters there made little use, except for building and fencing, of the rich store of hard woods—cedar, lignum vitae, mahogany, and red ebony; of dye woods—braziletto and fustic (logwood was not indigenous, coming in later, 1715); or of pimento and anotto, all of which afterward

1. Called by the English St. Iago de la Vega at first and afterward Spanish Town (Cundall, *A Brief Account of King's House, Spanish Town*, 1929; *The King's House and The King's Square, Spanish Town*, by H. C. Corlette, 1932, chiefly architectural). There is reason to think the town was called "St. Iago" even before the English took the island. *Venables Narrative*, p. 138; *Camden Miscellany*, XIII, "Spaniard's Narrative," p. 1.

2. Cundall, *Jamaica under the Spaniards*, pp. 40-41.

became of great importance. Cattle and pigs ran wild in the woods and were killed rather for their skins than their flesh. In 1611 the inhabitants were estimated[1] at something over fifteen hundred—523 native white men and women, 173 native white children, 107 free negroes, 74 Arawâks or aboriginals, 588 slaves, and 75 foreigners, probably Portuguese.[2] As time went on the area of occupancy widened, particularly to the east and west of Villa de la Vega, and the number increased of sugar plantations, ranches and ranges for cattle, and cacao groves and walks belonging to the richer people and of small farms and holdings occupied by the poorer folk. Horses, cattle, cows, hogs, goats, and sheep, pasturing on the outskirts of the town or running wild over the savannahs or in the woods, multiplied, and colts, donkeys, dogs, cats, ducks, guinea-hens, and other fowl, tame and wild, became a part of the island's animal kingdom. There was only one town—Villa de la Vega—where the well-to-do planters lived when away from their ranches, made up of an indeterminate number of houses—some say 400 to 500, others 1000—scatteringly built, very low on account of the hurricanes, many of which were of brick and timber covered with tile, others—the poorer sort both in towns and in country—of clay and reeds or bamboo. Jackson described the place as "a faire Towne consisting of four or five hundred houses, built for the most part with Canes, overcast with mortar and lime, and covered with Tyle."[3] In the seventeenth century only sea-level lands were available for settlement and there in largest

1. Letter from Bernardo de Balbuena, abbot of Jamaica, to the king, July, 1611, printed in Cundall, pp. 33–38. Balbuena is called by a Spanish writer "most illustrious Doctor don Bernardo de Valbuena, bishop of Porto Rico, previously abbot of [Jamaica], *Camden Miscellany*, XIII, 13. The first resident abbot, who died in 1606, was Francisco Marques de Villalobos. He lived for twenty-five years at Villa de la Vega. For the early history of the abbacy see Wright, in *English Historical Review*, XXXVI, 74–75; and on Balbuena, Van Horne, *Bernardo de Balbuena in Jamaica*, a paper reprinted from *The Gleaner*, Kingston, June, July, 1934.

2. The presence of Portuguese in the island is attested by Venables (*Narrative*, p. 47), who says that Don Acosta, "one of the best men amongst them," but deemed a traitor by the Spaniards, was a Portuguese (pp. 39, 99). The Arawâks were the descendants of those who greeted Columbus on his arrival. They were an inoffensive agricultural people, who had been enslaved by the Spaniards, some to work on the crown plantations and the haciendas of the wealthier settlers and others to be sold as slaves for cash in Santo Domingo and elsewhere. In the long run they were practically exterminated because of their uselessness as agricultural laborers, and negroes were imported very early to take their places. There could have been very few Arawâks in 1655, if forty-four years before there were only seventy-four on the island. Arawâks are to be found today in British Guiana.

3. "Voyage of Captain William Jackson," *Camden Miscellany*, XIII, 18.

part were located the small farms, ranches, ranges, and plantations (*estancias* and *haciendas*) which had been the centers of Spanish life during the century and a half of Spanish occupation. The greater part of the island was at that time, either barren, rocky, or heavily wooded, unplantable, wild and difficult of penetration, accessible chiefly by trails that were tortuous and obscure, easily protected and ideal for ambuscades. Thither the Spanish and negro defenders withdrew, during the greater part of the four years while the English were besieging the island, and there later the Maroons—some of whom were descendants of the Spanish and English negro slaves, while others were runaways from the English plantations—took refuge, living in a state often of savagery, a constant menace to the planters of the coast, who were in perennial fear of them and ever ready to pass laws controlling their movements and checking their depredations.[1]

Jamaica had never been a metal producing island and its value to its possessors, whether Spanish or English, lay in the variety of its staple products, its abundance of horses and cattle, and its surplus of beef and pork for the provisioning of ships and the stocking of commissariats in time of war. Hence its chief activity lay in the field of agriculture and stock-farming, in ploughing the fields and reaping the harvest, in felling the hardwood timber, in clearing the scrub and bush for pasture, and in opening up the lowlands for the cultivation of Indian corn, cassava, sugar, tobacco, and cacao, the last named called in 1668 "the best commodity of the island." As a plantation colony in the eighteenth century, Jamaica was never equal to Barbados, though its economic stability was greater and more lasting because of the diversity of its products.[2]

Thus Jamaica under the Spaniards was an agricultural colony,

1. On the dangers from rebellious and runaway negroes, *Calendar State Papers, Colonial,* 1661–1668, §§1038, 1049; 1689–1692, §1041; 1692–1696, §§1602, 1603; 1704–1705, pp. 224, 394; 1712–1714, pp. 313–314; 1714–1715, pp. 134, 154 (at that time the number of negroes was estimated at 60,000 "very insolent," and the whites able to bear arms at 2000). Leslie, *A New History of Jamaica* (1740), pp. 252–253; R. C. Dallas, *History of the Maroons* (1803), two vols., with folding map, and Bryan Edwards and Sir William Young, *An Historical Survey of the Island of Saint Domingo, together with an Account of the Maroon Negroes in the Island of Jamaica* (1801). The novel *Cudjo's Cave* concerns the insurrection of 1690 (*Calendar State Papers, Colonial,* 1689–1692, p. 316).

2. Yet Jamaica in the seventeenth and even in the eighteenth century was dependent, in common with the other British islands, though never to the same extent, on New England for provisions, *ibid.,* 1677–1680, §811 and elsewhere.

the only one of the kind that Spain ever possessed in the New World. But, as Whistler wrote in his journal, the people as a whole were lazy, had little ambition to be rich, and would take no pains to plant and cultivate their properties, though the soil would bear anything indigenous to a tropical country. There were many fresh rivers and three excellent harbors on the south side and one on the north, though slight use was made of them. In these early years Jamaica was a poor and much neglected land, insufficiently developed and badly manned for defense. This was the Spanish possession that Penn and Venables now proposed to attack.[1]

Historically speaking, the importance of the island to England of the seventeenth century lay not in its internal economy but in its external relations. It was located in the heart of Spain's colonial possessions and was in a position, as a contemporary puts it, "to gaule [the Spaniards] on every side."[2] Seated in the center of the Caribbean it was a favorable starting point for the sensational exploits of pirates, buccaneers, and privateers, who were engaged in cruising, marooning, and fighting, and in plundering and burning Spanish towns.[3] More important still was its usefulness as the center of trade

1. In 1916 the Institute of Jamaica at Kingston obtained through Miss Irene A. Wright a collection of transcripts of documents in the Archivo General de Indias at Seville relating to the Spanish period of Jamaica's history. These documents in translation form the basis of Mr. Cundall's volume, *Jamaica under the Spaniards*, published in 1919, and of Miss Wright's "Early History of Jamaica, 1511–1536," in the *English Historical Review*, XXVI (1921), 70–95, and "The Spanish Resistance to the English Occupation of Jamaica, 1655–1660," in *Transactions*, Royal Historical Society, fourth series, XIII, 117–147. The entrance of the United States into the war brought further effort to a close and the work has not been resumed, though it is doubtful if there are many documents remaining at Seville, untranscribed, that relate to the subject. One of the transcripts in the Institute, containing an account by a Spanish ecclesiastic, Captain Julian de Castilla, of the seizure of the island by the English fleet and army, May 10, 1655, to July 3, 1656, has since been printed by Miss Wright in *Camden Miscellany*, XIII (1924), under the title "The English Conquest of Jamaica." To this account, which is unique because it is the only Spanish narrative of events, may be added (1) the brief statements in *Venables Narrative* and its appendices (pp. 35–39, 136–137, 162–169), (2) the vivid picture given by Francis Barrington in his letters to an unknown correspondent, written from Villa de la Vega in July, 1655 (Historical Manuscripts Commission, *Seventh Report*, pp. 573–575), and (3) the "Attempt on the Island of Jamaica and taking of the Town of St. Jago de la Vega . . . and a full description thereof," in *A Book of the Continuation of Foreign Passages* (London, 1657).

2. *Calendar State Papers, Colonial*, 1704–1705, p. 208.

3. It was no accident that the Jamaican act for the suppression of piracy (1684) should have become the model for similar acts in other colonies. It was viewed so favorably in England as to be sent to all the colonies as a model to be followed (for example, *Calendar State Papers*, 1681–1685, §1592; 1697–1698, §310; *North Caro-*

with the Spanish Main and the channel through which pieces of eight, plate, and pigs of silver went to the English colonies and to England. The situation is well presented in the following quotation from *Tom Cringle's Log:* "The whole of the trade of Terra Firma, from Port Cavello down to Chagres, the greater part of the trade of the islands of Cuba and San Domingo and even that of Lima and San Blas, and the other ports of the Pacific, carried on across the isthmus of Darien, centred in Kingston. . . . The result of this princely traffic, more magnificent than that of Tyre, was a stream of gold and silver flowing into the Bank of England, to the extent of three millions of pounds sterling annually, in return for British manufactures; thus supplying the sinews of war to the government at home and, besides the advantage of so large a mart, the employing an immense amount of British tonnage and many thousand seamen; and in numberless ways opening up new outlets to British enterprise and capital."[1] Thus the world of the western Caribbean and Spanish mainland—Cartagena, Porto Bello, Vera Cruz, Darien, with both coasts of South America, Buenos Aires, La Guaira, Porto Cavello, Maracaibo, Santa Martha, on the east, and Valparaiso, Lima, Panama, and San Blas on the west—became to Englishmen, at home and in the colonies, a region, though still somewhat mysterious, one with which they could do and were doing a thriving and lucrative trade.

On the afternoon of May 9, 1655, two fishermen turtling off Morant Point descried a fleet of thirty-eight vessels,[2] with some smaller craft, pinnaces and doggers, sailing westward with Jamaica as their objective. Eager to report the news to the governor, the fishermen hastened to Villa de la Vega and gave the alarm only a

---

lina Colonial Records, I, 347–348; *Journals,* South Carolina, 1698, pp. 13, 14, 15, 16, 35). The law was suggested as early as 1678, passed for the first time July 2, 1681 (*ibid.,* 1681–1685, §160), but on orders from England was amended by the omission of the clause regarding the guilt of persons accessory and repassed in 1684 (*Laws of Jamaica passed April 17, 1684,* MDCLXXXIV, pp. 19–23; *Laws of Jamaica,* 1737, pp. 11–13) as the Act for the restraining and punishing Privateers and Pirates. Bartholomew Sharp, Every, Kidd, Bannister, Coxon, and others, all of them had some connection with Jamaica and Port Royal.

1. [Michael Scott], *Tom Cringle's Log* (ed. 1836), pp. 110–111. Compare Governor Lyttelton's account sent in to the Privy Council after he had reached London in June, 1664. *Calendar State Papers, Colonial,* 1661–1668, §§744, 812.

2. The list is given in *Memorials of Sir William Penn,* II, 17–18. Sedgwick arrived with eight ships and 800 men on October 1, 1655, and Brayne with another fleet in 1657.

short time before the fleet reached Kingston harbor. Resistance was useless. On board the vessels were perhaps six thousand men, under Venables, with a sea-regiment of one thousand more, while opposed were less than two hundred men guarding a series of three small breastworks, with three mounted guns, that defended the western end of the harbor known as Passage Fort.[1] The forts were easily taken by one of the smaller vessels of the fleet, leaving the English in possession of the harbor, the beach, and the defenses. The infantry, landing at Passage Fort, took up its march the next morning toward Villa de la Vega, about six miles away, and occupied it without opposition. Most of the prosperous residents were absent on their plantations and the remainder ran away to the mountains, carrying off such of their goods and treasures as they could take with them.

The governor, Don Juan Ramirez, in a wretched condition of ill health (he died the following September, while on his way to Campeche, whither the English transported him), had removed to a farm and sugar plantation about three miles away, but when negotiations with intermediaries proved unsatisfactory, on the insistent demand of General Venables, he consented to negotiate in person the terms of surrender. These terms, in one particular at least, closely resemble those which the Spaniards had offered the English after their capture of Old Providence Island. Everything of value—instruments of war, shipping, merchandise, and of course the land itself—was to be handed over to the English, the inhabitants of the better sort being allowed to depart whither they pleased with only their wearing apparel, books, writings, and provisions for the journey. The meaner folk, artisans and the like, were to remain, provided they accepted English rule. These terms were agreed to and during the year Venables began the distribution of the lands along the southern coast and the assignment of farms, ranches, and plantations to officers of the army.[2] The scramble for allotments in Jamaica during the next decade discloses the interest in the colonies

1. Watts, *Les Colonies anglaises*, p. 192.
2. Barrington wrote his cousin, Sir John Barrington, in 1657, "I have in this little time brought a plantation into handsome condition, ready to receive what servants shall be sent me from England . . . I have a good stock of cattle and sheep sufficient to undertake a sugar work, were my purse as able" (p. 575). He repeated several times his faith in the future and believed that so "gallant" an island would prove of great value to England. Time was to demonstrate the correctness of this prophecy, but unfortunately Barrington himself did not live to have a share in it. He was shot and killed in 1660 (*Calendar State Papers, Colonial*, 1675–1676, §328).

beyond the sea that was being aroused at home among merchants, military officers, and country gentlemen. Jamaica as a conquered land was at the disposal of its conqueror and in the imagination of Englishmen offered a new and inviting opportunity for the acquiring of land and the opening of trade, from both of which profits were expected to accrue. As a reward for his coöperation and support, Martin Noell in 1655 was granted 20,000 acres with certain carefully defined privileges, and at the same time Cromwell promised any one who would go to the island grants on the same terms whereon to live and plant. Probably for many years the system of land distribution was very faulty and allotments were held under orders of survey without much legal formality.[1]

Cromwell in his proclamation of October 10, 1655, declared that by the providence of God, Jamaica was in the possession of the Protectorate, and urged upon the people of "the English islands and colonies" the desirability of removing thither, promising them land, protection, and many privileges. But Jamaica was far from being a completely conquered territory lying freely at the disposal of the Protector, and had the New Englanders, particularly those of New Haven, accepted Cromwell's terms of removal, they would have found themselves involved for four long years in trouble, misery, and possible death to an extent unknown in the land from which they came.[2] The Spaniards almost at once repudiated the terms of surrender, showing that Ramirez had but a slender hold upon the Jamaican "grandees" and possessed no way of compelling them to accept English rule. During the three depressing years which remained to him of life Cromwell must have realized that "to clear the Jamaica business" was costing his government large sums of money it could not afford for new fleets and supplies, and the people of England enormous losses in officers and men. The New Haveners had some knowledge of the facts, but they did not know half of what they escaped when they refused to migrate. Though many of

In 1661 the widow of Major General Fortescue sent in a petition that two plantations (which had been allotted to her husband and upon which he had erected "at great charges" sugar works and cacao walks) be granted her and her children for their maintenance (*ibid.*, §§155, 156).

1. Long, *History of Jamaica*, I, 214–216; *Calendar State Papers, Colonial*, 1675–1676, p. 101. Noell's interests in the island were looked after by Major Richard Povey, the brother of his fellow worker Thomas Povey.

2. Strong, "Forgotten Danger," *Report*, American Historical Association, 1898, pp. 90–93.

the richer Spanish inhabitants fled from the island, going chiefly to Cuba, others, backed by large numbers of negroes and mulattoes, carried on a harrassing guerilla warfare from ambush and by direct attack, slaughtering the soldiers singly and in groups, whenever the latter strayed or straggled beyond their lines in the search for food or endeavored to penetrate the mountain region in revengeful pursuit of warring bands. To add to the horrors of the situation the soldiers suffered frightfully from tropical diseases such as dysentery and yellow fever, and the reports sent to old England and New England gave gloomy pictures of sickness, death, and burials. Scurvy, dysentery or the bloody flux, bad food, and plain starvation all took their toll. Wrote one observer in 1655, when an epidemic of yellow fever ravaged the island, "Wee have lost halfe our armie from our first landing in Spaniola, when we were 8000, besides 1000 or more seamen in armes. Never did my eyes see such a sickly time, nor soe many funerals, and graves all the towne over that is a very Golgotha." Another believed that "since he came to this place not less than 700 men are laid in the grave; the greatest part of the army now sick, and many of the new Regiment [the 800 men under Colonel Humphries that arrived with Sedgwick, October 1, 1655] that landed in much health, about fifty of them are dead. Unless God in his mercy stay his hand it will be very sad with us." Still another speaks of "the raging fury of mortality in the army which is almost destroyed."[1] On July 15, 1655, sick and utterly worn out, Venables returned to England, where he was thrown into the Tower for leaving the island without the Protector's license. Penn had already gone, to be incarcerated in the same place for the same reason. In the island death followed death. First died Major General Fortescue, whom Venables had left in command of the army; then his successor, Brayne; and later Major General Robert Sedgwick sent over in 1655. Scores of under-officers succumbed to the plague and the mortality among the rank and file exceeds belief. This state of things

1. *Venables Narrative*, p. 142; *Calendar State Papers, Colonial*, 1675–1676, pp. 104, 109, 267. "Sickness and indisposition of body, many times accompanied with death, have been most men's inseparable companions." From Surgeon General Clerke, "Those whom the virulence of the plague spared, suffered from pests—ticks, horse-lice, scurvy, nits, mosquitoes (the bite of which poisoned the part of the body bitten), niguas, lice . . . there was no relief from so great misfortune" ("The English Conquest of Jamaica," p. 20, *Camden Miscellany*, XIII). "Also great increase of vermin, such as cockroaches, weevils, ants, earwigs, mites and such like" (*Calendar State Papers, Colonial*, 1675–1676, p. 111).

prevailed for the first two years and a half, after which the sickness somewhat abated and the soldiers, having become in some measure acclimated and growing less averse to the demands of an agricultural life,[1] conditions began to improve.

While the army on shore was facing its three years' task of subduing the enemy and completing the conquest of the island, the Protector in proclamations and instructions was urging on the good work and endeavoring to provide additional men and ships to aid in the land campaign. In the meantime Goodson with the ships was engaging in a series of enterprises at sea, designed to round out Cromwell's original plan of conquest and add the wealth of Spain to the poverty-stricken treasury. In the late summer of 1655 he went with a flotilla of eight or ten vessels to lie before Cartagena and Porto Bello, for the purpose of intercepting Spanish ships and seizing booty. But the venturesome attempt brought in no returns to the Cromwellian exchequer. Again he despatched two ships to the north side of the island to prevent the rich planters from escaping with their treasure to Cuba and to cut off communication thence and possible aid. But the planters eluded him and the insurgents continued to make Cuba their headquarters, even though the governor there brought down maledictions on his head by refusing to help them recapture the island. Again Goodson sent fourteen vessels to Havana, in order to intercept any vessels of the plate fleet that might attempt to leave that harbor, after their annual conjunction there in preparation for the homeward voyage, and he planned to station other vessels in advantageous positions along the sailing routes in order to lay under contribution the whole Spanish trade. But though he succeeded in taking a few prisoners he failed to capture a single important prize and Cromwell's treasury remained as empty as before.[2]

1. In 1655 Goodson had reported that "the soldiers cannot be brought to plant or at least very little." The next year Captain Harrison said "the soldiers are being employed in planting, and it is not relished by many, about twenty-five per cent of them ran from their colours but were retaken and some of them executed" (ibid., pp. 104, 109, §279).

2. Goodson planned to send two frigates and a ketch to lie before Santo Domingo, five and a ketch before Cartagena, five before Havana, and two and a ketch off the north keys of Cuba. The last named were to impede the trade and to give intelligence of the arrival of any Spanish fleet. The vessels off Cartagena were to intercept the trade with Spain, Angola, Caracas, etc., and to be ready to assist the army in Jamaica; those on the north side of Cuba to cut off the trade of Santiago, Cavello, Principe, and that between the Canaries, Spain, and New Spain and Havana (ibid.,

The failures were not due wholly to faulty strategy. The ships of the fleet were all of them in a bad condition: the hulls were eaten by the worm, some almost honeycombed thereby; the sails, with which the vessels had been "meanly fitted" at the start, were worn and rotten from long use and constant wetting; and the equipment was wanting in powder, shot, guns, cordage, tar, ironwork, and ship's tools. Moreover the complement of sailors was inadequate, many had died or been drowned, others were sick, while those that were able seamen were "very poor creatures," boys often, incapable of handling sails or manning the small boats. Ship carpenters were too few and repairs were left undone. Provisions got scarce and such as were on hand were sometimes good but more often bad. Vermin were present everywhere. Furthermore, navigation in Caribbean waters was difficult, the routes were unfamiliar to the steersmen, and as charts and rutters were imperfect or wanting many ships went aground.[1] Major General Sedgwick disliked thoroughly the whole semi-piratical business and thought that "this kind of marooning cruizing West India trade of plundering and burning of towns, though it hath been long practiced in these parts, yet is not honorable for a princely navy, neither was it, I think, the work designed though perhaps it may be tolerated at present." He believed that God was highly displeased with the way things were being done, but hoped that He would "spare and pity a poor sinful people."[2]

After the banishment of Governor Ramirez, the command of the Spanish forces fell upon Don Francisco de Proenza, Ramirez' maistro de campo, who had taken part in the early negotiations. But Proenza was nearly blind, suffering from ague, and so tormented by a fistula that he was incapacitated for campaigning. His place was taken by Cristóbal Ysassi Arnaldo, a relative, whose appointment to the command made the whole insurgent movement something of a family affair.[3] Ysassi was not a trained soldier, but at this juncture he

239). This programme was never carried out but it discloses well the ends which the "Western Design" was expected to reach. This ambitious plan, in Sedgwick's words, used in connection with one of the expeditions, "produced little profit to the State" (*ibid*, p. 103).

1. *Ibid.*, §§239, 260, 275, and elsewhere.

2. *Ibid.*, p. 103. Despite what Sedgwick thought, the instructions of October 10, 1655, to Major General Fortescue are perfectly definite on this point: "Power and authority to land men upon territories claimed by the Spaniards, to take their ports, castles, and places of strength, and to pursue, kill and destroy all who oppose them."

3. *Transactions,* Royal Historical Society, 4th series, XIII, 118, note 1.

did the best he could. He took his stand at Guatibacoa, in the general vicinity of Old Harbor, some eight leagues southwest of Villa de la Vega, and with help received from Cartagena, Porto Rico, Cuba, Mexico, and Hispaniola, and with the support of the negroes and mulattoes—the best fighting men on the Spanish side—set out to make all the trouble possible for the English. He devastated ranches and burned their buildings and drove the English from their cultivated fields, interfering by every means available to prevent the continuance of settled agricultural life, until during the year 1657 he was finally driven off by General D'Oyley, Brayne's successor in command, and compelled to change his tactics. He retreated to the northern mountains as better suited for defense and offense and more convenient for giving and receiving advice and help from Mexico and Cuba. The king of Spain placed upon the Duke of Albuquerque, governor of Mexico, the responsibility of recovering Jamaica and the first relief force, made up of men from Mexico, Cuba, Porto Rico, and Santo Domingo, with a few refugee Jamaicans, reached the island in July, 1657,[1] and joined Ysassi at his northern headquarters. This shift of position made a guerilla warfare more effective, for as Francis Barrington wrote, "Such is the enemy amongst us they will not stand a shot, but so unknown are their abiding places that we cannot find them out."

Brayne before his death named as his successor Edward D'Oyley, captain and colonel and the man before all others to whom the English owed their final victory.[2] D'Oyley was a hardened campaigner, apparently immune to disease. Having driven Ysassi from Guatibacoa he was prepared to carry the war into the northern country. Ysassi had his troubles, for the men of the new relief force were discontented and already quarreling among themselves, his own supplies and equipment were insufficient; many of his men were without shoes and adequate clothing; some of his leaders were not to be depended on; and at one time more than two hundred soldiers and colonists deserted and escaped to Cuba, leaving him shorn of half his strength. He could get no certain promise of help from the Cuban governor. In the summer of 1657, D'Oyley very secretly sent a force over the mountains and attacked him in his fort near St. Ann, then followed up this maneuvre with a sea expedition, which

1. Cundall, *Jamaica under the Spaniards*, p. 83.

2. Cundall, *The Governors of Jamaica in the Seventeenth Century, with Eleven Portraits and Seventeen other Illustrations* (London, 1936), I. "Edward Doyley."

landing near Chorreras (Ocho Rios) was able by a flank movement to win a complete victory over the Spanish relief party, November 2, 1657.[1] The advantage thus gained was secured the following year by an attack (June 26, 1658) upon Ysassi's Camp de la Concepción at Rio Nuevo, a fort on the north coast, east of St. Ann's Bay, where reinforcements, sent from Mexico by way of Cuba, were entrenched. The attempt was successful and the Spaniards retreated into the woods.[2]

Despite these victories, the situation of the English forces in Jamaica during the years 1658 and 1659 and part of the winter of 1660 was precarious in the extreme. Though the health of the soldiers and sailors was improving and the area of planting was gradually widening, provisions were still very scarce and the depression in England, combined with the confusion following the death of Cromwell and the accession to power of his incompetent son, Richard, made it difficult for the government to keep up the supply of ships, stores, and money that Jamaica woefully needed.[3] So discouraging were the reports received from the island that the English authorities were at times almost ready to abandon the enterprise and to let Jamaica fall back once more into the hands of the Spaniards. There can be little doubt that had Spain undertaken wholeheartedly the invasion of which there were frequent rumors at the time, she would have been successful. But she was about at the end of her tether and the finances of the Spanish kingdom were in an even more desperate state than were those of the Protectorate.[4] That the

1. An account of these engagements is given by D'Oyley himself in *A Narrative of the great Success God hath been pleased to give his Highnesses forces in Jamaica against the King of Spain's forces; together with a true relation of the Spanish losing their Plate fleete, as it was communicated in a letter from the Governor of Jamaica*, signed Edward Doyley, Cagway Harbor, February 3, 1657[8] (London, 1658).

2. For D'Oyley's version of this battle, Thurloe, *State Papers*, VII, 260–262; for the Spanish version, Cundall, *Jamaica under the Spaniards*, pp. 73–78. *Calendar State Papers, Colonial*, 1675–1676, §305, adds something. The accounts differ considerably.

3. For the situation in 1659–1660, see Stock, *Debates*, I, 265–268; and for a Spanish report of conditions about the same time, Cundall, *Jamaica under the Spaniards*, pp. 85–86.

4. The financial and naval strength of Spain was vastly weakened at this juncture by Blake's victory on April 20, 1657, over the Spanish West Indian fleet, laden with treasure and merchandise. A narrative of this success, with an account of the ships captured, sunk, or burned, is given in *An Order of Parliament for a Day of Publicke Thanksgiving . . . for the Great Success God hath been pleased to give the Navy of His Commonwealth under the command of General Blake against the Spaniard.* [Together with] *A Narrative*, etc., London, 1657. There are lives of Blake by C. D. Curtis and Colonel Roger Beadon, each issued in 1935. Neither of them is entirely

English were able to retain Jamaica as a colonial possession was largely due to the fact that the Spanish government was unable to carry out a consistently aggressive policy. Spain's failure to recover Jamaica marked her decline as a great power, just as the winning and retention of Jamaica marked the beginning of England's rise to commercial and colonial preëminence.[1]

One of Jamaica's greatest needs, as we have already seen, was an increase in her population, for the wide reaches of level land along the southern coast were so sparsely occupied as to be incapable of proper protection. Ranches and farms were widely separated and the soil, everywhere fertile, was insufficiently cultivated. These conditions had been realized as early as 1655, when Cromwell did everything he could to encourage the peopling of the island. He offered to all who would go the protection of the state, a sufficient supply of land, and a tenure free of rents and services for a reasonable length of time. He promised them free denizenship and all privileges such as were enjoyed by Englishmen at home.[2] If he could get Puritans, he preferred them, for they were the right sort to help in carrying out his plan of Protestantizing the conquered territory. How eager the Cromwellian Council of State was to get godly men appears from the attempt made in 1656 to rescue the unfortunate

satisfactory. By 1661 Spain had no fleet, except the feeble galleys of Naples and Sicily, and her exchequer was empty. The heavy losses at sea and the failure of the war with Portugal had reduced her almost to the last extremity. Because of her wars on land she had paid little attention to the sea, and as her dominions were widespread the loss of her "wooden bridges"—her ships—rendered her helpless.

1. A little knowledge of European history is essential here. Portugal had won her independence in 1642 and for twenty years Spain tried to get her back, an effort that was practically ended when England came to Portugal's assistance in 1662, and Charles II married Catherine of Braganza. Spain had been carrying on a long and costly war with France—an aftermath of the Thirty Years' War—which ended in the humiliating treaty of the Pyrenees in 1659. She was steadily declining in power, wealth, and influence, and her failure to recover Jamaica, as later her failure to reconquer Portugal, was due to her exhaustion. The waning strength of the Spanish monarchy under Charles II, who succeeded Philip IV, was a contributory cause of the War of the Spanish Succession (1702–1713), from which Great Britain emerged as the first of the maritime and colonizing powers. Hence the events accompanying and following the taking of Jamaica mark the beginning of a new era not only in England's colonial methods and policy but in the character of colonial settlement in America after that date.

2. Calendar State Papers, Colonial, 1675–1676, §229; Steele, Tudor and Stuart Proclamations, I, nos. 3059, 3346; Long, History of Jamaica, I, 213–215. The proclamation printed in Long has special reference to the plans of the few English merchants who were behind Cromwell in the undertaking. Martin Noell sent over a considerable number of servants, who suffered severely during the plague.

settlers on the barren rock of Eleuthera and to bring them to Jamaica as a leavening influence.[1] Two hundred and fifty people came from Bermuda, fourteen hundred from Nevis, led by their governor, Luke Stokes, a company that settled at Morant Point and lost half its numbers by death within a year. Also during this period and afterward an indeterminate body of emigrants came from Barbados, part of them as soldiers and part as small planters forced out of their holdings by engrossing sugar planters who were setting up large estates. In 1657, the year after their first arrival in Boston, even a few Quakers came who worried D'Oyley by their insistence on the right of propaganda and their circulating, according to their custom, of various forms of literature on behalf of their cause.[2]

The military contest was now gradually approaching its end. At a council held by the insurgents at Chorreras (Ocho Rios), February 22, 1660, the Spanish leaders recommended the abandonment of the island, largely because of the growing disaffections of the negroes, who had been their best allies. Terms of capitulation were drawn up. Ysassi, after another defeat at D'Oyley's hands on the 26th, gave up the struggle and in May removed to Cuba, where he continued to make strenuous but unsuccessful efforts to persuade Don Pedro de Morales, the governor there, to give him aid. Morales, however, not only refused any further assistance but even went so far as to forbid Ysassi to return to Jamaica. Then and not till then did the insurgent leader realize that his cause was lost and that there was nothing more to be done. All further efforts that he or anyone else might wish to make to recover the island were stopped by England's proclamation of September 7, 1660, announcing a cessation of hostilities and the end of the war with Spain which Cromwell had declared in 1655.[3]

Thus almost coincident with the restoration of Charles II to the English throne, Jamaica passed from the hands of Spain and without further bloodshed became a permanent English possession. For the first time in her history England had acquired by conquest a distant territory, far removed across a wide ocean, and situated in

1. *Calendar State Papers, Colonial*, 1574–1660, p. 453. The Eleutheran episode is mentioned in Vol. I, 233, and note 4.

2. Thurloe, *State Papers*, VI, 834. Modyford afterward wrote of "the rude roughness of the sect's temper" in Jamaica (*Calendar State Papers, Colonial*, 1661–1668, §739) and laws were passed in 1665 against them (§962).

3. Davenport, *European Treaties*, II, 57, note 4.

the very heart of the Spanish sphere of colonial control in the Caribbean. Charles II and his ministers, returning to power, found themselves with an island on their hands, in the capture of which they had had no part and which probably for the moment at least they did not want. With a depleted treasury—and one that was to remain depleted during most of the reign—they were confronted with a problem that was colonial, not domestic or foreign or entirely commercial, the solution of which at the time may not have seemed very important. What possible advantage to a government, facing all sorts of difficulties both at home and abroad, could be this distant island, thinly populated, undeveloped agriculturally, and certain for many years to be a drain on the exchequer, without any adequate returns to compensate for the expenditure involved? But the matter was not one that the government was free to decide of its own independent will. Forces were already at work driving on to a decision those in authority, who in executive office as well as in parliament were realizing that there was something new in the air shaping England's destiny in the field of commercial and colonial expansion. When in 1661 a bill was brought into the House of Commons for the annexing of Dunkirk and Jamaica to the crown of England, it was announced as having "the most universal consent and approbation from the whole nation that ever any bill could be attended with," and despite the opposition of the Spanish ambassador the bill was passed and supplies voted for the establishment of civil government in the island. Fears that Spain, dissatisfied, might at any time endeavor to retake the island were not entirely stilled, either in England or Jamaica, until in 1670 the Spanish government in formal treaty relinquished its pretensions and in explicit and comprehensive language acknowledged England's undoubted right to all regions occupied by her own subjects in America.[1] By that

1. *Ibid.*, 189, 194; Stock, *Debates*, I, 288. It is an illuminating fact, illustrative of England's new and expanding interests, that at about the same time (1661–1664) Dunkirk, Mardyck, Tangier, Bombay, Jamaica, and New Netherland should have been annexed as outlying possessions, either incorporated into the realm or recognized as belonging to the crown of England—the first two in Flanders taken from Spain in 1658; the third in Morocco; the fourth in India by marriage treaty with Portugal; the fifth in the Caribbean by conquest from Spain, and the sixth on the mainland of America by conquest from the Dutch. These accessions in five different parts of the world, inconceivable as having been acquired under the early Stuarts, are all manifestations of a new and ambitious spirit that, more or less unobserved at the time, was stirring at the opening of the reign of Charles II. Something will be said on this

time, beginning with the establishment of civil government in 1661, the island of Jamaica, first under D'Oyley, then under Lord Windsor and his successor, Sir Charles Lyttelton, and for seven years under Sir Thomas Modyford, had become firmly organized as an efficiently administered royal colony, differing from others of the same type only in the fact that it had been in origin a conquered territory, and in the further fact that during its early years its agricultural welfare was hampered by the easy gains from buccaneering expeditions against Spanish towns and fleets.[1]

Inconsiderable as may have seemed the results of this audacious but ill-planned expedition of 1654, which started out for the conquest of Spain in the New World and ended with the winning of but a single island, in reality the promoters builded better than they knew. Jamaica became the largest and most important of all England's West India possessions, and as time went on it justified in more ways than one the confidence of those who at the beginning of the king's reign strongly urged its retention. Its location was advantageous, its productivity encouraging, its staples were many and varied, and, as its population grew, its capacity to consume the manufactured goods of the mother country was continually increasing. It became the center of the trade with the Spanish colonies, the distributing agency for the negroes supplied by the Royal African Company, and the channel through which flowed a constant stream, chiefly of silver bullion and coin, that spread in many directions, toward England in largest part but toward the continental American colonies also.[2] Even in the seventeenth century the northern continental colonies were as familiar with Port Royal and Kingston in Jamaica as they were with Basseterre in St. Kitts, St. John's in Antigua, and Bridgetown on Carlisle Bay in Barbados, and in the eighteenth century they were probably more familiar with Jamaica than they were with many of the ports of their own continental

subject in the next chapter, for the situation is important as affecting the whole course of English colonization in America after 1660.

1. Whitson (Mrs. A. J. Butterfield), *The Constitutional History of Jamaica* (1929). D'Oyley had been chosen governor on the death of General Brayne, but without a commission. As during that time to February 8, 1661, when he was formally commissioned by Charles II, he had been "compelled to inflict punishments upon mutinous and seditious persons to prevent anarchy," he petitioned in 1664 for the royal pardon, which was granted (*Calendar State Papers, Colonial, 1661–1668*, §§703, 704). On the appointees mentioned above, see Cundall, *Governors of Jamaica*.

2. Nettels, *The Money Supply of the American Colonies before 1720* (1934), ch. I.

seaboard, for through Jamaica they derived large quantities of their silver money, as Spanish pieces of eight were the current coin of the island and remained so for a century.

Jamaica's many diversified connections brought it frequently into the field of diplomatic controversy, and the rapidly expanding prosperity of its planters disturbed quite often its own domestic serenity and gave rise to local disputes and factional rivalries that color the history of the island's popular assembly and of that assembly's relations with the royal governor and with England.[1] Nevertheless the acquirement of the island, at a critical time in the shaping of England's policy, was a determining factor in strengthening that policy on its commercial and colonial sides, and in so doing influenced the later careers of all England's colonies, continental and island alike.

1. The history of similar disputes in the continental colonies, from New Hampshire to the Carolinas, is frequently clarified by reference to the constitutional troubles in Jamaica and other of the island colonies.

CHAPTER II

ROUGH SHAPING A POLICY: II. NEW NETHER-LAND AND THE ROYAL COMMISSION OF 1664

HARDLY had the news of the success of the expedition of 1654 in capturing Jamaica reached England than those of the merchants who had been interested in its inception sprang into action. Martin Noell and others, who had served as contractors under Desborough and were financially involved in the undertaking, now saw their chance of rewards and profit. With the huge moneyed resources of London behind them they were already deeply involved in financing trade and industry and were exerting every effort to swing Cromwellian policy more and more to their advantage. With the Western Design many of them were in accord, however much or little they may have cared for its religious aspects, for they saw in the enlargement of England's possessions in the sub-tropical Caribbean, with its rich supplies of products that England was already demanding—sugar, cacao, cotton, ginger, pepper, and dye woods—a new plantation area within which to exercise their energies and from which to expect quick returns. Trade, though never seriously affected by the civil wars, was beginning to revive as the victories of the Commonwealth brought a measure of peace on land and sea, and the treaties of 1654, with Sweden, Portugal, and Denmark enlarged their freedom of commercial intercourse. With the widening opportunities thus spread before them these men were becoming dissatisfied with the management of foreign trade and commerce and with the way the colonies had thus far been left pretty much to themselves. They were beginning to formulate ideas of their own as to how England should profit from the emergency confronting her. They did not wish to mingle business with either religion or politics and hoped to be able to arouse the interest of the Protector in foreign and colonial trade far enough to impress upon him its importance and its vital interest to the nation. Of a distinctly modern type were these men.

There were two ways of taking advantage of the new conditions, one private, with the coöperation of the state, somewhat after the fashion of the earlier commercial enterprises; the other public, by persuading the government to adopt a clear-cut colonial policy of oversight and administration. These men were willing to combine as merchants, either voluntarily or in a corporate capacity, to finance and carry through undertakings of a trading character, rather for mercantile than colonizing ends. There is nothing to show that Maurice Thompson, Thomas Aldherne, Martin Noell, Thomas Povey, and their associates and partners wished to become colonizers themselves—this they would leave to those of higher rank who could obtain patents from the king—but they certainly wanted to secure for themselves as large a share as possible of the trade in the New World. They dabbled in politics only so far as to influence appointments to office in Barbados, the Leeward Islands, Jamaica, Virginia, and Newfoundland, which they thought might be to their advantage, and in manipulating such appointments they often proved themselves to be very shrewd politicians.

With profit as their object, in the years from 1657 to 1659—an unfortunate time as it happened, for these were years of financial depression—they organized a Nova Scotia company, for trade in furs and skins in Acadia and up the St. Lawrence, which began well but was unsuccessful in the long run and involved the partners in heavy losses. About the same time they initiated a much more ambitious scheme, which was no less than the formation of a West India Company, to be patterned after the English East India Company, and the Dutch West India Company, and incorporated as a joint-stock by act of parliament. The object sought was the advancement of trade and, incidentally, the prosecution of the war with Spain in order that "those oppressed People (who are withheld from Trade though to their extreme suffering and disadvantage)" might be released "from the Tyranny [of Spain] now upon them." Unlike their forerunners of half a century before they had little or no interest in the conversion of the heathen or the extension of Christianity, for no such group of motives appears in their draft of a charter such as influenced Cromwell to embark on his "Western Design." They saw in conquest merely an enlargement of their money-making opportunities and were actuated by that most modern of maxims "Trade follows the flag." But the plan, which was drawn up in the form of a bill to be laid before parliament, was thwarted by the dissolution of that body, March 16, 1660, and by the return of the king the following May. No attempt was made to revive it. With the peace of the Pyrenees between Spain and France in 1659 and the proclamation by Charles II in 1660 of a cessation of hostilities, legitimate warfare against Spain in the Caribbean ended, though privateering continued on an elaborate scale for the rest of the century. The abiding hostility toward the old enemy, born of that feeling of religious enmity and moral indignation which had been so powerful a factor since the days of the Elizabethans, was gradually fading away and in its stead appeared an equally abiding desire to strip the declining empire of its wealth, either by capturing its galleons or by interfering with its trade.[1]

In the second place, the capture of Jamaica brought to the front the whole question of colonial regulation and control. During the early Stuart period and the Interregnum the strong arm of the government rarely reached out over the ocean and the colonies were either neglected or ignored. Decentralization ruled, partly because such distant lands had hardly become objects of state interest and partly because both the early Stuarts and Cromwell had other and

1. Andrews, *British Committees,* pp. 53–55. The documents in the case can be found in Egerton, 2395, ff. 87–93, 101–110, 202; Additional Manuscripts, 11410, 11411; and *Calendar State Papers, Colonial,* 1574–1660, pp. 475, 477. For a brief modern treatment, Newton, *Colonial Activities,* pp. 324–end.

The contents of the Povey collections, now in the British Museum with transcripts in the Library of Congress, deserve a thoroughgoing examination in the interest of the trading activities and ambitions of the London merchants of this period. There was not a colony (except perhaps Connecticut and Rhode Island) or a part of the north Atlantic world that did not come within the range of their survey— Massachusetts Bay, generally called "New England," Bermuda, Barbados, Antigua, St. Christopher, Nevis, Montserrat, Jamaica, as well as Canada, Newfoundland, Nova Scotia, Florida, Surinam, Guinea, and the Spanish possessions. The principals in the West India Company were Francis Lord Willoughby, Martin Noell, Thomas Povey, and Captain William Watts. Stephen Winthrop, the brother of John Winthrop, Jr. (in 1657 governor of Connecticut) and of Henry Winthrop (in Barbados and formerly assistant to Governor Charles Wolverston there), was one of them. Maurice Thompson, of a family of sectaries, to which group belonged many of the merchants, was trading to India, Canada, Barbados, and Guinea, and doing an early business in negroes (Historical Manuscripts Commission, *Portland,* II, 28–31). Martin Noell seems occasionally to have engaged in transactions that were of an even more sinister character (*ibid., Seventh Report,* pp. 117a, July 13, 1656; 133 ab, 1657–1658; *Calendar Clarendon Papers,* IV, 170, 177; Stock, *Debates,* I, 247–263), though we do not know all the facts in the case. Before 1665, when he and his wife died of the plague, he was virtually bankrupt, having made loans to the Protectorate that were never repaid (Ashley, *Financial and Commercial Policy,* p. 102).

more exacting things to think of. But now the merchants, viewing with lively expectation the first great break in the Spanish line, were demanding that a more centralized policy be adopted and that "his Highnesses Privy Council" pay more attention to colonial affairs. To these demands the council listened and in 1655 appointed a committee of its own members to carry into effect the decision that Jamaica be retained and to report on the needs of the colony. But soon a more important step was taken. On July 15, 1656, Cromwell erected a select advisory council of officers and London merchants to take general cognizance of all matters that concerned "his Highness in Jamaica and the West Indies," and of this council Thomas Povey, Tobias Bridges, Stephen Winthrop, Richard Sydenham, and R. Bowes (whose place was taken by Martin Noell in 1658) formed what came to be known as the "Committee for the Affairs of America." This council or committee was the forerunner of the select councils that were appointed in 1660 and again in 1670 of trade and for foreign plantations and of the Lords of Trade and the Board of Trade later. It lasted as an active body until March, 1660, investigating and discussing with seriousness and care colonial questions that came before it. Even after its members ceased to meet as a body Povey, its chairman, continued to make reports almost until the time the king landed at Dover.[1] He it was who during the last years of the Protectorate, when the government was in confusion and dejection was widespread, worked hard and long to prevent those in authority from letting Jamaica go and drew up "overtures," which he presented first to the Protector and later to Charles II, urging the adoption of a centralized system of colonial management. These "overtures," ignored as they had to be during the irresolute and unstable rule of Richard Cromwell, were taken up after the Restoration and given practical application in the instructions to the special councils of 1660.[2] The foundations of the old English colonial system

1. Andrews, *British Committees,* pp. 45–47; Egerton, 2395, ff. 123, 136, 142, 147–151, 157, 158, 243, 244, 263. The Privy Council in 1660 appointed a committee of its own, called the "Committee to consider the business of Jamaica," that lasted at least until 1666. This committee took over a part of the business that had been in the hands of the Cromwellian committee on the Affairs of America, of which Povey was the chairman, and thus properly speaking was its successor in so far as the affairs of Jamaica were concerned (*Acts Privy Council, Colonial,* I, §§491, 500, 522, 538, 539, 552, 556, 625, 630, 634, 635, 679). It shows the importance of the Jamaica issue that such a committee should be appointed.

2. Andrews, *British Committees,* pp. 55–60; Watts, *Les Colonies anglaises,* pp. 359–365.

were laid under Cromwell and there is no break in the continuity as we pass from the Protectorate to the monarchy. The Englishmen of 1660 were the same men who since the planning of the Western Design and the capture of Jamaica had become possessed of a new idea, as they looked out over the expanding colonial area and saw there new potentialities for trade and the enlargement of shipping and the mercantile marine. They were beginning to think of the plantations in terms of new staple products, and of the wide seas in terms of more ships and more seamen. As they viewed the region from Nova Scotia to the West Indies they began vaguely to believe not only that native products might be found there of a sort that England needed, but that other products also, by a method of transplanting or cultivation, might be profitably grown to the advantage of the merchant and the state. They were already thinking of mulberry trees and silk in Virginia and of spices in the West Indies[1] and under the pressure of these convictions they awaited the opportunity which the restoration of the monarchy might provide.

It was inevitable that the king and his councillors should come under the influence of these same ideas. They were returning to a depleted treasury and to a land where royalist estates, both lay and clerical, had been confiscated and sold during the period of Puritan supremacy. Though many of these estates were eventually taken out of the hands of the purchasers and restored to their original owners or to the latter's descendants, there were others bought during the Interregnum, by merchants who after 1660 supported the king and therefore could not be deprived of their property, however much the government may have been bent on revenge. The land issue was the more important in that the desire for profit from trade among the merchants was matched by an equal desire among the landowners for profit from new estates. The lords, old and new, were developing a business shrewdness and love of money foreign to the manorial lords of medieval times. It has been well said that "by the time of the Commonwealth, men were beginning to reckon prosperity in terms of pounds sterling, and were becoming used to

---

1. Egerton, 2395, ff. 336, 339; *Acts Privy Council, Colonial*, I, §630. Samuel Hartlib was a leading advocate of the introduction of silk worms and bees into Virginia, *A Rare and New Discovery* (London, 1652); *Legacie of Husbandry* (London, 1652), preface, an enlargement of *A Discourse of Husbandry; The Reformed Virginia Silkworm* (1655), and *The Reformed Commonwealth of Bees* (1655). Governor Sir William Berkeley reported in 1666 that progress had been made there in the raising of silk, flax, and hemp. *Calendar State Papers, Colonial*, 1661-1668, §1241.

the idea of sacrificing human life to the deity of increased production."[1] The law of self-interest which dominated the eighteenth century was already influencing men in almost all walks of life, a fact that must be taken into account if we are to understand many of the motives at work leading to settlement during this second period of the seventeenth century. The years of the Interregnum are remarkable in more ways than one, in that they bear witness not only to the growing power of the merchant and tradesmen classes but also to the changes taking place in the views of the lords and tenantry of England. Men were becoming hard-headed, greedy, money-loving, and practical, with a more or less unimaginative view of life and its opportunities, not only in the fields of industry and trade but in the care of the poor and the management of land also. Henry Bennett, when English resident in Spain, 1660, is reported to have said that "in London at present the only thing they cared about was gold."

The financial situation is important. Charles II faced a deficit of three million pounds. Of this sum two millions were an inheritance from the Puritans, all of which, with the exception of the more than nine months' pay due the army and navy, was promptly repudiated by the Convention Parliament. This body sat from April 25 to December 29, 1660, and tried to find a solution of the problems of debt and maintenance. It assumed the public and private debts of Charles II, but, because it as well as its successors could never find the necessary money, these debts remained unpaid, except as far as the king paid them out of his own resources, just as he was obliged to pay the sums he had borrowed during his exile. Financially, conditions were very bad and they did not improve as time went on. Parliament made an annual grant of £1,200,000 but left it to the king to collect, which the latter did only in part, for no one had sufficient money wherewith to meet assessments in full. It also granted him the revenues from excise and customs, and he had in addition, by virtue of his rights as a landed proprietor, the receipts from his royal manors, which had been restored to him on his accession. Large numbers of these manors, however, he was obliged to turn over to his creditors or to sell whenever he was short of ready cash; and from the rest, what with the falling off of rents and payments, the rise of prices, and the dearness of food and forage, brought in such inadequate returns that he was forced to rely, even for his personal

1. James, *Social Policy during the Puritan Revolution*, p. 111.

and court expenses, largely on the grants from parliament. This dependence was increased when in 1660 parliament forced him to give up certain of his minor revenues,[1] the most important of which were the returns from the royal right of purveyance, from knight service tenures, and from the court of wards and liveries.[2] The need of money with which to run court and kingdom was felt from the time of the king's return until the Stop of the Exchequer in 1672, the latter being merely an enforced declaration of bankruptcy, such as had been hanging over the kingdom for twelve years. It is said that at the end of that time Charles was in debt to the extent of from two to two and a quarter millions of pounds sterling, only a very small part of which had been wasted on favorites. Constitutionally speaking, the debt was the king's, and not that of parliament or the nation.[3] To meet the emergency trade and customs offered the best chance for an enlargement of the revenues. From the first the king's advisers stressed the necessity of cultivating these productive sources of income and lent willing ears to the overtures of the merchants with their suggestions regarding the wealth to be derived therefrom. Parliament passed the navigation act of 1660 and the king erected special councils for the oversight of trade and foreign plantations.[4] Though these measures were largely maritime and mercantile, in the ends sought they had important colonial aspects. By them the colonies, to an extent unknown before, were drawn within the orbit of England's commercial interests, and an increase in the number of these colonies made powerful appeals to those

1. What these lesser revenues were can be learned from Ogg, *Charles II*, I, 158. For the subject in general see Dr. Shaw in "Beginnings of the National Debt," *Owens College Studies*, and in the same writer's invaluable introductions to the earlier volumes of the *Calendar of Treasury Books*, which have effected a complete revision of opinion regarding the finances of Charles II.

2. The abolition of the court of wards and liveries was opposed by some of the high churchmen, who wished the education of wards to be turned over to the bishops, deans, and chapters of the Church of England, as an effectual way of stopping popery. *Calendar Clarendon Papers*, IV, 486; *Life of Barwick*, p. 478.

3. To understand the financial situation during the Restoration the reader of today must realize that the king was still expected to live and run the kingdom from his own resources. The fixed revenue was his; the responsibility for its management was his; the lord high treasurer was merely his "servant"; the army and navy, the civil service, the foreign ambassadors and other diplomatic agents were his; and the judges and the courts were his also. Thus in regulating his expenditure he was dealing with what was constitutionally his own. The only power that could restrain him was parliament and during his reign as well as that of William III, parliament held itself in no way accountable for the civil costs of running the country.

4. See Note at the end of this chapter and Vol. IV for a fuller discussion.

whose eagerness for land had now something of a speculative urge behind it, because to the profits from the soil were added possible profits from trade also. In keeping with the mood of the Restoration era, colonizing—though in some of its later manifestations it showed traces of the old adventurous spirit and bore marks of the former religious zeal—became henceforth in large part a practical and business-like affair. Also—and this was a matter of importance—the older colonies founded before 1640, as well as the newly-acquired Jamaica, were rapidly growing in population, a fact that might make them increasingly useful in advancing England's commercial prosperity.

The older colonies were passing out of their infant beginnings into maturity. Connecticut and Rhode Island, receiving legal recognition at the hands of the crown in the form of royal charters, began their inconspicuous careers as autonomous communities, largely outside the range of English knowledge and control. New Haven, always legally and economically strengthless, finally gave up under pressure from Connecticut a hopeless struggle to establish an ultra-orthodox Puritan community on the shores of Long Island Sound. Barbados succeeded in throwing off permanently the burden of a proprietary prerogative and, shouldering in its place the heavy financial obligation of the four and a half per cent duty, which the Leeward Islands later assumed, was rapidly becoming a prosperous sugar producing island. Maryland, emerging from the difficulties into which she had been plunged during the English civil wars and Interregnum entered upon a period of almost unrestricted proprietary rule under the aegis of a favoring Stuart monarchy and spent the next thirty years in a successful effort to throw off the personal dominance of the Baltimore family.

In the case of Massachusetts Bay the situation was even more noteworthy. Effectively screened by the waters of the Atlantic from the intrusion of English influences and completely out of touch with the new spirit of toleration and compromise that was gaining ground in England under the Restoration she continued to adhere with the utmost tenacity to the programmes and principles of the founders of 1630. By the Cambridge Platform of 1648 her leaders defined their orthodoxy in such rigorous and unyielding terms as to threaten the New England way of the churches with almost complete ossification, despite the compromise called the Half Way Covenant adopted by the Synod of 1662 and certain concessions grudgingly made regarding the franchise.[1] In so doing they stifled dissent and prevented a prolongation of religious warfare, but at the same time, in the face of a changing world of ideas, they were planting the seeds of trouble to come. In defiance of Cromwell and the victory of the tolerant Independents over the uncompromising Presbyterians in England and unaffected by the twenty-five years of suffering which were teaching Englishmen the need of mutual forbearance at home they remained unprogressive and isolated from the world around them. In defiance of their own charter they proclaimed the colony's independence in 1652 and for thirty years endeavored to exercise all the privileges of religious and political sovereignty. In defiance of the authority of king and parliament they claimed the right to go their own way without regard to royal decrees or parliamentary statutes. However convincingly the situation can be explained from the point of view of religious convictions, the eventual issue was inevitable. The plans of the English government, which, as regards commerce and the colonies, were in the making after 1660, could not be set aside even by what the Massachusetts Puritans believed were the commands of God. In the final test the divine intervention, upon which many relied for protection, failed to materialize. The seemingly inflexible system broke under pressure from the executive authorities at home and the colony lost its charter in 1684. The new charter of 1691 destroyed the supremacy of the Puritan oligarchy and to all intents and purposes reduced the commonwealth to the status of a royal colony.

The process of transforming Jamaica from a military to a civil state went steadily on. Favorable terms of land distribution were offered to all who would go over from England and the hope was expressed (a hope well conceived but never fulfilled) that only well-disposed people would be encouraged to migrate and no jail-birds or indentured servants be sent to distress the island. The soldiers were already settling down, turning their swords into ploughshares and their spears into pruning hooks, and very matter of fact efforts were being made to induce emigration from Barbados and other islands

1. Perry Miller, *Orthodoxy in Massachusetts*, pp. 309–313; Walker, *Congregationalists*, pp. 172–173.

nearby. When Modyford went to Jamaica as governor in 1662 he took upward of eight hundred people with him—mostly small free planters, whose going was much resented by their employers in Barbados. In 1667 six hundred people, driven out by the French from Montserrat, fled to the island, "extremely plundered, even to their very shirts," and a few years later twelve hundred arrived from Surinam. Though the ease with which fortunes were made in privateering diverted many of these from the irksome tillage of the soil, nevertheless Jamaica progressed rapidly, sugar, indigo, and cacao proving profitable staples, until gradually the memory of disease and starvation grew dim as plenty and health began to get the upper hand. A survey made in 1670 showed 717 families and 7,898 persons living in six parishes on the south side, with at least 20,000 acres patented on the north side in the remaining four parishes. Besides there were 2500 more people engaged in water transportation. It was estimated that there were fifty-seven sugar works, forty-seven cacao walks, forty-nine indigo farms; that the mountains were full not only of pimento or allspice trees but also of an "indestroyable" number of hard woods and dyeing woods; and that the savannahs were rich in pasturage for cattle, sheep, goats, and hogs.[1] There was no apparent winter, only "a perpetual spring," with excessive rains in but two months, May and November. To prospec-

---

1. *Calendar State Papers, Colonial,* 1669–1674, §§270, 271. These figures were sent over by Modyford and were probably intentionally exaggerated. Later reports comment on the reckless and disorderly way that land grants were made in Modyford's time and the great need of re-surveys and a proper reservation of quit-rents to the king and of acres set apart for king, church, and public. Modyford's reports were evidently phrased so as to impress the Restoration government with the value of Jamaica as a revenue-producing island and must be read with that idea in mind Mrs. Butterfield, one of my former students under the Commonwealth Fund, is at present engaged in bringing order out of chaos among certain groups of Jamaican papers. She has succeeded in having the most neglected of them transferred from Kingston to Spanish Town, where quarters have been provided for her. Regarding the evidence from the land records she writes me, "From what I have seen I think there was a great deal of land-grabbing and speculation in the island in the 17th century. . . . Modyford, Molesworth, and one or two others seem to have been leaders of the business." The map in Ogilby's *America* (1671), pp. 336–337, is much more to be depended on for accuracy than are Modyford's reports. Its entries of names, locations, and number of plantations—whether sugar, indigo, cacao, or cotton—seem authoritative. The map shows also the number of colonels, captains, majors, lieutenants, and ensigns who settled down to plantation life. Ogilby was the geographer royal and the draughtsman of a well-known atlas, and he must have had his own sources of information.

tive settlers no small part of the attractiveness of the island lay in the grant of liberty of conscience to those who believed in God and the free exercise of the Christian religion to all "modest and tender people" who would make Jamaica their permanent home.[1]

Under the stimulus of the hopeful prospects that the new situation in America opened to all, men with titles to colonial soil brought out and polished up their claims. The fourth earl of Stirling refurbished his ancestral rights to Long Island, based on the distribution of 1635 by the Council for New England, but was soon thrust out of court by the Duke of York, who bought him off, but, as happened with many ducal and royal pensions and annuities, never paid for his purchase.[2] The Duke and Duchess of Hamilton sought to recover the region granted the old duke by the council covering the region between the Connecticut River and Narragansett Bay, known to them as the county of New Cambridge. They hoped to receive quit-rents from tenants in the territory, but nothing came of the effort, partly because of the opposition of Connecticut and partly because the royal commissioners sent over in 1664–1665 reported against a revival of the title on the ground that James, Marquis of Hamilton, had never sent over any servant, agent, or planter to take possession of the territory.[3] Similarly, the Mason and Gorges heirs, Robert Mason and Ferdinando Gorges, tried, and with somewhat better success, to obtain possession of lands in New Hampshire and Maine, the former basing his claim on grants from the Council for

1. *Calendar State Papers, Colonial*, 1661–1668, §§374, 630, 635, pp. 187, 193. Charles II, in his declaration from Breda April 4, 1660, and in a second declaration, December 6, 1661, recommended a measure of freedom for all religions in England and it was hoped, particularly by the Roman Catholics, that liberty of conscience would be granted by parliament to all professing any religion without distinction. But the proposal was defeated partly by the opposition of Clarendon. The Act of Uniformity was passed in 1662 (14 Charles II, c. 4) and though king and House of Lords later recommended some moderation and indulgence in the enforcement of the law the House of Commons insisted on its rigid maintenance and refused to admit any right of dispensation except by itself (*Commons' Journal*, VIII, 442–443). Nevertheless the king in all colonial charters granted after this date and in all instructions issued and orders given, enforced liberty of conscience in the colonies. The colonies were his and the Act of Uniformity did not extend beyond the realm.

2. Calder, in *Essays in Colonial History*, pp. 92–93; Bond, *Quit-Rents*, pp. 41, note, 52–60; *Calendar State Papers, Colonial*, 1661–1668, §98. See above, Vol. II, 225, note 1.

3. *Calendar State Papers, Colonial*, 1661–1668, §§735, i, 1089, i; *New York Colonial Documents*, III, 107. Above, Vol. I, 417.

New England, the latter on the royal charter of 1639. Robert Mason, surrendering his patent in 1664, eventually recovered title to the soil, though it is doubtful if he ever received any quit-rents from the inhabitants and had to be content with such profits as could be derived from sales. The government as distinct from the soil was taken into the hands of the crown in 1679 and the territory became the royal province of New Hampshire.[1] Ferdinando Gorges, the younger, secured the restitution of Maine but his commissioners were put out by the Puritans, restored by the royal commissioners of 1665, and again displaced when, to the great displeasure of the crown, Maine was purchased by Massachusetts from Gorges in 1678. Gorges tried to recover his province in 1691 when it became known that the Lords of Trade were to return it to Massachusetts by the charter of that year, but he failed, perhaps in part because he was an absentee Barbadian planter and at one time agent in England for the Leeward Islands, and in part because the Lords of Trade were already convinced that private proprietary colonies and particularly the private colony of an absentee lord was certain to be disadvantageous to the crown.[2]

There were other claimants also. Sometime before 1662 the Hopton title to lands in Virginia, which "by reason of the late unhappy and unsettled times [the grantees] could not plant or enjoy" was assigned to Sir Humphrey Hooke and other eminent citizens of London employed as agents in seating the territory. These agents obtained from the crown instructions to the governor and council of Virginia that they be given all assistance in the work of planting and of receiving all the rents and profits from it. But the Virginians did not take kindly to this arrangement and the grantees surrendering their patent received a new one, May 8, 1669, to such of them as were alive and to the assignees of those deceased, giving them ex-

1. Hammond, "The Mason Title," *Proceedings,* American Antiquarian Society, October, 1916, pp. 245–263; *New York Colonial Documents,* III, 101–102. For the later history of the Mason grant, Bouton, *History of Concord,* and Greene, *Boundary Lines of Old Groton.* The case can be followed in *Acts Privy Council, Colonial,* II, §§1014, 1050, 1109, 1116, 1155, 1199, 1289, 1293, and in the volumes to 1679 of the *Calendar State Papers, Colonial,* especially, 1661–1668, §706; 1677–1680, §§996, 1036. Also *Collections,* Massachusetts Historical Society, 3d series, VIII, 238–242.

2. *Calendar State Papers, Colonial, passim* to 1692. Gorges was in England during these years, an absentee landlord from Barbados (*ibid.,* 1669–1674, §442). Later he became the agent of Governor Stapleton (Penson, *The Colonial Agents of the West Indies,* index).

tensive proprietary rights to the soil of Virginia.[1] This grant was
never acted on and in 1673 it was renewed to Arlington and Culpeper, on the same terms, except that arrears of rent should date only
from May 8, 1669. The Virginians sought to ward off the danger
by petitioning for an incorporation and charter of their own which
should enable them to buy out the patentees. But the effort, which
might otherwise have been successful, was ended by Bacon's Rebellion the next year and the grant remained to become the basis of the
later Fairfax estate.[2] None of these were colonies or even the beginning of colonies; all (except perhaps that of Gorges) had to do only
with the soil and its profits. They show, however, a marked revival
of interest at this time in the possibility of revenue from lands in
America and represent the hopes that many had, and were to continue to have, of rich rewards from the possession of proprietary
estates there.

Charles II, none better, knew the value of favors to those who had
befriended him and aided him in exile. Hopton was living with
Hyde at St. Helier's, Isle of Jersey, at the time of the Virginia
grant of 1649, and was one of the king's most ardent supporters. Sir
William Davenant, poet laureate under Charles I, was one of the
few men among the king's supporters who kept up his energy and
self-respect during these distressing years, and as a reward Charles
in 1649 appointed him treasurer of Virginia in place of Sir John
Berkeley, whom he had originally named to the post in order to get
rid of William Claiborne, because of the latter's loyalty to parliament. Later in 1650 he made Davenant governor of Maryland, but
Davenant, setting sail in May of that year, ended his career as a
colonizer by being captured in the Channel and thrown into Cowes
Castle.[3] As king of Scotland and still legally the king of England,
Charles maintained in exile his court and council, kept together the
"small family" of gentlemen that had been assigned to him by his
father, had his officers of state and other "servants," retained the
seals in his possession,[4] and possessed the nucleus of an army. He

1. *Calendar State Papers, Colonial,* 1661–1668, §§391, 520, 1513; 1669–1674, §§63,
145, 146.
2. *Ibid.,* 1669–1674, §§769, 770; *Acts Privy Council, Colonial,* I, §1045. For the
later history of this grant, above, Vol. II, 233–238.
3. Harbage, *Sir William Davenant: Poet Adventurer, 1606–1668* (1934); *Calendar
Clarendon Papers,* IV, 637.
4. Not the great seal of England, of course, that was in the hands of the Puritan
authorities in control at Whitehall.

was constantly asked for offices and grants, not only by those who were with him during his wanderings, but also by royalists in England who continued to visit him or communicate with him (despite the efforts of the Puritan government to prevent it), or else made contributions to his cause.[1] He issued many commissions, licenses, and letters patent to his friends, both lay and secular, created baronets and knights bachelors, and even peers, as when in 1658 he made Sir John Berkeley a baron, Baron Berkeley of Stratton in Cornwall.[2]

Among those closest to him was Sir Edward Hyde, his chancellor of the exchequer and in 1657 his lord chancellor and afterward Lord Clarendon, who remained with him or near him throughout his life on the Continent. In exile, too, was the Duke of York, his brother, a lad of but fourteen years at the time of his father's execution, who had fled from England to The Hague in 1648. He and the king were never on congenial terms, partly because of the duke's liking for intrigue and partly because of his more affluent circumstances, due to pay received for military service under the Spanish crown, which enabled him to set up a rival court at Brussels at a time when Charles was much alone and in want and had to sell his jewels to support himself. Until a reconciliation was effected in 1658, the brothers and their followers formed in a mild way two rival factions,[3] traces of which continued throughout the twenty-five years of the king's reign. Associated with the duke as his secretary, treasurer, and financial manager was Sir John Berkeley, whom Charles at one time sequestered from attendance on his master for six months, though he eventually restored him to favor. Hyde, a stern and restless man, often petulant and arbitrary, did not like either Berkeley or the duke, even though the latter was afterward to marry his own daughter, partly because Berkeley sided with the duke against himself and the king and partly because in the reaching of important decisions and the distribution of important favors, the ducal group, holding together, showed greater determination

1. *Calendar Clarendon Papers*, IV, 170, 196, 246.

2. "From the Victory of *Stratton*, two of the great Commanders that shared in it were successively created Barons of *Stratton* in *Cornwall*, Sir *Ralph Hopton* and Sir *John Berkley*, on the Honour's being extinct at Lord *Hopton's* death." *Life of Barwick*, p. 192, note.

3. "Never was little family so torn into so many Pieces and Factions. The Duke [of York] was very young, yet loving Intrigue so well that He was too much inclined to hearten any man, who had the confidence to make bold Propositions to him," Clarendon, *Life*, I, 241.

and possessed a stronger collective will than did Hyde and King Charles. In the ducal group were Richard Nicolls, called the duke's "servant," who ran many of the duke's errands and was afterward one of the grooms of his bedchamber, and William Coventry who, after 1660, was the duke's secretary in England. Sir George Carteret was on better terms with both sides, having entertained Hyde at Castle Elizabeth in Jersey for more than two years and on one occasion in an emergency having turned out his own family to make room for the duke and his retainers. In a similar position was Henry Bennett, afterward Earl of Arlington and secretary of state, and Lord Craven, whose devotion to the king's aunt, the queen of Bohemia, whose friendship for her son, Prince Rupert,[1] and whose many loans of money to the king, despite his own heavy losses in estates during the Interregnum, foreshadowed high preferment in the years to come. After the return of the king, General Monck, Anthony Ashley Cooper, and George Downing, all of whom had played important parts and held important offices under the Protectorate, received many rewards for their change of allegiance. There were others as well, who on returning to England after lean years on the Continent "had the keener appetites and the stronger Presumption to push on their Fortunes (as They called it) in the Infancy of their Master's Restoration that other men might not be preferred before them, who had not borne the heat of the day as they had done."[2]

For the first few years after his restoration Charles had very little to give in the way of money rewards. In one of his first speeches to parliament he said "I have not so much money in my purse as when I came to you . . . nor have I been able to give my brother one shilling since I came into England, nor to keep any Table in My House, but what I eat myself; and that which troubles me most is to see many of you come to Me at Whitehall and to think that you must go somewhere else to seek your Dinner."[3] But he could recom-

---

1. On Prince Rupert, *Memoirs* (Warburton ed.), three vols., 1849.
2. Clarendon, *Life*, II, 3.
3. *His Majesties Gracious Speech to Both Houses of Parliament, August 29, 1660.* A contemporary printed quarto. The speech is printed also, with many variations, in Bryant, *Letters of King Charles II*, p. 103. The Venetian resident reporting on this speech said: His Majesty "made a long speech, showing how he was pinched for money; since his return he had supported himself with the money sent to him abroad by parliament; he had given nothing to his brothers because he had not the means; the customs revenues assigned to his person were absorbed by the fleet." *Calendar Venetian Papers*, 1659–1661, p. 195. Other references to "the shortness of cash at Court" are, *ibid.*, pp. 187, 277, 300; 1661–1664, pp. vii, viii, ix, x, 24, 75, 164, 202.

pense his friends and supporters with offices and honors and with grants and gifts which cost him nothing. He could not give away freely his royal manors, as he needed himself the returns from all that he was able to retain, meager though these returns were, but he could make grants of land from the royal demesne in America, of which there were large areas still unoccupied. To this form of largesse he was inclined, not so much by his own will as by the suggestion and insistence of others. The first of such favors was the grant of that wide-stretching area to the south of Virginia that had first attracted the attention of Lord Baltimore, then of Sir Robert Heath, and in 1632 of Lord Maltravers, the last of whom made a serious effort to settle the territory.[1] This enterprise we shall discuss in a later chapter.

But a greater adventure in the field of colonial expansion was soon to come. For years the supremacy of the Dutch had been a source of irritation to the English merchants and had led to incrimination and conflicts that grew in intensity as the importance of trade became a major concern to those in England who looked to their own immediate trade profits and their country's commercial and colonial future. By 1650 the carrying trade of the world was in Dutch hands and Dutch ships were engaged in traffic with the English colonies in America, notably in Barbados and the Leeward Islands, where the connection of Sir William Courteen with Holland had been largely responsible for the beginning of the Dutch interest in that quarter. The planters were supplied not only with their clothing, implements, and provisions cheaper and on better terms by the Dutch than by the English, but they were also able to obtain their knowledge of sugar raising from the Dutch in Brazil and their tobacco seed and other seeds and roots from the Dutch husbandmen in Essequibo and Surinam. The prohibitory act of 1650 and the

1. As the Heath patent, which had been assigned to Maltravers and in part, according to his own statement, to one Samuel Vassall who had undertaken to settle the country and regarding whom we shall have something to say later, showed signs of awakening, it was stilled forever by order of council, which ordered the attorney general to quash it by process of law. Furthermore, the council at the time laid down the general rule that "no grant of any Foreign Plantation shall pass the Great Seal in future without a clause that if within a certain number of years no plantation be made the said grant shall become voyd" (*Calendar State Papers, Colonial*, 1661–1668, §§426, 525; *Acts Privy Council, Colonial*, I, §§594, 604). No such clause was introduced, as far as I know, into any of the later proprietary charters, though the same statement is to be found in the royal instructions to the commissioners sent over in 1664 (*New York Colonial Documents*, III, 56 [7]).

navigation act of 1651, both directed against the Hollanders and the Hamburgers, had had little influence in checking the traffic and one of the crying complaints of those who were bewailing the decay of trade was that the Dutch were the great obstacle in the way of England's commercial advancement. In the North Sea fisheries the Dutch boats were trespassing on English waters and pushing their field of operations to the very shores of England herself.[1]

Of even greater consequence was the rivalry of the Dutch and English for the control of the trade in negroes, on the coast of Guinea, which became singularly important as the island colonies more and more demanded slave labor for the upkeep of their sugar and other plantations. The African trade had been started very early by sundry London merchants, Sir Nicholas Crispe and others, who had sent ships there, built a fort and warehouses, and given the traffic a good start. During the Interregnum other merchants, John Young and Company among them, took it up, shipping to Guinea English manufactures and returning with slaves and gold (guineas). But the Dutch West India Company was also there and carrying on the better trade, and for some years Dutch and English had been engaged in a petty warfare, each side retaliating on the other, seizing ships, imprisoning men, and confiscating goods. To aid in winning ascendancy in these northern and central parts of the African coast the Morocco Company was formed in 1661, with the Duke of York and Lord Willoughby at its head, which received a grant of the region from Casablanca to Cape Blanco (34°–20°), supplemented two years later by the acquisition of Tangier. It was, therefore, eminently desirable that the Guinea region be made secure if possible for English trade and something of an official warrant be given to the proceedings of one Captain Robert Holmes, commander of some of his majesty's ships on the coast of Africa, who had been committing acts against the Dutch that, in their interference with the freedom of trade in those parts and affronts to a people with whom England was at peace, were dangerously near piracy.[2] So unscrupulous were these acts that later, in August, 1661, Charles II, who had little sympathy with the high-handed policy of the ducal group at court and in the City, the slogan of which was *Delenda est*

---

1. A chapter on The Dutch Rivalry will appear in the next volume.
2. *Calendar State Papers, Colonial*, 1661–1668, §954. For the situation as regards England, Portugal, and the Dutch in 1661 see the *Calendar Venetian Papers*, 1661–1664, pp. xxxviii–xl.

Carthago, felt called upon to disclaim them. To strengthen the English position, the Company of Royal Adventurers to Africa had been formed, December 8, 1660, with the Duke of York as its active and energetic head and all the region from Cape Blanco south to the Cape of Good Hope as its territory. Later this company surrendered its charter and on January 10, 1663, was reincorporated as the Royal African Company, with a complete monopoly of trade in negro slaves, elephants' teeth (ivory), red wood, hides, wax, gums, grains, and other commodities of the country. Though incorporated to last for a thousand years, the company actually lost its monopoly in 1698, but continued to do business, though a number of times remodeled, for a century and a half. It was a factor of tremendous importance in our colonial history, in that the very being of the plantation colonies depended on an ample supply of negro labor.[1]

In the forging of these instruments of aggressive action against the commercial leadership of the Dutch we see the handiwork of the merchants of London, aided and abetted by Sir George Downing, who had been resident minister at The Hague to the States General of Holland both during the Protectorate and under the Restoration. Downing, son of Emmanuel Downing and nephew of John Winthrop, the elder, had been one of the first graduates of Harvard College and afterward became closely identified with the customs and the treasury in England. He was a "voluminous" speaker and writer, obsessed with the idea of driving the Dutch from the commercial and colonial fields. He and the merchants omitted no opportunity, and had omitted none for ten years, to iterate and reiterate the importance of ending the Dutch supremacy,

1. Zook, "Company of Royal Adventurers Trading into Africa, 1660–1672" (*Journal of Negro History,* IV, no. 2, April, 1919. Dr. Zook in conjunction with Miss Elizabeth Donnan is preparing a history of the Royal African Company); Thurloe, *State Papers,* V, 429–432, and index under "Holland"; *New York Colonial Documents,* II, 243, 245, 255, 261–271, 281, 285–286, 298–304; *Calendar State Papers, Colonial,* 1661–1668, §§205, 206, 383, p. 117, §§408, 543, 545, 618, 663. There exist a great many Downing broadsides and manifestoes, in print and manuscript, in English and Dutch, many of which will be found in the Public Record Office, others, with the Dutch rejoinders, in *New York Colonial Documents,* II. The language employed is always extravagant and menacing, showing Downing's temper and implacable attitude. His tone became somewhat milder in 1664, perhaps in the hope that, despite the English determination to oust the Dutch from Guinea and New Netherland, the disagreements could be settled without resort to war. This somewhat more moderate expression of opinion can be seen in his pamphlet of 1665 replying to the Dutch answer to his Memorial of December 20, 1664, *A Reply . . . to the Remarks of the Deputies of the Estates General* (London, 1665).

and Downing in paper after paper, sometimes in Dutch and sometimes in English, showed how easily this could be done. Though at first these men made little impression on the king and Clarendon they won over the Duke of York and others of the court group, who were impatient for action and who, in common with Downing, the merchants, and the factors and agents of the Royal African Company and the Royal Fishery Company, were already dubbing as "insolencies" the efforts the Dutch were making to retaliate on their molestors.

The Duke of York was the leader of the group, which included Downing in Holland and Coventry, Berkeley, and Bennett at the court in Whitehall. He had been appointed lord high admiral in January, 1660, though he exercised the functions of his office only from the time of his brother's accession, when on July 4 of that year his appointment was confirmed by order in council. Under him were Lord Berkeley, Sir William Penn, and for a time Peter Pett, all of whom with Carteret, the treasurer and Sir William Batten, the surveyor, constituted the principal officers of the navy, or navy board, with Samuel Pepys, clerk of the acts. In his capacity as lord high admiral and in conjunction with the navy board he controlled the operations of the navy in all its aspects, devoting himself with great energy to the task of putting the king's ships in proper condition, scrutinizing expenses, eliminating waste, and seeing that contracts were fairly given out and honestly executed.[1] He was no figurehead in the enterprises with which his name is connected, for he worked hard and without scruple in his desire to advance England's interests at sea and in trade and in the many commercial spheres of influence. He accompanied the fleet in person at the outbreak of the second Dutch war, April 20, 1665, handing over his shore duties for the time being to the Duke of Albemarle. Thus he was in a position to use the ships much as he liked and in a mood to listen with sympathy and responsiveness to the grievances of the merchants and others against the Dutch wherever found—in Guinea, the North Sea, the Caribbean, and New Netherland on the American mainland.

Nowhere in the west were the Dutch more firmly intrenched than at New Amsterdam, the center and the heart of a wide trading area

1. *Memoirs of the English Affairs chiefly Naval from the year 1660 to 1673, written by his Royal Highness James Duke of York.* This volume contains letters from the duke to various officials. As lord high admiral he had to do only with the navy and not with the High Court of Admiralty or with the beginnings of vice-admiralty jurisdiction in the colonies.

that in claim at least embraced the three rivers, the Hudson, the Delaware, and the Connecticut. How soon and from whom the duke first heard of the quarrels taking place there between the Dutch and the English is not quite clear, but it must have been sometime in the year 1663. Maverick in New Amsterdam was writing letters to the Earl of Clarendon, though neither he nor the lord chancellor were as bitter toward the Dutch as were Downing and the merchants who were for immediate and aggressive action.[1] Nevertheless they were in the main favorable to the general plan. Where the duke led, the king and Clarendon, hesitating but not unwilling, were bound to follow. More directly influential was Colonel John Scott, who came to England in the interest of the Atherton Company some time in 1662 and remained until the autumn of 1663.[2] While in England he brought the grievances of the English inhabitants of Long Island to the attention of the council for foreign plantations, of which Lord Berkeley was president at the time and Colleton, Noell, Kendall, and Diggs, merchants and promoters all of them, were the only members present. After Scott's return he wrote to Joseph Williamson, undersecretary of state, enclosing a letter from a committee of the aggrieved and "enslaved" inhabitants, full of protests against the Dutch. The matter was referred to Berkeley, Carteret, and Coventry for report. These men, all in close touch with the duke, must have had before them as their sources of information the evidence furnished by Scott and Maverick, petitions from the Long Islanders, possibly a communication from Baltimore's privy council concerning the Dutch and the Delaware lands,[3] data supplied by the farmers of the customs, and probably a "brief narrative" prepared (or at least ordered to be prepared, as the docu-

---

1. *Collections,* New York Historical Society, 1869, pp. 21, 32, 38, 43; Osgood, *American Colonies in the Seventeenth Century,* III, 159–160.

2. Scott had already aroused the wrath and fears of the magistrates of the Dutch towns on Long Island, who charged him and his "attendant mob" with pursuing them "by fire and sword, yea running those through who will say that we are not seated on king's ground, etc." (*New York Colonial Documents,* II, 374). In February, 1664, he had come to some sort of an understanding with Stuyvesant and he confidently hoped that were the Dutch reduced to the authority of the king of England he would be allowed to control the region beyond the East River (*Calendar State Papers, Colonial,* 1661–1668, pp. 226–227; *New York Colonial Documents,* II, 393–394). He may have aspired to even a larger propriety of his own (*ibid.,* III, 105). He was destined to be grievously disappointed when the duke appropriated all the territory to himself. *New Netherland* (Original Narratives), pp. 411–412; 462–463; *New York Colonial Documents,* II, 234, 374, 393–409, 480–481.

3. *Maryland Archives,* III, 426–428.

ment is no longer extant) by Scott, Maverick, and George Baxter,[1] an Englishman of influence in the Dutch province. This narrative was intended to set forth the king's title to New Netherland, the Dutch intrusion, the state of the Dutch trade, the strength and form of government at New Amsterdam, and the best way to get rid of the Dutch occupation. The committee reported, January 29, 1664, recounting the encroachments of the Dutch and recommending immediate action.[2]

The plot against the Dutch at New Amsterdam now moved rapidly to its consummation. Whatever the ethics in the case may have been the logic of the situation was irresistible. England had thrown down her challenge and in a half unconscious way was rough shaping a policy in the decision to retain Jamaica, in the navigation act of 1660, in the grant of the region between Virginia and the Spaniards in "Florida" to eight friends of the king (to be discussed in a later chapter on the beginnings of Carolina), and in the recognition of the importance of foreign trade and the customs accruing therefrom as assets of prime consequence to the crown. Though more than thirty years were to elapse before consolidation of control was to become even approximately complete and though complete consolidation was never attained as far as the American continental colonies were concerned, nevertheless the adoption of a policy of centralization as most conducive to England's colonial and commercial success in the future was already becoming inevitable. At first, however, it was scarcely recognizable as such in the presence of the weightier diplomatic relationships that were engaging the attention of the king and his advisers during these four epochal years.

Berkeley, Carteret, and Coventry sent in their report on January 29, 1664, and Downing continued to issue memorials and write let-

1. Above, Vol. II, 46, 47 n.

2. *Calendar State Papers, Colonial,* 1661–1668, §§98, 510, 603, 622, 647; *New York Colonial Documents,* III, 46, 47, 48, 49, 86. Scott went to England at the end of 1662 and remained there until the autumn of the next year, when he returned to Long Island (*ibid.,* II, 363). There he resumed his efforts to erect a propriety. Connecticut complained of these efforts in February, 1663 (*ibid.,* III, 86), because Scott had persuaded the people of Hempstead to throw off their allegiance to Connecticut and set him up as "president" of a sort of little republic consisting of the English towns of western Long Island. He claimed that Connecticut's charter did not include Long Island. Connecticut arrested him and threw him into jail in Hartford, whence he petitioned the colony for release, "having run himself into a Labyrinth of misery by the villanie of bad Instruments as well as his corrupt nature," etc. (Connecticut Archives, Towns and Lands, I, nos. 11–38).

ters demanding satisfaction and reparation for Dutch insults. The decision to send commissioners and a fleet to New England and New Netherland must have been reached soon after, for before February was ended money had been allotted, vessels provided, men mustered, and arms, ammunition, and equipment prepared.[1] On April 21 the House of Commons resolved that the "wrongs, dishonours and indignities done to his Majesty by the subjects of the United Provinces" in India, Africa, and America were so flagrant and the "damages, affronts and injuries done by them" to the merchants were so obstructive of foreign trade that the house "would support the king with life and fortune against all opposition." Thus the king, parliament, and the duke, Downing, and the merchants were at last in accord in supporting the conspiracy and there can be little doubt but that the gentry at large, as far as they knew what was happening, were as eager as the others to see the programme carried out in full.

The months of February, March, and April must have been a busy time with those responsible for the undertaking and because there are no other than official references to the activities behind the scenes the preparations must have been made with considerable secrecy. Rumors of the projected invasion, to which hardly any attention at all was paid in England outside the group concerned, reached both New England and New Amsterdam and were confirmed when the king in royal letters to each of the New England colonies sent word of the appointment of the commissioners and the reasons therefor and bade each coöperate with them to the fullness of its power. He notified Massachusetts of the proposed reduction of New Netherland and took occasion to remind that evasive commonwealth of his dissatisfaction with its former attitude and his expectation that it would do better in the future.[2] But what the

1. The Venetian resident does not mention the expedition to New Netherland until October, 1664, long after the capture of New Amsterdam, and he apparently knew nothing about it at the time it took place. To him the troubles with the Dutch were all due to the Guinea situation (*Calendar Venetian Papers*, 1664–1666, pp. 47–49). Even after the capture had been effected Downing told De Witt in Holland that the driving of the Dutch out of New Netherland "was not true and that it could not be," though of course he knew it was true. The resident not without reason called Downing "cunning" and spoke of the "secrets of this government" as "impenetrable."

2. The king informed Massachusetts that her reply of November 25, 1662, to his letter of the June 28 before had not answered his expectations and he hoped for a stricter obedience this time to his commands (*New York Colonial Documents*, III, 63). In this he was sadly disillusioned. Massachusetts had no intention, if she could

king did not tell either Massachusetts or the other colonies was the disposition he had already made of the territory to be conquered and of such other adjacent territories as he considered within his right to give away. More than seven weeks before he wrote his letters to New England, acting undoubtedly under pressure from the Duke of York and his allies, he promised to make his brother the absolute proprietor of a strangely assorted group of lands, some of which were to be his by right of conquest, some by a more dubious but at least a defensible title, and some by no title at all if a previous royal grant be construed as having legal validity. The passage of the duke's charter through the seals was started early in March, the "warrant to prepare" (based on the petition which probably the duke had drawn up with the advice of lawyers) is undated but the king's bill was engrossed March 8. By special instruction under the king's sign manual the bill was to pass "by immediate warrant"; it reached the signet office March 10 and the privy seal office on March 12. The privy seal was prepared on the same day—the date of the enrollment[1]—and the great seal must have been attached at once. Thus the essential steps in the issue of this patent—an extraordinary document when one considers the date of its issue, which was after not before the Interregnum and at about the same time with the grant of the remarkably liberal charters to Connecticut and Rhode Island—occupied but four days, an unprecedented event.

The grouping of lands thus given away to form a ducal propriety was unlike anything hitherto known in English America. The lands were widely scattered, the boundaries almost grotesque in their contours, and the territory without symmetry or uniformity of race, religion, or products of the soil. They included Maine between the Ste. Croix and Kennebec rivers and northward to the St. Lawrence; Long Island, Martha's Vineyard, and Nantucket; and all the region from the Connecticut River to the Delaware and northward to and including Albany. Later there was added, as part of the territory taken from the Dutch, the west bank of the Delaware, thus shutting out the Maryland claim which Baltimore continued vigorously to defend. The title to the Maine section remained always insecure and was destined to be a bone of contention between France and Eng-

help herself, of obeying a royal command or of admitting the right of any royal commissioner to interfere in her affairs.

1. Patent Rolls, 16 Carolus II, pt. 8, no. 6; *New York Colonial Documents,* II, 295–298.

land for many years to come; that to Long Island was based on an incompleted purchase by the duke from Stirling and Berkeley,[1] with Martha's Vineyard, Nantucket, and other islands thrown in;[2] that to the region west from the Connecticut River was a clear violation of the Connecticut charter, granted less than two years before. One marvels at the indifference or ignorance of the English chancery officials and even more at the mental confusion of this young prince, only thirty years old, and of those who gave him their advice. The propriety of New York, in the territory granted and the powers conferred, is the worst example in the history of English colonization of a proprietary lordship, which the proprietor himself never even visited, which was administered entirely by executive agents, and in the government of which the people of the province were not allowed to have a share.

1. On February 18, 1662, the Earl of Stirling sold to Lord Berkeley for £3500 one half of the lands in New England and Long Island, which he claimed by virtue of the patent to his grandfather from the Council for New England, April 23, 1635. But Berkeley was unable to get from Charles II a confirmation of this purchase, in the form of a proprietary charter, just why we do not know, unless it be that the Duke of York had already made known his wish for a grant of colonial territory. Berkeley, evidently not wishing to be out of pocket by the transaction joined with Stirling in 1663 and petitioned for a new grant, but the solicitor general, Sir Heneage Finch, decided that the old title was sufficient. Berkeley then came to an understanding with the duke, who promised to pay Stirling the £3500 himself, evidently borrowing the money from his father-in-law, the Earl of Clarendon. Stirling then surrendered his patent and the way was cleared for the royal grant of March 12, 1664. But James never paid Stirling the £3500 and after his own patent had passed the seals found himself in possession of a territory to which the earl had a title not yet fully extinguished. He was therefore obliged to compensate both Stirling and Berkeley. He met his obligation to Stirling by promising him an annuity of £300 out of the net profits of his province, but as there never were any net profits Stirling received nothing and petitioned the Treasury in 1687 for payment (*Calendar Treasury Books*, VIII, pt. III, pp. 1174–1175; *ibid.*, IX, 237. A petition of 1760 puts the amount at £7000, *New York Documents*, VII, 430–432; *Board of Trade Journal*, 1759–1763, p. 128). He compensated Berkeley by giving him an undivided half of the region between the Hudson and the Delaware; but he did nothing for Stirling. Neither Berkeley nor Stirling had any interest in colonization as such. They, as well as the duke, Scott, and Sir Robert Carr, sought lands in America for financial ends only. Carr wanted a patent for a propriety on the Delaware as well as a governorship in Maine, and Scott, as we have seen, aimed at a propriety on Long Island. Perhaps Scott even dreamed of obtaining the very patent that the Duke of York received.

2. For Thomas Mayhew's claim to jurisdiction over Martha's Vineyard, Nantucket, and adjoining islands see *Executive Council Minutes of New York, 1668–1673* (Paltsits ed.), I, 97, 345–377. Thomas Mayhew, Jr., claimed jurisdiction over Nantucket by his father's purchase from Stirling's agent, James Forret, October 13, 1641, and over Martha's Vineyard by a similar purchase from Richard Vines, steward general and agent of Ferdinando Gorges, October 25 of the same year. In neither case was the grant more than a deed of land; it conveyed no rights of jurisdiction or government.

On April 2 James named his faithful adherent, Richard Nicolls, deputy governor of a region still claimed by and in the possession of the Dutch, and on the 23d the king made him the head of the commission of inquiry, the other members of which were Carr, Cartwright, and Maverick. Their business was to visit all the New England colonies, hear complaints from those who had already begun to voice their grievances, especially in Massachusetts, and to reduce all local activities to the rules prescribed by the several charters.[1] For their services they were to be given £200 apiece, but it is doubtful if they ever received it, unless it was paid from the duke's privy purse. There is no record of payment out of the exchequer. Maverick must have relished with grim enjoyment the opportunity thus furnished by the king of looking into the way Massachusetts had been conducting her government, for these commissioners were invested with wide powers to bring the whole of New England more directly

1. The instructions and secret instructions are in *New York Colonial Documents,* III, 51–65. A preliminary statement of purpose, which if drawn up by Lord Clarendon shows that the king and Clarendon were committed to the conspiracy, is in *Calendar State Papers, Colonial,* 1661–1668, §706. The reference to the charters in the instructions makes it clear that the terms of the Connecticut charter, as well as those of the charters of Massachusetts and Rhode Island, against the former of which the instructions were specially directed, were familiar to the officials in England and that "authentick coppyes" of them were brought by the commissioners to New England. Why then were the boundaries in the Connecticut charter either wittingly or unwittingly violated in 1664? Are we to draw any inferences from the fact that Charles II was reported to have declared himself deceived by those boundaries and that Joseph Williamson in 1663 should have entered in one of his many note-books (*ibid.,* §623) the item "The boundary of Connecticut is forfeited?" Williamson made many curious mistakes in his entries, but he must have had some reason for his statement. Are we justified in assuming (from the boundaries inserted in the duke's charter, which it must be remembered embraced the entire New Haven jurisdiction and all of the Connecticut colony west of the Connecticut River and on Long Island) that the English authorities did not realize the fact that they had already granted Connecticut the same territory? If so then the remark of Connecticut's fathers to the Dutch commissioners in October, 1663, that if Connecticut did not adhere with the utmost strictness to the boundaries of her charter she would "incur the king's displeasure" (*New Netherland,* Original Narratives, p. 436) has an odd sound. They were of course right in saying that they had the prior claim, but they were past masters in the art of shifting responsibility and the grant to the duke in 1664 must have come to them as a great shock, since it cut away the entire ground of their argument based on what they called "the king's displeasure." Unless the English officials were incredibly unobservant they must have known that after March 12, 1664, the king had been pleased to place the New Haven colony and all the Connecticut towns west of the Connecticut River under the authority of two jurisdictions, a situation so anomalous that one would suppose even they would have noticed it, unless they had taken a different view of the Connecticut boundaries from that held in the colony itself. See below, p. 62, note 1.

under the king's authority. This process of centralizing control was
carried a step farther by arrangements which were in the making
for the surrender of the Mason and Gorges patents and the transforming of New Hampshire and western Maine into a separate royal
propriety between Massachusetts and that portion of the ducal
grant which lay farther to the east. The object in so doing was to
render this region contributory to the improvement in trade, under
the regulations laid down in the acts of trade and navigation.

But the main object of the expedition was the reduction of the
Dutch colony to "an entire submission and obedience" to the king
and his government on the ground that the Dutch were interlopers
on English territory. After a tedious voyage of ten weeks, two of
the four frigates under the command of Captain Hugh Hyde
reached Boston, July 20, the others arriving soon after. On August
18 they entered Nyack or Gravesend Bay, in the Narrows just north
of Coney Island, and Nicolls first issued proclamations offering
favorable terms to the Dutch towns on Long Island and to the
burghers of New Amsterdam itself.[1] He then sent word to Peter
Stuyvesant, director or governor of New Netherland, demanding
the surrender of all the towns, forts, and other places of strength
possessed by the Dutch. Stuyvesant, though long forewarned of the
danger,[2] at first scornfully refused to surrender and played for time.
A three days' delay was agreed on (August 24–27), during which
time the English troops were landed at Gravesend, whence they
advanced to the ferry (connecting Breuckelen with New Amsterdam) ready to cross the East River, while the frigates after reducing
Staten Island advanced up the bay, one vessel anchoring off Nut
Island and two others passing in front of the fort under full sail
with guns trained on the fort ready to begin a bombardment.[3] The
Dutch situation was desperate. The frigates blocked the harbor; the
fort, at the lower end of Manhattan Island, was wholly inadequate
to withstand an attack;[4] the supply of powder, both at Manhattan

1. *New York Colonial Documents*, II, 410–411, 443.
2. The danger from the English was anticipated by Stuyvesant after knowing of
the Connecticut charter of 1662 and particularly after the failure of the October negotiations of 1663 (below, p. 62, note 1). This fact is made clear from his letter to the
directors of the West India Company, November 10, 1664 (*New York Colonial
Documents*, II, 484).
3. *Calendar State Papers, Colonial*, 1661–1668, §788; *New York Colonial Documents*, II, 371; *New Netherland* (Original Narratives), pp. 414–415, 452, 460.
4. The fort was begun in 1626 and largely rebuilt ten years later. In 1646 Father

and at Fort Orange, was nearly exhausted; water and provisions[1] were insufficient to last out a siege; and the town council and burghers were all for a compliance.[2] New Amsterdam was defended by only about one hundred and fifty regular soldiers and perhaps two hundred and fifty to three hundred men capable of bearing arms, while on the other side were four hundred soldiers supplemented by volunteers from New England and the Long Island villages, together with Colonel John Scott and his horse and foot, all of whom were encamped on the Long Island shore ready to cooperate. With them were Governor John Winthrop and his son, Samuel Wyllys and Captain Thomas Clarke representing Connecticut, Captain John Pynchon, who lived at Springfield, representing the Massachusetts general court, and some one not named from Plymouth. Four of these men with Sir Robert Carr of the commissioners were deputed by Nicolls to act on his behalf. On August 22, Winthrop had written a private letter to Stuyvesant, making an urgent plea advising him to surrender[3]—a letter which Stuyvesant read to the council of burghers. When Stuyvesant attempted to argue the pros and cons of the matter he was told by the commissioners that the English had come to execute orders and not to discuss them, and very reluctantly, and to the great wrath of the Dutch West India Company afterward, he finally gave way and surrendered the fort without firing a gun. The terms were agreed upon August 27/September 7, and signed at Stuyvesant's farmhouse by Nicolls, Carr, and

Jogues reported it as crumbling away and Stuyvesant in 1647 said that it resembled "more a molehill than a fortress, without gates, the walls and bastions trodden under foot by men and cattle." In 1650 it had "not one gun carriage or one piece of cannon in a suitable frame or on a good platform." The responsibility for this state of things lay not with the governor and burghers of New Amsterdam but with the West India Company or with the States General of Holland, both of whom scandalously neglected the settlement. Within the fort were the governor's house, the double-roofed church (Dutch Reformed, Calvinist) with its square tower, barracks, prison, gallows, and whipping post. It was without well or cistern. For the fort at the time of the surrender, *New York Colonial Documents*, II, 440–441, and for later descriptions, *Calendar State Papers, Colonial*, 1685–1689, p. 326; *New York Colonial Documents*, II, 260, 390, 429; III, 260, 589, 590–591; *Documentary History of New York*, IV, 6, 8, 16, 20.

1. For the powder, *New York Colonial Documents*, II, 366, 372, 460–462; for the provisions, *New Netherland* (Original Narratives), pp. 461–462; *New York Colonial Documents*, II, 367, 373–374, 420–421, 429–440.

2. Letter of the Town Council, 1664, *ibid.*, pp. 451–453; *Records of New Amsterdam*, V, 114–116. This letter, which contains an account of the surrender, was sent to the directors in Holland after that event had taken place.

3. Winthrop's letter is printed in Stokes, *Iconography*, IV, 240–241.

Cartwright for the English, by five of the burghers and Domine Megapolensis for the Dutch, and by Winthrop, Wyllys, Clarke, and Pynchon for the New Englanders.[1] Stuyvesant refused to sign. Within two hours, according to the articles, after the signatures were appended, the fort and town of New Amsterdam were to be delivered into the hands of Colonel Richard Nicolls, "by the service of such as shall be by him deputed by his hand and seal."[2] In the next month, September, Cartwright took Fort Orange, and in October, with unnecessary tactlessness and brutality, Carr with his son Captain John Carr and Ensign Arthur Stock, reduced Fort Casimir on the Delaware (erected in 1651 to take the place of Fort Nassau), which in 1657 had been handed over to the city of Amsterdam for a large sum of money by the bankrupt West India Company and colonized and administered by that city under the name of the town

1. The presence of the Connecticut men was the logical consequence of the negotiations which had been carried on in Hartford, October 19 to 23, 1663, between Van Ruyven, Van Cortlandt, and Lawrence for the Dutch and "old" Matthew Allyn (d. 1671), "young" John Allyn (d. 1696), and John Talcott, appointed by the general court of Connecticut, in the course of which the Connecticut committee, standing firmly on the exact language of the patent, refused to be bound by the terms of the boundary agreement of 1650, which had been broken almost as soon as it was made (New York Colonial Documents, XIII, 64–65). They insisted on their full right to accept the surrender of the English towns of western Long Island and Westchester (Oostdorp or Vreeland), which had already revolted from New Netherland, giving as their reason that they could not restrain these towns from so doing, but forgetting to mention the fact that the colony itself had instigated the revolt by sending deputations among them for the purpose. The committee took the ground that should the commissioners of the United Colonies decide against them Connecticut would withdraw from the confederation, and should the Dutch try to put down the revolts she would protect the towns and bloodshed would follow. Stuyvesant called the attitude of the Hartford committee "unrighteous, stubborn, impudent and pertinacious" and spoke bitterly of the Englishman's "insatiable desire of possessing that which is ours." From this and other evidence it is clear that Winthrop did not construe the patent as authorizing the absorption of either Rhode Island, New Haven, or New Netherland. The matter was, however, taken entirely out of his hands by the general court of the colony (New Netherland, Original Narratives, pp. 436–439, 440, 462–463).

2. A straightforward account of the surrender of New Amsterdam is in Brodhead, History, I, 736–745. But it was written eighty-three years ago and needs to be supplemented by more recently discovered evidence, all of which may be found in Stokes, Iconography, VI, 18–20. Nicolls's letter to Stuyvesant, August 25, 1664, and Stuyvesant's reply are in New York State Library, History Bulletin, 2, pp. 86–92. The articles of surrender are printed in New York Colonial Documents, II, 250–253; New York State Library, History Bulletin, 2, pp. 95–98; and Brodhead, History, I, 762–763. A Dutch broadside is given in Paltsits, Executive Council Minutes, I, 65. Stuyvesant's story of the surrender and of the torn Winthrop letter, much dramatized by historians, is in New York Colonial Documents, II, 445–446.

of New Amstel (New Castle).¹ The conquest of New Netherland was complete. New Amsterdam became New York, Long Island, Yorkshire, and the region between the Hudson and the Delaware, Albania. Fort Amsterdam was renamed Fort James.

Though the change of masters throughout New Netherland was successfully accomplished, the investigation by the commissioners into the affairs of New England was very largely a failure. Their mission was "to remove all jealousies and misunderstandings" and to arouse among the peoples of the different colonies feelings of mutual confidence, respect, and forbearance. They were to inquire into the governments, particularly that of Massachusetts, to see if they were conforming to the provisions of their respective charters— copies of which the commissioners brought with them—and to report on the desirability of issuing new or explanatory patents in cases where evasions and departures were manifest. They were to sit as a royal court of appeal and to hear and determine grievances, some thirty of which, as it happened, were brought to their attention during the period of their activity; and above all, they were to investigate and determine how far the colonists were obeying the navigation act of 1660. The letters which the king sent to the individual colonies were couched in tactful and mollifying terms, designed to allay any fears that might arise of malevolence in the royal mind, and were intentionally tender in the desire of the English authorities to avoid anything that might further inflame the sensitive feelings and touchy humors that Englishmen well knew already existed in New England.²

1. Brodhead, *History*, I, 629–633. The documents in the case are in *New York Colonial Documents*, II, 2–246.

2. A brief itinerary will show the movements of the commissioners. New Amsterdam was taken August 27, 1664. Toward the end of the year Cartwright and Maverick left for Boston, taking up their residence in the house of Captain Breedon, a merchant and royalist sympathizer, at one time (1661) governor of Acadia. They were able to accomplish little or nothing, even personally, because Cartwright had the gout and Maverick spent his time visiting old friends, and still less officially because Nicolls was detained in New York and Carr was still on the Delaware. The latter reached Boston, February 5, but Nicolls did not arrive until May. About February 20 Maverick, Cartwright, and Carr went to Plymouth, then to Rhode Island, and finally to Connecticut, at each of which places they were well received. Returning to Boston April 13 and 14, they were joined by Nicolls early in May, just before the meeting of the general court time, and they fought out the issue during the ensuing three weeks, that is, until about May 30. Then Nicolls hurried back to New York, because of the "high and mighty threats" uttered by the Dutch West India Company and an expected attack on New York by de Ruyter which did not material-

But neither the time, the occasion, nor the men were favorable to a successful performance of this extraordinarily delicate task. It was undertaken in the first full flush of the Restoration, when Massachusetts at least was fearful of what the king intended to do and was determined to resist to the bitter end any encroachment upon what she considered her charter rights. As English finances were low, the commissioners were always cramped for money wherewith to meet expenses and were annoyed at the delays encountered because of the charges involved and the eventual exhaustion of their means and their credit. The attempt to combine two antagonistic enterprises, one military and hostile, the other peaceful and conciliatory, in the hands of a single group of men, three of whom were soldiers, was almost certain to end in disaster on the pacific side. Likewise, the men selected, with the single exception of Richard Nicolls, who was overburdened with his duties at New York, were far from always wise in their method of procedure. The one civilian, Maverick, had old-time grievances against Massachusetts and was charged by Governor Bellingham and the Bostonians with being their "professed enemy," with calling the officials in Massachusetts traitors, and with uttering threats against the commonwealth as a "state" offering "civility" only and not obedience to the crown.[1] The distances were

---

ize as the Dutch admiral went to Barbados instead. The three others went north, by way of Salem, Ipswich, and Newbury to Portsmouth and the Piscataqua (*Calendar State Papers, Colonial*, 1661–1668, §§1009, 1010, 1015, 1021, 1024, i, ii, iii) and then on into the province of Maine (*New York Colonial Documents*, III, 107–108). They were back in Boston before July 26. Cartwright sailed thence for England with Captain Gillam (below, p. 226) but his vessel was captured by a Dutch privateer and all the papers sent over by the commission were lost. He was put ashore in Spain and made his way to England, where he was living on the Strand in 1667 (*Calendar State Papers, Colonial*, 1661–1668, §1612, where the address is given). Carr, sick, lingered on in New York, hoping for a patent granting him land either on the Delaware or in the King's Province or for an appointment as governor of Maine, none of which he got. He left New York in October, 1667, went to England, but died soon after at Bristol. His son, Captain John Carr, remained in New York, as did many another soldier of the regiments brought over, and became commander on the Delaware under Nicolls. Maverick returned to New York in October, 1666, and there continued to reside with his mother in a house in Broadway given him by the Duke of York (*Calendar State Papers, Colonial*, 1661–1668, §1288; *New York Colonial Documents*, III, 160–162; Paltsits, *Executive Council Minutes*, I, 37, 92, 161, 168). A number of documents relating to the movements and work of the commissioners may be found in New York State Library, *History Bulletin*, 2, pp. 72–79, 93.

1. Cartwright, February 7, 1664, wrote Secretary Bennett that there was "some ground to fear that the phancy of a commonwealth is yet in some of their braines" (*New York Colonial Documents*, III, 89).

great for, with the exception of New Hampshire and Maine, the journeys had to be made by water, and as the instructions required that no important decisions should be reached without the presence of Nicolls, it happened that only for about three weeks were the commissioners able to act all together. Connecticut refused to accept one of these decisions regarding her boundary with Rhode Island because it did not bear Nicolls's signature.

The questions involved were many: the boundaries between Connecticut and New York, between Connecticut and Rhode Island, and between Rhode Island and Plymouth; the disposal of the Narragansett territory; and more important than either of these the whole issue of the region of New Hampshire and Maine and the ousting of Massachusetts from exercising jurisdiction in that quarter. This last point opened up the question of Massachusetts' northern boundary and the interpretation of her charter. In 1652 the general court had construed the three miles north of the Merrimac to mean "three miles northward of the most northerly part or branch" of that river and it sent surveyors to set a bound mark there, at nearly the 43° 30' parallel, which, carried eastwardly, brought New Hampshire and the province of Maine within the Massachusetts bounds. Even more important was the question of the right of the king's commissioners to hear cases on appeal from the courts of the New England colonies and to decide cases of grievance that came before them by petition.[1] Plymouth, Rhode Island, and Connecticut brought forward a few complaints, but not many, and seemed to have had no objection to

1. There were four cases in Massachusetts. That of one John Porter, Jr., who had been put in Boston jail for "rebellion against his parents," sentenced to be hung, taken to the gallows with the rope around his neck, reprieved, and given thirty-nine stripes. Breaking jail he petitioned for a hearing (Calendar State Papers, Colonial, 1661–1668, §§969, 996, 1089, II, IV; New York Colonial Documents, III, 95–96, 107). That of the merchant Thomas Deane, a member of the Atherton Company, and others, in the case of the ship Oleron (New York Colonial Documents, II, 271; Calendar State Papers, Colonial, 1661–1668, §§1002, 1007, 1089, p. 344; Paltsits, Executive Council Minutes, I, 186). That of Abraham Corbett who was charged with being responsible for stirring up disaffection in New Hampshire (Calendar State Papers, Colonial, 1661–1668, §§1064, 1069, 1077, 1089, XII, XIII). That of the Narragansett sachems, who in 1664 surrendered themselves to the protection of the crown before the commissioners (preliminary to the erection of the King's Province) because of "violence and injustice" from Massachusetts (ibid., pp. 300, 342). One case is recorded from Connecticut, that of William Morton of New London, charged with treasonable utterances (Acts Privy Council, Colonial, I, §632; New York Colonial Documents, III, 97). On the work of the commission, see Hutchinson, History (Mayo ed.), I, 198–217.

the presence or procedure of the commissioners. Plymouth won them over to her own view regarding her boundaries, but was too poor and weak to resist their other demands, and it may be was hoping that compliance would bring her the long desired charter.[1] Connecticut and Rhode Island were too grateful for their charters recently received to make trouble for the crown and except in the matter of boundaries had no deep-seated grievances. But with Massachusetts the case was different. The colony was prosperous, powerful, and determined. It had thus far met with no serious check in its progress toward complete freedom from political and religious intervention from without and it did not propose at this juncture to yield in any particular to the authority of the royal commissioners. It declared itself to be a "free state" and believed that any concessions would endanger its charter, bring upon its people new and heavy financial burdens, and undermine the foundations of the model church and community which God had erected in the wilderness of America. It possessed, as Bellingham wrote, a passionate solicitude for its "liberties," that is, for the right to do as it pleased, both within and without its borders, to its own advantage and the disadvantage of its neighbors. The word "liberty" has many convenient meanings.

The clash which ensued in May, 1665, between the four commissioners and the general court of Massachusetts and the maneuvers employed by that colony, during the months that followed, to checkmate the activities of Maverick and Carr in New Hampshire and Maine have a certain dramatic quality, for the court even went so far as to order out the train bands to obstruct the commissioners. In argument it rested its case on the charter of 1629, not as that document actually was but as the colony had interpreted it to be during the preceding thirty-six years. It ignored what the commissioners constantly pointed out in their verbal and written statements that the king had not resigned his sovereignty over the Massachusetts people and that if they strove to grasp too much they might in the end "hold but a little," that the king who granted the charter might also take it away. Several times in their letters home the commissioners recommended that the charter be annulled, saying that nothing could be done with so refractory and presumptuous a community until its main defense was broken down. Even Clarendon was provoked enough to warn the colony that if it did not obey the king's commands it would have cause to repent its presumption, for the king would not "sette down by the affronts which he had received."[1] The strongest argument in the colony's favor lay in the personality of the commissioners. Massachusetts might have been willing to trust Nicolls, but it would not trust Carr, Cartwright, or Maverick, and whatever may have been its opinion regarding the king's sovereignty, it had no doubt whatever of the utter unwisdom of letting these men tamper with the exercise of justice in the colony.[2] To do so might end in the overthrow of a system which the leaders believed had the approval of the Most High.

One sees in all these proceedings and in those of the ensuing twenty years a desperate effort on the part of the Massachusetts commonwealth to save what the Puritans had come to America to establish. Had the commonwealth confined the enforcement of its "liberties" to its own internal affairs and interpreted these "liberties" less offensively in its relations with its neighbors; had the leaders not aroused the enmity of those about them by their aggressive demands in the matter of the boundaries; and had the general court been more tactful in its replies, less casuistical in its arguments, and less dilatory in its proceedings, Massachusetts might have continued, as did Connecticut, to enjoy the privileges she prized so highly. But in grasping so much and failing to see that a measure of adaptation was necessary in order to meet the demands of England's programme in matters of trade and defense, she eventually lost her charter, as the commissioners hoped that she would. Only by shrewd diplomacy, after the Dominion of New England had fallen in 1689, was she able to recover a part of what she had lost. But the greater part, the independence and self-control which she had enjoyed for more than half a century as a self-contained Puritan commonwealth, was gone forever.

These events of the years 1664 and 1665 were but the logical consequence of the policy that England had been slowly shaping during the preceding ten years and are clearly anticipatory of further development along the same line of centralized control. The continuance of Nicolls as commissioner to inspect the king's affairs in New England and the suggestion that he be made governor general of all New England, with Cartwright the major general in command of

1. *New York Colonial Documents*, III, 116.
2. In its reply to charges Massachusetts said that the commissioners "put their spurs too hard to the horses' side before they were got into the saddle" (*ibid.*, 142).

all the forces there, looks back to the appointment of Gorges which failed and on to that of Andros which succeeded temporarily. The mission of the commissioners prepared the way for the coming of Edward Randolph and the accumulating of evidence to show that Massachusetts was not conforming to the rules and regulations which England was laying down in the interest of her foreign trade. These men were the first of that long line of investigators sent over during the next half century to investigate colonial affairs, and their reports were always colored by their loyalty to England's plan regarding the place the colonies should occupy in her colonial scheme. The constant recommendations of the commissioners of 1664–1665 that Massachusetts be punished by the withdrawal of her charter forecast the actual annulment of 1684. The wrangling over New Hampshire and western Maine made inevitable the erection of New Hampshire as a separate royal colony in 1679, and one is tempted to believe that had any solution been possible of the troublesome problem of what to do with Maine, the five little towns that lay between the Piscataqua and the Kennebec would not have been returned to the jurisdiction of Massachusetts in 1691.

To every student of our colonial history the gradual process whereby England worked out her colonial as over against her commercial programme, though the two can hardly be treated separately, the story of the capture of Jamaica and New Netherland and of the activities of the commissioners of 1664 is exceedingly suggestive. These events were neither whimsical nor accidental, they were parts of a definite purpose that was inaugurated during the years of the Protectorate and continued after the Restoration on into the century that followed. The retention of Jamaica, the reduction of New Netherland, the regulation of Massachusetts and Bermuda, and the erection of the Dominion of New England are but early manifestations of England's effort, carried on into the eighteenth century, to complete the centralizing process by royalizing all the private colonies, corporate and proprietary, and thus concentrating colonial control in the king's hand. Behind this effort, which was never completely successful, lay the inexorable demands, as England saw them, of trade, commerce, and sea power, and the necessity of subordinating her colonies, as the other maritime powers of Europe were doing at the same time with theirs, to the higher welfare of the parent state.

NOTE: This point will be discussed from a somewhat different point of view in the next volume, but a few words about it may be said here. From the time of the king's arrival in England Charles II manifested a great desire "to improve the general Trafficke and Trade of the kingdom and upon all occasions conferred with the most active Merchants upon it and offered all that he could contribute to the Advancement thereof . . . the Increasing whereof [he] was to endeavor with all possible Solicitude which [could] make this nation flourish" (Clarendon, *Life*, II, 149, 152, 374; *Notes which passed at Meetings of the Privy Council between Charles II and the Earl of Clarendon*, pp. 25, 28).

Parliament was also much concerned regarding the apparent decay of trade during the years 1660 to 1663, and caused careful inquiry to be made into the causes of it. After 1663 the special council of trade sat at Whitehall and the House of Commons resolved that there should be such an inquiry. Consequently the council summoned representatives of the merchants to lay before it an account of the reasons why trade was obstructed with proposals for a remedy. This the merchants did at length (*Calendar State Papers, Domestic*, 1663–1664, p. 531), in the course of which they stressed not only the general importance of trade to the kingdom but also the new interest aroused in the plantations old and new, not as colonies or areas of land but as adjuncts of trade. It was no accident that Mun's *English Treasure by Foreign Trade*, written in 1630, should have now been published for the first time, edited by his son, John. It became the text-book of the merchants. Sir Richard Ford, who was often consulted by James, Duke of York (Clark, *Life*, I, 399), received permission to print it as "the most rational and demonstrative he had ever heard."

The negotiations with Portugal were in part directed against Spain but in larger part they were undertaken in the interest of England's trade. Portugal promised to grant England free trade with Brazil and by surrendering Bombay gave her a wider and more secure trade in the East Indies. The cession of Tangier Clarendon believed would "give the Law to all the trade of the Mediterranean." The king in an address to parliament said that the new acquisitions, Dunkirk, Mardyck, Tangier, Jamaica, and Bombay, should be esteemed "as Jewels of an immense magnitude in the Royal Diadem; and though they were a present expense, they were like in a short time, with God's blessing, to bring vast Advantages to the Trade, Navigation, Wealth and Honour of the King and his Kingdom" (*ibid.*, p. 313. For "A Short discours" to the same effect, *Calendar State Papers, Colonial*, 1661–1668, §267). On the importance of Tangier, as Englishmen of the day saw it, one should consult *A Discourse touching Tanger, in a Letter to a Person of Quality* (1680, preface dated October 20, 1679), in which the writer argues against the surrender of Tangier by showing (or endeavoring to show) that its possession would give England dominance along the northern African coast as against the Algerines with whom England had been at war for twenty-five years. The same point is brought out in *The Present Interest of Tangier* (1690, after the surrender), and is stressed in the debates before the House of Commons, November 17, 1680, on "His Majesty's Message about Tangier," *Select Debates in the House of Commons, 1680* (London, 1681), pp. 106–128. The surrender is dealt with in Historical Manuscripts Commission, *Dartmouth*, I, and *The Tangier Papers of Samuel Pepys* (Naval Records Society). Pepys had been treasurer of Tangier as had Thomas Povey before him and among the commissioners were Thomas Povey, Lord Craven, and John Lord Berkeley. Of the "Jewels" mentioned above only Jamaica remained permanently either as a part of the realm or in the king's hands. Dunkirk and Mardyck were sold to France, a sale which aroused the wrath of Spain and was very unpopular in England; Bombay was turned over to the East India Company; and in 1683 Tangier, which had proved a source of constant irritation, loss, and expense, was given up to Morocco, and in the present century after prolonged negotiations, 1923–1925, 1926–1928, was internationalized in 1929.

CHAPTER III

A DUTCH PROVINCE AND A DUCAL PROPRIETY

THE history of New York from 1664 to 1691 offers us for solution no problem of settlement such as we have met with in the case of each of the other colonies. The land was already occupied by a diverse people with well established forms of government and habits of life and there was no need of increasing the population by any such artificial means as had been tried out in Jamaica. The Dutch territory had been annexed to the crown with a minimum of bloodshed (and even that minimum might have been avoided had Carr been less impetuous on the Delaware), so that the conquest left but a slight aftermath of rancor and bitterness. The Dutch, English, and Swedes were racially and religiously kindred peoples, with the Dutch preponderating in numbers, and all were content to continue their personal and regional activities pretty much as before. Inevitably there ensued a certain amount of friction, due to the fact of conquest and to differences of opinion arising out of the circumstances of origin and the varieties of custom which represented the traditions and practices of their respective homelands, but such friction wore away as time and the common welfare brought all the inhabitants into a more or less common accord.

The situation was a peculiar one, unlike anything elsewhere existing. The Duke of York became the proprietor, not only of an oddly fashioned territorial area but of an equally strange assortment of peoples—Dutch, English, French, Swedes, and Finns—whose antecedents were their own and who were now brought together under a lordship, invested with absolute power and authority to govern them, under the terms of a proprietary charter, pretty much as it pleased. The question naturally arises, as to whether the duke, through his deputy governors, upon whom rested the burden of resolving these complex conditions, could execute his legal powers with sufficient tact and forebearance to reconcile the prevailing dissimilarities of experience and conviction and so to remove discontent and prevent revolt. Or would the propriety of New York go the way of the propriety of Maryland and eventually be transformed into a royal colony of the usual type? The problem was rendered the more difficult by the omission from the duke's charter of any mention of a popular assembly, such as Baltimore was obliged to summon. It was, however, simplified by certain other weighty circumstances which do not appear in Maryland's history. In the first place the Duke of York never visited his province, and so family influence, which played so baneful a part in Baltimore's government of Maryland, was entirely absent from New York. Secondly, the duke gave away a large section of his territory and thus narrowed the area of his propriety, by withdrawing the lands between the Hudson and the Delaware from under the ducal control. Thirdly, the duke never imposed an oath of fidelity upon all his people, as did Baltimore; he allowed all writs and processes to run in the king's name as Baltimore did not; and he never attempted to apply, as Baltimore did frequently, coercive methods of government and forms of land relationship that savored of medievalism. Fourthly, the accession of the duke to the throne of England automatically converted his propriety into a royal colony, though not one necessarily in which popular representation had a place. And, lastly, the downfall of the Dominion of New England, of which New York was integrally a part, but Maryland was not, left the province shorn of its official strength, an easy prey to insurgent attack.

The island of Manhattan, where the Dutch were in control for nearly forty years, was first discovered, but not occupied, by Henry Hudson, September 12, 1609. It was seen also by Christiaensen and Adriaen Block in 1613, who sailed past it far up the river to Castle Island, where on the east bank of the Hudson—a site that in 1617 was given up for another on the west side where Albany now stands —they built Fort Nassau, or Orange as it came to be called. There Block constructed the *Unrest* in 1613-1614, after his own vessel had been destroyed by fire.[1] It was seen also by Thomas Dermer in 1620.[2] But no certain evidence of the occupation of Manhattan itself appears before 1626, for up to that time all the trading and wintering activities, as we shall see, had been either along the Delaware or along the upper reaches of the Hudson, whither trading vessels had gone, some in the interest of the New Netherland Company (until

1. De Laet, *New World* (Original Narratives), p. 47. De Laet was a director and the historian of the Dutch West India Company.
2. Brodhead, *History of New York*, I, 92–94.

the expiration of its charter in 1618) and some independently after that date. But permanent settlement, even at Fort Orange, was not assured until a corporate body stronger than the New Netherland Company and with more certain resources came into existence. This was the Dutch West India Company, founded on June 3, 1621, which, with a working capital in hand, was equipped ready for action by August, 1623.[1] In the spring of 1624, after a winter of preparation, this company sent over as director of the projected colony, Cornelis Jacobsen May, with thirty families, Dutch and Walloon, some of whom went to Fort Orange and others to the Delaware; and during the same year it continued to ship settlers, livestock, and implements of husbandry until the nucleus of a colony had been formed. Thus the first permanent settlement within the borders of the present state of New York was made at Fort Orange in 1624 by Dutch and Walloon families, all of whom were engaged in agriculture and barter with the Indians. In addition there were also a few men in a small fort on Nut (Governor's) Island and a few families living isolated lives on the Delaware.[2] Of these small and scattered

1. Van Laer, *Van Rensselaer Bowier Manuscripts,* pp. 86–115, for the charter, text and translation. A readily accessible account of the company is by Professor Barnouw in *History of the State of New York* (1933), I, 217–258. The leading Dutch authority on the subject is Dr. S. van Brakel in *De Hollandsche Handelscompagnieën der Zeventiende eeuw* (1908) and "Compagnie (West Indische)" in *Encyclopaedie van Nederlandisch West-Indische* (1914), pp. 212–225, with an elaborate bibliography to 1913. See also, Geyl, *The Netherlands Divided,* 1609–1648 (1936), pp. 189–209.

2. The date of the settlement of New Amsterdam and the circumstances attending it have been the subjects of much controversy. The statements made by Miss Green (*Walloon Founding of New Amsterdam,* 1916) that the beginning of occupation by the Walloons "was never abandoned or interrupted but has steadily grown into the metropolis of the western world" (p. 47), and "the establishment, by this same French Protestant band, of the first permanent, crop-raising, town-building settlement, never since destroyed or abandoned, upon the . . . site of the greatest city in the western hemisphere" (p. 76) must be rejected as resting upon no sufficient historical foundation (Bayer, *The Belgians: First Settlers of New York and the Middle States,* 1925, adds nothing by the way of proof). The Walloons under Jesse de Forest first went to Guiana in 1623, where De Forest died. Another group ("mostly Walloons," says Wassenaer in his *Historisch Verhael,* Original Narratives, *New Netherland* p. 75) went out (as noted in the text) with one of the ships of the Dutch West India Company, under Cornelis Jacobsen May, in the spring of 1624. There were thirty families in all, Dutch and Walloon. Some of them went to Fort Nassau, near the site of the present Albany, others to the Delaware, where they erected a fort, also called Nassau, on the eastern bank of the river in what is now Gloucester County, New Jersey. That any of them settled on Manhattan Island or went across the Hellegat (the name given for many years to the East River) to Long Island is unproven (yet see Stokes, *Iconography,* IV, 64). Apparently the only basis for such conjecture is the existence today of the name "Walebought" or "Wallabout" (Waal-bogt, mean-

groups May remained the director until he returned to Holland in November of that year.

More active preparations were made in the winter following, for the company was determined to strengthen the Fort Orange colony by whatever was necessary for its welfare. It sent out an extraordinary shipment in three vessels and a "yacht" in April, 1625, particularly of horses and cattle for breeding and multiplying, hogs and sheep, hay, seeds, ploughs and other agricultural implements. Country people also went along, including six completely equipped families, to the number of forty-five individuals. Other vessels followed until the population was increased to two hundred souls. Some of the cattle were first pastured on Nut Island, then transferred to Manhattan, and finally, twenty of them having died cropping noxious weeds where New York now stands, they were all taken up the river for the use of the colonists there. Willem Verhulst, sent out as the supercargo on the voyage, became the second director, with instructions to deliberate and, with the coöperation of councillors, to act upon all matters of importance. With him, as a voluntary passenger and councillor, went one Peter Minuit, of French Huguenot or Walloon descent from Wesel, in the duchy of Cleves, destined, after his return to Holland in the autumn, to go back the next year as a passenger, and eventually to become the third director. Verhulst's instructions were signed by three of the later patroons, Albert Coenraets, Samuel Godyn, and Kiliaen van Rensselaer.[1] Probably in one of the ships of 1625 went Cryn Fredericksen, an engineer

ing Walloon's Cove) in Brooklyn where the Navy Yard is now located. We do not know how early the name got fastened on the place, but it was during the Dutch period certainly, for the name appears in the Nicolls map of about 1665 (Paltsits, *Executive Council Minutes,* pocket map) and is mentioned in a Nicolls grant, February 18, 1667, "of land lying in the Wallebogt, within the limits of a certain village now known by the name of New Bedford in the West Riding of Yorkshire upon Long Island" (Huntington Library). Michaëlius tells us, as of the year 1628, that "a portion of the Walloons [are] going back to the Fatherland, either because their years here are expired or else because some are not very serviceable to the Company" and that "some of them live far away" (*New Netherland,* Original Narratives, p. 125). The name might equally well have had a later origin and have been due to Walloons settling there after their return from the Delaware.

1. Paltsits, "Founding of New Amsterdam in 1626," *Proceedings,* American Antiquarian Society, April, 1924, pp. 39–65. Mr. Paltsits disposes finally of the fictitious Argall settlement of 1613 and does not even mention the Walloon claim. For an argument in favor of settlement in July, 1625, Stokes, *Iconography,* VI, 12–13. The instructions to Verhulst are given in *Documents relating to New Netherland* (Huntington Library publication), documents, C, D, January, April, 1625.

and surveyor, who was ordered to stake out a blockhouse (later Fort Amsterdam), "planned to be of large dimensions," in a place suitable for dwellings, pastures, and cultivated fields, at some healthful spot near the entrance of the river, well provided with water and timber for fuel and building and adjacent to streams supplied with fish.[1] Thus the way was all set for the greater migration to come, which was to result in the founding of New Amsterdam.

On December 19, 1625, the *Sea-mew*, Adriaen Jones captain, sailed from Amsterdam (leaving the Texel, January 9, 1626), bearing Minuit and a new body of emigrants brought together by the directors of the company for the purpose of carrying out and completing the instructions already given to Verhulst and Fredericksen. The vessel reached Manhattan on May 4, 1626.[2] There the emigrants found the site prepared at the lower end of the island, where the blockhouse was going up, and during the summer and autumn they succeeded in erecting nearly thirty houses, built of unpeeled logs and thatched with reed, on the west side of the island, running north and south, above the unfinished fort, with a counting house of stone under construction, a bark windmill for sawing lumber, and another for grinding corn. As Verhulst had mismanaged things badly (he was shipped back to Holland in disgrace in September), the local councillors persuaded Minuit to take his place, and the latter sent for his wife with the intention of remaining permanently in the colony. He purchased the island of the native Manhates,[3] after whom Manhattan (Manatus) was named, changed the title of the place to New Amsterdam, and then set about reinforcing the settlement by withdrawing the inhabitants from Fort Orange and the

---

1. Wassenaer's *Historisch Verhael*, p. 83; *Documents relating to New Netherland*, document E. Fredericksen surveyed Rensselaerswyck also. *Van Rensselaer Bowier Manuscripts*, p. 617.

2. These are the dates given by Wassenaer, pp. 87, 88, and in the *Van Rensselaer Bowier Manuscripts*, p. 686, and if correct make the voyage of the *Sea-mew* a very long one, lasting nearly four months. The route is not known, but was very likely the same as that taken by May in 1624—to the Canary Islands and thence across the Atlantic, though May, starting in the spring, reached Manhattan in about two months. Michaëlius thought his voyage long though it lasted only six weeks. Other voyages took from three to five months, *Van Rensselaer Bowier*, pp. 355–389, 645, 580–603. "A happy voyage" was from six to eight weeks.

3. This famous purchase of Manhattan Island for sixty guilders, or about twenty-four dollars, was by order of the directors in Holland, in their instructions to Verhulst. The money was paid in the usual form of trading goods, knives, beads, and trinkets. An entry in the council minutes, April 9, 1670, says "the Records shews it [Manhattan] was bought and paid for 44 yeares agoe."

Delaware, and consolidating all in one place.[1] A few men—probably fifteen or sixteen—were left up the river under a commander appointed by Minuit, but the others were brought down "in order to strengthen with people the colony near the Manhates," who unlike the Mohawks in the north "were becoming more and more accustomed to strangers."[2]

New Netherland was a colony or province founded and controlled by a Dutch trading company, chartered by their High Mightinesses the States General of the Netherlands. Legally it was in exactly the same class with Virginia and Bermuda, the colonies of trading companies chartered by the king of England. But there were differences of fundamental importance. Whereas after 1612 the Virginia Company was an open corporation, controlled in England by a governor, council, and general court of its members, that of New Netherland was managed at home by five chambers, located in different cities and parts of the Dutch republic, which delegated their powers of government to a board or college of nineteen (the Nineteen), sitting at Amsterdam, made up of representatives from each chamber, a close and select body, with the delegates from the chamber of Amsterdam itself holding the preferred positions, those from Zealand next. This group of nineteen men served the purpose of a general assembly of the company; its orders had to be obeyed by all the chambers and many were the opportunities offered for objections and answers, for there was among the other chambers jealousy of the powerful Amsterdam group, similar to that which existed in England between the outports and London. In case of a deadlock the issue could be referred to the States General at The Hague, which was supreme in matters of sovereignty and jurisdiction. The

1. There is some doubt as to whether all the Walloons on the South River were removed in 1626 (Brodhead, *History of New York*, I, 160 note, 205 note, 225). De Vries says that there were no families at Fort Nassau in 1633 (*New Netherland*, Original Narratives, pp. 226–227, 260, 313–314; *Collections*, New York Historical Society, 2d series, III, 1–129). Another Dutch colony on the Delaware was started in 1631 as a patroonship for Godyn and partners. It was wiped out by the Indians.

2. Minuit soon after his arrival was obliged to go to Fort Orange to investigate the death of Krieckebeeck, the *commis* there, who had been killed in attempting to aid the Mohicans against the Mohawks (Wassenaer, pp. 84–85; *Documents relating to New Netherland*, document F). Bastiaen Janseen Krol, who had come over in 1626 as *kranck-besoecker* or comforter of the sick (a feature of every Dutch Reformed Church in Holland), became the *commis* after Krieckebeeck's death. After Minuit's recall in 1632 he was appointed emergency director general of the colony and served until the arrival of Wouter van Twiller in 1633.

chief concern of the company was conquest and trade not colonization, and the end it sought profit rather than homes. The directors,
throughout the entire period of Dutch occupation, considered only
their own advantage—often the advantage of powerful individual
merchants—and not the welfare of the people of their province. Instead of having one center of colonizing activity, as was the case
with the Virginia and Bermuda companies, the Dutch West India
Company was chartered to promote trade throughout the entire
western world, wherever the directors could find an opening.[1] Their
claims ranged in Africa from Guinea to the Cape of Good Hope,
and in America from Newfoundland to the Straits of Magellan; but
in actual operations these claims were limited to the Gulf of Guinea,
to the region from Buzzard's Bay to the Delaware, to certain islands
in the Caribbean—Saba, St. Eustatius, St. Martin, Curaçao, and on
the South American mainland to Surinam and the Brazil coast, of
a portion of which they were in control from 1630–1635 to 1654.
Among the many parts of this diversified area, New Netherland
was but one of the sources of wealth and was looked upon, until
the years just before the surrender, as the least profitable and most
expensive of them all.[2] Hence arose the complaint, many times repeated, that the directors in the Netherlands neglected the province
on the Hudson and seemingly cared little for the prosperity of its
people.[3]

The province itself was not a single compact area of territory as
were the colonies of the English in Virginia, Bermuda, and New

1. See preamble to the charter (*Van Rensselaer Bowier*, pp. 89–90; *New York
Colonial Documents* II, 510, 511).

2. Dr. van Brakel in his article in the *Encyclopaedie* referred to above, says that
from 1661 to 1664 New Netherland was the most prosperous colony the company
possessed (p. 216b). It is difficult to determine, and I have seen no satisfactory attempt to determine, the actual value of New Netherland to the Dutch West India
Company at any time. That there was profit from the furs sent down from Esopus
and Fort Orange is clear, but that these furs met the expenses incurred is more than
doubtful. In 1664 Stuyvesant made the statement that the company had spent 1,200,-
000 guilders more than it received (O'Callaghan, *History of New Netherland*, II,
505–508). The province cannot have been considered by the States General the valuable possession that the company and the merchants thought it or an effort would
have been made to obtain its restoration in 1667, and it would not have been so
readily given back to England in 1674 (*New York Colonial Documents*, II, 510, 511–
513, 517, 541–542, 545, 730–731, 738–740). Stuyvesant charged the company with
misinformation and misconstruction of the reports that it received (*ibid.*, 444).

3. "Representation of New Netherland," *New Netherland* (Original Narratives),
pp. 316, 317, 347, 373.

England. It was rather a series of trading posts on the Hudson at Fort Orange, Esopus, and Manhattan, on the South or Delaware River at Swaanendael, Fort Nassau, and Fort Casimir, on the Connecticut at Fort Hope, all widely separated, difficult of easy access, and incapable of adequate defense. The situation was the more serious in that the remoter of these outlying posts occupied disputed territory and brought the New Netherlanders and consequently the company into conflict with the English in New England and on Long Island and with the Swedes and Marylanders on the Delaware.[1] Structurally the province was always weak, and, because underpopulated, was incapable of long resistance in case of attack. The strength of the Dutch position was further undermined by the fact that the West India Company had no definite patent of land that determined the boundaries of New Netherland, such as was to be found in each of the charters granted to the English colonies by the English crown, for the charter of the company contains no statement of the exact region within which it was to operate.[2]

Apart from the patroonships, to be discussed later, and the forts on the Delaware and Connecticut rivers, which added but little to the vigor and profitableness of the province, there were, north of Manhattan and New Harlem, but two posts, both on the upper Hudson. These were Fort Orange, a trading center dealing in beaver, otter, muskrat, and deerskins, and Esopus, halfway down, where was a small fort and (a few miles inland) about sixty Dutch families engaged in agriculture and the fur trade.[3] Each of these forts had to be supplied with soldiers, kept in repair, and constantly supervised. Each was an isolated outpost particularly in winter, in constant danger from the Indians, and a costly expedient in furthering the trade which the company favored. Thus, in the last analysis, the heart of New Netherland was New Amsterdam at the lowest point of Manhattan Island, to which may be added the villages and farms on Long Island and Staten Island, along the Harlem, and on the Jersey shore. Of all these New Amsterdam was the only one that was substantial and dependable.

1. *Ibid.*, pp. 304–316.

2. The omission from the charter of 1621 of any mention of New Netherland or any definition of boundaries was made much of by the Connecticut committee in its debate with the commissioners from New Amsterdam, October, 1663 (above, p. 62, note 1). Connecticut had an iron-clad statement of boundaries to fall back on. The same was true, but less convincingly, in the case of Baltimore.

3. "Description of Manhattan," *New Netherland* (Original Narratives), p. 422.

Just as New Netherland was unlike anything that the English possessed as a colony, so New Amsterdam bore no resemblance to a New England town. Instead of homesteads clustering about a church and a village green, the Dutch houses adjoined a fort, within which were the governor's house, the church, barracks, a prison, the whipping post and gallows, while nearby were the two windmills. The houses extended northward toward the wall or palisade, built in 1653, with its five or six bastions (Wall Street), beyond which was the "gut," dry at low water, but navigable for small boats at high tide, and crossed by two large bridges and three small ones (Broad Street). Beyond the palisade and the canal were bouweries (farms) and plantations, widely scattered, chiefly along the eastern and western sides of the island, perhaps fifty in number,[1] from the meager soil of which the occupiers in part obtained their living, while their cattle went at large in the woods covering the island. In the town itself the chief employment was in trade, for those that lived there planted and sowed very little.[2] The inhabitants numbered about three hundred in 1630, four hundred and fifty in 1646, fifteen hundred for New Amsterdam alone in 1664, and for the whole province less than seven thousand in the same year.[3] If we are to believe Domine Michaëlius they were a rough and unrestrained people, much given to quarreling and drunkenness.[4] The slow increase in the population contrasts strikingly with the rapid peopling of New England, where the numbers at the time of the conquest stood to those of New Netherland in the ratio of not less

1. Map of Joan Vingboom, 1639, reproduced in Van Winkle, *Manhattan, 1624–1639* (1916), from the original in the Library of Congress and enlarged, delineated, and the names rendered into English in a separate folding map. A plantation was a small estate of about five acres upon which tobacco or Indian corn was grown. It might in time expand into a farm or bouwerie, much larger in size, upon which a variety of agricultural staples was produced. There were nearly fifty such outlying holdings on Manhattan above New Amsterdam, which are described in Van Winkle and in Stokes, *Iconography*, VI.

2. *New Netherland* (Original Narratives), p. 424.

3. Maverick, who had lived in New Amsterdam and knew the place well, wrote Clarendon about 1661 as follows: "For the Dutch I know by credible information they have not of theire owne Nation, fourteene hundred wᶜʰ can beare armes, and there are neare fower hundred able English men wᶜʰ live amongst them." *Collections*, New York Historical Society, 1869, p. 21.

4. Valentine's *Manual of the Common Council of New York* for 1861 contains extracts of court actions during the Dutch period, which disclose the frequency and variety of infractions of the peace. The Dutch may have been phlegmatic and complacent, but there were certainly among them many who were disorderly and quarrelsome.

than ten to one.[1] The reason for this contrast and its significance will appear later.

Little by little, though very slowly, settlement was effected on the lands across the rivers and around the bay. Territory was acquired by purchase from the Indians, either by the governor or by private individuals, and there came into existence, often in the face of many hindrances and setbacks, the villages of Breuckelen, Bushwick, Ameersfort, Midwout, and New Utrecht (the Five Dutch Towns), Flatbush, Flushing, and Gravesend (Lady Moody's settlement) on Long Island, with the English villages of Hempstead (Heemstede), Jamaica (Rustdorp), Oyster Bay, Huntington, and Setauket farther to the eastward. At the upper end of Manhattan was New Harlem and beyond the Harlem River was Eastdorp or Vreeland (Westchester), on Staten Island De Vries plantation and later the patroonship of Cornelis Melyn, and across the North River, Bergen. No one of the Dutch villages was sufficiently populous or sufficiently secure to add much to the strength or protection of the province, being in some instances distinctly a source of weakness on account of the danger from Indian attacks along the frontier. Shortly before the conquest revolts, instigated by emissaries from Connecticut, took place in Eastdorp, Midwout, Middleburg, and Jamaica. Colonel John Scott, acting at first under Connecticut's auspices, was able to combine Hempstead, Gravesend, Flushing, Middleburg, Jamaica, and Oyster Bay into a sort of confederation against the Dutch, which later, without regard to Connecticut's aspirations, he attempted to erect into an independent propriety of which he should be the head. But his American career was stopped by the grant to the Duke of York.[2]

The very slow increase in population, of which the local authorities constantly complained, was caused, to no inconsiderable extent,

1. Stuyvesant put the ratio at 50 to 1 in his "Report" of 1665, but in his "Answer" of 1666 he gives it more correctly as 10 to 1 (*New Netherland*, Original Narratives, p. 459; *New York Colonial Documents*, II, 443). Population figures for the seventeenth century are little to be relied on. For instance undersecretary Williamson entered in his note-book, 1665, that New England had 27,000 fighting men. Probably all New England at that date had less than 50,000 people.

2. On Scott's activities on Long Island (already frequently noted) see further *New York Colonial Documents*, II, 234, 480–481, 487, 507, 509; *New Netherland* (Original Narratives), pp. 462–463; Brodhead, *History*, I, 725–727. When Connecticut found that Scott was acting in his own interests and not in hers, she had him arrested, taken to Hartford, and there imprisoned. Above, pp. 54, note 2, 55, note 2.

by the policy of the directors at home. The corrosive element that worked its deleterious effects on New Netherland was the determination of the Board of Nineteen to make profitable trade and not agricultural colonization the object of the company's efforts. The same policy that was operating in other fields of Dutch West Indian activity was applied to New Netherland also, where the profits were so meager or so often non-existent that the directors were unwilling to spend more money upon the peopling of the province than they had to. They were not disposed to draw upon the company's exchequer to meet the expenses of transportation, equipment, and support such as would be necessary for the establishment and upkeep of agricultural communities requiring farmers, livestock, seeds, clothing, and the tools of husbandry. In such colonies, with their planting and reaping, they saw only rivals cutting into the business of barter with the Indians, diverting the attention of the settlers from trade to the soil. Such a one-sided policy had its inevitable consequences. As the object of the directors was in largest part to seek adequate returns on the company's investment from traffic in furs rather than the raising of agricultural staples, so the object of many an individual in the province, from the governor down, was to seek his own fortune, by fair means if possible, if not by less defensible measures. Thus there never developed in New Netherland anything quite comparable with the community spirit of the New England towns, according to which the private advantages of the individual were subordinated to the welfare of the whole. The cohesive binding effects of a common religion, a common racial origin, and a common civil purpose were entirely wanting. Furthermore the company's monopoly of trade till 1647, New Amsterdam's monopoly of the staple, and the dependence of all the outlying forts and communities upon the chief town as the emporium of the province worked to the advantage of the official and business class rather than the agricultural, while a tendency toward engrossing, forestalling, and regrating among the merchants made for disparities of wealth. Also the heavy import and export duties worked hardship upon the poorer classes by the raising of prices and brought many a complaint from the New England merchants trading with New Amsterdam, who threatened retaliation. Though the taxes, customs dues, and excise were probably but little heavier than elsewhere, they served to hinder the cause of an open and free trade and so to narrow the range of Manhattan's commercial connections. After 1657 no one could trade with New Netherland without a license.[1]

Among the stockholders in the company was one Kiliaen van Rensselaer, a jeweler of Amsterdam. He was a "participant" and early became one of the twenty Amsterdam directors, who made up the most influential of the chambers, controlling four-ninths of the capital of the company.[2] Convinced that hunting and trading alone as the sole source of wealth would only result in loss and damage, he advocated the restricting of the fur trade and the setting up of private agricultural communities, partly to aid in colonizing the province and partly to make New Amsterdam a supply station of grain, cattle, and provisions for ships going to the West Indies. He argued that ships could thus refit without returning to the Netherlands and in so doing save the cost and avoid the danger of two long ocean voyages. He was opposed, and continued to be opposed, by those among the directors who were profiting by contracts for supplies and equipment at home; but he found support among others who saw in the plan a means whereby the region might be settled at the least expense to the company, because if the company was prepared to grant such privileges as would attract private capital to the undertaking, the costs would be borne by private individuals.[3] These men drew up a remarkable paper, defining the kind of agricultural colonies they wished to establish and outlining in great detail the conditions under which they should be managed. This paper, the contents of which, after long negotiation, were approved

1. *New Netherland* (Original Narratives), p. 371. After 1657 a license of twenty guilders had to be paid for the small burgher right which entitled "arriving traders" and natives properly qualified to carry on business in New Amsterdam. The great burgher right, costing fifty guilders, was required of all who held office, such as burgomasters, schepens, schouts, director and councillors, clergymen, and military officers.

2. The stockholders in Holland were represented by the "participants," who were men of wealth, each of whom had contributed not less than 6000 guilders. They had no part in the day by day management of the company's business, which was looked after by the Nineteen, but they were consulted on important matters of fiscal policy. In 1623 the stockholders were given permanent representation on the board of directors, by an agreement reached on June 21 of that year, allowing certain vacancies to be filled from the group of "participants," by plurality of votes in designated chambers (*Van Rensselaer Bowier*, pp. 46–47, 131, §v). Thus Van Rensselaer was at the same time a stockholder, a "participant" (the first to be received into the Amsterdam chamber), and a director of the Amsterdam chamber until he withdrew in 1631.

3. *Ibid.*, pp. 47–48, 235–236.

by the Board of Nineteen and confirmed by the States General on June 7, 1629, is known as the charter of Freedoms and Exemptions.[1]

In general the plan was not unlike that adopted by the English commercial corporations, when they wanted to encourage groups of associates among their own members to set up private colonies to supplement the work of the companies themselves.[2] But in details there were important differences. The Dutch undertakers had to be "participants" of the company and were to be called "patroons," their colonies taking the form of feudal estates—each a "perpetual fief" and "perpetual inheritance," with its promoter in full possession of feudal rights.[3] The patroonships were under the supreme jurisdiction of the States General and loosely under that of the West India Company, as appears from the fact that the officials in New Amsterdam could consider those in charge at Rensselaerswyck as "merely subordinates of the company."[4] Nevertheless, in point of fact, local control and jurisdiction in this patroonship were rarely restricted by any outside authority. Title to the soil was vested in partnerships or companies,[5] not unlike the "associates" of the English system, each member of which had certain share rights, which he could sell, alienate, or leave by will, as a whole or in fractional parts. The partners were at first from among the patroons themselves, few in number, who became subscribers to the fund for the upkeep of the

1. *Ibid.*, pp. 137–153 and notes 6 and 6a.   2. Above, Vol. I, 127–132.

3. See Van Rensselaer's letters of January 25 and February 4 and 5, 1641; *Van Rensselaer Bowier*, pp. 520–524, 528–534, 535–539, and §§vi and vii of the Freedoms and Exemptions. These feudal rights included high, middle, and low jurisdiction, with full control over fishing, fowling, and grinding corn. "Courts of the patroons" are mentioned in the charter but not specifically as courts baron and leet and there is no reason to believe that any courts corresponding to them ever existed in New Netherland. Van Rensselaer quoting "professors at Leyden" said that "feudal rights" were seldom met with in the province of Holland, though they were common enough in Gelderland. Local courts of justice were held at Rensselaerswyck, presided over by the schepens, and appeal was allowed to the governor and council at New Amsterdam in all cases involving more than fifty guilders (*Van Rensselaer Bowier*, pp. 415, 476; Freedoms and Exemptions, §xx). Probably these courts settled questions in dispute between lord and farmer and farmer and farmer and were not unlike the local courts of a New England town. They probably also took account of matters touching local administration, which were handled by reason, honest judgment, and common sense (*ibid.*, pp. 30, 62–63; for the schepen's oath, p. 203). Van Rensselaer discouraged as far as he could appeals to the governor and council at New Amsterdam, largely on account of the time and expense involved (See *Minutes of the Court of Rensselaerswyck, 1648–1652*, Van Laer ed., 1922).

4. *New Netherland* (Original Narratives), p. 368.

5. Mention is made of "Albert Coenraets and Company" (*Van Rensselaer Bowier*, p. 156). The partners are also called *co-fratres* and *socii*.

patroonship. In the case of Rensselaerswyck, the partners early became involved in a dispute as to their respective rights. Did each partner have high jurisdiction as well as rights in the soil or was high jurisdiction indivisible, as Van Rensselaer claimed, vested only in himself as the sole recipient of letters of enfeoffment from the company?[1] The patroons were strictly bound by the terms of the Freedoms and Exemptions, which allowed them extensive trading rights, though even as early as 1633 Van Rensselaer thought these rights too limited and the patroon's powers too restricted.[2] They had to recognize above all the staple-privilege of New Amsterdam and in case of death their heirs had to do homage to the company and pay twenty guilders in order to obtain a renewal of the enfeoffment.[3]

Rensselaerswyck[4] was the only patroonship that succeeded and continued to survive as a feudal propriety, though in reality its feudal characteristics were never conspicuous. All the others were either abandoned, transferred to the company, or continued as ordinary estates of land.[5] Of their history we know very little but of

1. "The first combination of colonies in New Netherland and the shares each partner is to have in them" is given in *ibid.*, pp. 164–165. At first Rensselaerswyck had four partners, Van Rensselaer, Coenraets, Godyn, and Blommaert, holding five shares of which Van Rensselaer had two. All these partners bore the expense in proportion to their shares. Later Van Rensselaer increased his shares to three, so that he might not be outvoted, and in 1643, in order to keep strangers out of the business, he admitted his mother-in-law to an equal share with the other "participants." At that time the stock was divided into tenths, of which Van Rensselaer had six. On the shares, *ibid.*, pp. 517, 518, 521, 531, 533, 534, 536–539; on the question of jurisdiction, pp. 468–471, 479, 504, 522, 529, 724; on the *venia testandi*, pp. 524, 536–539. Van Rensselaer was determined to keep high jurisdiction in his own hands, allowing two-tenth shares to exercise middle jurisdiction, and one-tenth low jurisdiction. He would not consent that high jurisdiction could be divided.

2. *Ibid.*, pp. 237, 242.   3. *Ibid.*, pp. 140–141 (§§v, vi).

4. "Rensselaerswyck" is the original spelling, used by the patroon himself.

5. Michiel de Pauw (Pavonia [for the name, *Proceedings,* New Jersey Historical Society, 1st ser., IX, 35–38], 1630, across the North River from Manhattan, also Staten Island, sold, 1633. The name Paulus Hook is the English form of the Dutch Powles Hook, from Michiel de Pauw); Samuel Godyn, Samuel Blommaert, and associates (Swaanendael, 1631, at Whorekill on the west side of Delaware Bay, sold, July, 1634); Albert Coenraets Burgh (east side of Delaware Bay, November 1, 1629, never occupied, sold to company); Samuel Blommaert (on the Connecticut River, 1629, never occupied); Kiliaen van Rensselaer (upper Hudson, 1629, the only patroonship that survived). In addition there were at least five lesser patroonships, hardly more than estates of land though they carried legally all the feudal privileges of the others. These five were the patroonship of David de Vries (Vriesendael, 1640, in the neighborhood of Tappan along the Hudson, which was abandoned at the time of Kiefft's Indian war); that of Cornelis Melyn (Staten Island, 1640, the government but not the land transferred to the company, June 3, 1659); that of Meyndert Meyndertsen

Rensselaerswyck we know a great deal. Through agents in 1630 and 1631 Van Rensselaer bought lands on the west side of the upper Hudson and gradually enlarged the area until he and his partners possessed a territory running up and down on both sides of the river, including Castle Island, and extending north on the west side until it surrounded Fort Orange, which remained the sole possession of the company within the colony of Rensselaerswyck. Adjacent to it was the hamlet of Beverwyck which was already beginning to take shape and was destined to become in time the independent incorporated city of Albany.[1] Kiliaen himself never visited New Netherland, but continued to reside in Amsterdam, ruling his colony from afar as an absentee patroon, by means of a *commis* or agent in charge, with an under-*commis,* a schout, the head officer who also administered justice, and five schepens or councillors, the last two of whom (schout and schepens) were authorized to wear insignia of their office.[2] To all these, each of whom took an oath of loyalty to himself, the patroon gave frequent instructions regarding the conduct of his business. He sent over, sometimes in the ships of the company and sometimes in other vessels, goods in great variety, horses, mares, cattle, cows, implements of all kinds for farming pur-

van Keren (Achter Col, 1641, in the valley of the Hackensack); that of Adriaen van der Donck, schout at Rensselaerswyck, who in 1645 took up a patroonship north of the Harlem, purchasing land "as far as Papirinemen, called by our people in spite of the devil" (Spyt den Duyvel) and fastening on the territory the name "de Jonkeer's Landt" (Yonkers); and, lastly, that of the Rev. Francis Doughty and associates at Maspet, 1642, eighty persons in all, the area amounting to 13,000 acres, which though called a patroonship never was such in reality and was soon broken up by the Indians (*Collections,* New York Historical Society, 2d series, II, 301, 333; Thompson, *Long Island,* Werner ed., III, 48–51, where the patent is given). These five and perhaps others were granted under the new Freedoms and Exemptions adopted by the company in 1639 and confirmed by the States General in June, 1640, which reduced the size of the patroonships though without changing their character, provided for smaller grants to free colonists, and liberalized the commercial privileges. Van Rensselaer protested against these concessions, though they were designed to aid in peopling the province, because he thought they would conflict with his trading profits (Brodhead, *History,* I, 311–312; O'Callaghan, *History,* I, 218–222; *Van Rensselaer Bowier,* p. 237–238, 424–425, 463–465, 466, 500). There is a short article on the patroonships in the *Quarterly Journal* of the New York State Historical Association, XII, no. 3, and among the *Publications* of The Order of Colonial Lords of Manors in America are pamphlets on the patroonships of Rensselaer and Melyn, nos. 2 and 9.

1. There is a description of Rensselaerswyck in 1634 in *Van Rensselaer Bowier,* pp. 306–312. See also Nissenson, *The Patroon's Domain* (1937).

2. *Ibid.,* pp. 204–205, 251. The insignia were a silver plated rapier, a baldric, and a black hat with plumes.

poses, millstones for a grist mill, materials for a saw mill, vats for brewing, iron and coal for the smithies, brick and tiles for building (though early he hoped to make brick in the colony), and he despatched at his own expense farmers, servants, and laborers.[1] He wrote letters constantly, long and prolix and badly arranged, which occasionally drew from those who received them expressions of dismay and must have made it difficult at times for his officials to know just what it was that Kiliaen wanted.[2] He conducted his propriety as a farming colony, cultivating a part himself and leasing other parts to farmers, of whom there were six on the east side in 1639, and in 1651 sixteen on both sides of the river and on the islands;[3] but by reason of his attempt to run the colony from across the water he became involved in constant altercations. Disputes were common with his farmers about leases, profits (of which he claimed half), and the payment of tithes; with his officials, whom he charged with extravagance and neglect of his orders, while studying their own benefit and advancement; and with Governor Kiefft at New Amsterdam about sending goods up the river, with successive *commisen* at Fort Orange over the fur supply, and with both regarding payment for the delivery of grain. He had trouble with the company regarding the use of its ships also. In general he complained of his own people, because they would hunt and trap, contrary to his express commands, for he wanted them to obtain furs only by barter; and he inveighed against interlopers, because in their search for peltries they trespassed on his property. It is hard to believe that he reaped anything but trouble as the reward for all his labors.[4]

In the meantime the province itself progressed but slowly. Occupying its territory were the functionaries, farmers, and laborers of the patroon at Rensselaerswyck numbering about one hundred in

1. *Ibid.*, pp. 523, 544, 644.   2. *Ibid.*, pp. 565, 568, 570.

3. *Ibid.*, pp. 453, 488. The sixteen are shown in an inventory of animals, farms, and farmers taken after the death of Kiliaen and the entrance of his son, Johannes, into the property (pp. 732–743). The estate had not been well managed for some years and affairs were in a confused condition (pp. 616, 621). A hearing was had in 1646 before the States General, between the remaining partners and the guardians of the young Johannes, which ended in favor of the new patroon.

4. For further details regarding the Rensselaer colony see *Court Minutes of Fort Orange and the Village of Beverwyck*, 1652–1680, two vols. (1920, 1923); *Court Minutes of Rensselaerswyck, Albany, and Schenectady*, 1668–1685, three vols. (1926–1932); *Correspondence of Jeremias van Rensselaer*, 1651–1674 (1932); and *Correspondence of Maria van Rensselaer*, 1669–1689 (1935), all translated and edited by A. J. F. van Laer.

1646; the officials and their subordinates at such forts, towns, and settled districts as were in the immediate hands of the company; a considerable body of free residents—"free men" or "free merchants" —who had come over on their own account and at their own expense and had been allotted land in full ownership by the company; many mechanics and retailers in New Amsterdam; and a large number of individuals in service under masters. Racially these people were of great variety, Dutch, Walloons, French, English, Portuguese, and, after 1655, Swedes and Finns. There were a few Jews, and many negroes from Brazil and elsewhere.[1] Domine Megapolensis divided those who lived on the island of Manhattan and its environs into two groups: "first, Christians—at least so called; second, Indians," in great variety and with forms of language that the domine tried to master but with difficulty. Father Jogues commented on the "confusion of tongues" in the province as depriving the people there of great benefits and likened the spirit created thereby to the "arrogance of Babel."[2] The official form of church discipline and polity was that of the Dutch Reformed Church, Calvinist, but there were in the province Lutherans, English Puritans or Independents, Quakers, Anabaptists or Mennonites, and a number of Roman Catholics. A spirit of intolerance prevailed on the part of the Calvinists toward the Lutherans, the Quakers, and other sectaries, an intolerance so strikingly in contrast with the liberalism of the home country that in 1663 the company took occasion to reprimand Stuyvesant on the ground that the "consciences of men should be free and unshackled."[3] Of schools and schoolmasters there was a great dearth.[4]

The government of the province was in the hands of a director general and his subordinate officials, not one of whom, with the

---

1. New Netherland (Original Narratives), pp. 329, 392, 407, 408; New York Colonial Documents, II, 31.

2. New Netherland (Original Narratives), pp. 172, 253. "On the island of Manhate, and in its environs, there may well be four or five hundred men of different sects and nations: the Director General told me [in 1646] that there were men of eighteen different languages; they are scattered here and there on the river, above and below, as the beauty and convenience of the spot has invited each to settle: some mechanics, however, who ply their trade, are ranged under the fort; all the others are exposed to the incursions of the natives" (pp. 259–260). A recent life of Father Jogues, by John J. Birch (1936), bears the title, The Saint of the Wilderness: St. Isaac Jogues, S. J. Earlier lives are by Felix Martin (1885) and F. Talbot (1935).

3. Ibid., pp. 260, 392, 393, 400 notes, 401–402, 404.

4. Ibid., pp. 398–399.

single exception of Peter Minuit (1626-1632), who afterward went over to the Swedes, was able to conduct himself so as to avoid serious criticism. Bastiaen Janseen Krol (March, 1632—April, 1633) a thirteen months' temporary appointee, was succeeded by Wouter van Twiller (1633-1638), a nephew of Van Rensselaer's, who was raised from an office clerkship in Amsterdam to be the governor of a province. He was charged with pride and vainglory, with indolence and carelessness, with drunkenness "as long as there is any wine," and with hostility toward religion. Van Rensselaer wrote him reprimanding him for his bad habits and poor judgment and warning him of the results.[1] Better times for the company began after 1635, with the completion of the conquest of Brazil and the establishment there of stable government. The stock was increased by one-third and the directors planned to take up the affairs of New Netherland with renewed diligence, reducing the monopoly and increasing the population, but it made a serious mistake when it sent out as the successor of Van Twiller one Willem Kiefft, a merchant of Amsterdam with none too savory a career behind him, but with something of a reputation for experience and capacity.

Whatever may be the truth of the charges of rapacity, drunkenness, uncontrolled passion, and overbearance that were brought against Kiefft—and they are very substantial and from the mouths of many reliable witnesses—one thing is quite certain, that the evil of the Indian war, for which he and his secretary Van Tienhoven were largely responsible, lived after him and was in no slight degree responsible for the failure of the company's efforts to build up the colony. The region from Fort Orange to the Delaware was singularly open to Indian attacks and there had been many murders committed during the years since 1630—at Fort Orange, Swaanendael, and on Staten Island. In 1643, partly to take revenge for outrages committed and partly to obtain a tribute which he claimed the company ordered him to exact, but which his enemies said he intended to keep for himself, Kiefft began a war against the Indians which, lasting until 1645, desolated the province, destroyed farms and crops, and brought heavy loss to the people in killed and wounded. The Indians, well supplied with guns and ammunition (though selling

1. *Van Rensselaer Bowier*, pp. 271-272. Van Twiller remained in the province for a year after his dismissal, then returned to the Netherlands, married there, and in 1646 was appointed one of the guardians of the young Johannes.

arms to them was strictly forbidden both at Rensselaerswyck and at New Amsterdam)[1] wreaked a vicious vengeance and were only subdued and compelled to sue for peace after the whole force of the province had been thrown against them.[2] For more than three years all progress was at a standstill, population decreased, trade fell off, and a feeling of hopelessness and despair settled upon the province, penetrating Manhattan as well as the devastated regions and driving back to Holland many a Dutchman who saw no future for himself and his family in a colony of so many disasters. Gradually during 1645 peace was made with the various tribes on Long Island and beyond the Hudson, but it left the province weakened in man power and financially insecure. The sanguine expectations of 1637 remained unfulfilled and the company saw the specter of bankruptcy threatening its existence as a solvent corporation. The Indian war ended Kiefft's career as a colonial governor. His life too ended in 1647, for he embarked for home in the *Princess Amelia,* which foundered off the coast of Wales, and was drowned with eighty other persons.[3] To take his place the directors sought the best man they could find, and they thought they had discovered him in Peter Stuyvesant, at one time (1643-1644) the governor of the Dutch island of Curaçao and adjacent islands, where he had managed affairs with dexterity and had displayed some of the arts of a Roman proconsul. Ambitious to maintain the colonial area under Dutch control he had conducted (March–April 16, 1644) an expedition for the relief of certain Dutch colonists at St. Martin, who were threatened by the Portu-

---

1. *Ibid.,* pp. 426, 565. Approved by the company under certain restrictions (*New Netherland,* Original Narratives, p. 344).

2. A brief statement can be found of the beginning of the war in De Vries' notes, 1642, and an elaborate description of its course in "Journal of New Netherland," 1647, which covers the years after 1641 (*ibid.,* pp. 213–215, 273–284). Some additional facts are given in *Documentary History of New York,* IV, 102–106. The latter account throws the blame for beginning the war upon the secretary, Van Tienhoven. Information regarding the Indians of the Hudson River valley and the regions adjacent to New Amsterdam and New York can be obtained from the contemporary writings of Denton, Miller, and Wolley and the narratives printed in *New Netherland* (Original Narratives). A useful modern treatise, giving a history of the local Indian wars from earliest times to 1788, is by Ruttenber, *History of the Indian Tribes of Hudson's River* (1872).

3. *Documentary History of New York,* IV, 111–112; *Calendar State Papers, Colonial,* 1661–1668, §1531. Winthrop heard of the event and saw in it "an observable hand of God against the Dutch," a special mark of the Lord's favor to his poor people of Massachusetts and "displeasure toward such as have opposed and injured them." *Journal,* II, 333.

guese, and there he was wounded in the leg while unsuccessfully attempting to capture a fort which was in the hands of the enemy.[1] Having had his leg amputated at Curaçao, he returned to Holland, where he was selected by the directors as a suitable man for their purpose. Sent out in 1647 as governor of New Netherland, Curaçao, and other adjacent Dutch islands in the Caribbean, all of which he had to look after and defend, he entered upon a period of storm and stress that lasted for seventeen years, until the capture of New Amsterdam in 1664.

There is no opportunity here to examine and comment on the charges which were brought against these men, particularly those against Stuyvesant.[2] De Vries in 1633, when he had only Van Twiller to talk about, said that the company appointed as superior officers "persons who never had command in their lives," and he wondered that the directors should "send such fools into this country who knew nothing except to drink."[3] Later (1642) he added that directors were sent to the province whether they were fit or not, and in this he was corroborated by others, who added that these men, employes of the company, returned home when their time was out, having accomplished nothing of importance.[4] A later representation, made in 1649, which contains a bitter attack on both Kiefft and Stuyvesant and is so full of revolting details of the war as to be almost unbelievable, calls Stuyvesant "an unlicked bear," and so overstates the case as to destroy one's confidence in its reliability. These men cannot have been so utterly and inconceivably bad as their enemies made them out to be, and Stuyvesant presented a dignified and impressive defense of his directorship before the company

1. There are documents relating to Stuyvesant's career while at Curaçao and his attack on St. Martin in Wright (ed.), *Nederlandsche Zeewaarders op de Eilanden in de Caraïbische Zee* (etc.), 1621–1648(9), Part II, 1635–1648(9), X, pp. 101–153 (documents in Spanish, translated into Dutch). This second volume was issued by the Historisch Genootschap, Utrecht, in 1935. There is a biography of Stuyvesant in the *Dictionary of American Biography*, by Victor H. Paltsits.

2. The charges are given at great length and with much verbosity in "The Representation of New Netherland," 1649 (*New Netherland,* Original Narratives, pp. 320–327), followed by Van Tienhoven's answer, which is more temperately and concisely written (pp. 359–365). Whatever we may think of Van Tienhoven's morals we must acknowledge that he made the most of his opportunity. Even his enemies allowed that he was "cautious, subtle, intelligent and sharp witted" (*ibid.,* 340). Contemporary accounts of Kiefft's conduct are usually hostile, for example, *Documentary History of New York,* IV, 101–112.

3. *New Netherland* (Original Narratives), pp. 191, 215.

4. *Ibid.,* pp. 215, 321.

in 1665. It must be remembered that he had been governor of Curaçao, a small island, where, in order to make his administration profitable to the shareholders, he had ruled as an autocrat, in the interest not of the islanders but of the company. Perhaps then it is not strange that he should have pursued a similar course in New Netherland, though conditions within and the surroundings without were entirely different. Then, too, it must be remembered that the community at New Amsterdam was not composed of men inclined to peace, harmony, and compromise. Endless quarreling went on and was pursued with the more vigor because those who took part in them were frequently in their cups. The hostilities became the more bitter because of the intolerance displayed by the Calvinists toward the Lutherans and their persecution of the radical religious groups.

One considerable charge—upon which comment was made contemporaneously and has been frequently repeated by later writers—concerned the absence for many years of any satisfactory form of popular representation, whereby the colonists might share in government and give effective voice to their many grievances. Until 1641 all the governors, from Minuit to Kiefft, had managed affairs with the advice of one or more councillors, appointed either by the company or by the governor himself.[1] But in August of that year, because of the impending trouble with the Indians—which two years later reached the stage of active warfare—Kiefft sought the co-operation of the heads of families of Manhattan and its neighborhood, who gathered at the fort and chose twelve men (the Twelve) to advise him what to do. He received the recommendations of these men, who at first counselled delay but as the situation grew worse consented to reprisals; and having got what he wanted he had no further use for them. But in 1643, when affairs were not progressing as favorably as he wished, he called the commonalty together again. This time, in a more determined mood, the burghers and farmers elected eight men (the Eight), whom Kiefft was not able to manage so easily. They not only had a part in the conduct of the war, but they opposed the governor in matters of civil concern and by their direct appeals, twice repeated, to the company at home were largely

1. *Ibid.*, p. 332. Kiefft had only one "councillor," La Montagne, a Huguenot physician, whom he selected himself. With him in consultation were also the fiscal, the secretary, and occasionally other officers of the company.

responsible for obtaining his recall in 1647. The success in this issue made a continuance of popular coöperation inevitable, so that almost immediately after Stuyvesant's arrival, when the town and province generally were found in so ruinous a state as to call for increased taxation and the help of the community in rebuilding, the new governor consented to another election. In August, 1647 (Stuyvesant arrived in May), the Dutch householders of Manhattan, Breuckelen, Ameersfort, and Pavonia (the English in the province, with one exception, having no part in the movement) met and elected eighteen men, who selected nine of their number, three from the merchants, two from the burghers, and four from the farmers, constituting the Nine, to advise and share in promoting the general welfare. These men were to meet only when summoned and, nominating their own successors, to continue until lawfully dismissed. Their functions, partly judicial, were largely consultatory, and the governor and his council were free to accept or reject as they pleased whatever the Nine, sitting with the governor as their presiding officer, might see fit to recommend. Needless to say Stuyvesant was inclined to tolerate them as long as they agreed with him, but he soon found himself involved in troublesome disagreements, because the board was only too ready with complaints and with remedies for a general betterment of conditions. It appealed twice to the company at home, sending over two of its number with a representation signed by eleven men, to answer whom Stuyvesant despatched Van Tienhoven, the secretary, with evidence in his own favor. The efforts of the Nine had a measure of success, for the directors of the company, acting under the influence of the Amsterdam chamber, granted to both town and province sundry new and desirable privileges. But Stuyvesant, though seriously concerned for the restoration of prosperity, objected to any curtailment of his executive prerogatives, and did so with such a violent display of temper and such a vigorous outburst of language that in the eyes of posterity his turbulence has tended to overshadow his really considerable qualities as an administrator. Though the Nine represented a distinct advance over the Twelve and the Eight in the direction of permanence and popular coöperation, and though the town of New Amsterdam obtained advantages that gave the burghers there a certain amount of direct control over its affairs, the discord was never stilled and the line of separation between the governor on one side and the leading burghers on the other remained unchanged to the end.[1] What would have happened in the long run had the English conquest never taken place cannot even be conjectured. As it was the English success put an end to the Dutch rule in New Nether-land; but as long as the province remained a dependency of an in-corporated trading company at home—a status which the Nine in their representation of 1649–1650 hoped the States General would bring to an end—it may well be doubted, judging from the history of the Dutch administration in the East, if any elaborate form of self-government would ever have been introduced. Self-administra-tion and self-taxation, similar to the practices which obtained in the cities of the Netherlands, might have come, but that anything com-parable with the law-making and money-appropriating powers of the assemblies in the English colonies of the eighteenth century should have evolved is unlikely.[2]

In the face of the danger that encompassed the province in 1664 the situation confronting the Dutch in New Netherland was hopeless, and the reasons why it fell such an easy prey to the Eng-lish attack are clear. Without depending more than is safely believ-able on the contemporary charges and counter-charges—for which corroborative evidence is for the most part wanting—certain subver-sive and enfeebling conditions are manifest. The province never lived up to the motto of the States General, "Union makes strength," for it was without unity, homogeneity, or compactness, either in race, religion, territorial settlement, or types of local organization and government. The distant colony of Rensselaerswyck added nothing to its cohesiveness, for not only was there bickering within

1. The chief documents in the case are to be found in *New York Colonial Docu-ments,* I, with satisfactory accounts in O'Callaghan and Brodhead. There is also an excellent description in *History of the State of New York* (1933), I, 277–282, 300–317. The Nine drew up the "Representation" noted above. The indifference of the English towns on Long Island may have been due to the fact that they were allowed by the Dutch to govern themselves. George Baxter wrote to Winthrop in March, 1650, that these towns had ample privileges of self-government, liberty of conscience "according to the custom of Holland," and control of all cases of justice under fifty guilders (*Collections,* Massachusetts Historical Society, fifth series, I, 370). Probably John Scott and Connecticut had a good deal to do with their later uneasiness.

2. Three gatherings of delegates from towns adjacent to New Amsterdam were held, one on December 10, 1653, one on November 3, 1663, and a third on March 19, 1664. Each of these assemblies was called for a special purpose in a time of crisis, to consider the state of the province and to promise support. No one of them was summoned a second time or had any right to come together again. Brodhead, *History,* I, 570–575, 722, 728–731.

the patroonship but there was constant friction between Van Rensselaer and the *commis* at Fort Orange and the director at New Amsterdam, and the sparseness of the population of his propriety made
assistance thence in time of need practically impossible. In the province itself there was always present a measure of hostility between
the minority interested in their personal profits and the majority
favoring farming and agriculture. Socially, there existed a disparity
between the general run of the people, both within and without
New Amsterdam, that is, between those who were poor, simple, and
uninformed, and the merchant and burgher classes, who mainly,
though not in all cases, favored trade rather than population and
were charged with practices that were oppressive to their less privileged neighbors.

The company did little to advance the general welfare. To be
sure, it claimed to have done what it could,[1] but its management was
in the interest of the few rather than the many. Also its attitude
toward some of the colony's more vital needs was one partly of
indifference and partly of necessity, because after 1645 it became
heavily involved financially and wholly bankrupt after 1654 when
its trade with Guinea fell off and it lost Brazil, up to that time its
best market. It was never successful in the men it sent over to direct
the affairs of New Netherland, for even after all allowances are
made for personal likes and dislikes, it is evident that Van Twiller
and Kiefft were incompetent and that Stuyvesant was headstrong
and dictatorial. The executives of the province, all of them, were
invested with more authority than was good for their souls. The
province was governed from above and not from below; the administration was autocratic and not popular; the burghers had little to
say regarding the methods employed, and for two decades before
the conquest, their grievances were the order of the day. In the
complaints which they made they declared that greed was the motive determining the policy of the company and its agents; that
taxes were imposed without regard to the popular ability to pay;
that money was constantly going out and never coming in; that
trade restrictions encouraged monopoly, injuring legitimate business
and encouraging smuggling and traffic in contraband; and that the
directors at home displayed little interest in the time-honored doctrine, the safety of the people is the supreme law. They said that

1. *New Netherland* (Original Narratives), pp. 371, 374.

little had been accomplished in the way of public works—only a tavern, a church, a town hall, a market, a palisade, a few wharves, and a few bridges; that the fort was neglected; that scarcely anything had been accomplished in the way of community needs for social betterment, such as disclosed the presence of an awakened public spirit.

The strength of the province was sadly undermined by the hostile attacks of the Indians, who up the river, on the other side of the Hudson, in Long Island, Staten Island, and north of the Harlem were frequently engaged in raids of one kind or another, a series of tragic encounters that culminated in the disastrous war of 1643. This conflict left the province battered and unnerved. The peace that followed lasted for ten years but was again broken at a time when, in 1655, Stuyvesant, after spending seven months of the previous year in Curaçao,[1] was engaged in the capture of the Swedish settlements on the Delaware, a bloodless but expensive campaign, the cost of which had to be met in 1657 by turning over Fort Casimir to the city of Amsterdam for the founding of New Amstel (New Castle). Then it was that in revenge for outrages committed by the English, the Indians began a new reign of terror, forcing the outlying farmers to seek refuge behind the palisade, compelling the Long Island towns to appeal to Stuyvesant for aid, and even invading New Amsterdam itself. In 1663, the village of Esopus, lying in an unprotected region north of Manhattan, because of which, though protected by a fort, it had suffered much at the hands of the savages, was attacked in a peculiarly atrocious manner, and despite vigorous resistance, involving three aggressive expeditions, was rendered helpless as an asset of strength to the province. Altogether the Indian wars cost the company heavily in money and men, diverted the attention of the provincial officials from domestic needs, and stripped the open country of its inhabitants, thus rendering easier encroachments by the English on the east, who were already crowding on into the territory claimed by the Dutch.

The Dutch claim was vast in extent and wholly indefinite as to boundaries, for the latter rested on no certain foundation, the charter

1. This visit to Curaçao was made at the time of the Western Expedition sent out by Cromwell, and some of the Dutch ships captured by the English fleet in that year and following years were those which Stuyvesant sent from Curaçao in the effort to enlarge the trade of that island and so to help the company which was facing heavy losses.

to the West India Company mentioning limits in general terms, with rights of possession based on occupation only—all in contrast with the carefully worded clauses of the English charters which were generally very definite. Whatever may be the ethics in the case, it is impossible to subscribe to Brodhead's statement that "the title which Holland acquired to New Netherland—as far east at any rate as Buzzard's Bay—was as just and valid as any of which the history of the world contains a record."[1] The claims of the English, whether valid or not, were based at any rate on exact statements and were followed up by permanent settlement. To people seeking homes rather than the profits of trade, particularly when those people were Puritans, acting under the guidance of the Almighty,[2] expansion was inevitable, whether to the northward, as with Massachusetts, or to the westward, as with New Haven and Connecticut. This growth, which was grimly though not quite accurately described by the Dutch as an "insatiable desire [of the English] to possess that which is ours," was slow but steady in southwestern Connecticut and Long Island and led to Stuyvesant's well-known attempt in 1650 to obtain an agreement on a boundary line running through Oyster Bay and Greenwich.[3] His failure to accomplish his purpose became evident in 1653 when Connecticut's and New Haven's plan of invading New Netherland came to light and fell through only because Massachusetts refused to coöperate and because peace was made the next year between England and Holland. Connecticut seized Fort Hope in 1654; New Haven talked of a settlement on the Delaware; John

1. *Commemorative Oration* (1864), p. 11. Mr. Brodhead's services to history are beyond praise, but his interpretation of the course of events in New Netherland is unrestrained in its defense of the Dutch and their claims and unduly flattering in its estimate of the general situation in the province. In the stress which his treatment lays on "popular rights" it bears the earmarks of the time when it was published (1853). In these respects the *Oration* is even more eulogistic than the *History*.

2. The Venetian resident in England, commenting on the "sectaries," voiced a general opinion when he said that they "all claim to be saints and that all they do is by divine inspiration" (*Calendar Venetian Papers,* 1661–1664, p. 205). The "sectaries" thus characterized were "the Anabaptists, Independents, Brownists, Levellers, Seekers and Quakers, people governed by their own fantasies, who claim to have the spirit of God" (*ibid.,* p. 86).

3. Papers relating to the locating of this line, which was eventually agreed to in Holland but never in England, and to other phases of the controversy between the Dutch and the English at this time can be found in Hazard, *State Papers,* taken from the records of the New England Confederation. They were reprinted in 1811, in *Collections,* New York Historical Society, first series, I, 189–303. All have since been printed in volumes IX and X of the Plymouth Colony Records.

Pynchon from Springfield advanced his trading posts into the region behind Rensselaerswyck; New Haven established a trading post up the Housatonic at Derby; and the commissioners of the New England Confederation considered the possibility of disputing the Dutch monopoly of the Indian trade on the upper Hudson and Mohawk rivers.[1] On the other side of the water, running concurrently with the aggressive actions of the New England colonists, the Cromwellian government continued to seize Dutch ships in the West Indies for trading contrary to the navigation act of 1651, sided with the Portuguese in their recovery of Brazil, and disputed with the Dutch their right to a monopoly of business in Guinea and along the African coast. The two movements worked in close accord. Connecticut sent her agents beyond the Oyster Bay–Greenwich line into Westchester and western Long Island; John Scott coöperated with a "confederation" of the six English towns already formed there,[2] raised a troop of horse, and tried, but unsuccessfully, to bring under its authority the five Dutch towns that lay to the west along the East River;[3] while Maverick and perhaps Scott himself, both on visits to England after 1660, presented the situation to the English authorities of the Restoration and urged action. The sequel has already been told. An English fleet captured New Amsterdam in 1664 and by further conquest within the year reduced the whole of New Netherland to the authority of the English crown.

Though outwardly the result seemed to show merely a shift of masters, for the territory and the population remained intact, in fact it involved changes of great significance. What had been the property of a trading company, with its multiple board of directors and its complicated system of chambers, became the feudal domain of a proprietary lord, possessed by grant from the king of England along with full and absolute authority to govern the people who lived there as a matter of proprietary control. It must be remembered, first, that the charter thus conveyed by one young man of thirty-four to an-

1. Buffinton, "New England and the Western Fur Trade, 1629–1675," *Publications,* Colonial Society of Massachusetts, XVIII, 160–192.

2. Hempstead (1644), Gravesend (1645), Flushing (1645), Newtown (1652), Oyster Bay (1653), and Jamaica (1656).

3. Breuckelen (1646), Midwout (Flatbush, 1652, 1654), Ameersfort (Flatlands, 1633, 1654), New Utrecht (1659–1661), Boswyck (Bushwyck, 1661). The first three were granted municipal privileges in 1654; the last two were under the jurisdiction of the others.

other young man of thirty was drawn up in great haste, for it passed through the seals in less than four days, and secondly that it was the only charter in our colonial history which was issued to a member of the royal family, a possible heir to the throne. These peculiar conditions explain, in part at least, why the document is the shortest of all the colonial charters and contains the fewest restrictions of any upon the powers which the grantee might exercise. Within the territory taken from the Dutch and the supplemental territory to the northward belonging to the down-east mainland of New England, the Duke of York was empowered to rule unhampered by any counterbalancing agency in the form of a popular assembly such as might limit his complete independence of action. He could control all appointments, make all laws and ordinances—provided they were in conformity with those of England—and determine all judicial matters, capital and criminal, civil and marine, except in cases of appeal, which the king reserved to himself, his heirs and successors. He was to have entire command of the trade of his propriety, could fix the customs dues, regulate the granting and assigning of lands, and take all necessary measures in case of attack. In the event of rebellion, insurrection, or mutiny his appointees could exercise all the powers of lieutenants in the counties of England, as defined by their commissions or the acts of parliament. And as if these carefully defined functions were not enough, the charter declared, by implication, that in all things essential to the good of the inhabitants the duke might exercise discretion, even though the charter were silent, and that in the matter of the boundaries he might ignore all patents and grants hitherto made to any bodies politic or corporate.[1] As the lands were to be held in free and common socage, all that the duke was to render in recognition of the king's paramount lordship was forty beaver skins yearly, whenever they should be demanded. There is nothing to show that these skins were ever presented at Greenwich as were the two Indian arrows by Lord Baltimore at Windsor Castle.

Though literally interpreted the duke's charter contains the most extreme expression of proprietary authority to be found in any of the feudal grants of soil and government in English America, and

1. This remarkable clause in the duke's charter of 1664 would seem to be directed definitely against Connecticut, and might be construed as a deliberate denial of Connecticut's claim.

though the administration under it is sometimes characterized by our historians as arbitrary and despotic, it may be doubted whether the powers actually exercised by James and his appointees were any-where near as absolute as were those of the Maryland proprietors at the same time. There was no palatine clause in his charter. Except in the one matter of a representative assembly, which the duke was not obliged to summon and did not cause to be summoned until 1683, the general management of the governors resident in the colony—Nicolls, Lovelace, Andros, and Dongan—was always in-tended to be as nearly in the interest of the inhabitants as the charter would allow. According to the duke's own instructions, the people were to be "treated with all humanity and gentleness that can con-sist with the honour and safety" of the government and Andros was specially enjoined to administer the propriety "for the encourage-ment of Planters and Plantations and the improvement of trade, and commerce, and for the preservation of religion justice and equity."[1] There is nothing to show that either Andros or the others departed from a line of conduct determined by these precepts or within the province itself acted in a harsh or tyrannical manner. A government need not be despotic because it is cast in an executive mold.

Never in the ducal proprietorship was there any attempt, as was made in Maryland, to claim the proprietary prerogative as a family right at the expense of the king on one side or the body of the people on the other, or to concentrate the control of governmental and mili-tary offices in the hands of the proprietor, his relatives, and sup-porters. Though an oath of fealty was required of councillors and officials in New York,[2] there is no evidence that the people at large swore fidelity or were required to do more than render obedience to those whom the duke set in office over them. An oath of alle-giance to the crown was enforced from the beginning and all writs, warrants, and executions ran in the king's name and not in that of the duke. Furthermore the king controlled the military forces in the garrisons and forts (though not the militia), making allowances for all military charges up to a certain point, above which the province or the duke himself was expected to supply the funds. The form of the government was executive throughout and the indefinite lan-

1. *New York Colonial Documents*, III, 216, 237.
2. *Ibid.*, 218.

guage of the charter left the duke free to determine what that form should be. His governors all had councils, selected, as far as we have definite information about them, from among the leading men of the place, not to exceed ten in the case of Andros and Dongan, who were specially instructed to choose all magistrates and officers of justice from among those persons "wch have most reputacon both for their abilities and integrity and for that reason most acceptable to the inhabitants." Liberty of conscience was guaranteed to all persons of what religion soever, and in the distribution of land Andros was told to be as liberal as were the neighboring colonies of New England and Maryland, in order that planters might have the same inducements to settle in New York as they would have anywhere else.

But New York was a propriety not a self-governing colony and the duke's interest in it, before all else, was material and financial. He wanted a considerable profit if he could get it, if not he wanted that the costs of government should be so far kept down as to help him to reap some advantages in return for all the trouble and expense that he had been at in protecting the colony. For that reason he retained in his own hands the appointment of customs officials and with his advisers in England scrutinized the balance sheets showing the state of the province on the financial side. He established the customs rates both for exports and imports and insisted that payment should be made in cash or goods ad valorem. He had in England not only his secretary, treasurer, and auditor and receiver general, but also his attorney and solicitor general, constituting a small board of commissioners, who were appointed after the restoration in 1674, to act as an advisory council, particularly in connection with matters of law and policy, giving the duke their opinion on such suggestions for change and improvement as were made by the governors in their reports.[1] He rarely, if ever, acted

1. These advisers were at first Sir Francis Winnington and Sir John Churchill, eminent lawyers and king's counsellors of their day, who served as the duke's attorney general and solicitor general, and together were known as his "commissioners." Later, September, 1677, Sir George Jeffreys, of the "bloody assizes," took Winnington's place, and he and Churchill served until the duke became king. Their last recorded acts (March 2, 1683, August 22, 26, and December 4, 1684) were to prepare a deed confirming to the proprietors of East New Jersey the powers granted to Carteret; to discuss with the proprietors of East New Jersey the bringing of their colony under the government of New York; to approve the charter and laws passed by the assembly of 1683; and to take into consideration the general welfare of the province, regarding which they declared it to be impossible for them at so great a

alone, but depended on the advice of his commissioners, even at times calling upon others also for their approval and consent. On doubtful points he seems always to have been guided by the opinions of his counsellors.

That the duke took an immediate and personal interest in his possession is everywhere apparent. The affairs of this distant propriety engaged but remotely the attention of those in office at Whitehall who were concerned for the administration of England and her colonies. Once in the duke's hands, except for a few particulars already noticed—those embodied in the charter and others connected with defense—he and his governors were made responsible for its management. He directed its policy, read the correspondence, wrote letters, either in his own hand or in the hand of Sir John Werden, his secretary, or Sir Allen Apsley, his treasurer, issued orders and instructions, and kept himself posted as to the returns from rents, revenues, profits, and perquisites. After the appointment by the crown of William Blathwayt in England as auditor general of the plantation revenues, he sent over John Lewen as his personal auditor on the spot to make inquiry into the state of affairs in the province, because he was beginning to fear that his failure, since 1674, to obtain any income from his property was due to the prevalence of carelessness, error, and fraud whereby his rights were "damnified."[1] As Sir John Werden said in a letter to Governor Andros, May 24, 1680, shortly before the latter's recall "the Cheife thing we inquire after is the chardge and revenue of your government, of wch we have met with calculacons soe vastly differing from your acc^{ts} as on the one side we have not yet sufficient evidence to believe them certaine, soe on the other we cannot but be sollicitous to have a strict enquiry made into the businesse by a person wholely unconcerned." Andros was recalled in 1680 and made a vigorous defense of his administration against Lewen's charges of collusion on the part of collectors and disobedience on the part of the merchants, and of extravagance, theft, and evasion on the part of the government.

But whatever may be the merits and demerits of charge and de-

distance "to judge of every particular worke," and so they were obliged to leave decisions "wholely to [the governor's] prudence." *Calendar State Papers, Colonial,* 1681–1685, §§985, 1841; *New York Colonial Documents,* III, 348, 353.

1. *Ibid.,* 279–282. For Lewen's report, 302–308, and Andros's answer, 308–313, 314–316. The duke's commissioners exculpated Andros and probably with justice. *Calendar State Papers, Colonial,* 1681–1685, §1415.

fense, one thing is certain—the duke was not receiving from his estate in America what he thought were his rightful and just dues. The fundamental reasons for this failure seem clear. A ducal domain, such as that of New York, from which revenue was to be extracted, was as foreign to the spirit and trend of the times as was the equally incongruous lordship that the Baltimores were endeavoring to maintain in Maryland during these same eventful years. Its problems were becoming too intricate and formidable to be handled by a private proprietor, however well intentioned, living three thousand miles away. Taxes and customs dues, rents and manorial payments imposed and exacted by an authority outside the colony, in comparison with practices prevailing in England where parliament controlled the purse and of the nearby New England colonies where proprietary tenures did not exist, were easily construed as arbitrary and unjust. New York was gradually ceasing to be a propriety except in name. In fact it was becoming a small, subordinate commonwealth, presenting problems to its governor and other officials that were troublesome to solve because they concerned a community of freemen and not a proprietary estate of land. The duke's appointees were trying to perform the impossible feat of serving two masters and, as might have been expected, there arose charges and countercharges, complaints and justifications that were impossible to determine because of the duality of interests. The governors could not satisfy both duke and people, and the collectors—particularly William Dyer (1674–1683)—were helpless in their efforts to enforce regulations that the merchants and planters were unwilling to obey.[1] There was corruption enough, for it was an age of corruption, but ducal control on one side and official inefficiency and neglect, connivance and greed on the other are not enough to explain the troubles that arose in New York during the period of the duke's proprietorship.

1. In the bill or accusation brought by the grand jury against William Dyer the charge was "high treason" against the crown for imposing unlawful customs in the interest of the Duke of York. Dyer denied the jurisdiction of the special court of assizes and was remanded to England for trial. The case is important as showing the efforts of the merchants to break an appointee of the duke who was trying to serve his master. It was referred to the Privy Council, which in turn handed it over to the Lords of Trade. As the complainant, Samuel Winder, did not appear, though advertised for, the charge was dismissed. Dyer was acquitted and later appointed surveyor general (New York Colonial Documents, III, 287–289; 318–321; Collections, New York Historical Society, 1912, pp. 10–14; Calendar State Papers, Colonial, 1681–1688, index; Acts Privy Council, Colonial, II, 47). Also see below, p. 110, note 2.

Colonel Richard Nicolls, the duke's first appointee, entered upon the government of a territory which was even more scattered than that with which the directors of New Netherland had been called upon to cope, but it was a territory that was perfectly well defined as to its boundaries, as the territory of New Netherland never was. In addition to the towns at the western end of Long Island and to the lands along the Hudson and the Delaware, which had been about all that was of importance to the Dutch, New York took in half of Connecticut, the whole of Long Island, the whole of New Jersey, an undefined stretch along the western side of the Delaware, the territory of eastern Maine extending northward to the St. Lawrence, and all the islands, except Block Island, from Cape Cod to Cape May. This area was soon reduced by the loss of New Jersey, granted to Berkeley and Carteret; by Connecticut's western half, which in 1667 Nicolls and the surviving commissioners gave back to that colony; and by the lands along the western bank of the Delaware, which as we shall see later became the subject of a prolonged dispute with Lord Baltimore arising out of attempts which the New York governors made to issue patents within the territory. Such a strangely outstretched and elongated area, with a length of boundary lines out of all proportion to the extent of land embraced within its limits, offered very serious obstacles in the way of population, cultivation, and defense. There were no peoples east of the Kennebec except the Indians and possibly a few itinerant fishermen who were always ready to abandon their locations whenever threatened with Indian attacks. Up the Hudson were the Dutch, at Esopus, Rensselaerswyck, and Schenectady,[1] Dutch and English were on Long Island, occupied chiefly in making ends meet by cultivating the poor soil; while those at the eastern end were occupied with fishing also.[2] On Manhattan and in the present Westchester County was the larg-

---

1. Schenectady was founded by Arent van Curler in 1661–1662 (*New York Colonial Documents*, XIII, 219). His name, in the form "Corlear," was given by the Indians to the governors of New York, so highly was he esteemed. The town, which was at first a Dutch frontier trading post, was sacked and burned in 1690, a terrifying witness to the fact that during the period from 1664 to 1700, at least, further expansion up the Hudson or Mohawk rivers was impossible on account of the French and Indian menace. *Documentary History of New York*, I, 302–306; II, index, under "Schenectady."

2. "The people of L. Island are very poor and labour only to get bread and clothing, without hopes of ever seeing a penny of monies" (*New York Colonial Documents*, III, 106). "Long Island is very poor and inconsiderable" (*ibid.*, 174).

est group of all, of which the Dutch constituted three fourths, the English less than a quarter, and the French and other nationalities the remainder.[1] Every one of the governors from Nicolls to Dongan bewailed the loss to the duke of the rich lands between the Hudson and the Delaware and Andros and Dongan particularly resented the commissioners having given back to Connecticut all her lands east of a line drawn at Mamaroneck, November 30, 1667. Andros had said that it was impossible for his government to subsist without the addition of Connecticut and Dongan hoped that the Puritan colony would soon be added to New York, "the Centre of all His [Majesty's] Dominions in America."[2] This problem of the boundaries was a never-ending source of trouble to the governors, because

1. In 1681 it was said that New York at that time was "most settled" by Dutchmen, *New York Colonial Documents,* III, 298.

2. In 1667, after an examination of both charters and a hearing of both sides of the case, the remaining commissioners placed the western Connecticut boundary line at Mamaroneck, approximately twenty miles east from any part of the Hudson River (*Annual Report,* New York State Historian, 1896, pp. 143–144). Nicolls recognized the fact that the Connecticut charter antedated that of the Duke of York by two years and believed that to deprive Connecticut of her lands as far east as the Connecticut River would lead "to the utter ruin of that colony" and be a manifest "breach of their late patent." Lovelace agreed with Nicolls. Connecticut accepted the agreement as final, though she considered the drawing of the western line "short of its extent in oᵣ understandings," and thanked both Nicolls and Lovelace for their neighborly conduct. But the Duke of York looked on the decision as only temporary and after the restoration of his province in 1674 paid no attention to the commissioners' decision and in accord with the wording of the boundaries in the new charter instructed Andros to take possession. The latter, obedient to orders (as befitted a soldier), made an imperative demand upon the colony for the surrender of the territory, and, when the general court refused, appeared at Saybrook with an armed force, "so convinced was he that [the annexation of Connecticut] was necessary for New York" (*Calendar State Papers, Colonial,* 1685–1688, p. 334). Then ensued the incident of Andros with his soldiers and Captain Bull at the head of a Connecticut trainband, though the story of the drumming ordered by Bull to drown out the reading of the charter and Andros's commission, seems to be a later invention. *Connecticut Colonial Records,* 1665–1678, pp. 333, 341–345, 572, appendix, nos. xvi, xix; Trumbull, *History of Connecticut,* I, 343–347.

Nicolls had suggested as early as 1665 that the only way out of the dilemma of the patents was to force all New England to submit to the authority of the Duke of York ("to bring down the pride of Massachusetts" as well as to consolidate the governments and improve the revenue), a prophetic anticipation of the Dominion of New England. There can be no doubt that the urgings of Andros and Dongan for the annexation of Connecticut and New Jersey and their conviction that the government of New York would never be able to support itself unless this were done was one reason for the decision reached by James II and the Lords of Trade to try the dominion experiment in 1686. *Documentary History of New York,* I, 150–153, 155, 174, 187; *New York Colonial Documents,* III, 106, 113–114, 136, 230–231, 247, 260.

it involved them in encounters with Maryland, the Jerseys,[1] and Connecticut that brought upon them at times the charge of acting in an arbitrary and offensive manner.

Defense was a greater and more continuous burden than even were the boundaries. Nicolls, while serving in his dual capacity as governor and commissioner, was unable to find opportunity to co-operate with his fellow commissioners for more than a brief length of time. He was called back to New York because of an attack threatened by the Dutch fleet under De Ruyter—but which as it happened never came off—and because of the aggressive activities of the French in Canada, traders like the English for beaver and furs, who in their determination to punish their inveterate enemies, the Mohawks, with whom they were at war, invaded territories claimed by the English king, without his knowledge or consent. Nicolls set on foot a counter-plan for the reduction of Canada and called on the New England colonies for aid; but both Massachusetts and Connecticut, after conferring with each other and with Sir Thomas Temple, governor of Nova Scotia, considered the plan too hazardous "in respect of the difficulty (if not impossibility) of a land march over the rocky mountains and howling desarts about fower hundred miles."[2] Massachusetts too had her eastern Indians to contend with and Connecticut could spare few men from their harvesting, being without servants to carry on the labor and without ammunition or money with which to buy it, and, for an attack by sea, entirely without ships. Therefore on the assurance of the Marquis de Tracy, governor general of Canada, that the expedition against the Indians was without warlike intent against the English, Nicolls gave up the project.

Internal conditions were no less perplexing. Nicolls was inclined

1. The trouble with the Jerseys was largely financial and commercial, arising out of the disputed claim as to whether West Jersey was exempt from the payment to the duke of duties on goods brought up the Delaware, and whether East New Jersey controlled New York harbor as far out as where the bay joined the sea at Sandy Hook. In the latter case the East New Jersey government, on the ground that its territory ran up the west bank of the Hudson for some miles above Manhattan, denied that their vessels coming within the bay had to stop at New York and pay customs, insisting that such vessels could go straight on to East New Jersey's port, Perth Amboy, and be entered there. New York contested this claim, but in the end (1700) lost out, a decision being rendered in England favorable to East New Jersey, too late to be of much service to that province (below, pp. 180–181).

2. *Massachusetts Colonial Records,* IV, part ii, p. 328; *New York Colonial Documents,* III, 137–138, 154–156.

to peace and desired that those over whom he ruled should be satisfied and contented. He realized, as did his successor Lovelace, that if he were to settle the arrears of pay due the soldiers he had brought over and maintain the forts from Albany to the Delaware, money and credit were necessary and that if the province was to be made self-supporting, trade and shipping would have to be encouraged. Therefore his attitude toward the Dutch, in accordance with the terms laid down in the articles of capitulation, was conciliatory in the extreme. By these articles the States General of Holland and the Dutch West India Company were guaranteed all their rights of property in New Netherland, and the people of the province, whatever their nationality, were to continue as free denizens, to enjoy unmolested their lands, houses, goods, and ships, to have entire liberty of conscience, and, in their private concerns, to be governed at least temporarily by the manners and customs of their own country.[1]

In matters of trade, dearer to the heart of a Dutchman than any political advantages, direct intercourse with Holland was to last only for six months after the surrender, but Stuyvesant, who elected to remain in New York and wanted to pass freely to and from Holland, hoped that the time might be extended. He made an appeal to the Duke of York and also to the Privy Council, on the ground that the issue was one which concerned the kingdom of England as well as the duke's propriety, asking that when the six months period had expired the Dutch might be allowed to trade freely with their correspondents in the Netherlands, to send thither what goods they pleased, and to receive in return goods from their own country and in their own ships. The Privy Council referred the request to its own committee on plantations and acting on that committee's recommendation agreed, October 23, 1667, that the Dutch in New York might send three ships a year for seven years. But in 1668 the king set up a new and special council of merchants to concern itself with trade and plantations and this council, listening with approval to a vigorous protest from the merchants of the City of London against the concession, sent in a report advocating withdrawal of the privilege. The Privy Council, responding favorably to this report, revoked the permit, November 18, 1668.[2] From that time for-

1. *New York Colonial Documents,* II, 250–253.

2. *Ibid.,* 163–167; *Acts Privy Council, Colonial,* I, §§730, 731, 812; *Calendar State Papers, Colonial,* 1661–1668, §§1602, 1603, 1613, 1874, 1875; Andrews, *British Committees,* pp. 91–93.

ward all the traders of New York, Dutch and English, were subject in every respect to the navigation act of 1663, which forbade the colonists to enter into any direct commercial communication with the European continent.

To the Dutch, a trading people, commercial advantages were paramount, but to the English, agriculturally inclined, political benefits, such as were enjoyed by their neighbors of New England, were of even greater significance. The Dutch towns in New Netherland had never possessed local self-government. They had never had popular elections, town meetings, or community solidarity. Their magistracies were of the nature of close corporations and ultimate authority was from above and not from below.[1] Therefore the only change made by the articles of surrender was the grant to the town of New Amsterdam of the right to choose deputies who were "to have free voices in all public affairs." Though Nicolls went as far as he could in the process of Anglicizing the administration of the province and of introducing features of English political practice,[2] he was prevented from meeting in full the desire of the people of the Long Island towns, for self-government, because he had no authority under the charter or by virtue of his own instructions to call a general assembly made up of representatives elected by the people of the towns for the purpose of controlling especially taxation, as those towns wished. The best that he could do was to draw up a code of laws—known as the Duke's Laws—the different sections of which in many parts were taken, but with important modifications, from the New England codes.[3] These laws, which were designed especially for the population of Long Island—overwhelmingly English by race and closely attached to New England by sympathies—were approved at a meeting of thirty-four deputies from seventeen towns, thirteen English and four Dutch, at Hempstead, March 1, 1665. But during the ensuing eighteen years the Long Islanders, par-

1. McKinley, "English and Dutch Towns of New Netherland," *American Historical Review*, VI, 7–9.

2. The same, "Transition from Dutch to English Rule in New York," *ibid.*, 697.

3. *Ibid.*, 705–720, a thoroughgoing analysis and exposition of these laws. Dr. McKinley says: "If the laws be grouped together according to subject matter instead of the alphabetical arrangement, they will be found to contain a civil and criminal code, elaborate provisions concerning local government, and a general provincial organization of the courts and the militia." He then proceeds to make a comparison of the two extant copies of the laws with the codes of Massachusetts of 1660 and of New Haven of 1656, to show (1) the omission of New England features; (2) the introduction of Dutch customs; and (3) the insertion of wholly new provisions.

ticularly those of the eastern end, continually expressed dissatisfaction with the curtailment of their political privileges and frequently objected to the imposition of taxes without popular consent.[1]

Nicolls, weary of his office with its perplexing responsibilities at New York and the burden of looking after four widely scattered forts, especially the most troublesome one at Albany;[2] tired of supervising the affairs of a territory extending from Schenectady to the Delaware and from Long Island to Martha's Vineyard and Maine— in the latter of which the "usurpation" of Massachusetts aroused his wrath—asked as early as November, 1665, to be relieved of his post. He was hampered by want of money, worn out with his controversies with neighboring colonies, harrassed by the dangers from the French and Indians, and overworked with the correspondence which his varied activities obliged him to conduct However, he remained until August or September, 1668, and then returned to England to take up his former post as one of the grooms of the duke's bedchamber. Several months before his departure he welcomed his successor, Colonel Francis Lovelace, and willingly handed over to him the duties and unfulfilled promises of his office. Lovelace, an exile for a time on the Continent with Charles II, had, like Nicolls, received his appointment as a reward of loyalty,[3] and now for a few months under the guidance of Nicolls and in sympathy with his methods and plans began a five years' tenure with an amicable desire to govern wisely and well.[4]

1. *New York Colonial Documents*, XIV, 564–566; III, 91. Westchester was the only town outside Long Island that was represented. See the list of deputies, New York State Library, *History Bulletin*, 2, p. 156.

2. Instructions for the captain of the fort at Albany were drawn up by Nicolls and Lovelace jointly in August, 1668. The captain was strictly charged "to read them over frequently and not to follow y^r owne humo^r but my orders." He was not to listen to tales of the Dutch being disaffected to the English, "for generally wee cannot expect they love us," but to wait for sufficient testimony of words or actions "tending to the Breach of Peace or scandalous defamaĉon." *Executive Council Minutes*, II, 387–390.

3. Lovelace had gone to Virginia in 1650 but returned in 1652. Possibly his brief residence in America had something to do with his being selected as governor (*Virginia Magazine*, XVII, 288–291). The biography in the *D. N. B.* has been entirely superseded by that in the *D. A. B.*, an admirable article by Victor H. Paltsits.

4. In the instructions noted above Lovelace said that, inasmuch as several complaints had been brought to his attention against the burghers of New York, "some of them very meane in their nature, others of some yeares standing all tending but to the unsettling of men's mindes: And rising up those Seedes of distrust and Jealousie amongst us, which above all things ought principally to be avoided," he would proclaim "a Generall Amnistia and Oblivion." *Executive Council Minutes*, II, 389–390.

Lovelace, a less able but no less conscientious man than Nicolls, was called upon to meet the same problems connected with the duke's boundary claims that Nicolls had faced and left unsolved. He postponed settling the boundary line with Connecticut, in spite of the fact that Nicolls had agreed with that colony to run the boundary line from Mamaroneck to the Hudson River; and he passed on to the duke for decision the claim that Massachusetts made relating to the extension of her western line as far as the upper Hudson and the right to use that river for "free Egress and Regress" and the transportation of people and goods.[1] Lovelace also had a somewhat acrimonious controversy with James Carteret, a son of Sir George Carteret, who had become involved in a revolt of the towns of East Jersey against the proprietors, in the course of which Lovelace hinted at the duke's rightful title to the government there and warned Carteret to keep away from Staten Island, which, he insisted, was within the duke's propriety. He took pains to complete the purchase of that island from the Indians and declared for full right of possession, granting land and settling families there, a right that the Jersey proprietors continued to dispute for the ensuing twenty years.[2] In the face of Maryland's pretenses he endeavored to bring the Whorekill region under the jurisdiction of the Duke of York; and because of an insurrection led by a man known as the "Long Finn" at Christina in August, 1669, for the purpose of bringing the region once more under Swedish control,[3] he took strenuous measures to repair the fortifications at New Castle, a town which in 1672 he erected into a corporation or bailiwick. On the ground that the boundaries of the duke's patent covered all the islands from Cape Cod to Cape May (except Block Island) he granted away Prudence Island in Narragansett Bay and so got into trouble with Rhode Island, and had a long controversy with the Mayhews and others of Martha's Vineyard, Nantucket, and adjoining islands over the question of title and jurisdiction.[4] Thus in one way or another he ran the gamut of the boundaries and obeyed as far as he could

1. Ibid., II, 662–666.

2. Ibid., I, 129–130, 337–344; II, 449, 487, 494, 715–725; New York Colonial Documents, III, 354.

3. Executive Council Minutes, I, 124–125, 309–323; II, 669; New York Colonial Documents, XII, 463–472.

4. Executive Council Minutes, I, 96–99, 345–377; New York Colonial Documents, XIV, 635–636.

the proprietor's instructions. Only with Maine, as far as we know, he had nothing to do.

In domestic concerns he was active and in the main successful. He developed Esopus, which was renamed Kingston; enlarged the boundaries of other towns and started new plantations; organized more efficiently his council, court of general assize, and sundry commissions concerned with local bounds and land disputes. He encouraged shipbuilding and the fisheries—whale and cod; widened trading privileges and licensed free trade in furs. He and his council issued many orders for the repression of crime—theft of hogs, boats and canoes and the sale of powder and liquor to the Indians; eased, as far as comported with the costs of government, the burden of taxation and customs dues; and intervened in ecclesiastical matters, when the churches could not settle their difficulties for themselves. New York did not progress rapidly under Lovelace but it did progress.

While the governor's relations with the Dutch and other nationalities was not unfriendly, his attempting to bring into line the English towns on Long Island produced trouble reminiscent of Nicolls' experience with the Duke's Laws and clearly linked with events to come. There were two groups of these towns: Hempstead, Jamaica, Gravesend, Flushing, Newtown, Huntington, Setauket or Brookhaven, and Oyster Bay toward the western end and Southampton, Easthampton, and Southold in the east. Though all these towns had self-governing privileges, the people in them were discontented because the governor and council at New York exercised executive powers over them in matters of trade, in the levying and collecting of the public rates, and in the enforcement of the Duke's Laws. Some of these towns had begun to murmur even before Nicolls left the colony, the inhabitants of Southampton, Easthampton, and Southold refusing to choose constables and overseers or to pay their rates, and a few in Hempstead refusing to do the same. They claimed that they were "inslav'd under an Arbitrary Power." Elsewhere there was resistance to the duke's authority and an unwillingness to hold office. Lovelace inherited this unpleasant business, which he could neither avoid nor settle except in accordance with the terms of his instructions, because, like the other governors, he was involved in one phase of a time-honored conflict between an executive and a popular form of government. To a petition from Hempstead in

1669, for a redress of grievances and a right to share in the making of laws, Lovelace could make but one answer—the inhabitants of the towns must render obedience to the duke's authority without protest. When in 1670 the governor and council voted an extraordinary tax for the repair of the fort, the opposition flamed up anew and so vehement were the addresses sent in by Flushing, Hempstead, and Jamaica that the court of sessions sitting at Gravesend denounced them as "false scandalous illegal and seditious" and ordered that they be openly and publicly burned before the town house in New York. In 1672 the far eastern towns, remote, inaccessible, and completely out of touch with the ducal system of government, begged the Privy Council in England that they might be annexed to Connecticut or, if that were not feasible, that they might be set apart as a corporate colony by themselves. The petition was considered by the council and handed on to the special council for foreign plantations, but though reference is made to it in the journal of that body nothing more seems to have been done about it, either because it was considered the duke's business and not the king's or because an issue geographically so remote and beyond the ken of the members was lost to sight in the presence of weightier matters.[1] As with the disfranchised freemen of Maryland so with the unfranchised people of Long Island, both were denied, as they profoundly believed, the "rights of English subjects" (or "the libertys of Englishmen" as a protest from Huntington actually stated it), and both were asserting that the proprietor and his governors were exercising wider powers than the king himself possessed in England, an assertion which meant much to the people of Easthampton, who refused to accept the duke and acknowledged only the king as their sovereign.[2] And they were right. What they were to do about it the sequel will show.

1. *New York Colonial Documents*, III, 197–198; XIV, 574–575, 577, 578, 580, 582, 584, 631–633, 646, 647; *Executive Council Minutes*, II, 485–487, 524–525; *Acts Privy Council, Colonial*, I, §942; *Calendar State Papers, Colonial*, 1669–1674, §§875, 875, i; Andrews, *British Committees*, p. 143.

2. One should study the terms of the true bill found by the grand jury against William Dyer, the duke's collector of customs, for traitorous conduct against the king, in order to grasp the intensity of feeling that prevailed against the duke in 1681. Dyer was charged with acting "Contrary to the Greate Charter of Liberties, Contrary to the Peticon of Right, and Contrary to other Statutes in these Cases made and Provided, and Contrary to the Honor and Peace the most Soverigne Lord the King that now is his Crowne and Dignity" (*New York Colonial Documents*, III, 289; "Proceedings of the General Court of Assizes," *Collections*, New York Historical So-

The recapture of New York by the Dutch, July 30, 1673, and the restoration of Dutch rule there for a little more than a year, until November 10, 1674,[1] changed in no material way the course of events. Lovelace, disgraced and broken by the loss not only of the province but also of his own property and the duke's good will,[2] was succeeded by Major Edmund Andros, a soldier and an aristocrat who had served in the West Indies and had held important office in his ancestral home in the island of Guernsey. Trained by experience to obey his superiors and to command those placed in authority under him and a seigneur by birth and instinct—the seigneur of Sausmarez—he was admirably fitted to carry out the duke's instructions. These instructions, based on the new charter granted the duke June 29, 1674—new only in time not in content—made no concessions in the matters of boundary or popular assembly and were in no way affected by the events of the preceding ten years. The duke was willing to do what he could for the prosperity of his people and to treat them "with humanity and gentleness," but he demanded from them obedience and loyalty as of tenants to a lord. To him New York was still not a royal colony but a personal propriety, its boundaries were what the charter stated them to be, its laws were those of 1665, open only to such modification as Andros and his council might think necessary, its form of government was to remain the same as that against which the Long Islanders had protested, and taxes and customs dues were to be determined by himself and his advisers and not by the people who paid them. The duke knew that he was making no profit from his investment, though the province seemed to be paying for itself, but as yet he had not come to realize just where the trouble lay.

ciety, 1912, p. 11). Here is a clear case of conflict between the "rights of Englishmen" and the duke's prerogative, the opportunity having been furnished by the expiration of the period set by the duke during which the customs were to be in force. The grand jury took advantage of the occasion to present also the grievances of the colony and to insist that "in point of government" the people should be granted equal rights with their "fellow Brethren and subjects of the Realme of England In or Neighboring Plantacons" and be allowed to have an assembly "Duly elected by the Freholders of this collony," "Proceedings," as above, pp. 14–15.

1. The fort was surrendered October 31, 1674. For documents relating to the surrender and the restoration, *Documentary History of New York,* III, 67–100, and *New York Colonial Documents,* III, 198–214.

2. The Duke of York claimed that Lovelace owed him £7000 at the expiration of his governorship and he ordered Andros to seize whatever of Lovelace's property he could find in the province.

At the outset Andros displayed great activity and a determination to live up to the duke's expectations. When the towns at the eastern end of Long Island refused to acknowledge his authority, he proclaimed the inhabitants rebels and threatened to compel them by force to obey, at the same time sending letters to Governor John Winthrop, Jr. (December 4, 28, 1674) warning him that Connecticut must stop countenancing and supporting the duke's rebellious people.[1] Later, May 1, 1675, he wrote other and still more vigorous letters to Winthrop and the council of Connecticut demanding the surrender of all Connecticut's territory west of the river and despatched a special agent to deliver these letters at Hartford. Declaring the colony's reply to his demand to be "insignificant" and "no sufficient answer," he followed up the correspondence with the expedition to Saybrook, to which reference has already been made.[2] But the outbreak of King Philip's war postponed all further action on his part. In 1680 he laid claim to Fisher's Island and granted a patent to lands east of the Connecticut line as agreed to by the king's commissioners in 1667, to both of which maneuvers Connecticut vehemently objected; and so the controversy went on.[3]

Very soon after his arrival Andros seems to have got some inkling of the popular desire for a general assembly and to have become himself sufficiently impressed and probably annoyed by it to write the duke in November and December that it existed, but, adding, that as it lay altogether outside his instructions it had received no encouragement from him. The duke in reply commended him for his good judgment and said that notwithstanding such assemblies existed in neighboring colonies (and in this he was referring not only to New England but to New Jersey also), they did not comport with the form of government established in New York and were not necessary "for the ease or redress of any grievance" that might arise. Evidently he had not yet grasped the idea that to the Long Islanders laws and taxes were more important than grievances, and that his refusal to heed the popular demand may have had something to do with the paucity of his profits. Andros, sensing the

---

1. *New York Colonial Documents*, XIV, 681–685.

2. *Connecticut Colonial Records*, 1665–1677, appendix, no. xvi; *New York Colonial Documents*, XIV, 688–689, 763–764. Above, p. 103, note 2.

3. *Ibid.*, 763–764; *Connecticut Colonial Records*, 1678–1689, 64, 100, appendix, nos. xxiii, xl.

seriousness of the situation,[1] presented the matter anew in later letters and with better results. In January, 1676, the duke replied in an oft-quoted passage: "I have formerly writt to you touching Assemblyes in those countreys and have since observed what severall of your lattest letters hint about that matter. But unless you had offered what qualificacons are usual and proper to such Assemblyes, I cannot but suspect they would be of dangerous consequence, nothing being more knowne than the aptness of such bodyes to assume to themselves many priviledges wch prove destructive to, or very oft disturbe, the peace of the governm^t wherein they are allowed. Neither do I see any use of them wch is not as well provided for, whilst you and your Councell govern according to the laws established . . . But howsoever if you continue of the same opinion, I shall be ready to consider of any proposalls you shall send to that purpose."

This is not the reply of a bigoted man or of one who having convictions is unwilling to modify them. James may have been a zealot but he was not unjust and he had good advisers. After Andros's return in 1681, leaving the government in the hands of Lieutenant Brockholls, the duke consulted with his secretary and his two commissioners to such good effect that the former, Sir John Werden, could write to Brockholls (the duke being in Scotland at the time), "Though I cannot yet positively assure you that it will be so, yet I may hint to you that we believe his R^ll H^s will condescend to the desires of that Colony in granting them equall priviledges in chooseing an Assembly &^c as the other English plantations in America have," on certain conditions of raising money for the maintenance of the garrison and the government. It is quite likely that the financial situation, which continued to be very bad, as much as any

---

1. On the growth of popular discontent during this period see O'Callaghan, *Origin of Legislative Assemblies in the State of New York* (1861), pp. 5–16. Meetings of deputies from several of the central English towns had been held as early as December, 1663, to consult regarding the general good (*Jamaica Records*, I, 25), and again in 1669 regarding "greivanenses" to be presented to Lovelace by petition (*ibid.,* 43, 45). Protests were made in 1670 against paying a rate levied by governor and council for the repair of the fort (*ibid.,* 47–48; *Huntington Records*, I, 163–164). In 1681 deputies from a number of towns met at Huntington to agitate for their "Just Libertys, to present grievances, and to pray for relief" (*Oyster Bay Records*, I, 245–246; *Hempstead Town Records*, September 26, 1681; Proceedings, General Court of Assizes, *Collections*, New York Historical Society, 1912, pp. 17, 25). Thus the disquietude, which eventually brought about the calling of an assembly in 1683 had been active for twenty years.

change of conviction may have been the determining factor. The duke on his return from Scotland confirmed Werden's conditional promise and himself wrote Brockholls that he intended "to establish such a forme of governm^t at New Yorke as shall have all the advantages and priviledges to the inhabitants and traders there, wch His Ma^{ts} other plantacons in America doe enjoy, particularly in the chooseing of an Assembly," provided funds shall be raised not only to meet the costs of administration but also to pay off the arrears resulting from past failures to collect the public revenue. And, he added, "I seeke the common good and protection of that countrey and the increase of their trade, before [any] advantages to myselfe in the matter."[1] It was becoming clear to the duke and very clear to his commissioners and others of his personal staff, that the colony could no longer be kept going as a mere propriety. They were all becoming convinced that the coöperation and aid of the inhabitants must be sought and obtained, at least as far as defense and public revenue were concerned, if the government was to continue and the territory to be maintained intact. When this decision was reached the beginning of the end of the proprietary prerogative was at hand; but the end itself was not quite yet.

Andros was succeeded by Colonel Thomas Dongan, an Irishman, a soldier and a Roman Catholic, friend and co-religionist of the duke and of exactly his own age, who for three years had been lieutenant governor of Tangier. The duke, true to his promise, wrote into Dongan's instructions (or his commissioners did so for him, which is the same thing) the following statement, "I have thought fitt that there shall be a Gen^{ll} Assembly of all the Freeholders by the p^{r}sons who they shall choose to rep^{r}sent them in ord^r to consulting wth yor-selfe and the said Councill what laws are fitt and necessary to be made and established for the good weale and governm^t of the said Colony and its Dependencyes, and of all the inhabitants thereof." This assembly was to pass laws, which to be effective had to receive the assent of the governor and the confirmation of the duke. It was to raise money but was not going to be allowed to spend it, and was to regulate the customs dues, none of which could be demanded or received except as enacted and established by act of assembly. The governor was authorized to summon, adjourn, and dissolve that body as he should see reason and cause. Acting under this definite

1. *New York Colonial Documents*, III, 235, 317, 318.

order from the duke, Dongan and his council issued the necessary writs on September 13, 1683, and on October 17 there met at New York for the first time in the history of the province as a whole a gathering of representatives, not of the people at large but of the landed classes, who alone had the right to vote.[1] There were present in the fort at New York seventeen deputies: two each from the three ridings of Long Island, including Fisher's Island, Shelter or Silvester's Island, and Gardiner's Island; one from Martha's Vineyard, Nantucket, and the Elizabeth Islands; one from Staten Island; two from Esopus and its neighboring villages; two from Albany and Rensselaerswyck; one from Schenectady; and four from New York and Harlem. Pemaquid and its dependencies were authorized to send one representative, but even if there had been any freeholders in that remote section of the country, time and distance would have been insuperable obstacles to service and attendance.[2] Who the men were composing the assembly we do not know, all the information furnished is that they were "mostly Dutch," a somewhat remarkable statement in view of the familiarity of those who drew up the "Charter" and framed its laws to accord with Magna Carta, the Confirmation of the Charters, the Petition of Right, and the navigation acts—all leading English documents. The assembly consisted of Governor Dongan, five members of the legislative council, and the

1. The right to vote everywhere in the colonies at this time was restricted to freeholders, that is, to the possessors of estates in fee simple. This had probably always been true in Rhode Island, and in Connecticut certainly since 1657. It was probably true in Massachusetts, where it is difficult to believe that any church member could have been landless; it was true in the Jerseys and the Carolinas, and since 1670 and 1671 it had been true in Virginia and Maryland also. New York was but following the general rule when it stated that "none but freeholders were to vote," and when on September 13, 1683, the governor and council sent warrants to the sheriffs "to warne the ffreeholders" to choose in a definitely stated way two deputies from each district or riding (New York State Library, *Report*, 1902, p. 34; for the warrants O'Callaghan, *Origin*, pp. 16–17). In the "Charter of Libertyes and Privileges" a freeholder is defined as "one who is soe understood according to the Lawes of England." When Nicolls called for the election of deputies to meet at Hempstead (above, p. 106), he placed the voting in the hands of "all persons according to their estates," that is, freeholders (New York State Library, *History Bulletin*, 2, pp. 154, 155). In the instructions to the royal governors, from 1696 to 1761, appears this phrase: "You shall take care that the members of the assembly be elected only by freeholders, as being most agreeable to the customs of this Kingdom, to which you are to conform as near as may be" (Labaree, *Royal Instructions*, I, 93). A campaign broadside, issued February 25, 1818, to the Freeholders of Westmorland, England, contains this sentence: "The Freeholders of past times knew that their rights were most likely to repose in safety under the state of rank and property." See below, p. 287, note 1.

2. There was only a fort at Pemaquid, with officers and twenty men in pay.

seventeen deputies. No record of proceedings remains. We know that Matthias Nicolls, a relative of Colonel Richard Nicolls, was elected speaker and John Spragg clerk; that parliamentary procedure was followed in the reading and passing of laws; and that the members sat for three weeks, until November 3, and passed fifteen measures, the so-called "Charter" and fourteen laws.[1] A second session was called October 4 which lasted until the 29th and adopted some thirty more measures,[2] after which it adjourned to meet the following year. But before the time of meeting came Charles II had died and Governor Dongan, believing that this event terminated the continuance of the assembly, dissolved it by proclamation, August 13, 1685, and issued writs for a new election.[3] The second body met October 20, 1685, elected William Pinhorne, speaker, and Robert Hammond or Hammill, clerk, sat but one session and passed six acts.[4] On October 29 it adjourned until September 25 of the following year, but before that day arrived it was further adjourned, September 6, 1686, and dissolved the following January. It never met again.

Thus the first general assembly of the province of New York sat for three sessions, nearly eight weeks altogether, and passed fifty laws, all of which received the approval of James, as duke and king, and became, temporarily at least, the laws of the province supplemental to the Duke's Laws of 1665. The king's approval, given in the new instructions to Dongan of May 29, 1686,[5] was but provisional, however, to apply only until Dongan and his council should pass other laws in the king's name to take the place of those passed by the assembly. This the governor and council did in a number of instances during the remaining years of Dongan's administration,[6] which legally came to an end with the issue of the commission to Andros, as governor general of the Dominion of New England, April 4, 1688, but not actually until the following August. Thus the laws in force in the colony until 1691 were the Duke's Laws of 1665, those of the general assembly, 1683–1685, and such additional or sub-

1. *Laws of the Colony of New York*, I, 111–142.
2. *Ibid.*, 143–173.   3. O'Callaghan, *Origin*, pp. 20–21.
4. *Laws of the Colony of New York*, I, 173–177.
5. *New York Colonial Documents*, III, 369–375, §13.
6. Minutes of council, December 9, 1686, to August 2, 1688, are printed in O'Callaghan, *Origin*, pp. 25–32. A calendar of the council meetings, 1668–1783, is to be found in New York State Library, *History Bulletin*, 6.

stitute measures as were passed by the governor and council, 1665–1688,[1] a collection made up of a strange mixture of executive ordinances and legislative acts.

The "Charter of Libertyes and Privileges" was no doubt in large part the work of, or at least was inspired by, Matthias Nicolls, the speaker, formerly secretary of the province, twice mayor of New York, judge in the court of assizes, a lawyer by training and profession, and the reputed compiler of the Duke's Laws. It bears the marks of one familiar with English constitutional and legal history and in sympathy with some of the ideas and practices of the Interregnum. In its thirty paragraphs it presents a bill of rights and the outlines of a constitution for the province, slightly perfectionist perhaps, in that it contains a few powers and privileges unknown to the other colonies,[2] but in no way utopian, because everything in it was based on practical experience. The "Charter" and the laws were sent to England in December, 1683, by Captain Mark Talbot of the royal navy, and after consideration by the duke and his personal advisers, was signed and sealed by him and countersigned by his secretary, Sir John Werden, on October 4, 1684, ready to be registered by his auditor Aldworth and then to be delivered to Captain Talbot for transmission to New York.[3] There is nothing to show that the duke was insincere in approving the charter or had any intention, in 1684, of discontinuing the meetings of the general assembly of New York. In such important matters as this he did not act alone but in conjunction with his secretary and commissioners, and though these men in conference doubtless recommended amendments, they were manifestly willing that the experiment of a consti-

1. What these laws were can be seen in *Annual Report*, New York State Historian, 1896, pp. 145–180.

2. Note the "Observations" upon the charter, *New York Colonial Documents*, III, 357–359, drawn up possibly at the request of the Lords of Trade either by the crown lawyers or some other official adviser, and read at the meeting of that body, March 3, 1685. The objections do not seem very serious, the most significant being the use of the phrase "and the people met in General Assembly" instead of merely "the General Assembly" as was the customary form. Just what the assembly meant here by the word "people" it is impossible to say, unless it were employing the word in the sense implied in the "Agreement of the People" of 1649 in England. Probably it was only a comprehensive word for "freeholders," for even the Cromwellian franchise was confined to property holders. Above, p. 115, note 1.

3. The document containing this important information was inadvertently omitted from the *New York Colonial Documents*, but a copy of it was later obtained by Mr. Brodhead and printed in *The Historical Magazine*, first series, VI, 233 (1862).

tution or charter for New York should be tried. Once the duke had given way in the matter of his "full and absolute power and authority" there was no possible reason why he should wish to return to it merely as a matter of personal contrariness.[1]

Why then was the "Charter" with the duke's approval never sent back to New York? The assembly was allowed to continue, its laws were confirmed, and not until January, 1687, was it finally brought to an end. During these years something was happening to disturb the serenity of the situation in New York and New England and to cut across the normal development of each of the colonies. This new and anomalous something was the Dominion of New England, a form of consolidation which had been more or less in the minds of the duke and his governors for a long time. The loss of the Jerseys, western Connecticut, and the region west of the Delaware; the unprofitableness of Long Island; the worthlessness of Maine—all these had provoked the governors to recommend at every opportunity the recovery of the lost territories. But inasmuch as the consolidation under consideration could not be effected by friendly agreement with Baltimore, Penn, Connecticut, and the East New Jersey proprietors—for no one of these would yield to New York's demands —it became necessary to charge them all with "stretching their privileges as New England had done" and by legal means to transform the region into a royal domain. There were other and weightier reasons, too, for the erection of the Dominion of New England, more directly connected with the disciplining of Massachusetts, the promoting of trade, and the ensuring of adequate defense, but the New York situation was undoubtedly an important contributing cause, as the

1. I carry no brief for the Stuarts, but the facts speak for themselves. At the very time when the Duke of York was approving the charter for New York, Charles II, who had already allowed a popular assembly to be convened in New Hampshire, was authorizing the calling of an assembly of the freeholders in Bermuda also (above, Vol. I, 243-244). Duke and king in matters of this kind did not act alone—the duke acted with the advice of his secretary and commissioners; the king with that of his secretaries, the Privy Council, and the Lords of Trade. Some of the older comments on the "despotism" of the Stuarts are almost naïve and as historical statements are even more arbitrary and prejudiced than anything charged against the Stuarts themselves. There is no proof whatever that the duke "never willingly consented to the concession of a representative assembly" or in doing so "feigned a virtue though he had it not," as Dr. O'Callaghan says. There is no doubt that financial troubles in the province finally broke down the ducal prerogative, but to say that the duke agreed to the calling of an assembly in 1683 in order to provide the duchess with pocket money in January, 1668 (gossip of Thomas Povey quoted by Pepys), is a conclusion that contradicts itself (O'Callaghan, Origin, p. 23).

sequence of events will show. Three weeks after the New York "Charter" was sealed but not sent, the charter of Massachusetts was annulled. On February 6, 1685, the Duke of York became King of England, and in May the governor and council of New York and the mayor of the city sent addresses of condolence, the latter reminding the king of what he knew already that it would be for the ease and safety of his subjects and his royal interest and service to reunite Delaware and the Jerseys to New York and to enlarge that province to the eastward, that is, to take back western Connecticut. In July, the letter from the mayor having been read, the Lords of Trade agreed to ask the attorney general to consider the grants and proprieties of East and West New Jersey and Delaware and to enter writs of quo warranto against the proprietors thereof, and four days later, adding Connecticut and Rhode Island to the list, at the request of Edward Randolph, the board so reported to the Privy Council. The latter, adding Maryland also to the list, on account of the trouble with Baltimore, approved the report and ordered the issue of the writs. What thoughts were in the duke's mind on the subject of the New York "Charter" between October, 1684, when he freely and, as far as we know, willingly ratified the document, and February, 1685, when he became king are beyond our finding out, but certain is it that the vacation of the Massachusetts Bay charter improved, as nothing had done before, the chances of immediate consolidation and therefore helps to explain the attitude of James as king toward the situation in New York. As it was evident that were consolidation effected, the New York "Charter" would be useless, it was not sent back to the colony; and in May, 1686, it was finally disallowed by the Privy Council, on recommendation from the Lords of Trade, after the working plans for the dominion had been finally decided on.[1]

The idea of the "Dominion" was not new, for something of the kind had been in the air since the time of Nicolls, and the duke, ever concerned for his revenues, must frequently have thought about it as one after another of his governors reminded him of the scantiness and inadequacy of his province. He instructed Andros in 1674 to gather up as much as he could of the lost territory and restore it

1. Board of Trade Journal, V, 162–163 (inadequately calendared); *Calendar State Papers, Colonial*, 1685–1688, §§279, 282, 283; *Acts Privy Council, Colonial*, II, §§194, 195. The full report of the Lords of Trade is in C. O. 324:4, pp. 230–231; *Maryland Archives*, V, 445.

to New York, and in his instructions to Dongan he called for exact maps of all his territories, evidently with the idea of seeing just where his lands lay. These maps he received in 1687. After 1684 and particularly after he became king in February, 1685, he agreed to an enlargement of the plan of consolidation and the selection of Massachusetts instead of New York as the center of the Dominion. That he was far more interested in the idea than ever had been Charles II, who had no vested property at stake in America, appears from the fact that he was present at every meeting of the Privy Council at which the new scheme was discussed.[1]

Thus the accession of the Duke of York to the throne of England had vital consequences for the province of New York. In the first place it changed its legal status from a ducal seignory to a royal colony, a change which removed it, constitutionally speaking, from the overlordship of the duke and his advisers and made it henceforth subordinate to the king, Privy Council, secretaries of state, and other branches of the executive government in England. Thither in the future all letters and accounts were to be sent and thence all orders and instructions were to come, as in the case of the other royal colonies. In the plantation office from this time forward New York was to have a place of its own in the files, and no longer to be listed among the proprieties. In the second place Dongan's pleading for more territory on account of the narrow bounds within which the people were "cooped up" and his constant iteration in letters written and reports rendered between 1686 and 1688 of his inability to run the province on the revenues he had[2] was in part, at least, responsible for the addition of New York and the Jerseys to the Dominion of New England in 1688 and the issue of a new commission to Andros designed to cover these territories. In helping to bring about this important modification in the relation to its neighbors of the New York province, which though still in the king's hand was for three years to be but an administrative part of a larger organization, Dongan was signing his own death warrant as governor, for he was superseded, April 7, 1688, by Sir Edmund Andros, who for more than a year had been governor general of the Dominion of

1. This fact does not appear in the *Calendar of State Papers, Colonial*, but is conspicuous in the original minutes of proceedings.
2. *New York Colonial Documents*, III, 391, 397, 406, 415-416, 420, 422, 423, 424-425, 429, 492.

New England, and Francis Nicholson took his place in New York under the title of lieutenant governor.

During the nearly seven years of his governorship (1681–1688), Dongan had proved an able administrator and despite his fears to the contrary New York had prospered under his hand. Serving first the duke and then the king he showed himself efficient, just, and conciliatory, though at times perhaps over-inclined to leniency, loyally devoted to his superiors in England and equally faithful to the people he governed. He encouraged land grants, thereby enlarging the area of cultivation and increasing the quit-rents due the duke; stimulated settlement; and, following the example of Nicolls and Lovelace, erected numerous manors,[1] partly to strengthen the aristocratic element in the province as over against the refractory and levelling tendencies of the Long Island and Westchester towns, partly to bind leading men to himself and the duke by ties of feudal interest, and partly to reinforce the frontier against the Indians, as when he made Rensselaerswyck a manor, and to prevent the encroachments of Connecticut and East Jersey, as in the erection of manors in Westchester and Staten Island.[2] He granted also liberal charters to the cities of New York and Albany, taking the latter out of the hands of the Rensselaers, on the ground that the second most important town of the province and one that brought in a large part of the revenue should not be possessed by any particular men.[3] During these years he aided the centralizing processes that were already at work and brought into existence a strong group of aristocratic landholders. After the dissolution of the assembly, his government became once more executive and the king and his Privy Council had the ultimate control of all expenditures of money and other activities connected with the administration of provincial affairs and disclosed the same concern over the revenues that the duke had displayed before he became king. But on account of the frauds charged against Santen, the collector, Smith, the surveyor, and Harlow, the waiter and searcher, which led to their suspension and eventual dis-

1. See the *Publications* of The Order of Colonial Lords of Manors in America, twenty-five pamphlets, 1921–1934, with two others in preparation. In no. 23, "The Patroons and Lords of Manors of the Hudson," is a useful map of the patroonships, manors, and seigniories recognized by the Order.

2. Goebel, "Some Legal and Political Aspect of the Manors of New York" (no. 19 of the series mentioned above), p. 17.

3. *New York Colonial Documents,* III, 410–411.

missal, the returns still remained insufficient to maintain the government. The statement was made in 1689 that there were no net profits in that year out of New York.[1]

One reason for the inadequacy of the revenue was the heavy cost of defense, particularly in the repair and upkeep of the forts at Albany, New York, and Pemaquid, the last named of which Dongan would gladly have given to Massachusetts in exchange for land nearer home. The fort at New York had to be rebuilt against a possible attack by the French; and that at Albany, "as a frontier place both of the Indians and French," needed yearly renewal, constructed as it was of timber and not of stone, because it was the chief protection of the northern Dutch, who stood in constant fear of the diminution or loss of their one industry, traffic in furs. Dongan, who more than any of his predecessors except Andros understood the larger aspects of the French and Indian situation, relieved the pressure by treaties with the Iroquois, July and August, 1684, whereby the latter placed themselves under the sovereignty and protection "of the great sachem Charles that lives over the Great Lake," and submitted to the authority of the government of New York. For the next five years, though the prospect of a French invasion was always imminent, especially in 1686-1687, and Dongan was obliged to strain his resources[2] in order to hold the Indians to their allegiance, the French made little trouble and peace with the Indians was maintained.[3]

But if in its outward relations the province suffered only in anticipation of disaster, inwardly it was ripe for revolt. The English towns on Long Island were thoroughly alarmed at the dissolution of the general assembly and the return of the province to an executive form of government, while the merchants in the city, denying

1. *Ibid.*, 607.   2. *Calendar Treasury Books*, XIV, 329.
3. *Ibid.*, 429, 466-490, 503-536, 548-549. An understanding was reached with France at the end of 1687 (*ibid.*, 504-510). Dongan, still fearful, spent the winter of 1687-1688 at Albany with 400 foot, 50 horse, and 800 Indians, but nothing happened (511). Andros, after reaching Boston, in December, 1686, was even more the traveller. He remained in Boston until in 1688 he received his second commission, which he published in New York, September 11 of that year. From New York on the 15th he went to East Jersey, then to West Jersey on the 18th. Returning to New York he reached Albany on the 30th, where he had conferences with the Indians. Thence back to New York he journeyed overland to Boston, by way of Springfield, along the line of the Indian frontier, with the idea of looking into the disorders there in order to prevent if possible a second Indian war. In the April and May following he went north to Piscataqua and Pemaquid.

the legality of the customs levied and taxes imposed by fiat of the governor and council, considered reviving their former refusal to pay the dues demanded by the royal collector. The executive council, after 1688, resenting the annexation of New York to the Dominion of New England, declared that the inferiority of its position was leading to the ruin of the province, weakening its authority and estranging many men of influence whose coöperation was essential to an efficient control of seditious and rebellious movements in the city and elsewhere. Such subversive movements, largely under cover as yet, were the result of many causes, very much the same as those which were at work in Maryland, where conditions were more nearly analogous to those in New York than was the case with any other colony: fears of attack by French ships sailing up the harbor, with the fort so extraordinarily out of repair as to render resistance useless; fears of the Indians, both in New York and up the Hudson to Albany, where the inhabitants believed that the French were arousing the jealousies of the Indians and saw no other remedy for their decaying trade than the complete subjugation of Canada; and, finally, in some ways most important of all, fears for the safety of the Protestant religion, with a Roman Catholic on the throne of England and other Roman Catholics in office in the province—Dongan, the governor, Plowman, the collector, Baxter, in charge of the fort at Albany, Brockholls, major and former acting governor, and a few lesser men in minor offices, civil and military. It made no difference that in 1688 Dongan was superseded by Andros and Nicholson; that before 1689 Baxter and Russell, ensign in the garrison, had been dismissed; that later Plowman was put out of office; and that the total number of Roman Catholics in the province was very small in comparison with the Protestants of various denominations who made up the population. Dongan after his retirement to Hempstead was believed to be the center of Roman Catholic plots; Nicholson was charged with being secretly a Roman Catholic because he was twice seen in England kneeling when mass was celebrated;[1] the chaplain, Rev. Alexander Innes, was stamped "by outward pretence a Protestant but in effect a meere papist"; and even Andros did not escape condemnation as a Roman Catholic sympathizer. Among the unthinking mass of the people and even among those of position and influence who took their religion seriously, reports

1. *Documentary History*, II, 27.

from England had been ominous for a decade and the form such reports assumed in the province, enlarged and aggravated by local incoherence as well as by deliberate intent, developed a state of excitement that in extreme cases bordered on delusion. New York as an independent royal colony, even had it remained under an executive form of government, might have weathered the crisis for a longer time at least had not events in England and the neighboring colonies set the combustible material aflame.

In December, 1688, James II fled from England and in the February following the "great and glorious" revolution was completed by the offer of the crown to William and Mary as king and queen of England. In America the reaction to this event was immediate. Boston rose, seized and imprisoned Andros, and the Dominion of New England, resting only on the fiat of the crown and not on the sound foundation of popular approval, collapsed without hope of recovery. Each of the Dominion's component parts resumed its former state of independence and each in its own way reëstablished its previous system of government, while the Privy Council at home faced the difficult question of what was to be done to meet the French menace, now that weakness and dissension prevailed once more in New England and a declaration of war by Louis XIV was impending. Nicholson and his councillors in New York, left in an oddly anomalous position by the catastrophe to the Dominion, endeavored to carry on as best they could, though uncertain of their authority, because they were without orders from England either to proclaim the new sovereigns or to continue in command. Confronted with many "ill-affected and restless spirits" in the city they feared the worst, and Nicholson, a young man but thirty-four years old and none too tactful or discreet in his remarks,[1] did little to alleviate the critical situation.

The towns at the eastern end of Long Island, already planning to send a statement of grievances to England, together with other towns in Queens and Westchester counties, at once rose in revolt against the authority of the lieutenant governor, turned out ap-

1. For these remarks, as reported by Leisler's faithful adherents, Cuyler and Lodwyck, *Collections,* New York Historical Society, 1868, pp. 292–293, 295; *New York Colonial Documents,* III, 593–594. Whether Nicholson actually said what these men deposed is another matter. The effect in either case, however, would have been the same.

pointees of the central government and elected others to take their places.[1] Then on May 31, 1689, six weeks after the Boston uprising, while Nicholson, the mayor, aldermen and councillors, and some of the civil and military officials of the city were assembled at the town house to consult regarding the uproar and to take measures for the safety of the province,[2] a part of the militia, led by one of its officers, Jacob Leisler, took possession of the fort and defied the authorities.[3] On June 11 Nicholson, with the advice and consent of the council, left New York to go to England, for the purpose of entering complaint against the usurpers, leaving Leisler in full control at the head of a revolutionary government that had no legal right to exist. Leisler claimed that right as an emergency expedient to serve God and King William, to preserve the true Protestant religion, and to deliver the people of the province, whether they wanted or needed to be so delivered or not, from the creatures of King James, who had subverted their ancient privileges and were hostile to their religion and their liberty.[4] He wrote to Massachusetts, Connecticut, and Maryland for advice and assistance and received favorable replies, Connecticut sending a delegation which flattered his self-esteem by applauding his conduct and calling him the "noble

1. *Southampton Records*, p. 124; *New York Colonial Documents*, III, 575, 577 (declaration of the men of Southampton, Easthampton, and Huntington, May 10, 1689), 592. The town records contain few entries that show the influence of the revolutions in England and Massachusetts, the Huntington records being the only ones that refer to the larger events of the period (II, 29–33, 60 [Leisler's demands], 63, 71, 73–74 [address, April 15, 1690, acknowledging Leisler's authority], 84–86 [the same], 92 [welcome to Sloughter], 92–93 [deputies to assembly of 1691 and resolution regarding taxation]).

2. The proceedings are in the *Collections*, pp. 272–290. The opinion that Nicholson should go to England by the first ship to give an account "of the desperate and deplorable state of the government, and to pray for some immediate release" is on p. 270.

3. The progress of the rebellion can be followed in the *New York Colonial Documents*, III; *Documents relating to the History of New York*, II; *Collections*, New York Historical Society, 1868; *Calendar State Papers, Colonial, 1689–1692; Narratives of the Insurrections* (Original Narratives); *Minutes of the Common Council of the City of New York*, I, 207–213; and *Laws of the Colony of New York*, I, 219–220. The records of the towns, as far as they have been printed (Huntington, three vols., Jamaica, three vols., Oyster Bay, two vols., Southampton, one vol., Easthampton, five vols.), provide a certain amount of local detail, but not as much as one would expect, so largely are they taken up with local land distribution. A brief but discriminating biography of Leisler, by Stanley M. Pargellis, is in the *D. A. B.*

4. *New York Colonial Documents*, III, 583, 589, 608, 609, 610; *Documentary History*, II, 10, 11, 14, 29, 32, etc.

and Loyall Captⁿ Leisler whose loyalty, courage prudence pains and charge hath been grait."[1]

But Leisler needed something more warrantable than "the choice of the people of his Company,"[2] the commendation of his Protestant English neighbors, and the rough-handed and often brutal support of his soldiery. Without any instructions received directly from England he proclaimed their majesties, first in New York on June 22 and then in Albany on July 1,[3] fashioned an address to his sovereigns, and toward the end of June sent circular letters to the towns to elect delegates to a committee to meet in New York and consider ways and means for the maintenance of the revolutionary authority. Nine towns responded, though we are told that not a third of the people voted, and eighteen men were chosen, two of whom immediately withdrew. Thirteen appeared at the first meeting on June 27, and sat until August 15, issuing orders and looking after the finances, on the last day discoursing about their grievances, especially "the oppression and slavery imposed by the former governor and his council." The convention appointed ten men to serve as a committee of safety and the latter named Leisler commander in chief of the province, with power to act in legal, military, and administrative matters, they themselves remaining as his temporary council.[4] A definite revolutionary organization was now in being, which by various contrivances of intimidation stilled all resistance, throwing opposition leaders into prison and driving many out of the province or into hiding, thus bearing out the contention that the province was in the hands not only of those who stigmatized the upholders of the former government as Jacobites but also of Oliverians, some of whom were ready to declare that there had been no legal king in England since Oliver's day.[5]

But as yet there had been no sign from England to make known the intentions of the authorities there. Not until the end of July

1. New York Colonial Documents, III, 589; Documentary History of New York, II, 17; Connecticut Colonial Records, 1678–1689, pp. 255, 466–468.

2. New York Colonial Documents, III, 603.

3. Connecticut proclaimed William and Mary, June 13, 1689 (Connecticut Colonial Records, 1678–1689, p. 466).

4. Calendar State Papers, Colonial, 1689–1692, 352; New York Colonial Documents, III, 605; Documentary History, II, 23–24; Narratives of the Insurrections, pp. 328, note, 382. The Connecticut representatives, Fitch and Gold, were invited to be present at the first meeting and accepting the invitation took seats with the others.

5. New York Colonial Documents, III, 617.

did the Privy Council take action. Then at last it issued an order for the proclamation of their majesties in New York, and William III, through his secretary of state, addressed to Nicholson a letter authorizing and empowering him to take over the government as lieutenant governor under the king and to call to his assistance such of the freeholders and inhabitants as he thought fit for maintaining the welfare of the king's subjects there. Both order and letter were addressed to Nicholson or "in his absence to such as for the time being take care for Preserving the Peace and administering the Lawes of our said Province in New York in America."[1] These despatches were addressed to Nicholson, showing that the king and Privy Council considered him their official representative in the province, and the question naturally arises whether in his absence his councillors were similarly considered. That is not so clear. The mentioning of Nicholson by name might reasonably be construed as a kind of informal royal re-appointment or at least a recognition of him as the king's lieutenant governor continuing in office, with the king taking the place of his former superior, Andros, but such recognition was not accorded by name to his councillors, who were only de facto preservers of the peace and not very successful ones at that, being but the hold-overs from a defunct government. Had Nicholson remained in the province until December 11, 1689, when the despatches, brought by John Riggs from Boston, were received, the revolution might have come to an end then and there, at the command of a king whom Leisler always declared he was ready to

1. *Ibid.*, 605–606; *Documentary History*, II, 365–367. Similar documents, similarly addressed, were sent to the other colonies, *Pennsylvania Colonial Records*, I, 301; *Maryland Archives*, VIII, 167–168, 188–189, 236; Toppan, *Randolph*, IV, 290; *Calendar State Papers, Colonial*, 1661–1668, §214, ii; 1689–1692, §752; *Acts Privy Council, Colonial*, II, §312. To "such as for the time being," etc.; "to all to whom these presents shall come"; "to whome else it may there concerne"; or "to the Govʳ or Commander in chief of that Province for the time being"; were customary forms used in documents of this kind. (Compare Bulkeley's "Will and Doom," *Collections*, Connecticut Historical Society, III, 75, "To such as for the time being take care for preserving the peace and administering the laws. . . .") It had no special significance for New York (*Narratives of the Insurrections*, p. 338, note 2). It is, therefore, quite beside the mark to say, as does the writer (probably David Jamison, secretary of the council) of *A Letter from a Gentleman of New York* (*ibid.*, 365) that these despatches were sent in response to letters from Nicholson and his councillors, and that the latter were therefore the ones, in Nicholson's absence, authorized to preserve the peace. On the contrary Sloughter, council, and assembly, April 13, 1691, formally declared that the king's letter contained no "power or direction for the Government to the said Captain Leisler."

obey. But even this conclusion is doubtful as the revolution had made great progress since May 31 and Leisler, who had no respect whatever for Nicholson, might well have argued that as the English authorities were ignorant of the true state of the case the reasons which justified the revolt in the beginning still held good.

However that may be, the fact remains that Nicholson was not there and that his councillors were powerless. Leisler intercepted the despatches, read them, and interpreted them as applying to himself. He was the only one who was "preserving the peace," even though he was preserving it in his own peculiar way, with the aid of his soldiers—an armed peace enforced by an intolerant and abusive minority. His interpretation of the king's letter is of the utmost importance. From this time forward, until March, 1691, Leisler looked upon himself as the legally appointed head of the province, authorized by King William to take care of a government no longer revolutionary but constitutionally and lawfully established and warranted in its every act by the authority vested in him from England. We know that his claim was false, for neither king nor Privy Council ever intended to invest him with the powers he assumed; but the very ambiguity of the king's letter and the order in council lent a specious coloring of truth to his explanation of their meaning, which vastly strengthened his position in the eyes of his followers. Blame for the opportunity thus offered him must rest with the English authorities, just as the long continuance of his usurpation, lasting as it did altogether for nearly two years, was due to the incompetence of the Admiralty and the lack of any efficient coördination among the executive officials and departments of the crown.[1] The

---

1. A recital of dates is helpful here. The Lords of Trade took cognizance of the situation as early as July 19, *1689,* and on August 31, recommended sending a governor at once. Sloughter was selected September 24 and his commission approved, October 28; frigate ordered, same day; order repeated, December 30; privy seal, January 4, *1690;* order repeated, January 11; Admiralty acknowledges its receipt, January 14; Sloughter instructed to proceed at once, April 10; in meantime many petitions and letters received from New York urging haste; Lords of Trade report that province will be lost unless something is done, May 22, and continue so to report through the summer; Admiralty says frigate has been waiting two months, May 24; more urgent petitions from the province; Nicholson writing from Virginia, June 6, says that Sloughter should have arrived long before; Sloughter ready to go, August 28; Lords of Trade still urging, September 27; Sloughter sails from Cowes, November 29; reaches Bermuda, February 9, *1691;* his vessel wrecked; he remains there three weeks; reaches the Narrows, New York Harbor, March 18; the city, March 19. Sloughter said that his departure was "designedly delayed for six months," just why or how we do not know. In any case the incompetence of and

time was one of great confusion in the English and colonial worlds and the men in England holding responsible office, both civil and naval, often untrained and unfamiliar with their duties, were overwhelmed by the complexity of domestic and colonial concerns, which were thrown into worse confusion by the war with France.

We cannot enter here into an examination of the events of the period from December 11, 1689, until March 19, 1691,[1] although these events are of no little importance for colonial history. Leisler and many of his associates were crude in their methods, coarse in their speech and demeanor, and blustering in their efforts to overawe their opponents, but some of his followers were men of intelligence, wealth, and ability, playing important but less conspicuous rôles than did his chief ally Jacob Milborne or his dramshop agent Joost Stoll. Gouverneur, Edsall (who had an estate of fifteen hundred acres at Bergen Point), Delaney, Lodwyck, Daniel Denton of Jamaica (son of the Rev. Henry Denton of Wethersfield, Stamford, and Hempstead), Vermilye, Clarkson, Williams, and Beekman made less noise than some of the others or even than Leisler himself, but they were undoubtedly influential in shaping Leisler's policy, as many of them were members of the council which Leisler appointed December 11, 1689, after the receipt of the king's letter, to coöperate with him in the administration of the province.[2] The thirteen months of Leislerian government, from December 11, 1689, until March 19, 1691, was not a time of mob rule. Leisler and his associates showed not only vigor of action but also considerable capacity for administration, and allowed neither lawlessness nor anarchy to prevail. They organized a government, raised money, made a seal, issued commissions, erected courts, and put down riots. They sent Joost Stoll to England to obtain the king's approval of all that had been done and to ask for a regular commission and increased powers, but though Stoll's petition was read at a meeting of the Lords of Trade, nothing came of it, a fact which is sufficient evidence to prove that the king was not supporting Leisler and had

---

lack of coördination among the executive officials is manifest and, though ships were scarce at the time, the Admiralty must be charged with dilatoriness on an unexampled scale. See Neeser, "The British Naval Operations in the West Indies, 1650–1700," *Proceedings*, United States Naval Institute, November–December, 1914, for a survey of the general situation which made such botchery possible.

1. A detailed account is given in Brodhead's *History*, II, 571–637, strongly anti-Leislerian.

2. *Documentary History*, II, 45.

never intended to do so.[1] As commander in chief, by vote of his committee of safety, and acting governor, by virtue of his construction of the letter from King William, Leisler compelled Albany, after long resistance, to submit to his authority.[2] It yielded finally, not because it recognized Leisler's claim but from fear of Indian raids. He took up the war against the French and offered to join with the New England colonies in making an attack on Quebec, an enterprise that proved a complete fiasco. He appointed military officers, held courts martial, issued letters of marque, and created a commission which sat as a court of vice-admiralty for the trial of prizes taken from the enemy.

Most significant of all were his contacts with the other colonies. He entered into frequent communication with Massachusetts and Connecticut regarding the sending of military aid to Albany.[3] He wrote letters to Coode in Maryland, Colonel Nathaniel Bacon in Virginia—president of the council in the absence of Governor Effingham, Thomas Lloyd, president of the Pennsylvania provincial council,[4] Governor Robinson of Bermuda, and a number of times to Governor Stede of Barbados. The New England colonies, Maryland, and Barbados recognized his authority, particularly in connection with the war against the French and Indians, but neither New Jersey, Pennsylvania, nor Virginia would have any dealings with him until orders should come from the king. Barbados could do nothing to help, as Stede at the time was having his own troubles with the papists and was fighting the French in the West Indies. Bermuda was not sympathetic, but Robinson, the governor there, to the wrath of his council, sent twenty barrels of powder.[5] This remarkable effort

1. The situation in New York was not unlike that in Maryland, and Coode noticed the similarities when he wrote "Or circumstances are so alike and the common danger so threatening that we ought to stand together" (*Documentary History*, II, 42). But there were also important differences. Both revolutions were against prerogative government, Roman Catholics in office, and French and Indian attacks; both were typical as uprisings employing armed force, intimidation, arrests, and banishment, and the formation of committees or conventions, under leadership. But in Maryland there was an assembly as there was not in New York, and the revolt was against a proprietor and not an appointee of the crown. William could and did approve the movement in Maryland, but he could not approve that in New York because he deemed it an affront to the dignity of a crowned head, and in that respect William was as unyielding as ever his predecessor had been.

2. *Documentary History*, II, 80–156.

3. *New York Colonial Documents*, III, 731.

4. See below, p. 312, note 2.

5. *Calendar State Papers, Colonial*, 1689–1692, 945; *Documentary History*, II, 271,

at colonial coöperation, and the most statesmanlike effort of the kind up to this time in colonial history, is more noteworthy even than the formation of the New England Confederation because it had no religious motive behind it. It reached its climax in the conference of the "governors of several provinces" which Leisler called in April, 1690, immediately after the sacking of Schenectady, to meet at New York for the purpose of defending and checking the advance of the enemy.[1] Though many were called but few responded—only Massachusetts, Connecticut and Plymouth, the remaining members of the New England Confederation, who thus continued, as it were, the former gatherings of the commissioners of that Puritan experiment, with New York as an additional member. Though the commissioners promised that the New England colonies would send troops to Albany, Connecticut seems to have been the only one to do so, for Massachusetts and Plymouth were raising men for an expedition against the eastern Indians and the former was planning to send Sir William Phips against Port Royal in Nova Scotia, an undertaking which it carried out successfully.[2] The Connecticut troops at Albany soon became disgusted with Milborne, whom Leisler had placed at the head of the New York contingent, and stricken with smallpox, dysentery, and fever, lost faith in the enterprise. Those that survived returned.

Thus this first attempt at coöperation, even against the common enemy, ended in failure. How far this failure was due to military ineffectiveness and how far to loss of confidence in Leisler it is difficult to say. At the beginning there was a marked desire among the colonies for mutual understanding and neighborly intercourse. Leisler occupied a central and strategic position in New York and Albany for carrying on the war against the French and as long as he seemed to represent the prevailing dislike of prerogative government, fear of popery, and apprehension of danger from France there continued to exist a measure of unity and good will. But as the year 1690 wore on confidence became impaired and suspicions arose as to his motives. Riots and tumults increased in New York City, Albany raged inwardly but helplessly, and among the Long Island

272. Governor Robinson promised to send twenty barrels, but apparently Leisler got only ten of them.

1. *Ibid.*, 211, 227, 237–238, 239–240, 300; *New York Colonial Documents*, III, 732.

2. *Documentary History*, II, 259–260.

towns and in Connecticut the feeling spread that Leisler was pushing the war against the French in order to divert attention from the
discontent in city and province. Interest in the war and in Leisler
perceptibly waned and the material obstacles that would have rendered successful combination difficult in any case were supplemented
by a growing unwillingness to further Leisler's personal ambitions.[1]
In Massachusetts, Maryland, and Virginia men were waiting anxiously but hopefully for orders from England and in New York
especially Leisler's opponents were looking for relief to the arrival
of the new governor, whose appointment had been reported and
whose arrival was anxiously awaited.

Leisler, too, knew that the end of his tenure was approaching, but
he clung to power as long as he could. When Major Ingoldesby with
one of the regiments from England reached New York on January
29, 1691, seven weeks ahead of the newly appointed governor,
Sloughter, Leisler denied his right to issue orders, refused to surrender the fort, and vehemently negatived his request that his troops
be admitted within its precincts. This refusal was based on Leisler's
belief that Ingoldesby had no commission as commander in chief
from the king or instructions from Sloughter to supplant himself
as the king's deputy.[2] However, he and his council consented that
Ingoldesby should quarter his troops in the town, but they resented
hotly and with open hostility the very presence of the major and his
regiment and opposed by show of arms what they called his "illegal
unwarrantable and undue practices." To Leisler's wrath Ingoldesby
began to drum up forces on Long Island, to issue proclamations and
orders, and to perpetrate acts that were openly belligerent. Leisler
had three hundred men in the fort, while outside were the regulars

1. Note the letter of Livingston, town clerk and superintendent of Indian affairs
at Albany, May 9, 1690, to the government of Connecticut; the petition of the towns
of Hempstead, Jamaica, Flushing, and Newtown against Leisler's "tyrannical usurpation"; the protest of the magistrates of Westchester; and the declaration of the towns
of Ameersfort, Breuckelen, and Midwout (New York Colonial Documents, III, 728–
731, 754–756; Documentary History, II, 330–331, 336–337). Connecticut, who had
befriended Leisler from the beginning, was now charged by him with "breach of
covenant, insolent obtrusions," and "unconcerdness." Major General Winthrop, who
was in command of the Connecticut troops at Albany, was censured for "unaccount-
able and unchristian behaviour," and Livingston, who had opposed Leisler's usurpation of the government at Albany, was stigmatized as a Jacobite.

2. I have been unable to find any trace of such a commission, Narratives of the
Insurrection, p. 390, note 2; Documentary History, II, 320–321; Collections, 1868,
306–309.

and five hundred men from the surrounding towns, chiefly of Long Island. In an incautious moment Leisler's men fired on the king's troops, killing two and wounding seven, an overt act that brought upon him later the charge of felony. In the welter of recrimination that followed it is as impossible as it is unnecessary to apportion the blame.[1] Two men in command, neither of whom possessed certain authority, had come into conflict. Hatreds bit deep and each side charged the other with illegality. To the Leislerians, Ingoldesby and his associates were "papists" and "revengeful spirits" exceeding their powers; to the newcomers, Leisler was "a puny usurper" who was struggling to retain a position that he knew he must soon abandon. Neither showed restraint in language used or deeds committed or displayed any trace of the spirit of compromise or willingness to concede that the other had any rights worthy of recognition. Only the coming of the new governor could avert a civil war.

Sloughter finally reached New York in the evening of March 19, 1691, and after publishing his commission ordered Ingoldesby to demand at once the surrender of the fort. Three times did Ingoldesby make his demand and three times did Leisler refuse to recognize Ingoldesby's authority or to deliver up the fort at night, claiming that it was contrary to military rules to surrender a fort after dark. Later this refusal became the basis of the charge of treason. Leisler demanded that Sloughter either appear in person the next morning or at that time send a written order properly authenticated, promising, if this were done, he would obey the king's command. True to his promise, the next morning he surrendered and instead of being thanked for his "faithful service in defending the fort and province from the French and the treachery of Papists and Jacobites," as the writer of *Loyalty Vindicated* thought he should have been, he was arrested and brought to trial, with Milborne and eight others, for felony and treason.[2] The trial lasted from March 31

1. Compare, for example, the letter of the new collector, Chidley Brooke (*New York Colonial Documents*, III, 757–758), with the defense of Leisler in "Loyalty Vindicated" (*Narratives of the Insurrection*, pp. 390–392). It is impossible to reconcile the statements in these and other documents (*Documentary History*, II, 320–346; *Collections*, New York Historical Society, 1868, pp. 299–310). The situation represents a conflict of asserted authority which, legally speaking, neither side possessed.

2. *Documentary History*, II, 358–438; *Collections*, New York Historical Society, 1868, 310–365; both volumes containing numerous documents relating to the trial and its aftermath. The proceedings at the trial are in C. O. 5: 1037, no. 4, a transcript of which is in the Library of Congress. They are not printed in *New York*

to April 17, during which Edsall and Delaney were acquitted, Leisler and Milborne, refusing to plead and persisting in their refusal, were condemned to death, as were six others, Gouverneur, Beekman, Williams, Courteen, Vermilye, and Brazier. During the trial the court obtained from the governor and his council a definite statement that the despatches of 1689 contained no "power or direction for the Government to Captain Leisler," and later the House of Representatives passed a resolution embodying a similar opinion. Sloughter, very unwisely, urged on by the spirit of revenge existent among those whom Leisler had treated with contumely for over a year, signed the warrant for the execution of Leisler and Milborne, who were hanged, May 16, 1691, while the others were reprieved and eventually pardoned by the crown, March 15, 1694.[1] The act of execution was not only merciless but it was a blunder, for it kept alive the prevailing animosities for years to come, when amnesty might have worked for harmony and a measure of peace. Through the efforts of the sons of Leisler and Milborne and of the recently pardoned Abraham Gouverneur, aided by Massachusetts and her agents in England, who were thoroughly out of sympathy with the excesses of the anti-Leislerian party in New York under Governor Fletcher, Sloughter's successor,[2] parliament passed an act in 1695[3] reversing the decree of the New York court, removing the attainder, and restoring the blood and estates of the families of Leisler and Milborne. No one reading the act of parliament, whether he believes it to have been justly passed or not, can fail to see that it contains a good many misstatements of fact and was drafted by pronounced Leislerian partisans.

Leisler has always been a troublesome character to interpret because of the difficulties met in estimating his motives and accomplishments. He has been vehemently defended and venomously con-

Colonial Documents or elsewhere. Other copies are in C. O. 5: 1082, nos. 2, i–iv. The address, April 9, of governor, council, and general assembly, declaring that Leisler had no authority from the crown and for two years had usurped the government is in C. O. 5: 1037, no. 8, transcript in the Library of Congress. Resolutions of the House of Representatives, April 17, condemning Leisler are in the same, numbers 11, 12.

1. *New York Colonial Documents*, IV, 54–55; *Calendar State Papers, Colonial*, 1693–1696, 943. For a brief account of some of these men, *New York Colonial Documents*, IV, 212.

2. That Governor Phips of Massachusetts was strongly pro-Leislerian appears in his relations with Governor Fletcher of New York. *Ibid.*, IV, 5, 6, 8, 9, 10.

3. *Documentary History*, II, 435–437; *Calendar Treasury Books*, X, 65.

demned, especially by those who feel it their duty, in passing judgment on historical personages, to take either one side or the other.
There is no good reason in his case for either defense or attack.
Leisler in New York was in the same class with Fendall and Coode
in Maryland, Righton in Bermuda, the Milbornes in three colonies,
and others elsewhere less conspicuous because of less favoring circumstances—all of whom were men who came to the front in a time
of conflict between opposing systems of thought, governmental, social, and religious. Such men are bound to be fanatical in temperament, insensitive, prejudiced and often, though by no means always,
of low birth, crude, ignorant and unlearned, men whose emotions
are more highly developed than their intellects and who are profoundly assured of the rightness of their cause. The age that gave
them birth was one in which violent warfare was raging between
prerogative and popular government, between Roman Catholicism
and the Protestant and Dissenting sects, between England and
France for the first fruits of colonial enterprise. It was an age in
which convictions, rigid and partisan, were deeply rooted, when
enmities were easily aroused, when perils were immoderately exaggerated, particularly by those who lived in isolation and, often oppressed by poverty and the adversities of life, knew little of the world
at large.

There was not a colony that did not show some traces of this conflict, but in only two, New York and Maryland, did it reach a climax. These were the two colonies where proprietary prerogative
and Roman Catholic ascendancy seemed most conspicuous and dangerous and where popular unrest, brought about by belief in the
selfishness and indifference of the ruling classes, was most widely
spread. In New York the grouping of circumstances was unique.
The centering of the activities of the province at Manhattan, where
the fort was the heart of the government and where he who possessed it was in a peculiarly commanding situation; the heterogene-
ity of race and speech which rendered almost impossible the formation of an efficient and united opposition; the nearness of the self-
governing English towns within the province and the example of
the neighboring New England colonies and towns where popular
control prevailed; and, finally, the failure of the experiment with
an assembly in New York and the return to an executive form of
administration, all these circumstances made the conditions in New

York peculiar and unique. More immediately disruptive in their effects upon the course of events in the province were the revolutions of 1689 in England and Massachusetts; the downfall of the Dominion of New England which undermined the strength of the New York officials, none too competent or popular at best; the flight of the lieutenant governor and the reprehensible slowness of the home government in supplying his successor, leaving the province for nearly two years without a head. The combination of all these circumstances furnished an opportunity for someone to assume the leadership—someone possessed of boldness, confidence in the justness of his cause, acting in accord with the spirit of the English revolution, and holding certain definite notions regarding the rights of Englishmen and the defense of the reigning sovereigns as over against the discarded Stuarts.

Such a man was Leisler. He had courage, capacity for work, a forceful personality, and no little organizing ability. He found followers, not only among the working classes—the bricklayers, blockmakers, farmers, traders, officers of the militia, and roving agitators of the time, but also among the merchants, traders, and professional classes, notably the Dutch. In carrying out his ambitions he was domineering, revengeful, and often demagogic, proclaiming martial law, inflicting heavy penalties, and employing terrorizing methods. In defense of his usurpation he impressed upon his leadership the stamp first of a pseudo-popular consent, the consent of a small minority, and then of an equally fictitious royal approval, and built up his claim to govern on what he believed, or pretended to believe, was a royal mandate to him, as the king's lieutenant governor, which for the last thirteen months of his supremacy he made the cornerstone of his authority. Inevitably, as with leaders in all revolutions, his aspirations grew upon him and a zest for power became an increasingly dominant motive. As this tendency became manifest, his following, grown fearful, fell off; the towns in Queens County, Long Island, repudiated his claims and charged him with tyranny; the colony of Connecticut withdrew its support; and within Manhattan itself merchants and traders began to send urgent petitions to England against him. It is doubtful whether in any case he could have lasted much longer than he did, because he had become almost entirely dependent on his soldiers and the possession of the forts at Albany and the city of New York. The coming of the king's governor ended his career.

In the commission to Governor Sloughter, that passed the great seal, November 14, 1689, appears the following paragraph: "And we do hereby give and grant unto you full power and authority with the advice and consent of [your] Council from time to time as need shall require, to summon and call generall Assemblies of the Inhabitants being Freeholders within your Government, according to the usage of our other Plantations in America."[1] With the issue of this order and the calling of an assembly on April 9, 1691, for the first time under the direct authority of the English crown, the period of prerogative and executive government came to an end, New York entered the ranks of the regular royal colonies with governor, council, and popular assembly, and a new era in the history of the province began.

1. *New York Colonial Documents,* III, 624; *Calendar State Papers, Colonial,* 1693–1696, §1803.

CHAPTER IV

PROPRIETARY TROUBLES IN THE JERSEYS

THE struggle against proprietary rule in the Jerseys, though not as prolonged or as intense as that in Maryland, had peculiarities enough of its own to give it a well-defined place among the many efforts made in the seventeenth century to destroy the proprietary system altogether. In no other colony or province did there exist from the first the doubt which in the Jerseys clouded the title to proprietary government and persisted as a weakening factor throughout the entire period of proprietary control.

Three and a half months after the Duke of York received his own charter from the king he made over to his friends, John Lord Berkeley and Sir George Carteret—by a form of land conveyancing in common use in England known as lease and release[1]—that portion

1. The lease and release (established by statute, 27 Henry VIII, c. 10, for transferring uses into possession) was an ingenious contrivance in land conveyancing, which had become so popular in England as to supplant the deed of feoffment (the familiar livery of seisin and enrollment). It had become at this time the general mode of conveyancing, *inter vivos*, in free and common socage. Its application in the case of the Jerseys was as follows. The tenant (the duke) holding in fee simple (by the charter of 1664) bargained and sold (the lease or indenture of bargain and sale, *New Jersey Archives*, I, 8–10) for an amount of money stated in the indenture (ten shillings, which did not have to be actually paid) an estate, manor, or propriety (the land between the Hudson and Delaware rivers) with a sufficient reservation (a pepper corn) to constitute a use only. The day after the sealing of the lease, which made over to the lessees the use of the property, the release, or indenture of grant, release, and confirmation, was executed (June 23, the lease; June 24, the release) clearing the property of the lessor's right of reversion (the duke's right as symbolized by the pepper corn) and conveying it to the lessees, already possessing it for use, in as free and ample a manner as the lessor had it (the release, *New Jersey Archives*, I, 10–14). In this way the property was freed from the duke's reversionary right and Berkeley and Carteret were given possession, no longer for use but in fee simple. The indenture constituted, however, only a conveyance of land and in no way carried powers of government (Jacob, *Law Dictionary*, under "Lease"; Digby, *Law of Real Property*, 3d ed., pp. 322–323). The Duke of York had no right in law to divide the powers received from the crown and Berkeley and Carteret had no right to exercise any governmental powers whatever. The phrase "in as full and ample manner" can refer to nothing more than the profits from the land and not to taxes or customs dues which were collectible only by authority of government. When in 1718 the proprietors of the Carolinas executed a deed of lease and release to Sir Robert Mountgomery, the

of his propriety which lay between the Hudson and Delaware rivers. He may have parted with this valuable area at the request of the grantees themselves or he may have given it away on his own initiative, as he owed both men some return for favors received. On neither point have we information. Charles II had made the same two men, with six others, proprietors of a much larger tract of land south of Virginia only the year before, and as all of them were members of the king's court and were acting more or less in common in their desire to acquire territory on the mainland and islands of America, it is extremely probable that the proprietary form of colonization was frequently a subject of discussion among them. Just how much Berkeley and Carteret knew about the lands they received, either of the Carolinas or of the Jerseys, is problematical; but some information must have drifted in, for Colonel John Scott and Samuel Maverick had both been in England shortly before the grants were made and at the time when the plans for the conquest of New Netherland were beginning to take shape. The activities of the years 1663 and 1664 show that Englishmen at Whitehall and elsewhere had been learning a good deal about colonial geography since the capture of Jamaica, and though maps were few and imperfect and descriptions inaccurate and overdrawn, they could have made considerable progress with what was at hand.[1]

Carteret and Berkeley had been meeting with their fellow proprie-

attorney general said that they could not give away their rights of government (above, Vol. II, 227; *Calendar State Papers, Colonial,* 1717–1718, §459). When Captain Delavall made over lands in Harlem to his son-in-law, James Carteret (below, p. 149, note 1), he signed the lease but refused to sign the release until he was sure that Carteret was trustworthy (Riker, *Harlem,* revised ed., p. 339).

1. Unfortunately Taylor, *Late Tudor and Early Stuart Geography,* ends with 1650, but the work does give an account of such maps as were available in that year. Pepys tells us that in March, 1661, he found Sir William Coventry, who with Berkeley and Carteret was instructed in 1663 to make a report on New England and New Netherland, studying the map of Jamaica under the guidance of Sir William Penn; and we know that Speed's maps of America as well as of England, though made thirty or more years before, were frequently consulted. Dutch maps, too, such as would be known to Downing, must have been within reach, but at best the region between New England and Maryland and south of Virginia was unfamiliar territory. Ogilby's *America* did not appear until 1671, so it is not surprising that one of the first demands of the Carolina proprietors, May 23, 1663, was that maps should be obtained and printed (*North Carolina Colonial Records,* I, 34). A very spacious folding map, twenty-one by sixteen and a quarter inches within the border, was issued in 1682 with the caption "A New Description of Carolina by order of the Lords Proprietors" and is attached to the second issue of Wilson's *Account* (London, 1682). It was drawn by John Gascoyne and is commonly known as the Gascoyne Map. There is no refer-

tors of Carolina since the summer of 1663 and it is not impossible that their desire for a property of their own was stimulated by this association. However that may be, the fact remains that the "Concessions and Agreements," planned at the first meeting to encourage planters to migrate to Carolina, was taken over by them and issued for New Jersey, in somewhat shortened form and with slight changes of wording and rearrangement of text,[1] on February 10, 1665. The significance of this fact, among other significant features of the "Concessions," lies in the assumption by Berkeley and Carteret that they possessed identically the same powers in the Jerseys that in common with the other six men they possessed in Carolina, though in their own case they had merely an indenture conveying ownership of the soil. One of the problems of early New Jersey history is to discover why it was that for a period of thirty years the Duke of York should have connived at this state of things and have made no effort in England to legalize the pretensions of his friends by a royal confirmation under the great seal. He must have known that, technically speaking, he alone had governmental authority over the Jerseys and that he could part with it only by consent of the crown officially and formally expressed. In all other grants of soil only, such as those to Lord Fairfax and Lord Granville, no such claim to governmental rights within their respective districts was ever made or would have been allowed if it had been made, yet Berkeley and Carteret from the first acted as if their "lease and release" had all the value of a royal charter and declared themselves to be the "true and absolute lords proprietors of all the province of New Cæsaria or New Jersey." Legally speaking this declaration was never true.

Neither of these "true and absolute lords" had the slightest intention of going in person to his propriety. Following the example of their patron, who in 1664 had sent over Colonel Richard Nicolls as his governor, they selected as their governor Captain Philip Carteret,

ence in Wilson's pamphlet to the map, so that it must have been published separately and inserted in the pamphlet after the latter had been set up in type, by Larkin and Smith at the Elephant & Castle, Cornhill. It is mentioned by Thomas Ashe in his *Carolina*, which was published in the same year, and by Wilson in his statement of account, 1683, *North Carolina Colonial Records*, I, 344.

1. The Carolina "Concessions" are in *ibid.*, I, 79–92; those for New Jersey in Leaming and Spicer, *Grants and Concessions*, pp. 12–26; *New Jersey Archives*, I, 28–43. The two documents should be carefully compared.

Sir George's cousin,[1] a young man only twenty-six years of age, and having provided him with a body of carefully drawn instructions and a ship, the *Philip,* with about thirty people, gentlemen and servants largely from the Channel Islands, despatched him overseas in April, 1665. In May the vessel reached Virginia, where Carteret dallied for several weeks, during which time he forwarded letters to Boston and New York and kept Nicolls and others on the anxious seat waiting for the arrival of the first ship to reach New York since the surrender. Finally, July 29, the *Philip* sailed up New York harbor and a few days later passed through the Kill van Kull and cast anchor off the point known later as Elizabethport, a landing place selected probably for its convenience.[2]

The region henceforth to be known as New Jersey was but sparsely occupied at this time, chiefly in the northern part. On his arrival Carteret found at Elizabeth but four families living there and they were English. Had he extended his inquiries he would have gathered the following information about the remaining parts of the territory he was sent over to govern: (1) that scattered to the northward there were Dutch families, perhaps two hundred people altogether, some occupying a few places populous enough to be called villages, and others cultivating a few farms, purchased of the Indians, possession of which had been legalized by the Dutch governors and confirmed by Nicolls as one of the conditions of surrender; and (2) that there were no Dutch south of the Raritan until the lower Delaware was reached, where on the left bank were located a few Dutch families, subject as were all the rest to Berkeley and Carteret's authority, such as it was, and owing allegiance to the proprietors, as the latter interpreted the scope of their powers. He would have learned (3) that there were English Puritans living nearer at hand—well established at Middletown, Shrewsbury, and Woodbridge to the south and southeast and that plans were in the making for others to arrive the next year from the defunct New Haven jurisdiction settling as a Puritan town later to be called Newark. The former were small communities growing into towns and already equipped with rudimentary organs for self-government,[3]

1. *Proceedings,* New Jersey Historical Society, 2d ser., I, 31; 4th ser., IX, 328–333; Whitehead, *East Jersey,* 2d ed., pp. 106–108.

2. Whitehead, *East Jersey,* pp. 272–273, Silvestre Salisbury's deposition.

3. The settlement of Elizabethtown, Woodbridge, Shrewsbury, Piscataway, and

and they owed their origin and titles to grants from Nicolls, made after he became governor of New York and before he heard, in the summer of 1665, that the best part of his province had been given away to the duke's friends. Philip with his French background and proprietary commission may well have wondered how he was going to get along with these sectaries, whose practices were so entirely out of keeping with his own ideas and instructions and who were more than likely to make him trouble when he attempted to enforce the commands which the proprietors had imposed upon him. He faced in New Jersey much the same problem that the duke's governors in New York were to face in their relations with the English and Puritan towns on Long Island.

But in one respect these relations differed, though perhaps not as fundamentally as on the surface might seem to be the case. The Duke of York issued no such body of "Concessions" as those which the Carolina proprietors and Berkeley and Carteret drew up for their respective proprieties. Nicolls met this omission in part by his grants of self-government to the Long Island towns and by his recognition of liberty of conscience for all Christians. But he could not permit the calling of a representative assembly for the making of laws and the levying of taxes, because he was not authorized by the duke to do so. Berkeley and Carteret, on the other hand, who had shared, officially at least, in the making of the Carolina draft, were very liberal in their offers, induced thereto by the necessity, which they and all the Carolina proprietors must have felt but which the Duke of York did not feel, of persuading people from England, as well as from the colonies already established, to take up lands in New Jersey and to increase the population without which the propriety would be worthless.

These "Concessions" were probably based in part on the recom-

---

Newark was promoted by men either from New England or from the English towns of Long Island: Elizabethtown from Jamaica; Woodbridge and Piscataway from Massachusetts Bay and New Hampshire; Middletown and Shrewsbury from western Long Island, Shelter Island, and Newport, Rhode Island; and Newark from the defunct New Haven colony. The last named town was started in 1666, but did not become established until the next year. It was a typical New Haven community, with its fundamental articles, its town meetings, its customary methods of land distribution, and its rigid moral and theological codes ("Records of Newark," *Collections,* New Jersey Historical Society, VI). It was begun in response to Philip Carteret's publication of the proprietors' "Concessions," which were sent by special agents to New England and Long Island, soon after Carteret's arrival in 1665.

mendations of the Barbadian members, in part on certain ideals that were creeping into English thought at the time, and in part on the conviction that colonists could not be obtained unless very favorable conditions of settlement were offered them. Consequently the "Concessions" were made as attractive as possible. To all who swore allegiance to the king and faithfulness to the proprietors[1] were granted full freedom of conscience,[2] generous terms of land distribution— limited only by certain rules of seating—by the payment of a quit-rent and by the reservation in all towns of one-seventh part for the use of the proprietors; the privilege of appeal in cases of grievance; and most important of all the right of the freeholders to send deputies to a general assembly for the making of laws, the erection of courts, and the levying of taxes for general defense and the support of the government. Apart from the fundamental issue of the right of the proprietors to govern the country at all and the obligation of those residing there to obey established authority, the only clauses of the "Concessions" that were likely to stick in the throats of the settlers from New England and Long Island were those requiring an oath of fidelity and the payment of a quit-rent. These clauses as well as the fundamental issue of the proprietary prerogative were pregnant with trouble. But nothing happened until after the first assembly met in May, 1668, in summoning which Carteret could hopefully say that the province was "in a probable way of being populated, there being a considerable number of families already

---

1. The oaths of allegiance to the king and of fidelity to the proprietors are given in Leaming and Spicer, pp. 91–92, and the names of those who took them, 1665–1668, in *New Jersey Archives*, I, 48–51. The oath of fidelity to the proprietors should be compared with the similar oath to the proprietor of Maryland, which is far more severe in form and terrifying in the penalties imposed (above, Vol. II, 331, note 1). The New Jersey oath was very mild and imposed no penalties, but no one was entitled to be a freeholder until he had taken it (*ibid.*, I, 58–59).

2. The enjoyment after 1660 of fairly complete religious freedom in certain of the colonies for all who believed in God must have appealed very strongly to many in England and to some in New England, especially in Massachusetts Bay, where the orders of Charles II, issued in 1662, for a limited toleration and a widening of the franchise (*Calendar State Papers, Colonial*, 1661–1668, §314) were largely ignored. There was in reality little of the spirit of toleration in either Massachusetts or Connecticut, and as for England many may have felt as did the "fanatic" reported by Pepys as saying that those who desired toleration were "the true spirit of the nation, and the greater part of the nation too, who will have liberty of conscience in spite of the 'Act of Uniformity,' or they will die" (under date June 22, 1662). The truth is that the miseries of England after the Restoration were teaching the men there a lesson of mutual forbearance that was unknown in either Massachusetts or Connecticut.

settled in several parts of the same and many more that in a short tyme are to come and place themselves und^r this government."[1] He anticipated no obstacles in the way of a peaceful administration, knowing nothing, as yet, of the peculiar temperament of the Puritans or of their tenacious adherence to their own interpretation of a written or printed document, whether the Bible, the catechism, or a parchment bearing an official seal.

The assembly met on May 29. It was composed of the governor, seven councillors, and ten deputies from the towns of Bergen, Elizabethtown, Newark, and supposedly from Middletown including Shrewsbury. At later assemblies deputies came from the Delaware settlements also. The membership was a strange medley of French, Dutch, and English, the last named predominating—a fact which probably accounts for the strong Puritan coloring that was given to the laws passed, particularly to those concerning capital offenses. Carteret, quite unfamiliar with the various New England codes from which these capital penalties were taken, must have been not a little surprised at their character, just as he must have been somewhat taken aback at the desire of the members to go home, after sitting but four days, thus seeming to belie, in some measure at least, their much vaunted demand for popular representation in assembly. The members met again in November, and after that as a legally recognized body only in November, 1671. An assembly denounced by the proprietor as wholly unauthorized came together, May 14, 1672, but its records were suppressed and no new gathering was summoned until November 5, 1675.[2]

The trouble which this unauthorized assembly discloses was due in part to a disturbed condition of the province, brought about by Indian disorders similar to those that were menacing the frontiers of New York, but it was due in a greater part to a clashing of jurisdictions that arose from conflicting origins of title. Nicolls, before Philip Carteret had arrived to tell him of the separation of the Jerseys from New York, had issued many land patents within that part of the duke's domain which lay to the south and west of Staten Island, in the Raritan and Navesink regions. One of these patents— the Elizabethtown grant—was given to a group of men from Ja-

1. *New Jersey Archives*, I, 56–57.

2. Whitehead, *East Jersey*, p. 60, note 3, says that there are "intimations of several meetings during the intermediate period," and Governor Parker in the article mentioned below gives definite evidence for the meeting in November, 1671.

maica, December 1, 1664, and embraced the territory from the Raritan northward to "the first River wch sets westward out of Cull Bay," a boundary line in dispute, but commonly thought to be the Passaic. Another, known as the Monmouth grant, was issued April 5, 1665, in the interest of a group of Long Islanders from Gravesend and elsewhere. These Long Islanders immediately set on foot a movement which resulted in the settlements of Middletown, Shrewsbury, and Portland Point and the locating of scattered plantations here and there, within a section the boundaries of which, though very loosely stated, probably enclosed the whole of Monmouth and Ocean and parts of the modern counties of Middlesex and Mercer. According to this patent the people were authorized, among other things, to meet in a general assembly of their own, distinct from their town meetings, for the making of laws; to set up courts for the trial of petty causes; to be exempt from taxation for seven years; and to enjoy all the privileges and immunities common to the duke's subjects in New York.[1] Acting on these concessions the towns sent deputies to a gathering at Shrewsbury, December 12, 1667, and continued so to send for a number of years. This general assembly of the Monmouth region passed laws, dispensed justice, and laid down the conditions under which land could be held. Such an independent jurisdiction, similar to that which the towns of eastern Long Island had wanted and to that which the western Long Island towns had in mind when they lent themselves to the schemes of Colonel John Scott, was bound to come into conflict with the Carteret government. It is an interesting matter for speculation whether either of the assemblies had a strictly legal foundation. The Duke of York had received by his charter no right to delegate governmental powers, either to the New Jersey proprietors or through Nicolls to the grantees of the Monmouth Patent, and neither the assembly called by Carteret at Elizabethtown nor that of the Monmouth people at Shrewsbury had, strictly speaking, a legal right to convene.

1. The Monmouth Patent is in Leaming and Spicer, pp. 661-663; *New Jersey Archives*, I, 43-46. The confirmation by Carteret (May 28, 1672) is in Leaming and Spicer, pp. 663-664. The Elizabethtown Patent is in *ibid.*, pp. 671-673; *New Jersey Archives*, I, 14-19. These two grants, because of the disputes that arose regarding the proprietors' title to government as well as the soil, resulted, in the Monmouth case, in a rebellion that was partly responsible for the final surrender in 1702 and, in the Elizabethtown case, to litigation that lasted down to the Revolution.

When the Elizabethtown general assembly met in May, 1668, Middletown and Shrewsbury were represented by two of the original Monmouth patentees, James Glover and John Bowne, who took the oath to the proprietors. But the freeholders of the towns they represented repudiated, in town meeting, the right of these men to stand as deputies, on the ground that they had not been chosen by a sufficient number of voters. The freeholders declared that the towns would not be bound by anything these men might agree to in the assembly that would in any way infringe upon or violate their patent. They offered to send other delegates, properly elected, but in doing so would not suffer any of them to take an oath that would prejudice their rights as patentees, unless a reservation were inserted guaranteeing all that their patent allowed them. This demand for a reservation was a defiance of the proprietary authority and a contemning of the proprietor's own assembly. Consequently in November, 1668, when two new deputies appeared for Middletown and Shrewsbury and refused to take the oaths without the provisos or to submit to the proprietary laws and government, they were not allowed to take their seats. Answering this action of the governor and his council Middletown and Shrewsbury refused to pay the rates assessed at the previous meeting in May on the ground that the Monmouth Patent freed them from all payment of taxes until seven years had passed.[1] The assembly in its turn sent two of its members to collect the rates, by force if necessary, and to find out whether the revolting towns would or would not submit to the laws and government of the province. The insurgents answered that they would resist to the end distraint of goods and cattle and should anyone of their number be summoned to appear before the governor and his council to defend himself they would compensate him for time lost and would meet all charges and penalties. As this answer was a flat rejection of the proprietors and all their works, the Middletowners, in meeting assembled, defined their position and drew up a remarkable paper that shows, better than any other document of the period, the bewilderment of the Puritan in the presence of the absolute

1. Extracts from the town records of Middletown, October, November, 1668, February, March, 1669, December, 1671, are printed in an article by Governor Parker of New Jersey, "Monmouth during the Provincial Era," in *Proceedings,* New Jersey Historical Society, 2d ser., IV, 17–46. In the text the writer gives the date of the first meeting of the Monmouth general assembly as June, 1667, but the record reads, December 12, 1667, and Salter, *Old Monmouth,* says it met at Shrewsbury.

authority claimed by the proprietors and the hopelessness of any attempt at compromise between the principles underlying proprietary versus popular rule. The issues at stake were not confined to New Jersey; they were present wherever these irreconcilable ideas regarding government came into conflict, and in the seventeenth century, that was in a large majority of the colonies.[1]

In this Middletown paper the insurgents spoke of the proprietary prerogatives as something new and "soe obscure to us that at present we are ignorant what it is." Writs in his Majesty's name they were familiar with and understood, but what were writs in the name of the lord proprietor—that was something such as "we simple creatures never heard of before." How could Governor Carteret say that their patent (the Monmouth Patent) was of no account and that the lands they had purchased and held by deed in proper legal form were not theirs but belonged to the proprietors? How could the governor and council prohibit them from electing their own town officials or say that if they did so they would be "proceeded against as mutineers"? The lords proprietors seemed to be demanding not only absolute sovereignty but absolute propriety also, as if they alone were the ones from whom all lands "must be holden," thus transforming the people of the towns into "absolute tenants," who by the taking of oaths and the paying of quit-rents bound themselves to a submission that "would be a dishonor to him that gave it." They declared that they would not be violators of their patent and they refused to give up the right granted therein of making for themselves the "prudential lawes" that were so necessary for their safety. They resolutely asserted that they would not submit to the breaking down of their rights and privileges by swearing to the laws of another government which would not recognize either their patent or their liberties. They were willing to offer obedience in matters that lay outside the terms of their patent, provided some secure way "be thought of or projected" to guard their rights, but if such way could not be found then they were "resolved not to intangle" themselves "into any other interest appertaining to any men."

1. Parker's article, pp. 26–30. Vote of March 17, 1669. There is a document of a slightly earlier date, 1663, relating to a proposed and partly executed project for a settlement by New Englanders on the Cape Fear River (below, pp. 192–193). It is a chip from the same block as the Middletown protest and in the views presented regarding land titles and rights of government is a characteristic Puritan product (*North Carolina Colonial Records*, I, 36–39).

They were determined "(with the assistance of God) to stick" to their patent, as a trust committed to them, and, if need be, to appeal for remedy to the highest authority, that is, either to Berkeley and Carteret or even to the Duke of York himself. They hoped that their answer would be "presented to the general assembly in order to prevent misinformation."

Whether this paper was ever known to Carteret or whether the threat to appeal over his head to the proprietors or to the duke proved a deterrent cannot be known, but apparently nothing further happened until in 1670 the time came for collecting the quit-rents, as provided for in the "Concessions." These quit-rents the colonists who held by grant from Nicolls flatly refused to pay, because to do so would require that they take out special land patents from the proprietors through the governor, thus acknowledging Carteret's right to grant away their lands and imperilling their own title to full ownership. This title, derived from Nicolls, they insisted on and their assigns continued to insist on it during the long controversy that followed. The persons chiefly concerned were the patentees of the Monmouth and Elizabethtown grants, tracts of land that embraced some of the most valuable parts of the province and covered either wholly or in large part five counties of the present state of New Jersey.[1] The Newark settlers also, who had arrived in 1666 and taken up ground north of the Passaic, raised the same issue regarding ownership, though they offered to pay quit-rents, when the time came, in wheat but not in sterling. Many who were freeholders and had taken oaths to the proprietors accepted patents, but as there were others in large numbers who refused to take oaths or accept patents, confusion reigned and demonstrations were staged against the government.

The resistance took on a more argumentative and less spectacular form when in May, 1672, delegates from Elizabethtown, Newark, Woodbridge, Piscataway, and Bergen twice gathered in assembly at Elizabethtown (whether as a general assembly or not is uncertain), and there debated regarding "the safety of the country."[2] But as no writs had been issued and the governor and council were not present, the proceedings and acts of this body were deemed invalid and the records destroyed. In the effort to give their position

1. Tanner, *Province of New Jersey, 1664–1738*, p. 59.
2. *Newark Records*, p. 44, under date of May 13, 1672.

a measure of legality, because Philip Carteret would have nothing to do with them, they fastened on Captain James Carteret,[1] a son of the proprietor, who was at the time residing temporarily in Elizabethtown on his way to Carolina, where he had been named a landgrave under the Fundamental Constitutions issued in 1669 by the Carolina proprietors. Him they made their presiding officer, as they claimed they were authorized to do under that clause of the "Concessions," which said that should the governor wilfully refuse to be present then the deputies might themselves appoint a president during his absence.

The invitation to James Carteret was an act of defiance and in a way an act of rebellion, instigated by the insurgents for the purpose of securing their title to the lands they occupied. The assembly cannot be considered a legal body, even though the delegates styled it a

1. Hatfield, *History of Elizabeth*, pp. 143–155; Leaming and Spicer, pp. 31–41; *New Jersey Archives*, I, 89–109.

James Carteret, the second son of Sir George, was bred to the sea. Before 1671 he had been captain of a merchantman in the India service and had taken part in the attempted recovery of St. Christopher from the French in 1667. In 1671 he was made a landgrave of Carolina and, soon after, set out to inspect his propriety there. Because he was the bearer of letters from Berkeley and Carteret to Philip in New Jersey, he visited Elizabethtown and while there was invited by the insurgents to preside at their assembly. That he accepted the invitation out of any genuine interest in their cause is hardly possible; he may have had merely a dislike of Philip, whom he charged with many miscarriages in a letter written to Governor Lovelace of New York, June 14, 1672 (quoted in Riker, *Harlem,* revised ed., p. 322, note). In 1673 he married Frances Delavall, daughter of the mayor of New York, and resigning all his New Jersey pretensions at the command of his father, set out with his wife for Carolina. Captured by the Dutch fleet he was put on shore in Virginia and after the recovery of the province of New York from the Dutch returned to Manhattan and took up his residence in Harlem, where, as also in Albany, his father-in-law had landed property. He took some part in the public life of Harlem, but though possessed of ability and considerable resourcefulness his habits were against him. He had one son George and a daughter Elizabeth who married in the Isle of Jersey Philip Pipon as her second husband. James was probably thirty or a little more when in New Jersey. Regarding his character opinions differ. Hatfield and Riker think well of him. The latter, influenced no doubt by the sympathy which he shares with Hatfield for the so-called popular cause, calls him "a generous-hearted captain." Paltsits, on the other hand, accepting as credible the description of Carteret given by Jasper Danckaerts in his *Journal* (Original Narratives), pp. 66–67, as "a very profligate person," thinks him "a weakling and a rake, yet of 'good understanding.'" That he was a roysterer and a reprobate appears from the fact that his wife left him, his father-in-law distrusted him, and his father disowned and practically disinherited him (will in Riker, p. 311). On hearing of his father's death in 1680 he returned to England and died there soon after, hardly forty years old. Hatfield, *Elizabeth*, pp. 154–155; Riker, *Harlem*, pp. 321–323, 339–340, 359–360, 810–811; Paltsits, *Executive Council Minutes*, I, 129–130.

"general assembly," for the governor had not summoned it nor had the delegates taken the oath, as all members of a regular assembly were required to do. On the other hand, if it were merely an unauthorized convention, "disorderly Assembled" as the governor said, then the delegates had no right to appeal to the provision in the "Concessions" for their justification. In fact the situation had at last reached an impasse, from which the only escape was an appeal to England. Various addresses were immediately sent over presenting one side or the other of the issue in dispute, and early in July the governor with three of his councillors sailed to acquaint Sir George, at this time an old man some seventy-two or three years of age, regarding the state of affairs and to lay before him and Lord Berkeley the grievances of the province.

The result was a complete victory for the proprietary claim, as was bound to be the case. Sir George disavowed his son's conduct and ordered him to leave the province. The Duke of York, informed of the facts in the case, denied the validity of the Nicolls grants and thus swept the ground from under the feet of the insurgents by declaring that their titles were void in law. Both of the proprietors reaffirmed the true meaning and intent of the "Concessions" by stating that no one could be a freeholder or take any part in government who did not actually hold his lands by proprietary patent and pay the quit-rent. They also upheld the authority of their governor as over against the assembly and made him and his council the ultimate source of all title to the soil, thus repudiating any right that the assembly might claim to regulate the granting or laying out the lands of the province. Their objects in so doing were, of course, to make certain an adequate return from the quit-rents, and to reduce, as far as possible, the powers of the assembly in all that related to tenure, to civil, military, and judicial offices, and to rights of summons, adjournments, and dissolution. In the face of such a determined exhibition of proprietary authority the contentious towns submitted and a sort of general amnesty was tacitly agreed on "to prevent deriding or uttering words of reproach to any that had been guilty of the riot."[1] But the question of title still remained unsettled.

1. Whitehead, *East Jersey*, p. 73, quoting from the East New Jersey council records. (The printed journal of the governor and council does not begin until December, 1682.) Just what happened in the towns as the result of these proprietary commands it is impossible to say. The Monmouth people had taken no part in the insurgent movement and resting on a confirmation of their title by Philip Carteret, May 28, 1672,

The capture of New York by the Dutch in 1673 was accompanied and followed by a series of events, of considerable significance, in the history of the province. The conquest abrogated the English titles and the reconquest in 1674 nullified all that the Dutch had done to establish their own control over their former territory. It became necessary therefore for the king, after the treaty of Westminster had stipulated the restoration of New Netherland to the English crown, to reissue the charter to the Duke of York. It became necessary also for the duke to lease and release again the land across the Hudson to Berkeley and Carteret, and for the latter to confirm the "Concessions" of 1665 and such alterations as had been made in them by the "Explanations" of 1672. All this was done with one important difference. Between March 6, 1674, when the treaty of Westminster was ratified by the States General of Holland, and June 29, when the king issued his charter of renewal, John Lord Berkeley, sold out his proprietary rights for £1000, March 18, to one John Fenwick, acting for a fellow Quaker, Edward Byllinge, thus retiring permanently from the New Jersey scene.[1] A rearrangement

(a confirmation not easy to understand, as it was virtually repudiated by the proprietors in their declaration of the following December) probably maintained the *status quo* (for the confirmation, Leaming and Spicer, p. 663; *New Jersey Archives*, I, 38). Hatfield does not tell us what happened in Elizabethtown, but a letter from the proprietors, December 2, 1672, implies that no quit-rents had been paid up to that time (*ibid.*, 105–106). As to Woodbridge the record remains that the proprietors offered to resign a third of the quit-rents for seven years, presumably on condition that the inhabitants submitted (*Proceedings*, New Jersey Historical Society, 2d ser., I, 100–101; *New Jersey Archives*, I, 104–105). Whether they did submit and take out patents is not disclosed, though it is probable (see below). Newark had already promised (1670) to pay the quit-rent of half a penny an acre in wheat and did so certainly for a while (*Newark Records*, pp. 29, 30, 34–35, 41 ["the Lord rent"], 47), so that the question, as in fact everywhere, was not the payment but the title to the land. In July, 1673, the question of title had not been decided as far as Newark was concerned, and the town voted to send an agent to the proprietors "for the removing of the Grievances incumbent, and obtaining what may be necessary for the good of the Province and of this Plantation—in testimony of our Consent hereto and of our agreement" (*ibid.*, p. 50). The "Consent" evidently refers to the promise of 1670; the "agreement" to the fundamental agreement of 1666 (*ibid.*, pp. 3, 54, 97). In October of 1673 a committee was chosen "to take out the Patent in their names in the Town's Behalf" (*ibid.*, p. 52) "upon the Terms proposed" (56). In March, 1674, the town petitioned the governor and council for a confirmation of its lands (55), and in 1677 voted to ask for a "Charter" as good as was that of Woodbridge (71, 78, 90). The town patent was not finally obtained until 1713 (pp. 123, 124) after the proprietary government had come to an end.

1. Leaming and Spicer, p. 64; *New Jersey Archives*, I, 209; Danckaert's *Journal*, pp. 154–155. Fenwick said in 1679 that he bought Berkeley's share "with [his] own money" (Johnson, *Settlement of Salem*, p. 37).

took place all along the line. The king renewed the patent to the duke, who appointed Andros the governor of his province of New York; the duke released to Carteret alone not all New Jersey, but only the northern half, above a line drawn from Barnegat Creek on the ocean side to Rankokus Kill on the Delaware, leaving the lower half for the time being without renewal; Carteret recommissioned Philip as his governor and sent over new instructions, which included the modifications made in consequence of the disorders arising from the recent attempts to contest the proprietary land claims.[1] The situation underwent another change when Byllinge, threatened with bankruptcy,[2] transferred his rights to three fellow Quakers, William Penn, Gawan Lawrie, and Nicholas Lucas, the transaction having been already complicated because Byllinge had placed the management of his property in Fenwick's hands, offering him a tenth part if he would look after the actual business of settlement, thus making Fenwick a party to the transfer from Berkeley. In the end Fenwick was to prove a very disturbing factor in the history of West New Jersey.[3]

Thus the year 1674 showed a decided change in the status of New Jersey. Carteret became the sole proprietor of the eastern half and three Quakers were in possession as joint proprietors of the western portion and tenants in common with Carteret. But the Quakers had received no confirmation of their title from the duke, resting their rights solely on the bill of sale ("indenture of bargain and sale") from Berkeley, which ordinarily would be equivalent to a lease but in this case was manifestly intended to have the same effect as a

1. Leaming and Spicer, pp. 50–57. The other documents are printed both in Leaming and Spicer and in the *New Jersey Archives.*

2. 1674. Edward Byllinge on his debts. "To friends and people of all sorts whatsoever," debts having been run into by him and his late wife "in the presence of the mercy of Lord God" he hopes that "no reasonable nor tender-hearted man or woman will not too far oppress with their tongues him that's already overwhelmed in sorrow, neither anywise charge this my miscarriage upon the principal people of God called Quakers, for their principle is holy just and true and they are clear of these things." Historical Manuscripts Commission, *Pepys,* p. 268.

3. Harleian, 7001, ff. 300–301; Bowden, *History of the Society of Friends in America,* I, 391–392. It is not necessary here to enter upon an examination of the different phases of this Quaker proprietary land deal. For our purpose the important fact is that a group of three Quakers became the proprietors of nine-tenths of the region known as West New Jersey. I have discussed the subject briefly in my *Colonial Self Government,* pp. 114–117. There is an elaborate biography of Fenwick in *Proceedings,* New Jersey Historical Society, IV, 53–89.

lease and release.[1] Whether Berkeley could convey the propriety, "in as full, ample and beneficial Manner to all intents and purposes as the same was granted" to himself and Carteret was open to doubt, and therefore it was eminently desirable that the Quakers strengthen their title. This they did, first by arranging in London for a formal division of the territory, July 1, 1676, in what is known as the Quintipartite Deed between Carteret on one side and Penn, Lawrie, Lucas, and Byllinge on the other;[2] and, secondly, after four years waiting, by obtaining from the duke a confirmation in the form of an indenture, August 6, 1680, by which James "granted bargained sold and confirmed" to them and their heirs the entire region known as West New Jersey.[3] The line between the two provinces ran from Little Egg Harbor (the southern partition point) to the northernmost branch of the Delaware River (the northern partition point), the latter defined as that part of the river which was crossed by northern latitude forty-one forty. The two sections, though fairly equal in territorial area (if Staten Island be included in the eastern part, a matter of controversy to be referred to later), were very unequal in point of occupation and improvement, for the eastern part was populated, while the western part was a wilderness except for the land occupied by a few families along the lower reaches of the Delaware river and bay.[4]

But the shuffling of proprietary rights was not even yet complete. On January 13, 1680, Sir George Carteret died in his eightieth year. By his will be devised "all his Plantations of New Jersey" to his

1. Ruffhead and Morgan, *A New-Law Dictionary* (based upon Jacob), under "Bargain and Sale." The deed to Fenwick is called an "indenture of bargain and sale" (Leaming and Spicer, p. 64) and is spoken of as "duly enrolled in his Majesty's High Court of Chancery." It is odd that the Berkeley-Fenwick conveyance should have been by lease only, while that between Fenwick and the four Quakers should have been by lease and release.

2. The text of the Quintipartite Deed is in Leaming and Spicer, pp. 61–72; *New Jersey Archives*, I, 205–219.

3. *Ibid.*, I, 324–332. By this indenture the Duke of York made conveyance to six Quakers instead of the four mentioned in the Quintipartite Deed. The reason is that Fenwick, though beginning settlement in 1675, did not reach a final agreement with Byllinge until after the Quintipartite Deed had been executed, so that he was not a party to that deed. Later having become legally vested with his tenth part he would have been named in the duke's indenture had he not leased or mortgaged his share to creditors, John Eldridge and Edmond Warner, who were named in his place (Johnson, *Settlement of Salem*, pp. 56–63).

4. For the later history of this line see George H. Cook, "Explanatory Remarks with Maps," *Proceedings, Bi-Centennial Celebration, 1884*, pp. 50–55.

widow and a group of trustees, bidding them sell them for the purpose of paying his debts and legacies. In the execution of this trust,
Lady Elizabeth Carteret, the proprietrix, and the trustees, after an
unsuccessful attempt to dispose of the property privately, put it up
at public auction and it was bought in for £3400, peppercorn tenure,
by twelve men, mostly Quakers, including Penn, Byllinge, and
Lawrie. These men, having evidently committed themselves to a
greater expense than they could carry, at sundry times during the
year 1682, added others to their number, until the twelve became
twenty-four, organized as a voluntary association of proprietors for
the government of a province containing over five thousand souls
and for the managing of a land situation, already highly complicated. The Duke of York legalized the sale by a deed of release,
March 14, 1683, and the king added his confirmation the following
November.[1] Thus East New Jersey came under the control of
twenty-four "absolute proprietors," Englishmen and Scotsmen, who
as a group had little in common, possessed as they were of an oddly
assorted variety of political, social, and religious opinions. They
ranged from the aristocratic Roman Catholic Scottish earls of Perth
and Melfort, through Presbyterian and Covenanting lowlanders, to
the unpretentious Quaker merchants and liverymen of London.

---

1. Leaming and Spicer, pp. 141–150; *New Jersey Archives*, I, 383–394; *Calendar
State Papers, Colonial*, 1681–1685, §1411. The names of the twenty-four are given
in the release and biographies in Whitehead, *East Jersey*, pp. 170–181. Sixteen were
Englishmen, six Scots, and two resident merchants of Dublin. Of the Englishmen
one was a lawyer, one a "mariner," four were "gentlemen," five were merchants,
and five were engaged in trade, members probably of one or another of the liveries of
London. Among them were William Penn, Edward Byllinge, Thomas Rudyard, and
Gawan Lawrie, who was probably (in origin at least) a Scot and is placed among
the Scots in one of the lists (*New Jersey Archives*, I, 448). The Scots were the Earl
(later Duke) of Perth and his brother John Drummond, Viscount (later Earl) of
Melfort, Robert Barclay of Urie, the Quaker apologist, whose chief efforts seem to
have been directed toward inducing the persecuted Scottish Covenanters to emigrate,
and his brother David, Robert Gordon, a merchant, and Arent Sonmans or Sonnemans, a Dutch merchant from Rotterdam living in the lowlands, whose son Peter
afterward became an active land litigant. As time went on some sold out and others
bought in, bargaining for shares or fractions of shares. The number of "proprietaries"
or shares always remained the same, but the number of those who bought, inherited,
or were given fractional parts increased rapidly (for the proprietors in 1683, already
showing many new names, *New Jersey Archives*, I, 441–442; in 1684, Leaming and
Spicer, p. 195; in 1697, *New Jersey Archives*, II, 191; for the fractional distribution,
ibid., 528–530). The Scottish membership is discussed in Insh, *Scottish Colonial
Schemes;* in an article by Pryde, "The Scot in East New Jersey," *Proceedings*, New
Jersey Historical Society, 4th ser., XV, 1–39; and in "Unpublished Scots East Jersey
Proprietors' Letters," *ibid.*, VIII, 4–12.

Their financial interests ran from the five and a quarter "proprietaries" or shares eventually owned by the Sonmans family of Wallyford County, East Lothian, Scotland, to the tenth and even fortieth part into which a "proprietary" (meaning, in terms of land, ten thousand acres) might be divided for purposes of sale or inheritance. In actual operation the control of the government was in the hands of a few (a council representing at least a third of the proprietors), but the disposition of the lands was the concern of the many, who were all tenants in common of the soil, and occupied their time and attention for many years, leading to continuous controversy and the multiplication of law suits.

Outside the towns and to some extent within their boundaries the allotments were prodigal in plan and unmethodical in assignment. Sometimes the lands were sold to purchasers from other colonies, sometimes disposed of by the shareholders among themselves. No uniform rule was adopted, for the proprietors were unable to agree on any consistent course, so that metes and bounds became inextricably confused and continued to be confused for two centuries. Though surveyors were appointed they were rarely competent or efficient. Scores of grants were never surveyed at all, while those that were marked out were frequently inaccurately bounded because of faulty instruments, and at times were lost to sight entirely because of easily obliterated landmarks. Speculators sought lands for re-sale rather than improvement and often appropriated the best sites as more likely to be remunerative. The elaborate instructions, drawn up by the proprietors three thousand miles away, could not be applied with exactness and were rarely obeyed.[1] Even when attempts were made to enforce them the results were confused and often chaotic because those who had purchased of the Indians or held under the Nicolls patents—particularly the Elizabethtown associates—were determined to prevent the proprietors from trespassing

1. There are no less than sixteen papers of one kind or another, 1683–1700, that treat of the apportionment of the land and the collecting of quit-rents, beginning with the "Instructions for such as goe over in summer, 1683" (*Proceedings,* New Jersey Historical Society, 4th ser., VII, 4–11) and extending through the various instructions to the governors and the conditions of plantation (*New Jersey Archives,* I, 434–437, 447–454, 461–462, 470–474, 476–482, 486–487, 492–500, 503–504, 514–516; II, 84–86, 106–113, 124–129, 186–194, 209–213, 344–352; *Journal, passim*) to the end of the proprietary administration of government. The control of the unlocated lands of colony and state did not end in 1702 but has continued, normally at least, to the present day (below, p. 179, note 1).

on their territory and giving away or selling any of the lands within their tracts. Before the end of the century, litigation, destined to last throughout the colonial period, was well under way and turbulence, violence, and even riots foreshadowed an inauspicious future.[1]

These land troubles lay at the very heart of the East New Jersey situation, for they concerned not only the title to the soil but the right of the people at large to have a part in government as well. Those who had come from Long Island and New England and were accustomed to the land habits and governmental practices of the Puritan towns there claimed, not unnaturally, that the lands they had bought were their own and that they owed neither fidelity nor payment to a proprietor. They declared with vehemence that they were freeholders in their own right and not by virtue of any proprietary patent and they strongly objected to the demand, which the proprietors made of the king in 1688, that should the latter surrender their governmental rights to the crown, as they were asked to do at the time the Dominion of New England was established, they should be allowed to retain in East New Jersey the same property rights that were exercised by any lord of the manor in England.[2] These Puritans and their descendants, those who bought of them, and those who held similar views, formed the anti-proprietary party. Over against them were the upholders of the proprietary prerogative, who adhered strictly to the rules laid down in the "Concessions" and "Instructions," who called the Nicolls titles "crazy titles," even though agreeing to the confirmation of some of them, and held that all the lands of the province were legally the property of Berkeley and Carteret, who could dispose of them as they pleased.[3] They insisted further that no land constituted a freehold which was not held by proprietary patent and that the possession of such a patent carried with it the obligation of taking the oath of fidelity and paying a quit-rent. Only by patent could one be seised of a freehold and only by the possession of a freehold could one become a freeholder and therefore qualified to vote and serve as a deputy in the general assembly. The logic of the situation was inescapable, once one accepted the premises, for according to the argument those who denied the rights of the proprietors were automatically disfranchised, unable

1. For the later history of the proprietary land methods see Roome, *The Early Days and Early Surveys of East New Jersey; Board of Trade Journal*, 1749–1753, p. 69.

2. *Calendar State Papers, Colonial*, 1685–1688, §1690. See below, pp. 159, 179.

3. *Ibid.*, 1700, p. 726.

to elect or be elected, to sit in the assembly, or to hold office in the province. However much the disfranchised and their deputies might protest in speech or written paper, they were only "pretended Representatives," as Philip Carteret said in 1681, whose conduct was "a crying sin and doubtless will reach Heaven."[1] As far as the land question was concerned, the contest between the two groups went on unabated long after the proprietary government had come to an end, because the surrender in 1702 was of the government only and not of the soil. It was not finally terminated until the outbreak of the American Revolution.

The controversy over land ownership and its concomitant right to the franchise were not the only troubles that the proprietors were called upon to face in their efforts to populate and build up their province. They were unfortunate in possessing a propriety which had been carved from the larger province of New York and lay, as it were, under its shadow. With this powerful neighbor East New Jersey's relations were at all times strained and often exceedingly unfriendly. All the New York governors from Nicolls to Fletcher resented, and continued to resent, the loss of this portion of the duke's original area and were unceasing in their efforts to recover it and to bring it again under the duke's control. Though Nicolls and Lovelace expressed their indignation only in words, Andros began active operations, strengthened in his convictions by the events

1. Letter from Philip Carteret to Jonas Wood, Elizabethtown, November 19, 1681, containing a declaration by the governor and council of the proprietary rights as defined by the "Concessions" and "Instructions." This declaration is a very clear exposition of the proprietors' side of the case (Huntington Library, HM, 784). It was prepared to justify the dissolution of the house of deputies by the governor and council, November 2, 1681, to which the deputies strongly objected, and should be read in connection with the long controversy which took place between the governor and council and the deputies beginning with October 19 (*New York Colonial Documents*, III, 293–300). The deputies discovered, or thought they had discovered, a discrepancy between the "Concessions" of February 10, 1665, and the "Directions, Instructions, and Orders" of December 6, 1672, whereby the "ffreedomes and Priviledges of the People" were encroached on. In the acrimonious debate which followed this discovery the governor and council "lamented" that "the representatives should be soe shorte sighted that they cannot see that he which runnes may Read" and that as the representatives "bare the shape of men [they] should acknowledge [their] Error." To this the assembly replied that the "Lords would likely never have had a thought of such contradiction of themselves had it not been a bratt begotten in New Jersey to be fed with the groans and Oppressions of the People." The governor and council declared the house to be only a "Pretended house," because some of its members held land without a patent and had not taken the oath of fidelity. Therefore they dissolved it.

that followed the death of Sir George Carteret and the sale of the province in 1680. Then, challenging Philip Carteret's right to exercise authority and jurisdiction "over the king's subjects to their great disturbance in those parts within the bounds" of the duke's patent, he caused Carteret to be seized at Elizabethtown and brought to New York for trial, because the latter refused to deliver the government into Andros' hands. To the latter's disgust a New York jury, twice sent back to reconsider its verdict, declared that Carteret was not guilty of the charge against him.[1] Lady Elizabeth Carteret bade the East New Jerseyites take no orders from Andros and the duke disavowed his governor and recalled him, saying that he had given him no instructions that would warrant so drastic an action. Nevertheless, strictly interpreted, Andros had the law on his side, though in his manner of executing it he was wholly unjustified.

During the next few years the controversy took on a new form, one less governmental than military and commercial. Was East New Jersey, with its lower customs rates and its favorable opportunities for smuggling goods into New York, to be allowed to undermine the trade of the latter city? Was it to be allowed to cut down the revenues of the province at a time when the war with the French and Indians—the "Gallic peril"—was demanding unusual and costly expenditures for the protection of the frontier and the security of its outlying population? Many reasons were at work determining the answer. Dongan and the merchants stressed the trade issue. Others urged the annexation of East New Jersey to New York, in order to widen the area of supply that was absolutely necessary if New York were to prosper. The Privy Council and the Lords of Trade in England, for purposes of defense against the French, were already planning to unite into a single dominion under a single head all the colonies north of Virginia and both the Jerseys were included within the scheme. This plan, which was to result in the erection of the Dominion of New England, was well advanced in 1685, and on April 30, 1686, was recommended by the Privy Council. The business was pushed forward rapidly. The proprietors, upon whom the quo warrantos were served in England, bitterly objected to this attempt to deprive them of their property and in their replies to the Privy Council outlined at length the wrongs they had suffered at the

---

1. *New Jersey Archives,* I, 303–304, 315–316; Leaming and Spicer, pp. 675–686; Danckaerts, *Journal,* pp. 239–244.

hands of the New York authorities. They declared that if the Privy Council insisted they were willing to make, under pressure, a "voluntary" surrender of their governmental rights, but only on certain reservations of control and use of the soil.[1] Whether the king in council ever formally accepted these terms we do not know, for the details of the negotiations are nowhere given; but some understanding must have been reached, for in April, 1688, the surrender took place on the general ground "that many inconveniences and disorders [had] arisen from their [the proprietors'] pretended right to govern," thus showing that twenty-four years after the indenture of 1664 was issued to Berkeley and Carteret the official mind in England was convinced that the grant had been one of land only and not of government. In consequence of this surrender the governor and council of East New Jersey ceased to function, June 19, 1688. Andros, returning to America as the head of the new Dominion, visited the province, August 15, formally took over the administration, and departed the next day. For a period of more than four years, from the summer of 1688 to the autumn of 1692, when the proprietors resumed control, the province was without any resident central organization whatever.[2] Inevitably these years were a time of great confusion and neglect. The towns carried on in local affairs unmolested and those in them who opposed the proprietors—the anti-proprietor group—entrenched themselves more firmly than before. So much for the effect of the annexation of the Jerseys to the Dominion of New England in relaxing and weakening the proprietors' grip on their provinces. The troubles with New York on the commercial side, postponed for the moment by the larger issue, were, however, not yet over. The sequel of that story will be taken up in its proper place.

Even when in full possession of their propriety the twenty-four were none too successful in the men they selected to govern the province and whom they instructed to execute the rules and orders drawn up in England or Scotland for their guidance. The "Fundamental Constitutions" which they sent over in 1683 was a characteristic doctrinaire treatise of the period that proved wholly unwork-

1. *Calendar State Papers, Colonial,* 1685–1688, §§10, 23, 186, i, 261, 304, 319, 2112, pp. 322, 327, 433, 499. For the conditions and reservations of the proprietors, §§1014, 1342, 1690, 1737, 1822; *Calendar Treasury Books,* VIII, pp. 1627, 1995, 2057.
2. Leaming and Spicer, pp. 604–605; *New Jersey Archives,* XIII, 187; *New York Colonial Documents,* III, 554

able and was never put into practice;[1] while the many schemes laid down for the granting of land and the collecting of quit-rents, though less academic because based on proprietary experience elsewhere, were almost equally impracticable.[2] Attempts made to enforce them in East New Jersey kept the colonists there in such a constant state of uncertainty as to lead to discontent and at times to open rebellion. The first nominee as governor, Robert Barclay of Urie, controversialist and theologian, was hardly of the stuff from which colonial governors should be molded, and the proprietors seemed so well aware of his unfitness as an administrator that they allowed him to remain in Scotland for life and to name deputies for actual service in the province. Barclay appointed in succession four men, Thomas Rudyard, Gawan Lawrie, Lord Neill Campbell, and Andrew Hamilton, the first two of whom maintained with difficulty a measure of peace, while the third, in office but three months (October 20–December 28, 1686), though guided by the advice of a strong council, made little impression on the course of events. He soon returned to Scotland, nominating Hamilton as deputy governor in his place. This nomination was confirmed by Governor Barclay and Hamilton served as deputy until the surrender in 1688. Two years after Barclay's death in 1690, on the resumption of proprietary control in the province, he was commissioned chief governor and remained in office until 1698. Then doubts having arisen as to the right of a Scot to hold office in the colonies, because of certain words in the navigation act of 1696, he was supplanted[3] by Jeremiah Basse, himself a proprietor who had been the agent in West New Jersey for the West Jersey Society, of which more anon. Basse was a merchant living in Burlington, an active and none too scrupulous trouble maker, whose qualifications for the post are not readily apparent. If Hamilton's right to be governor was clouded by his Scottish birth that of Basse was always doubtful because his commission had been signed by only ten instead of sixteen proprietors, as their by-law demanded, and because neither he nor any of the other governors

1. In 1686 Deputy Governor Lawrie made inquiry as to "the scheme of Governm[t] formerly given them" and received from the house of deputies the answer that the Fundamental Constitutions "Did not agree w[th] the Constitu[c]on of this province and that they understood that the same were noe wise binding except past into a law by the General Assembly." *New Jersey Archives*, XIII, 158. See also *Journal of Governor and Council*, pp. 80, 125–126, 128, 131.

2. *Ibid.*, 162–163.

3. *Ibid.*, II, 176; *Calendar State Papers, Colonial*, 1696–1697, p. 565.

had met, to the satisfaction of the English authorities, all the requirements regarding oath, bond, and royal confirmation imposed by the navigation acts.[1] Basse's legal standing in the colony was never quite secure, for large numbers of the people of East and West New Jersey—of both of which provinces he was the governor—refused to accept him.[2] When therefore the crown lawyers finally decided that a man was not barred from colonial office because he was a Scotsman, the proprietors reinstated Hamilton. Basse retired to his plantation[3] and Hamilton remained as governor until his death in April, 1703.

Hamilton, Basse, and the proprietors of both East and West New Jersey fell on evil times, characterized, both within and without the provinces, by cross currents and violent controversies. Within, the people were divided into the Hamilton and Basse factions, corresponding closely to the proprietary and anti-proprietary parties, though political and religious factors entered in to prevent the groups from being identical. The Hamilton faction was the stronger and the more numerous in West New Jersey where the Quakers led by Samuel Jennings were determined to get rid of Basse, while the Basse faction dominated the eastern division where the land question was still a burning issue, as it had never been in the western section. Outside the province, the relations with New York, which had been strained for a quarter of a century, almost reached a break-

---

1. Leaming and Spicer, pp. 591–593, 605; *Journal*, p. 196.

2. Tanner, *Province of New Jersey*, p. 93; *Calendar State Papers, Colonial*, 1696–1697, §§814, 947. Little is known of Basse's antecedents. The statement, first made by Lewis Morris, his bitter opponent, and frequently repeated, that he was originally "an Anabaptist minister" (*New York Colonial Documents*, IV, 34; *Proceedings*, New Jersey Historical Society, IV, 120) does not comport very well with his own account of his early seafaring experiences, with his capture by pirates off Porto Rico, and with his intimate knowledge of pirates and piracy before 1697 (*Calendar State Papers, Colonial*, 1696–1697, §1203). He turned Anglican later and became a warden and lay reader in St. Mary's church at Burlington (Hills, *History of the Church at Burlington*, p. 233). In many ways his was a contradictory character, compact of self-confidence, strong partisanship, and a fondness for political intrigue, mixed with much piety and apparent good intentions. He never had the confidence of a majority of the New Jersey people and was always at odds with Bellomont, who called him "a known profligate fellow and remarkable for lying" (*New York Colonial Documents*, IV, 778; V, 205).

3. So said Randolph in 1698, but in 1702 the Board of Trade gave as one reason for not appointing him to the New Jersey council that he had no estate in the province that the board ever heard of (*Calendar State Papers, Colonial*, 1697–1698, §814; *New York Colonial Documents*, IV, 966). The board was wrong, Basse had property in the colony.

ing point with a quarrel over the eastern boundary and with the mimic commercial war, which found its cause in the determination of the proprietors to make Perth Amboy a port of entry on a par with the port of New York itself. The boundary issue, which concerned the ownership of Staten Island and adjoining waters, was not unlike, though on a smaller scale, that between Maryland and Pennsylvania, because there are those today who think that in each case the dispute should have been settled differently, and that just as parts of Pennsylvania and Delaware should belong to Maryland so of right Staten Island should be a part of New Jersey and the division of the waters should lie to the east and not the west of that island.[1]

The prolonged bickering which took place over the commercial status of Perth Amboy and the right of the proprietors to have a customs port independent of New York came to a head in 1698, when Bellomont ordered the seizure of the ship *Hester,* owned and freighted by Basse and his brother-in-law John Lofting, a merchant of London and one of the proprietors. The vessel had come in without entering at New York and was preparing to go out with the same disregard of New York's claim that its customs officials were the only ones qualified to give clearance papers. Bellomont offered to restore the ship if Basse would have her properly cleared, but Basse refused, saying that the proprietors had positively forbidden him "to enter, clear, give bond, security, or anything that [would] pay an acknowledgment [to the port of New York], either for the *Hester* or any other vessel.[2] Acting on the "positive and unanimous Opinions" of his council,[3] Basse not only made no attempt to retake the ship, but resolved not to meddle or concern himself in the matter, justifying himself by shifting all responsibility to the shoulders of the proprietors in England. But the latter made no headway in their attempt to obtain relief or to reach a compromise and were finally convinced that the only way to secure a decision binding on

1. *Proceedings,* New Jersey Historical Society, VIII; X, 89–158; I, 2d ser., 31–36. The agreement between New York and New Jersey in 1833, whereby the eastern boundary line of New Jersey was placed west of Staten Island, apparently rests on the presumption that the Kill van Kull is one of the mouths of the Hudson River. This view of the case was taken in New York in 1697, when the governor and council there demanded the right to collect customs duties on all goods belonging to East New Jersey "that came within the Hudson River" (*Calendar State Papers, Colonial,* 1696–1697, §1308). See below, pp. 180–181.

2. *Ibid.,* 1699, §116, iv, v.   3. *New Jersey Archives,* XIII, 244–245.

all would be for Basse and Lofting to bring an action of trover and conversion on a feigned issue before the court of king's bench at Westminster Hall. The trial took place during Easter term, 1700, Basse and Lofting, plaintiffs, versus Bellomont, defendant. The verdict of the jury was for the plaintiffs, with damages and costs amounting to £1890, a sum that was paid not by Bellomont but by the English Treasury itself.[1] The victory came, however, too late to be of service. Two years later the proprietors surrendered their provinces, and Perth Amboy, regarding whose commercial future so many hopes had been raised, sank into obscurity, completely overshadowed by her powerful neighbor.

In the meantime West New Jersey was receiving its meed of settlers and entering the group of the growing colonies. After Berkeley had sold his portion of the original grant to John Fenwick in trust for Edward Byllinge and before negotiations had been completed for the formal division of the territory by the Quintipartite Deed of 1676, Fenwick in the late summer of 1675 set sail from England in the *Griffith* (Captain Griffin, master), with his family and others, friends and servants, for the purpose of inspecting and occupying his new purchase. They landed in September or October on the eastern shore of the Delaware River, near the bend where the river opens into the bay, at a place which he called Salem. Two years later, after a series of troublesome disputes had been settled through Penn's mediation, other families arrived and there was set up an independent propriety or colony, with Fenwick as its lord and chief proprietor. Lands were obtained of the Indians and distributed to purchasers, some of whom, in order to provide funds for the voyage, had put down their money before Fenwick left England. Additional lands continued to be acquired and sold until Fenwick's death in December, 1683.[2]

The causes of the disputes just mentioned were various. At first Fenwick refused to accept the one-tenth share allotted him by Penn as his recompense for the trusteeship. He wanted two-tenths. Even after he had given way on this point he was obliged, on account of

---

1. See Note at the end of the chapter, and *Calendar Treasury Books,* XV, Index, s.v. "Bass."

2. Smith, *History of Nova-Caesaria* (1765, reprinted 1890), ch. V; Johnson, *First Settlement of Salem* (1839); the same, "Memoir of John Fenwicke," *Proceedings, New Jersey Historical Society* (1846), IV, 53–89; "Parentage of Fenwick," *Pennsylvania Magazine,* XLIX, L; Schourds, *Fenwick's Colony* (1876); "Fenwick's Proposal for Planting a Colony," *Pennsylvania Magazine,* VI, 86–90.

financial difficulties, to mortgage or lease what remained unsold of his tenth to two Quaker friends, Eldridge and Warner, thus impairing his own title. Furthermore, by Penn's decision, he was to be given £900 by Penn, Lucas, and Lawrie to compensate him for his outlay in buying the remaining nine-tenths, a sum that he thought inadequate on the ground that it cheated him out of the greater part of his estate. In the second place, he was determined to maintain his propriety—with its courts leet and baron, its payment of quit-rents, and its oath of fidelity[1]—as a separate community, outside of and independent of the proprietary control of the other nine-tenths. For six years he stood aloof, refusing to conform to the demands and to accept the authority of the West New Jersey proprietors. He charged them and their agents with frequent acts of injustice, physical and mental, and an unrighteous desire, very unbecoming of Quakers, to deprive him of what he considered his honest rights. The insecurity of his title was further emphasized by the aggressive policy of Andros of New York, who in December, 1676, caused him to be seized and taken prisoner, tried at a special court of assizes there, and found guilty of arrogating to himself, "without any Right or title," jurisdiction over territory that lay within the bounds and limits of the duke's patent.[2] Though Andros detained Fenwick in New York for a long period (Fenwick says "two years and about three months") he was compelled finally to let him go and, presumably instructed to that end by the duke, to forbear molesting him further. Not so forbearing, however, were the West New Jersey proprietors. They continued what Fenwick called "their illegal practices and designs," until, wearied and worn by the persistent contention, he made over on March 1, 1682, all the lands of his colony, except 150,000 acres, to Penn, whom he made the guardian of his children, and in 1683, only a few months before his death, accepted

1. That Fenwick intended his propriety to take on a manorial form appears from his erection of the manors of East Fenwick, West Fenwick, and Fenwick's Grove, and his appointment of the Swede, Erick Vearnens, as the reeve or bailiff of the West Fenwick manor. It appears also from the occasional references to courts leet and baron, to the steward of these courts, to the oath of "faithfulness" to himself, and to the rents as determined by the "Concessions" of 1665 (Johnson, *Salem*, pp. 24, 27, 34, 44, 65, 66–67; *Pennsylvania Magazine*, V, 329; *New Jersey Archives*, I, 371; XXI, 569). Fenwick's father was the lord of a manor in Northumberland.

2. Johnson, *Salem*, p. 38; *New Jersey Archives*, I, 186–192, 236–239; *Proceedings*, New Jersey Historical Society, II, 8–21, IV, 79–80; *New York Colonial Documents*, XII, 559, 565–569, 595–600, 602, 610.

an election as a deputy to the assembly at Burlington, thus recognizing the jurisdiction of that body over his own portion.[1] His efforts,
prolonged for eight years, to set up an independent propriety based
on a manorial plan had completely failed.

A final judgment in Fenwick's case is arrived at with difficulty
because of the obscurity that surrounds the various business transactions in which he was concerned. Did he out of his own pocket provide the money for the purchase of Berkeley's portion, as he says
he did, or did Byllinge put up the money and pay Fenwick for administering the property? If the former, then the understanding
must have been that Fenwick was to be in some way recouped for
his outlay; if the latter, as some New Jersey writers think (one of
them says bluntly, but without offering any proof therefor, "Byllinge
furnished the purchase money"),[2] then the transactions that followed
are not easy to understand. Byllinge's trustees—Penn, Lucas, and
Lawrie—later paid Fenwick £916 for nine-tenths of the land and
gave him in addition the remaining tenth, which in money would
be the equivalent of £100, the whole amounting to the £1000 paid
for the Berkeley property. In this case Fenwick could have had no
claim to anything more than his one-tenth.[3] But, as we have seen
already, the title even to the one-tenth was not clear, though Fenwick always seemed to ignore that fact. His mortgage or lease to
Eldridge and Warner, according to the view which they took of
the matter, gave them absolute ownership and deprived Fenwick
of all "title or equitable interest in any foot of land there."[4] This
lease, in a curiously roundabout way, Eldridge and Warner transferred to William Penn, thus placing him in possession of such parts

1. Leaming and Spicer, pp. 457, 469. John Fenwick and nine others appeared for
Salem tenth and "freely consented" to conform to the Fundamentals. The assembly
passed an act, "by agreement of John Fenwick and the people of Salem liberty,"
confirming Salem bounds, which were to "stand and be forever, to and for the only
use, behoof and benefit of the Freeholders of the said Town of Salem" (ibid., pp.
461–462). This confirmation placed Salem in a preferred position of semi-independ-
ence in the colony, with power to collect its own rates, to make laws for the general
good of its inhabitants, and to enjoy a separate jurisdiction of its own.

2. Proceedings, New Jersey Historical Society, new ser., XV, 534.

3. The statement of the trustees is to be found in a letter indited by Penn, Lawrie,
and Lucas to the members of the Society of Friends in 1676, printed in New Jersey
Archives, I, 231–235; Narratives of Early Pennsylvania, West New Jersey and Delaware (Original Narratives), pp. 182–185; and Pennsylvania Magazine, V, 316–319.
This letter does not, however, clear up all the disputed points. An outline of the
various transactions, 1674–1707, is in Pennsylvania Magazine, V, 327–328.

4. Harleian, 7001, f. 301b.

of Fenwick's tenth as had not already been granted away. If this statement of the case is correct, then Fenwick's charges against Penn seem unjustifiable, for it is quite manifest that Penn and his fellow trustees were suspicious of Fenwick and doubted his integrity. Final conclusions cannot be reached, for we have the evidence for only one side of the case. How much allowance is to be made for the irresistible desire, everywhere felt among these early colonists—whether Puritan, Quaker, or other—for possession of land in the wide spaces of the new world and how much for the less commendable motives underlying the desire to obtain and exercise political authority we cannot determine. Just as Rhode Island absorbed the Coddington colony and Connecticut absorbed New Haven, and just as Massachusetts annexed Maine, and New York prevented the erection of independent jurisdictions in Long Island, so the West New Jersey proprietors took over the Fenwick colony, not only because of what they claimed was their legal right but in the interest of unity and strength as well. A manorialized propriety, such as Fenwick conceived for western New Jersey, based on a defective title and modeled after a seignorial plan, could hardly have survived long in the face of the tide of popular opposition to proprietary and feudal forms of government everywhere rising in the English colonies of seventeenth-century America. The movements of the eighteenth century were against the king and his prerogatives; those of the century before were against proprietary rule.

According to Penn's decision, in the arbitration between Fenwick and Byllinge, the latter was to retain nine of the ten parts into which, as a matter of convenience, Berkeley's portion was divided. But Byllinge, in debt to many creditors, among whom were Lucas and Lawrie, made over his allotment to these two men, who with William Penn ("though every way unconcerned") were to serve as trustees until all Byllinge's obligations had been cleared. In persuance of their task they met a part of the debt by assignments of land in West New Jersey to certain of the creditors and other parts of the debt by the sale of land to two groups of Quakers—one from Yorkshire and the other from London—on whose behalf they sent over commissioners to prepare the way for settlement. The latter in 1677 laid out the town of Burlington and colonization followed. The first ship, the *Kent*,[1] brought over two hundred and thirty people, the

---

1. *New York Colonial Documents*, XII, 579.

second, the *Willing Mind,* brought sixty or seventy more, and the third, the flyboat *Martha,* added one hundred and fourteen. During the next year others arrived, until in Salem, Burlington, and the country about there may have been five hundred souls, almost all of whom were Quakers, for with the exception of the Swedes, Finns, and Dutch already there, nearly all of the early settlers of West New Jersey were members of the Society of Friends.

The plans drawn up for the government of this Quaker colony are of conspicuous importance. Among the many "concessions" that were wrought out during this era of fundamental ideas and agreements and fashioned in England for use in the colonies by those interested in the proprietary development of colonial grants, none are as worthy of study as are these. Broader and more liberal than the Berkeley and Carteret "Concessions" of 1665, far more appropriate and practical than the "Fundamental Constitutions" of 1683, these "Laws, Concessions, and Agreements" of March 3, 1677, in large part certainly the handiwork of Penn himself, differed from the others not only in the range and depth of their content but in the fact that before the *Kent* left England they were approved and signed by two hundred and twenty-five proprietors, freeholders, and inhabitants of the province of West New Jersey.[1] Not all the signers migrated but all were interested in one way or another in the new colony. This noteworthy document provided for entire liberty of conscience, security from illegal arrest, trial by jury, legal guaranty of individual rights, complete control of taxation by the representatives of the voters, a generous system of land grants with quit-rents payable to individual proprietors, recording of all deeds (an innovation not carried out effectively till after 1694), and above all else the calling of a general assembly, the members of which were to be either proprietors or freeholders, and the voters, balloting secretly, were to consist of the entire body of proprietors, freeholders, and inhabitants residing in the province. This assembly was to have supreme powers, with the right to appoint its own time of meeting, right of adjournment, freedom of speech, pay for members, and entire control over legislation within the limits laid down in these fundamentals. The place given to the people of the province appears from the privilege which was granted them of attending the assembly, if they wished to do so after debate was over, and witnessing

1. Leaming and Spicer, pp. 382–411; *New Jersey Archives,* I, 241–270.

the casting of votes and observing the attitude and inclinations of the members voting, a privilege that was extended in 1683 to allow anyone who desired to be present at the first meeting, "provided they stay not to impede the business."[1]

But it was one thing to draft such an idealistic system and quite another to get it to work and when at work to make it function properly. West New Jersey had first to reckon with Andros of New York before its people could settle down to an independent governmental existence. The duke had never confirmed the sale of the Berkeley portion and until he had done so Andros claimed the right to interfere in its affairs. He demanded the payment to New York of all customs dues on goods brought into the province and regularly for three years repeated his demand. In 1680 Byllinge entered a formal protest, asserting that West New Jersey was independent of New York's jurisdiction and therefore exempt from any customs duties that the governor and council there might impose. When the protest came into the hands of the Lords of Trade, they passed it on to the king's attorney general, Sir William Jones, who reported adversely to the duke. James, in compliance, instructed his own attorney general, Sir John Churchill, to prepare the desired document confirming the West New Jersey proprietors in the possession of their property.[2] This document was a release, drawn up on August 6, 1680, signed and sealed by the duke on September 3, though the royal confirmation did not come until two years later.[3] It was des-

1. Leaming and Spicer, p. 482. The suggestion has been made and with reason that the various "Concessions" and "Agreements" of this period represent an attempt to put into practical operation some of the political, social, and legal ideas contained in Harrington's *Oceana*, a book which had a considerable vogue in England after its first appearance in 1656 (H. F. Russell Smith, *Harrington and his Oceana, a Study of a 17th Century Utopia and its Influence in America*, 1914, ch. VIII). Mr. Smith thinks that Harrington influenced especially Shaftesbury, Penn, and Locke, "the three greatest prophets of civil and religious liberty in the age of Restoration." It is possible to believe that these three men were in large part the authors of the various documents of this kind to which reference is so often made in this volume. Mr. Smith's work is the outgrowth of an earlier essay, *The Theory of Religious Liberty in the Reigns of Charles II and James II* (1911).

2. *New Jersey Archives*, I, 323-324; *New York Colonial Documents*, III, 284-286; *Calendar State Papers, Colonial*, 1677-1680, §1479.

3. Byllinge's title is traced in C. O. 389:8, pp. 245-246. The king in his sign manual, after reciting his own grant to the Duke of York, says, "Our sayd Dearest Brother hath likewise given and granted part of the sayd lands called West New Jersey unto Edward Byllinge Gent with Powers necessary for the good Government thereof which Governm.t he the sayd Edward Bylinge intends to undertake himself in his own person. We do approve of that his undertaking and have thought fitt

patched by a ship which reached the province before the middle of October, and conveyed the news not only that the West New Jersey ports were legally free but also that James in confirming possession had settled the government on Byllinge himself.[1] The latter did not come over but appointed as his deputy Samuel Jennings, who had arrived in the colony the month before.

Jennings the next year summoned an assembly—"a general free assembly chosen by the free people" of the province—which, as its first act, defined the status and powers of the deputy governor and made it perfectly clear that he was lawfully to do nothing in the execution of his office without the consent of the popular body or against the liberties and properties of the people themselves. When this act was agreed to Jennings was formally acknowledged the deputy governor of the province.[2] The assembly, consisting of deputy governor, council, and deputies continued until 1701 to meet regularly every year at Burlington, in spring and autumn sessions, with the exception of the years 1686–1692 for which no records have been discovered. This general assembly selected the justices and all administrative officials and passed laws for the good of the colony. Probably before and certainly after 1683,[3] the electors were not all the male inhabitants but only the freeholders, and representation was by tenths until 1694 and after that by counties. The peculiarly Quakerish language of the original fundamentals soon disappeared from the wording of the acts and legislative procedure and enactments followed the customary form and phraseology common to

hereby to publish Our will and pleasure That all persons settled and Inhabiting or that hereafter shall settle and Inhabit within the limits of the s^d Province of West New Jersey do yeild all due regard to him the sayd Edward Bylyng as Governor, and to his Deputies and Agents, according to the powers and Authorityes legally granted unto him by our sayd Dearest Brother, with which Our Will and Pleasure We expect and require a ready complyance from all persons whom it may concerne as they tender Our Displeasure." November 15, 1683. Byllinge would appear, therefore, to have had some warrant for his exercise of the powers of government, but after all his warrant was no better than that of the East New Jersey proprietors, whose rights in this particular were denied as without legal standing. The various English authorities would seem to have been coördinating badly.

1. Robert Smythe writing to Byllinge, April 20, 1681, said, "Now that illegal impositions of customs is taken off, the port and country made free, and the government thereof settled on yourself," etc. *Proceedings,* New Jersey Historical Society, new ser., XV, 529.

2. Smith, *History of New Caesaria,* pp. 126–129; Leaming and Spicer, pp. 423–425.

3. *Ibid.,* p. 478.

similar bodies elsewhere. The freedom of the assembly as a popular body was seriously restricted by the fact that West New Jersey was a proprietary province and that the proprietors as well as the freeholders had a right to share in the government.

By the duke's release of 1680 Byllinge was recognized as the true and absolute proprietor of the province, but the same question came up that was raised in East New Jersey regarding his right to control the government. In 1683 the deputies "at an open and free conference" challenged his nomination of Jennings and themselves elected Jennings governor and chose the members of his council. They accompanied this challenge with the draft of a paper, to be submitted to the Friends in England, containing a statement of the case and the reasons why "the proprietors of this Province, with Edward Byllinge" should not be allowed to interfere with "the Peoples legal and equitable right to the Government."[1] They sent over Jennings, who was undoubtedly the leader in this revolt against proprietary interference, to negotiate and present the paper, and chose Thomas Olive governor in his place. But this effort to throw off the proprietary incubus failed. On November 15, 1683, Charles II confirmed the appointment of Byllinge as governor and the latter, ignoring Jennings and the deputies, sent over John Skene as his deputy and with him a "new charter" reinforcing the right of the proprietors to cast proxy votes in the assembly.[2] The deputies accepted Skene, "reserving their just Rights and Privileges," but they postponed consideration of Byllinge's "charter" and the matter of the proxies until a later time. Apparently they put it off permanently, for at this juncture the curtain drops on their proceedings for eight years. How much of this time was consumed in dissent and controversy and how much in a complete closing down of all legislative activities, due to the annexation of the province to the Do-

1. *Ibid.*, pp. 472, 483, 485, 490, 497, 499, 505. Governor Jennings and many other Quakers removed to Philadelphia where Jennings remained until 1698. What Gawan Lawrie thought about him can be inferred from the letter of James Claypoole to Lawrie, February 24, 1684, *Pennsylvania Magazine*, X, 408.

2. C. O. 389:8, pp. 245–246. The proceedings of assembly (Leaming and Spicer, p. 505) speak of the "new Grant from the late Duke of York (now king) of Soil and Government to Edward Byllinge, and also the Instrument from Edward Bylling, and Proprietors." The only document that appears to be extant corresponding to the "new Grant" is the king's confirmation of November 15, 1683 (above, p. 154). There may have been another grant from the Duke of York, but I have not been able to trace it or to find any further reference to it.

minion of New England in 1688 and other causes, there is no way of finding out. When the curtain rises the date is November 3, 1693, and the governor is Andrew Hamilton, the recently appointed governor of East New Jersey.

Briefly what had happened was this. In 1685 Byllinge died and two years later by deeds of lease and release his proprietary rights were purchased by Dr. Daniel Coxe,[1] a London physician and merchant, and a land promoter on a large scale. Governor Nicholson spoke of him as "an honest gentleman and a very good doctor." In consequence of this purchase Coxe became the heir to all Byllinge's property rights in West New Jersey and, after consultation with Byllinge's trustees and with members of the legal fraternity decided that he possessed rights of government also. Therefore he assumed the title of hereditary governor as well as that of chief proprietor. He even considered the possibility of going over to the colony himself and exercising the functions of governor in person, but was persuaded by his friends not to do so. He appointed at least two deputy governors, Hunloke and Tatham, but apparently made no effort to bring about a meeting of the "free general assembly," so that the serious objections raised at the time against Tatham as a Jacobite and High Churchman (if not a Roman Catholic) came from individuals and not from a legislative body. General affairs were managed by the deputy governor and his council and local affairs were looked after by the town and "tenth" authorities, who had been left undisturbed by Andros in 1688. The years from 1685 to 1692 seem to have been a time of proprietary executive government.[2] The distribution of land and the determining of land titles

1. Scull, "Biographical Notice," *Pennsylvania Magazine,* VII, 317–337. Coxe was born in 1640 and died in 1730. After Byllinge's death he wrote to the remaining proprietors giving the reasons for his purchase (Smith, *History of Nova-Caesaria,* p. 140, note K; *New Jersey Archives,* II, 4–9). The details of the purchase are too involved for examination here, but can be followed in *New Jersey Archives,* II, 47–56. Apparently Coxe bought a part of Byllinge's land in 1684, before Byllinge's death.

2. This conclusion seems justified by the complete absence not only of records of laws and proceedings but even of references to an assembly during these years. One is, therefore, perplexed by the following entry in one of the laws passed in 1693, "Whereas for several Years past, there hath been held Yearly and every Year at Burlington a General Assembly at two several Times in the Year," etc. (Leaming and Spicer, p. 510). Such a statement would seem to imply that the assembly had been meeting every year, but it may be merely a general remark covering past experience. The anti-renters said in 1700 that the proprietors had left the people without any government from 1689 to 1692 (*Calendar State Papers, Colonial,* 1700, §908, i) and we know that no general assemblies were called in any of the colonies that made

were in the hands of a council of proprietors, a body set up in the province, February 14, 1687-1688, to act on behalf of the widely scattered, unwieldy proprietary group, which as a whole had proved hopelessly incapable of coping with the rapidly increasing division and subdivision of proprietary shares.[1]

Coxe maintained his connection with West New Jersey for about five years, 1687-1692, and continued as one of the proprietors until the end. His holdings were large and he was assiduous in his efforts to lease or to sell, through his agents, John Tatham and others in Burlington, to all that he could. He issued alluring prospectuses for the purpose of attracting emigrants, planned to expand the whale and codfisheries already established at Cape May, to tap the fur traffic of the Northwest, and to start a "circular trade" between West New Jersey, the other colonies, and the West Indies. He began a fruit plantation at Cape May and a pottery at Burlington for "white and chiney ware" ("earthenware" it is elsewhere called), erected a pottery house in Burlington for the purpose, and sent over pottery workers from England to run it. He made the town of Burlington the residence of his deputy governor and land agents and the center of the industrial activity of the province and in so doing prepared the way for the grant to it of special self-governing privileges by the general assembly in 1693.[2]

But the whole undertaking proved too vast and intricate for one man to master. Meeting with ill success in his business ventures and discouraged by the annexation of the province to the Dominion of New England in 1688, he sold out, in the form of a tripartite indenture, March 4, 1692, to a group of forty-eight men, chiefly merchants of London, who took the name of the West Jersey Society, most of whose stockholders were members of the Church of England thereby

up the Dominion of New England. We have definite mention, however, of an assembly meeting in 1692 (Leaming and Spicer, pp. 513, 534; New York Colonial Documents, III, 840).

1. Smith, History of Nova-Caesaria, pp. 199–207.

2. "Dr. Daniel Coxe his account of New Jersey" and other documents from Bodleian, Rawlinson C, 128 ff. 42–47. Coxe estimated his various holdings at a million acres, of which 400,000 were surveyed and the Indian purchase complete, the remainder surveyed but not purchased. Further information can be obtained from New Jersey Archives, XXI, 315–317, 434–436. For the pottery enterprise, ibid., 440, where we are told that Coxe formed a partnership in London for the purpose and on August 23, 1688, arranged with William Gill, potter servant, to go over with John de Wilde of London, citizen and potter, as his assistant. See also Proceedings, New Jersey Historical Society, 2d ser., XII, 68–70.

destroying the Quaker supremacy in the western province. The price paid was £9800, of which £4800 was to be cash down on the delivery of the release and £5000 secured by a mortgage for one year on a third of the estate.[1] This society, itself the "governor and commander in chief," made Hamilton, also a proprietor, its deputy governor in the province (1692), thus bringing both the Jerseys under one executive head, and it authorized the summons of a general assembly on November 3, 1692, the first, as far as we know, in seven years. This assembly, composed of governor, council, and deputies, continued to meet annually in the spring until 1701.

Acting through this provincial body and other local agencies, the West Jersey Society accomplished much. It continued the work which Coxe had advanced of promoting the whale fishery, planned the erection of distilleries and the adding of wine and brandy to the colony's staples, and encouraged trading voyages, many of which had already been undertaken down the Delaware and coastwise as far south as Virginia. Sir Thomas Lane, the chief man of the society, formed a company in England for the production of naval stores. The real estate transactions of the society were continuous and without limit and the sales turnover frequent and almost bewildering. Through its resident factors-general, Jeremiah Basse, Nathaniel Westland, and, later, Andrew Hamilton, its trustee Thomas Revell, and its surveyor William Emley, it engaged in land sales not only in its own province, but in East New Jersey as well, where it owned two and a half shares in Middlesex and Somerset counties. It encouraged migration from nearby communities and from as far away as Connecticut and Bermuda, and it found purchasers for its land in nearly every colony of the day. It started a small boom in real estate on its reserved lands in Cape May county, where it sold to yeomen, mariners, sea-captains and others in the whale fishery, on easy terms calling for the payment of a small quit-rent, such as an ear of Indian

---

1. *New Jersey Archives,* II, 41–63; XXI, 316–317, 436–438, 454, where are given abstracts of the contents of the lease, which took the form of a tripartite indenture. Sir Thomas Lane, the first in the list of names, was an alderman of London, as was also Sir John More, who came into the society later (*ibid.,* XXI, 326, 327, 330). Gabriel Thomas dedicated to them and the rest of the West New Jersey proprietors his *Historical and Geographical Account* published in 1698 (*Proceedings,* New Jersey Historical Society, new ser., VIII, 1; *Narratives of Early Pennsylvania,* Original Narratives, p. 338). Paul Docminique, afterward (1714–1735) a member of the Board of Trade, was one of them, serving on their committees, and owning land in the province (*New Jersey Archives,* III, 51 and elsewhere; XXI, 331).

corn or a capon or two, "payable to the Society as Lords of the Mann^r of Cox Hall."[1]

The land arrangements under which the society operated were, generally speaking, more complicated than was the case in East New Jersey. The undivided areas were reckoned at one hundred shares of 13,000 acres each (a propriety equaling one one-hundredth of the province), while in East New Jersey the proprietary lands were rated at only twenty-four shares of 10,000 acres each. Titles in West New Jersey were derived from a greater variety and number of grantors, as proprietary ownership changed, split up, and fell into so many hands that at times it was difficult to trace the original source and ownership became uncertain and its background obscure. In both provinces sales of fractional parts—one thirty-sixth, one twenty-fourth, one half of one twentieth, or one eighth of one thirty-second of a share—appear among the entries. In the case of a plantation where minerals were evidently thought to exist, we find reservations or sales of one-eighth, seven-eighths, and three-eighths. For these and other reasons the land records of the province are a muddle of perplexity.

But to the proprietors, a large number of whom were common to the two groups,[2] though the membership was legally quite distinct, the problem of government ("the chiefest motive," said those of East New Jersey, "of purchasing the said province") was more trouble-some even than the confusion of the land system. In East New Jersey, according to the statement of the proprietors there, they had spent the greater part of their estates in planting and building up the country, without any returns whatever for their labor and costs. Not only were the anticipated receipts from patents and quit-rents disap-pointing but both groups were badly behind in their payment of the annual rent of ten nobles due the crown at Middle Temple Hall, London. With the financial situation thus depressing, unexpectedly the proprietors discovered a growing dissatisfaction among the au-

1. *Ibid.*, 458–459. There were many manors in East and West New Jersey, such as Tinton manor, Sonmans manor, Hutchinson's manor, and the Fenwick manors. These manors were probably little more than estates of land or plantations, though there are occasional references to courts leet and baron and of lands "late appendant to said manor" (*ibid.*, 518, 569). On the whalery, Leaming and Spicer, pp. 519–520.

2. The Board of Trade said in 1699 that the West New Jersey proprietors were "for the most part the same persons" as made up the East New Jersey group (*Calendar State Papers, Colonial*, 1699, p. 396).

thorities in England with the whole system of proprietary and corporate colonies and were called upon to face the determination of the Privy Council and the Board of Trade to enforce the navigation acts and for that purpose to get rid, if possible, of the private colonies altogether. This determination opened up the whole question of the right of proprietary government in the Jerseys.

Though the proprietors had convinced themselves that the right of government was legally lodged in their hands, albeit for a quarter of a century that right had been challenged in one quarter or another, they were now, almost for the first time, brought to realize how insecure that right, when brought to the test, really was.[1] When in 1699 they wanted to appoint Andrew Hamilton the governor of both provinces and to that end petitioned the Board of Trade asking for the king's approval, they were dismayed to learn that the board would make no recommendation to the crown until the question of government had been settled. They learned further that the board was thoroughly annoyed because of the conflict with New York over the Perth Amboy issue and because of the fact that the members of the East New Jersey group, both in England and America, were divided among themselves and were by no means agreed as to what governor to appoint. One faction desired the return of Hamilton and another favored Captain Andrew Bowne, a Middletown man probably related to John Bowne, one of those mixed up with the James Carteret affair. This second faction actually commissioned Bowne and sent him over to publish his authority. The Board of Trade was in something of a quandary. It saw in the prevailing discord among the proprietors ample evidence of incompetence and inefficiency and with its mind set on a more unified and centralized plan of colonial control it refused to do anything that would strengthen the proprietors in their rule of the Jerseys. Probably no one of the proprietary groups in America had so little to say in its own defense or was so hopelessly out of accord with the English

---

1. The proprietors of East New Jersey claimed that the question of the right to govern the province had been settled when Fletcher was appointed governor of New York. At that time Dr. Coxe had opposed the mention of West New Jersey as a dependency of New York and succeeded in having the name of the province left out of Fletcher's commission (*ibid.*, 1689–1692, §2071, i; 1699, §§229, 855; 1700, §985; 1701, §1082; *Acts Privy Council, Colonial*, II, §437). But the insertion of an equivalent phrase "the territory thereon depending" neutralized his success and left the question open.

policy of the time as were the proprietors of East and West New Jersey.[1]

In the provinces themselves conditions were even worse. The proprietors there, some of whom lived outside the Jerseys, were no more agreed on what they wanted than were their fellow proprietors in England and Scotland. The Hamilton group, which opposed Basse in West New Jersey and Bowne in East New Jersey were, all told, probably in the majority, overwhelmingly so in the west division. There the Quakers, led by Samuel Jennings, whom his opponents called "that bigoted Quaker," had come out for Hamilton and the king, and in their intense dislike of Basse had tried in 1698, after Basse had been appointed governor, to "overthrow the Government" at Burlington, driving Basse from office and putting Jennings in his place.[2] In East New Jersey the faction led by Bowne corresponded to the old anti-renters, that is, to those who held by title from Nicolls and by purchase from the Indians, against whom the proprietors had been compelled to proceed by distraint and eviction. The members of this group now sent petitions to England against Hamilton and in favor of Basse, fortifying their argument by references to Hamilton's failure to receive the king's approval and to the fact that as a Scot he was barred from holding office. One of these petitions was signed by two hundred and twenty-four persons and another from Elizabethtown by sixty-five. This faction may be called, if one likes, the popular party, but it must be remembered that, except for Middletown and Shrewsbury, the towns were by no means unanimous in their political affiliations and that the cohesive element binding the members of this party together was less political principle than the menace to their land titles, their pocket books, and their economic and social prosperity. Doubtless there were those among them of New England origin who objected to proprietary rule on principle as opposed to self-government and the rights of Englishmen. In this respect they were in the same class with their fellow insurgents of Maryland and New York.[3]

The result of these factional antagonisms was anarchy in the Jer-

1. The documents in the case may be found in *New Jersey Archives,* II, and the *Calendar State Papers, Colonial,* for the years from 1699 to 1701. A few of them are printed in Leaming and Spicer and in the *Journal,* pp. 228, 229–230, 231–233.

2. *New Jersey Archives,* XXI, 513; *Calendar State Papers, Colonial,* 1702, §928, i.

3. *New Jersey Archives,* II, 124–129; Leaming and Spicer, pp. 688–689; *Calendar State Papers, Colonial,* 1700, §908ƒ i; 1701, §§695, i, 855, i, 1052, 1053.

seys. Basse, who departed for England in December, 1699, reported that the province was in "great confusion" and, speaking for himself and his party, said that there existed a widespread desire among the inhabitants to get rid of the proprietors. Lewis Morris, who sided with Hamilton and the proprietors, declared, on the other hand, that the public peace was violated daily by turbulent people who were impatient of any government whatever and that justice was impeded by seditious complainants and mutinous malcontents, evidently referring to the maltreatment of the proprietors' sheriff by the anti-renters of Middletown, an incident that almost brought on a local war. Bowne and his associates charged the proprietors with arbitrary proceedings and said that the country was in a state of distraction, ready to rise "by whole towns" against their methods of suppressing opposition. All the proprietors could say in reply was that the trouble was fomented by "a few factious and mutinous people, impatient of any government . . . from a design to deprive [the proprietors] of their right to the soile and quit-rents of the Province and to strip His Majesty of his legal rights to that and other plantations and to render them independent of the Crown."[1]

On at least two occasions already the members of the Board of Trade had recommended first to the king (March 26, 1701) and then to the House of Lords (May 8) the resumption by the crown of all the private colonies. They now drew up with great care a special report on the situation in the Jerseys (October 2), and in it rehearsed the familiar facts of government and title, always referring to the proprietary claim to government as "pretended" only. They declared that the existing situation, if allowed to continue, would lead to the destruction of the colony, and that as the proprietors had expressed their willingness to surrender the government the time had come for the king to take over the provinces and to administer them through a governor appointed by himself. They explained that final action had been delayed because of certain conditions imposed by the proprietors relative to their property rights which the Board of Trade could not accept and they recommended that they be required to make an unconditional surrender, leaving all reservations to be

1. *Ibid.*, 1700, §§47, 670, i (attack on the sheriff). Compare the riotous proceedings in one court of sessions at Newark, September 30, 1700, and in another at Middletown, March 25, 1701, *ibid.*, 1701, §§695, vi, vii, 967 (Basse), 985 (proprietors); 1701, §§187, 745, i, ii, iii; Leaming and Spicer, p. 608.

acted on later.[1] The proprietors having agreed to the terms proposed, the articles of surrender were issued April 15, 1702, and accepted by the queen in council two days later.[2] The proprietors yielded up "all their pretences to the said powers of Government" without any reservations whatever, so that it was left to the authorities in England, in drawing up the instructions to the new governor, whoever he should be, to state what these reservations were. This was done in the instructions to Governor Cornbury of New York in 1703. The rule of the proprietors was over and after April 17, 1702, New Jersey became a royal colony of the usual type, with two peculiarities: one, that until 1738 the governor of New York was also the governor of New Jersey, but under a separate commission, so that the political independence of the colony was given legal recognition; and the other, that the meeting of the general assembly alternately at Perth Amboy and Burlington testified to the fact that for more than twenty-five years the Jerseys had been divided into two separate provinces, standing in the same class with Rhode Island and Connecticut as of dual origin, with two capitals during the colonial period and for many years thereafter.

Though giving up their rights of government the proprietors retained full possession of the soil of the provinces. Their ownership in this particular was recognized when in drawing up the instructions to Cornbury the Board of Trade ordered him to obtain from the first assembly called under his commission a law confirming "the right and property of the said general proprietors to the soil of the province . . . together with all such quit-rents as are due and all other privileges, excepting the right of government."[3] This instruction was obeyed and though the assembly was slow to respond and the matter had to be brought before the chancery court in 1745, without ever being judicially settled, the two boards of proprietors in England, perpetuated through their councils in the Jerseys, have continued to exist from that day to this. At the present writing their

1. These conditions may be found in Leaming and Spicer, pp. 589–591 (memorial of July 5, 1699); answer of the Board of Trade (*Calendar State Papers, Colonial,* 1699, §1006) with objections thereto. Lewis Morris on the same subject, §855.

2. Leaming and Spicer, pp. 609–618; *New Jersey Archives,* II, 452–462. King William died on March 8, 1702, so that the acceptance was by Queen Anne. Legally the surrender was in 1702, but as Cornbury did not receive his instructions to take over the government until July 29, 1703, the date 1703 is sometimes given (*New York Colonial Documents,* IV, 1069–1070).

3. *New Jersey Archives,* II, 517.

business has so far dwindled as to leave them little or nothing to do. For years the duties of the boards, which have never been incorporated but have come to be recognized as corporations "by prescription," have been to give quit-claim deeds to parties wishing to complete title. As there is very little unlocated land left, now that the boundary line with New York and the division line between East and West New Jersey have been finally settled, the state before long may purchase the maps and records of the boards and install them permanently at Trenton. When this has been done the boards of proprietors of East and West New Jersey will have come to the end of a long and noteworthy career, one that is unique in the history of our country.[1]

Whatever we may think of proprietary rule in general, there can be no doubt of the baneful results of the duke's casual and almost

1. The present councils or boards of proprietors trace back to the councils created in the provinces by the proprietors in England for the management of their lands in the Jerseys. The West New Jersey council was established, February 14, 1688, "to confirm title to the soil, adjust disputed boundaries, see that dividends of proprietary rights were properly made and disposed of, and to have general charge of the unappropriated lands of the province." It is accustomed to meet in April every year to elect members, five of whom are chosen on April 10 at Burlington and four on the 13th at Gloucester. A right of propriety consists in the ownership of a share or a portion of one of the one hundred shares into which Edward Byllinge's interest in the western division of New Jersey was divided. Meetings are held at Burlington on the first Tuesday of May, August, November, and February, formerly in a little one-storied brick building on Broad Street, now in the surveyor general's office, a new structure erected in 1913-1914. Its rights consist of titles to all "new" lands, that is, to lands, such as sandbars, formed by acts of nature, and to all remnants of land due to faulty surveys. It is usually unwilling that its records should be examined and charges high fees ($10.00) for a search among its papers. Dr. Stevenson speaks of it as "The Great New Jersey Trust." The East New Jersey council meets twice yearly and anyone holding a certain proportionate part of a share is entitled to attend. The annual meeting is held at Perth Amboy, where the records are kept in a small building immediately north of the city hall. A second meeting is held, October 15, at Newark in the rooms of the New Jersey Historical Society. The rights are similar to those of the West New Jersey council, but the charges for a search are lower. Probably both councils would be glad to sell their records to the state, but the price is high, and on this account members of the New Jersey state government would like to find a way whereby the papers could be legally confiscated and properly housed. *Bi-Centennial, Board of Proprietors, East New Jersey, November 25, 1884* (1885), with maps; "Providence Line, 1887," *Report* of the Committee to the Proprietors of West New Jersey, May 1, 1888, with maps; Stevenson, "The Great New Jersey Trust" and "Councils of Proprietors of New Jersey," *Proceedings,* New Jersey Historical Society, 3d ser., VI (1908), 130-135; VII (1913), 129-136; McGregor, "Board of Proprietors of East New Jersey," *ibid.,* new ser., VII (1922), 177-195; Craig, "Council of Proprietors of West Jersey, Origin and History, *Camden History,* Camden County Historical Society (1922), I, no. 3; "Council of Proprietors of West New Jersey," *Pennsylvania Magazine,* XVII, 496-503; private information, 1936.

haphazard grant of the Jerseys to Berkeley and Carteret, for it bene-
fited no one, not even the proprietors themselves, and brought only
trouble, confusion, and discord in its train. The uncertainty of the
right of government, the conflict over the land titles and quit-rents,
the loss of the territory to New York's great injury, the division into
two provinces and the consequent absence of a unified and centralized headship, the conflict over the commercial independence of
Perth Amboy and the ownership of Staten Island, the constant
change of proprietors, their want of agreement, and their lack of
interest for the most part in anything but the revenues from the
soil—all these things made the thirty-eight years of proprietary rule
a time of distraction that checked the normal development of both
provinces and left legacies of litigation lasting on indefinitely. Conspicuous as was the opposition in all the colonies outside Virginia
and New England to proprietary prerogative in matters of government, nowhere were the injurious results more apparent or the ends
sought more futile than in the accidental and whimsical gift of a
duke to his friends.

NOTE: This *cause célèbre*, which made quite a stir at the time among the executive
authorities in England, has hardly received the consideration that it deserves. A brief
chronological statement will help to a better understanding of it. Though the proprietors had sought to obtain the commercial independence of East New Jersey as
early as 1687, the question had not become a practical issue until England began,
toward the end of the century, to enforce more rigorously her customs policy. Andros
said in 1700 that during his governorship (1674–1680) all ships had been obliged
to enter and clear at the port of New York and that the same was true as late as
1688, when he visited the provinces as governor of the Dominion of New England
(*Calendar State Papers, Colonial*, 1700, §§149, 150. He repeated this statement in
his testimony at the time of the trial in England). But after 1692 the proprietors insisted that Perth Amboy was an independent port and refused to accede longer to
New York's demand that East New Jersey ships enter and clear at New York and pay
the local customs dues imposed by the New York assembly. In the summer of 1697
they petitioned the Treasury and the latter referred the petition to the commissioners
of the customs (*Calendar Treasury Books*, XI, 415). The commissioners reported on
August 31 that the issue was a purely local one and did not come under their cognizance (*ibid.*, 1696–1697, §1308), but, they added (in a later report of February 21,
1699), the fact that the Treasury, in its warrant of November 20, 1696, had set apart
Perth Amboy as a port for the collection of the plantation duty, did not exempt the
New Jersey inhabitants from paying local duties to New York, as the proprietors
hoped it did (Treasury 1: LIX, no. 61; *Calendar State Papers, Colonial*, 1699,
§117, i). The proprietors alarmed by this opinion petitioned the lords justices in
council and the petition was referred to the Board of Trade, September 23, 1697.
The proprietors sent a memorial to the board also, October 1, but the board, influenced by an opinion which it obtained from the attorney and solicitor general,
Trevor and Hawles, reported adversely to the proprietors' claim (*New Jersey*

Archives, II, 180–185) and the Privy Council approved the report (*Calendar State Papers, Colonial,* 1697–1698, §69). It ordered the board to instruct the New York governor to permit no goods to pass "up the Hudson River" but what had paid duty at New York City, a witness to the council's knowledge of Hudson River topography, on a par with that of the clerk who placed Perth Amboy "in the West Indies," *Calendar Treasury Books,* XV, 396.

Bellomont and his council, receiving this instruction, showed it to Basse, saying that they intended to construe the Kill van Kull as coming within the phrase "up the Hudson River." When therefore they heard that a vessel, the *Hester,* worth £1500, owned and freighted by Basse and his brother-in-law, John Lofting, one of the proprietors, and by Lofting's partners, had entered from England and was preparing to clear from Perth Amboy for England, loaded with pipe-staves and provisions, worth £800, without regard to New York's demand, they sent some forty or fifty soldiers from one of the independent companies of redcoats in the city to seize the vessel and bring it to New York. There it was condemned and sold by wick of candle to Abraham Depeyster for £315, New York money, the whole sum going to meet the costs of seizure and condemnation (*ibid.,* 1699, §215) and to pay the wages of master and seamen (§280). The proprietors outraged by this act of aggression, on March 9, 1699, again petitioned the Privy Council, protesting against the seizure and sale, and soon after sent in a new memorial to the Board of Trade, pointing out the errors and absurdities in its former report (§205). The board in a quandary, though rejecting all compromises, accepted as the only way out of the dilemma a suggestion which the proprietors had made that, as a last resort, the case be brought before the court of king's bench on a feigned issue, whereby a judicial determination might be had, not only regarding the port issue but regarding the government issue also (*ibid.,* 1699, §§272, 726; *New York Colonial Documents,* IV, 546; *New Jersey Archives,* II, 266–269; report of April 18, 1699; *Journal,* pp. 201–206, 217).

In the meantime Basse, out of office in New Jersey, had gone to England and with Lofting had petitioned the House of Commons for redress. Nothing came of this petition (*New York Colonial Documents,* IV, 605–606; *Calendar State Papers, Colonial,* 1700, §§113, 118; Stock, *Debates,* II, 354–355). Failing in this quarter, they came to an understanding with Bellomont's counsel in England regarding the trial at law, and in Easter term (May 10, 1700) brought an action of trover against Bellomont for the purpose of recovering damages equal to the value of the goods seized (*Calendar State Papers, Colonial,* 1700, §§197, 369, 425, 716, p. 693). The jury found for the plaintiffs, who recovered damages amounting to £1800, with costs of £90, which the Treasury, by warrant of July 17, 1700 (*Calendar Treasury Books,* XV, 63, 93, etc.), ordered paid out of the exchequer. The Board of Trade, chagrined at the outcome, told Bellomont that it could do no more for him. There is in C.O. 5:1044, no. 20, a clerk's report of the proceedings of this trial before the king's bench, with the arguments of the defense and brief rebuttals by the attorneys for the plaintiffs, and the charge of Chief Justice Holt to the jury. For Bellomont appeared the attorney and solicitor general and attorneys Conyers and Cooper; for Basse and Lofting Sergeant Darnell, Sir Bartholomew Shower, recorder of London, and Sir Thomas Powys, while Sir Edmund Andros ("Andrews" as the name is written) was called in and testified. The sympathies of the chief justice are clearly with the plaintiffs, as is seen in the questions which he asked the attorney and solicitor general and in his charge to the jury. He is not convinced that New York ever possessed any independent legislative jurisdiction over the Jerseys. The decision estopped New York from further action, thus confirming Perth Amboy as a free port and seemingly making it clear that the Kill van Kull did not lie either "up the Hudson River" or "within it," and that a vessel going to and from Perth Amboy was not "passing the River of New York" or coming "into the Hudson River," as the defendants claimed.

CHAPTER V

CAROLINA: THE BEGINNINGS

THE first few years of the reign of Charles II reveal incongruities in ideas and practices which, to a greater extent even than in the days of the early Stuarts, play an important part in the history of the American colonies. Charles II had been swept into power on a wave of reaction against the republican experiments of the Commonwealth and the Protectorate, which for the moment submerged the men responsible for them and gave renewed vitality to the doctrine of the divine right and supremacy of kingship. This revival manifested itself in the recrudescence of certain legal principles underlying the proprietary grants of the period, among which was belief in the royal ownership of all lands that remained ungranted by the crown in the *terra regis* of the New World, in the right of the king to do what he liked with his own, and in the prerogative of the king's advisers to say what form these grants should take. Sometimes these forms were archaic or even obsolete in that they revived models and formulae medieval in origin, but their importance for us lies in the fact that they testify to the weight given at the time to the king's royal will and pleasure, which in the first full flush of his newly acquired popularity was recognized by an overwhelming majority of the people of England as the spring of all action and the legal source of all authority. The charters and grants of 1662, 1663, and 1664, few in number but of great significance in colonial history, are in large part a result of this sudden transition from republicanism to monarchy.

The dissimilarities of the period are conspicuous. Shortly before the issue of the charters to the Carolina proprietors and the Duke of York, granting unoccupied and conquered territories in the New World, appeared the amazingly liberal charters to the people of Connecticut and Rhode Island; the struggle of the planters of Barbados to throw off the burden of proprietary rule, abetted in so doing by the king and his advisers; the determination of the merchants of London to make uniform the system of colonial administration, as shown in their petition to the councillors of the crown, urging them to bring all the colonies directly into the king's hand; and, lastly, the concession by all promoters of colonization of liberty of conscience to those who believed in God as an indispensable privilege offered to attract settlers.

The grant of 1663 to eight Carolina proprietors was no premeditated act of royal generosity to favorites whom a spendthrift king wished to reward. It was not a voluntary act but, like many other important measures of the early years of the reign, was something originated and put through by others and assented to by a king who seemed unable to refuse a request from those whose will and purpose were stronger than his own. Two groups of such men appear. One, the merchants and the planters' agents of the City of London, possessed of a cold, hard, self-satisfied commercial spirit, who greeted every fresh acquisition of territory—Jamaica, Bombay, Tangier, and New Netherland, located in four different parts of the world—as opening new markets for trade and profit;[1] the other, the group of courtier-promoters at Whitehall, led by the Duke of York, who were largely responsible for the founding of the Royal African Company and the Hudson's Bay Company,[2] for the seizure of New Netherland, the grant of the Jerseys, and the issue of the charters for the Carolinas and the Bahamas. Of the members of this group Sir Anthony Ashley Cooper (later, Anthony Lord Ashley and the Earl of Shaftesbury), influential at Whitehall and in affairs of state, was the most determined promoter.[3] In the case of the Carolinas he was himself stirred to action by two men, outside the Whitehall group, Sir John Colleton, a Barbadian planter, who probably originated the idea of obtaining a grant of land in the region south of Virginia, and Sir William Berkeley, former governor of Virginia and soon to be reappointed to the same post, who knew of attempts already

1. In Povey's "overtures" appears the phrase "and that the Several Pieces, and Colonies bee drawn and disposed into a more certaine, civill, and uniform waie of Government." The same idea appears in the royal instructions issued in 1660 for the select council for foreign plantations, and is to be found in a petition of March, 1661, presented by the planters of Barbados residing in London for "an immediate dependence on the crown." (Andrews, *British Committees*, p. 69; *Calendar State Papers, Colonial*, 1661–1668, §39.) The grants to proprietors were in direct contradiction of the principle laid down in Povey's recommendation and the instructions to the select council. The proprietary idea triumphed for the moment (note the proposed grant of Surinam to Willoughby in 1663 as a county palatine, *Calendar State Papers, Colonial*, 1661–1668, §§309, 451), but before the end of the century was officially discarded.

2. See Note at the end of this chapter.

3. Louise Fargo Brown, *The First Earl of Shaftesbury* (1933), ch. X.

made to occupy that portion of the region which lay north of Albemarle Sound.

These men were quite familiar with the colonial situation, particularly with that part of the colonial area which lay south of the Potomac and in the West Indies. Colleton, who had served the king during the civil wars, had found it expedient to retire to Barbados soon after 1650, had there established himself as a planter, and had lent his support to his kinsman Modyford in the confused political disturbances that followed. Opposing the king's reappointment of Willoughby as governor of Barbados, which was finally effected in 1663,[1] he had returned to England in 1660 and there continued his opposition in combination with a group of planters in London, who were strongly opposed to proprietary rule. He was appointed a member of the Royal African Company, and as one of the members of the select council for foreign plantations may well have come into contact with John Lord Berkeley, Sir George Carteret, the Earl of Craven, the Duke of Albemarle (Monck), the Earl of Clarendon, Sir Anthony Ashley Cooper, and Sir William Berkeley, all of whom were connected with the select councils, though probably few of them attended very often. Colleton had considerable property in Barbados as had Ashley also, but he never went back to the island, partly because of Willoughby's resumption of his proprietary prerogatives and partly because of the changing economic conditions there, due to the consolidation of estates, the increasing population, and the squeezing out of the smaller planters. Colleton was, therefore, in the mood for adventure and the trying out of an investment elsewhere.

Sir Anthony Ashley Cooper had lived from early years in something of a colonial atmosphere. His father had been a member of the Virginia Company of London, and he had married as his first wife the daughter of Lord Coventry, keeper of the great seal and father of Henry and William Coventry, who after the Restoration had much to do with colonial business. Though Ashley's main activities before 1660 had been confined to war and politics, when he was a member of councils of state in 1653, 1659, and 1660[2]—the last

1. See above, Vol. II, 266–267.
2. Christie, *Life of Anthony Ashley Cooper* (1871), I, 110, 177, 202, 203; Firth and Rait, *Acts and Ordinances,* II, 1273, 1274 (May 19, 1659), 1418 (February 25, 1660); Shaftesbury Papers, X, June 18, 1652, February 27, 1655, Deputy Keeper's *Report,* 33, p. 255.

two of which had been instructed (among other things) to promote trade and shipping—he had never lost sight of the possible advantages of contact with the overseas world. After the return of the king, the plantations became one of the absorbing interests of his life and he lent himself personally and officially to the furthering of their welfare. He served on the Privy Council committee and the select councils of 1660, and afterward, as the Earl of Shaftesbury, became the president of the consolidated council of 1672. At the same time he was constantly at hand for committee work in settling disputes and framing plans of government for Newfoundland, Maryland, Barbados, and Jamaica. Because of these contacts he came to know something about the conditions prevailing in every colony that England possessed. The range of his outlook and understanding can be gauged by the intelligent and broadminded body of instructions that he drew up, with the aid of Dr. Benjamin Worsley and John Locke, for the council of 1672, instructions which, based on earlier documents of a similar character, became the model and guide for later instructions during the more than a hundred years that followed. His interest in trade and plantations, though less spectacular than his interest in politics, has given him a place of first importance among the promoters of English colonization in America.

As early as 1646 Shaftesbury, then Sir Anthony Ashley Cooper, had invested money in Barbados and acquired a part share in a plantation located in St. George's parish with an agent in residence.[1] He had sent out servants and bonded himself for the charges, but the enterprise failed and in 1655 he sold the estate. The reason was probably the same as that which led Colleton to withdraw from the island—inability to compete with the larger and wealthier sugar planters who, endeavoring to increase their profits by absorbing the smaller estates, were bringing social and economic distress to the island.[2] When therefore Colleton and Ashley got together in London, with Sir William Berkeley at hand to provide the necessary information and Colleton's son Peter to furnish additional data, they took stock of the situation. Colleton had heard of the unoccupied area south of Virginia from captains who had sailed along the coast and had noticed its large navigable rivers and fertile lands, and their accounts made a strong appeal to one who like himself had

1. Christie, Life, appendix ii, pp. xxxiv–xxxvi; Brown, The First Earl, pp. 150–151.
2. Harlow, Barbados, pp. 306, 309, 340.

lived in a small arid island, where lands were falling into the hands of a few, and where the staple products were limited, in largest part, to sugar only. He hoped to start a migration on the part of those who were considering the necessity of removing to any nearby available land, Jamaica or elsewhere.

To carry out their purpose these men had to have a charter from the king; and if they were to obtain the sort of document they needed, they would be obliged to secure the support of men of higher rank than themselves. Unfortunately, they possessed dignities no more important than knighthood, and that title since the days of James I could always be bought for a price. Neither Colleton nor Sir William Berkeley was a peer of the realm or in office at White-hall, Westminster, or London, while Ashley, an old Presbyterian who had served the Commonwealth and the Protectorate, was not trusted by the royalists, despite his ability, knowledge of the world, and devotion to business, because they thought him self-seeking and without principle, honor, or conscience.[1] His very liberality, toler-ance in religious things, and philosophic idealism found no response among the reactionary members of the Cavalier Parliament. There-fore he, Colleton, and Berkeley needed the backing of others, of men whose place at court was recognized, whose control of office carried influence, and whose loyalty to prerogative was unimpeach-able. To this end they secured as co-petitioners with themselves the following friends of the king and the Duke of York. First, the Earl of Clarendon, who already had correspondents in Barbados and plantations in Jamaica, and was always willing to extend his hold-ings and increase his property whether in England or America. Sec-ond, the Earl of Albemarle,[2] with a reputation for parsimony and covetousness that made it natural for him to become interested in any scheme which would increase his wealth, and who was the more likely to favor the project because he had correspondents and

1. Clarendon wrote, "A. A. Cooper, who has been presented by General Monck under a special Recommendation was then too sworn of the Council, and the rather because having lately married the Niece of the Earl of Southampton [lord high treas-urer, Cooper's third marriage] . . . it was believed that his slippery Humour would be easily restrained and fixed by the Uncle." (*Life*, p. 12.) For a still more caustic judgment see *Memoirs of the Duke of York* (1729), pp. viii–ix. "Champion of the popular Faction," "the Hydra of the Populace," "a man violent in his Passions," "implacable in his malice" (the terms there used) apply chiefly to Cooper's career as Earl of Shaftesbury. For a well-balanced and reasonable estimate, Brown, *The First Earl*, pp. 305, 308.

2. Recent lives of Monck are by Warner and Davies (1936).

friends in Barbados and was related to both Colleton and Modyford. Third, John Lord Berkeley, Sir William's brother, one of the principal officers of the navy and the recipient of many indulgencies and opportunities for preferment. Fourth, Sir George Carteret, treasurer of the navy and vice-chamberlain of the household.[1] Lastly, the Earl of Craven, who later in the reign was to obtain high honors at the hand of the king. Though all these courtiers had large estates in England or Ireland, they were eager to join, energetically and with a measure of enthusiasm, in the work of advancing the new undertaking, and thus they became the leading men among those who formed the courtier-promoter group at Whitehall.

Plans must have been conceived as early as 1660, when Colleton, Modyford, and Sir William Berkeley were in London together, but the charter was not issued until March 24, 1663. Either the co-petitioners were slow in giving their adherence to the project, requiring as it did a considerable investment of money without certain or immediate returns, or, as is quite likely, Charles II may have been disinclined to follow, too complacently, the lead of the petitioners. In the end, however, just as was to be the case with the charter to the Duke of York and the taking of New Amsterdam, he was obliged to give way. One of the king's assets was his knowing when to yield, and one of his greatest liabilities was the importunity of his friends.

Unexpectedly, a month or two later, an unforeseen difficulty arose. Two claimants, acting quite independently, denied the validity of the grant on the ground of their prior right to the whole or a part of the territory. The Duke of Norfolk, son of Henry Lord Maltravers (who after 1646 had become the third earl of Arundel and Surrey and earl marshal of England), based his pretensions on an assignment of the "province of Carolana" to his father in 1632 by Sir Robert Heath, to whom the king had made over the territory in 1629. With the king's entire approbation, Heath had assigned the

---

1. The feeling of the king for Carteret was undoubtedly one of intimacy and affection. Unlike Berkeley, who was a good deal of a schemer for place, vain, and lacking in tact, Carteret was unselfish and by his willingness to put himself out to the advantage of others won the gratitude of both the king and the Duke of York. Charles wrote him in 1649, as follows: "Carteret, I will add this to you under my own hand that I can never forgett the good services you have done to my father and to me and if God bless me you shall find I do remember them to the advantage of you and yours; and for this you have the word of your very loving friend Charles R" (Additional Manuscripts, 27,402, f. 124).

property, but in what form this approbation was expressed we do not know. Norfolk's opponents said later that he had no patent and could show no documentary basis for his claim. From the beginning Maltravers had intended to send settlers into the territory, just as his friend Lord Baltimore was planning to do with Maryland before his death in that same year, but he was prevented from doing what he wanted until in 1637 he obtained a letter from Charles I instructing Governor Harvey of Virginia to set off for his use a portion of that colony's territory (which the council spoke of as "Lord Maltravers province of Carolana"), and to assist him in the work of planting. Maltravers commissioned Captain William Hawley to settle the southern part of the "province," giving him ten thousand acres of land and the title of deputy governor, and he also commissioned Captain Henry Hartwell to settle the northern part. Dr. Coxe in his *Carolana* tells us that Maltravers "at great expense planted several parts of the said country, and had effected much more had he not been prevented by the war with Scotland, in which he was general for King Charles; and afterwards by the civil war in England and the lunacy of his eldest son." That Maltravers ever actually sent colonists to occupy his "county of Norfolk" is uncertain, though Harvey issued the desired patent, erecting the county into a semi-independent propriety and commissioning Captain Hawley to act as its governor. Sir John Colleton once spoke of the plantation as having been "started by one M[r] Mariat, steward to the Duke of Norfolk,"[1] and it is quite possible that this was so, the settlers coming mainly from Virginia itself. The assignment by Heath in 1632, royal letters of 1637 and 1639, and the Harvey patent

1. The Privy Council said afterward that "no English whatsoever have by virtue of any such Graunte hitherto planted in the said Province" (*Acts Privy Council, Colonial*, I, §604). Maltravers had manifestly done nothing up to the time of the issue of Harvey's patent (January 22, 1638), and in that patent was given seven years in which to fulfil the conditions. The Scottish war began in 1639 and as Maltravers was drawn into it on the side of the king he could hardly have continued his preparations, though it is possible that Captain Hawley may have done something and that the duke's steward may have helped. Harvey's patent is a very interesting document. Maltravers was to hold his "county" of the king in free and common socage, with certain local privileges. In other respects he was to be subject to the authority of the Virginia general assembly (*North Carolina Colonial Records*, I, 14–16). There seem to have been two royal letters, one of 1637 and the other dated April 20, 1639 (*Virginia Council Minutes*, I, 492; Hening, *Statutes*, I, 552; *Virginia Magazine*, X, 272; XI, 48, 49; XII, 385; XIII, 392; XIV, 195).

of 1638 became a sufficient evidence for the claim that Maltravers' son now sought to revive.[1]

Even more interesting than the Maltravers' claim in throwing light on these early attempts at colonization is that brought forward by Samuel Vassall, a merchant of London of Huguenot descent, who was engaged in trade with various countries bordering on the North Atlantic. He was a member of the Massachusetts Bay Company, belonging to the extreme Puritan group, and a brother of William Vassall, who signed the Cambridge Agreement of 1629 and went with Winthrop to Massachusetts the next year.[2] He was also a partner in various trading enterprises with Maurice Thompson, merchant and Puritan zealot. His interest in Carolana, as a serious business proposition, seems to have been first aroused by Huguenots who escaped to England after the fall of La Rochelle, October 29, 1628, and who under the leadership of Captain Antoine de Sancé, an officer of Soubise's army, spent time and energy in formulating plans for a migration to Carolana. They acted under the authority of the patent to Heath, in obtaining which, October 30, 1629, Vassal and his Huguenot brethren had been the ones chiefly concerned.[3] With William Boswell, later Sir William and English

1. *Calendar State Papers, Colonial,* 1574–1660, p. 282; *Virginia Council Minutes,* I, 481, 482, 492; Coxe, *Carolana* (ed. 1840), p. 87; *Acts Privy Council, Colonial,* I, p. 240 (§10). The document printed in *ibid.,* pp. 238–241, is a report of the Dorset commission, of earlier date than that assigned to it in the Privy Council Register, 1632 instead of 1638 (not 1631, as given above, Vol. I, 201, note 3). It fixes the date when Maltravers received the transfer from Heath, and seems to show that Maltravers and George Calvert were working toward the same end at the same time, one forty-six years old and the other fifty-two. In C. O. 1:17, no. 39, fol. 101, and no. 39[1], fol. 102, are the proprietors' statements of the pretentions of Maltravers and Vassall. In the first document Mariot, the steward, is described as living "in Chancery Lane at the next door to the Harrowe" and as saying that he "had the patent and articles" in his possession. In the second, Vassal claimed to have "an Assignem^t from Sr Robt Heath for a tearme not yet Expyred." In the same, Mariot (or "Merriot," as it is spelled here) is called the duke's "Sollissiter."

2. For William Vassall, see above, Vol. I, index. Samuel had a son Henry, agent in London for the Cape Fear adventurers, who died in 1667, in the same year with his father. The John Vassall, planter of Barbados, who went with the Cape Fear company in 1664 and was appointed by the proprietors surveyor general for their county of Clarendon was a son of William Vassall, who himself had estates of considerable size in Jamaica.

3. The date of the charter, August 4, 1629, suggests this, but more conclusive is the statement in the charter itself, that Sir Robert Heath was planning "to lead thither a colony of men large and plentifull, professing the true religion." It was not Sir Robert who was planning to do this, but Samuel Vassall. As this was the year of the

ambassador at The Hague, Vassall and the Huguenots persuaded George, eighth Baron Berkeley of the Berkeley Hundred, to obtain, as the higher lord and proprietor, an enfeoffment of land[1] from Heath, on condition that the merchants would provide the men, ships, and equipment, all sharing in the profits, such as they were.[2] As far as we know nothing was done until 1632 and 1633, when one Henry Taverner, acting under orders from Vassall, set out from London to go to Virginia and thence to continue the voyage southward. Taverner went as far as the "St. Helena River," the first Englishman to see the region which was known at the time as "Florida als Carolana." In 1633 one Edward Kingswell, by arrangement with Vassall, went to Virginia prepared to carry a body of colonists into the territory; but for reasons undisclosed Vassall defaulted on his contract and Kingswell returned to bring his case before the Privy Council, the High Court of Admiralty, and the Laud Commission. Carolana remained as before a land unoccupied by Englishmen. But the grants and commitments under the Heath patent, regarding the nature of which we know very little, retained enough vitality in 1663 to warrant both the Duke of Norfolk and Samuel Vassall in bringing forward their claims to a share in the territory[3] which Charles II was granting to the eight proprietors.

Massachusetts Bay charter it is interesting to find Vassall backing a Puritan and a Huguenot enterprise at the same time.

1. The statute of Quia Emptores is not mentioned in the Heath patent, but from the language used it is evident that enfeoffment was not forbidden. The terms of the enfeoffment are given in *Calendar State Papers, Colonial*, 1574–1660, p. 115.

2. *Ibid.*, pp. 99, 102, 109, 110, 115, 120, 121, 129, 140–141, 145; *North Carolina Colonial Records*, I, 34–36. The years from 1628 to 1632 were a busy time in colonizing enterprise. Among the many activities of the period were the various West Indian and South American voyages, the grant to Plowden, the trading ventures to Canada and the capture of Quebec by the Kirkes, the founding of Massachusetts Bay, the ambitious projects of the Providence Company, Warwick's attempt to obtain a patent for lands in southern New England, and the notable transactions of Maltravers, Baltimore, and Gorges. No period of our colonial history of similar length can show as many colonizing and trading happenings of major importance as does this.

3. *Calendar State Papers, Colonial*, 1574–1660, pp. 190, 194, 197–199, 207; *Acts Privy Council, Colonial*, I, §§339, 340, 343, 350, 352–354; Examinations, High Court of Admiralty, 13:51, ff. 270, 436–437. Taverner was only thirty years old at the time. He sailed south, September, 1632, in the *George of London*, as far as St. Helena Sound, exploring parts of the coast as he went along. Returning early the next year, he gave Vassall a map and a description of the country. Encouraged by this reconnoiter Kingswell undertook a plantation in Carolana and contracted with Vassall for two vessels, the shallop, *Thomas of London*, Taverner, master, and the pinnace *Henry*, Orpheus Dunkin, master, together with servants, provisions, clothing, bedding, ironware, beads, and other trading goods. All these commodities were to be delivered

The two claims were presented June 10, 1663 to the Privy Council, which instructed Sir Geoffrey Palmer, the attorney general, to investigate the matter and at the same time ordered "all pretenders" to attend at the council chamber and to bring such evidence of title as they possessed in order to demonstrate their claims. After a careful examination of the witnesses and the exhibits and an equally careful consideration of the attorney general's report, the council found that "no English whatsoever have, by virtue of any such Graunts, hitherto Planted in the said Province" and decided for that reason that "such Letters Patent (if any were) are become voyd." Consequently it instructed the attorney general to take the proper legal steps voiding the patents and issued an order that henceforth no one was to molest the Carolina proprietors. The latter, therefore, went ahead with their plans for the planting of the province, fully confident of their right to do so.[1]

By the first charter, that of March 24, 1663, the validity of which was now satisfactorily established, eight men became the true and absolute lords proprietors of the region formerly granted to Sir Robert Heath, lying between the thirty-sixth and thirty-first degrees of northern latitude and extending westward to the "south seas." By the second charter, that of 1665, these bounds were pushed northward half a degree, that is, to Currituck Inlet, and southward a hundred miles below the present line between Georgia and Florida. As joint-proprietors these men held this enormous frontier domain as Heath had held it and as Baltimore was holding Maryland, under the princely Bishop of Durham clause, but like Baltimore and unlike Heath they held not in capite but in free and common socage, paying their twenty marks a year as Baltimore was paying his two In-

---

to George Menefie, Vassall's factor in Virginia, who was to provide additional passengers and equipment for the new plantation, of which Kingswell was to be the governor. Vassall defaulted at both ends of the contract, for reasons that are not clear, unless we accept a sickness of which he complained as more than a pretext. He failed to have ready the vessels at London and Kingswell was obliged to sail, October, 1633, in another ship, the *Mayflower*, Peter Andrews, master, with his wife, family, and forty servants. At Jamestown he waited in vain for the vessels promised by Vassall that were to take him to Carolana, and finally, in June, 1634, returned to England. Suit followed in 1635 and 1636. Vassall was condemned to pay damages, and failing to do so was committed to the Fleet in 1635 and to the Gatehouse in 1636. Still living in 1663 he entered his claim against the Carolina proprietors. For his career in general, see the *Dictionary of National Biography*.

1. *Acts Privy Council, Colonial*, I, §§594, 604; *North Carolina Colonial Records*, I, 42–43, 52–53.

dian arrows. The remaining terms, though more elaborately worded
in the Carolina charter, are much the same in all three, reproducing
the seignorial privileges of a baronial lord in England and at the
same time authorizing the summons of a law-making assembly of
the freemen or freeholders, a combination of the old and the new
that from an Englishman's point of view was in no way incongruous. The Carolina charter laid exceptional stress, as might have been
expected, upon towns, ports, trade, and commercial privileges and
provided for toleration in religious matters, despite "the unity and
uniformity established in this nation." Such indulgence and dispensation for those who worshipped God were conceded to all the
colonies after the Restoration and, as we have already seen, found
remarkable expression in this very year 1663 in the charter granted
to the inhabitants of Rhode Island. Unlike the members of the
Council for New England, which was the only collective body of
proprietors that had been brought into existence up to this time, the
Carolina proprietors were legally a feudal not a corporate group and
their shares were alienable and heritable, as those of the members
of the Council for New England were not, at least until after the
lands actually had been distributed. The territory of the Carolina
proprietors was never divided up among the members as was that
of the Council for New England and that of Berkeley and Carteret
in New Jersey. The only share that was ever set apart was that of
Lord Granville in 1744, long after the other proprietors had surrendered both government and soil to the crown. For a man who
paid almost no attention to his property in America, Lord Granville
was very tenacious of his proprietary rights.

The first meeting of the Carolina proprietors was held on May 23,
1663, and at that meeting plans were set on foot for spreading the
news of the grant as widely as possible that colonists might be induced to settle in the territory under such terms as the grantees
wished to lay down.[1] Maps were ordered to be made and invi-
tations were sent to New England and Barbados and later to Bermuda also. In New England a group was formed, composed partly
of persons from Massachusetts who started the movement, and

1. "A Declaration and Prospects," dated August 25, 1663, is given in *North Carolina Colonial Records*, I, 43–46, 53, but that there were earlier drafts is definitely
stated by the London adventurers and implied in the assertions of Modyford and
Colleton in Barbados. The "Declaration" mentioned above was prepared as an answer
to the paper of the New England adventurers.

partly of London merchants, which was known as "the adventurers for carrying on a plantation in Charles [Cape Fear] River on the coast of Florida." In Barbados, under the direction of Sir Thomas Modyford and Peter Colleton, to whom the proprietors had given authority to push the project in that quarter, a similar group was brought together, composed of Barbadians only. This group, some two hundred in number, was called the Barbadian Adventurers, each one of whom was expected to subscribe at least one thousand pounds of sugar, in return for which he was to receive five hundred acres of land in the distribution to "first settlers." Whether the "Adventurers about Cape Fear" in Boston and London, ever did anything more than organize will probably never be known, but certain is it that some time before 1663 a courageous company of New Englanders went to the Cape Fear, perhaps as an advance party, and settled down there with their equipment and livestock as a town community. Discouraged because of the seeming unhealthfulness and barrenness of the country they eventually deserted the place and went back to New England or migrated elsewhere.[1]

The activities of the Barbadians produced more substantial results. On receiving instructions from the proprietors, Modyford and Colleton marshaled the adventurers, raised funds, and in the summer of 1663 sent Captain William Hilton to spy out the land. Of Hilton's first voyage no account remains. Encouraged by Hilton's favorable reports and eager to offset the adverse comments of the New Englanders, the adventurers sent him off again, with two representatives or commissioners and twenty seamen, in the same ship as before, the *Adventure,* to reaffirm his first good impressions. Hilton sailed August 10, 1663, for the coast of "Florida als Carolana," explored St. Helena Sound and Parris Island, where he found a Spanish captain, Argüelles, and seven men, soldiers from St. Augustine, and a few Englishmen who had been wrecked on the coast a month before.[2] Sailing northward to the Cape Fear, he made his

1. In a "Brief Description of the Province of Carolina" (Carroll, *Collections,* I, 11) the date is given as May 29, 1664, and the number of New Englanders as 800.

2. Thirteen Englishmen survived the wreck, which occurred in July, 1633. Three of them were killed by the Indians and the remainder taken prisoner. *Charleston Year Book,* 1884, pp. 231, 232, 234, 237, 238; *Shaftesbury Papers,* p. 170. Hilton's journal is printed also in *ibid.,* pp. 18–25; *Early Carolina* (Original Narratives), pp. 33–55, and in part in *North Carolina Colonial Records,* I, 67–71. It is strange that in his journal Hilton should have made no mention of his first voyage, yet it seems to be well authenticated (*ibid.,* 40).

way up that river for a considerable distance, inspecting the lands on both sides and on his way back found at the mouth traces of the New England settlement in the form of surviving cattle and pigs. The notice fastened to a tree disparaging the country, which he called a scandalous writing, he must have seen on the previous voyage.[1] Returning to St. Helena he made a map and prepared a journal and then departed on his journey home, December 6, 1663, reaching Barbados on January 6 of the next year. He carried with him several of the natives, one of whom, an Indian chief, Shadoo, must in some way have found his way back to his Edisto home, for he was seen there by Robert Sandford when he made his tour of discovery in 1666.[2] He was also seen by the settlers later, when they arrived in 1670. It is quite possible and even probable that between 1663 and 1666 other ships were sent out from Barbados, of which no record remains.

The Barbadian Adventurers were greatly cheered by the favorable representation made by Hilton after his first voyage, in which he probably described the Cape Fear region in the language used after the second voyage as "good land and as well Timbered as any we have seen in any part of the world, sufficient to accommodate thousands of our *English* nation." Shortly after sending him out for the second time on August 10, they drew up, August 12, a series of preliminary promises to expectant settlers regarding government, trade, and the distribution of lands in the proposed plantation.[3] At the same time they formulated several proposals designed to make perfectly

1. It is unfortunate that more is not known of the New England enterprise, as throwing light on what a Puritan thought regarding a settlement of his own beyond his native heath. Evidently the Puritan exodus was mapped out on a large scale, for the adventurers intended to ask the proprietors not only for a grant of land but for extensive privileges such as would be in accord with their practices at home. They asked that their land titles be based on purchase and not on patent and that they themselves be granted full rights of self-government. It is possible that the scheme fell through not only because of the discouraging reports but also because the Puritans asked too much. The proprietors thought them not a very "fassil people." Their disparaging remarks were greatly resented by the Barbadians, and Robert Horne's description of the Cape Fear (*Early Carolina*, pp. 65–73; Carroll, *Collections*, II, 10–18) was undoubtedly written to counteract the effect of these remarks.

2. *Shaftesbury Papers*, pp. 64, 170.

3. *Charleston Year Book*, 1884, pp. 255–261. These promises included participation of all freeholders in the election of deputies to a general assembly, freedom of trade, immunity from customs, liberty of conscience, and other privileges such as were warranted by the proprietors' charter and represented what the Barbadians had been striving to obtain ever since their acceptance of the Ayscue terms of surrender in 1652.

clear to the proprietors in London what they expected to receive should they succeed in settling the country. They demanded permission to buy of the natives a tract thirty miles square controlled by what they proposed to call the "Corporation of the Barbados Adventurers," under which the colonists were to enjoy and exercise all the privileges and immunities granted the proprietors by the king, with a large measure of self-government similar to that of the city of Exeter. This corporation was to be the forerunner of other similar corporations to be colonized in the future by the "many hundreds of noble families and well experienced planters" that Modyford and Colleton saw in their minds' eye moving across the face of the waters from Barbados to Carolina. To these unexpected demands the proprietors replied with some asperity, bidding the Barbadians keep to the proposals already drawn up for the information of the New Englanders ("from the substance whereof we shall not receade"). For though they were willing to make reasonable concessions, they wished it distinctly understood that they, not the Barbadians, were laying down the conditions of settlement, and that they had no more use for a corporation like that of the city of Exeter than they had for a community like that of a New England town.[1] This answer ended all efforts that either the Barbadians or the New Englanders were to make of their own initiative for the settlement of Carolina and threw both responsibility and control squarely upon the shoulders of the proprietors, where it properly belonged.

After September, 1663, the attention of the proprietors had been centered largely upon the northern part of their territory, the part adjoining Virginia on the south. When, therefore, they learned that one of their number, Sir William Berkeley, was going back to that colony as governor, they instructed him to take charge of their business there, looking after the granting of land, the collecting of quit-rents, and the appointing of a governor and council. For some years Virginians, first as explorers and pioneers and then as families seeking land and homes, had been moving southward into the region lying along the northern shore of Albemarle Sound. At least as early as 1653 and in increasing numbers during the ten years that followed, forerunners had taken up their permanent abode there, and at the time when Sir William Berkeley received his instructions there was a sprinkling of settlers located between the Chowan River

and Currituck Inlet, living on small farms and plantations and raising livestock, tobacco and corn.[1] In October, 1664, soon after his
arrival, Berkeley, acting under authorization from his fellow proprietors, selected one William Drummond as governor of the province of Albemarle. In due time he was commissioned by the board
in England, but whether he completed the governmental organization of the province by the calling of a council and the summons of
an assembly is wholly uncertain, though he was warranted in doing
so by the Concessions and Agreements of 1665. Thus the province
of Albemarle, later to become the colony of North Carolina, was
started on its way, and the proprietors were able to show the king
that they were not sleeping upon his patent, but were "promoting
his service and his subjects profitt."[2]

There still remained the southern section, as yet without settlers,
and in its interest the proprietors renewed their negotiations with
the Barbadians for the purpose of carrying out their original plan.
A new group of nearly ninety Barbadian planters, with associates in
England, New England, the Leeward Islands, and Bermuda, was
brought together, headed by John Yeamans, a friend of Colleton's
and one of the former adventurers. This group employed Major
William Yeamans, a son of John, to act as their agent and to arrange
for the transportation of colonists to Port Royal on St. Helena
Sound or to some other good harbor below Cape Romainia (Cape
Carteret). To meet the new situation the proprietors issued the General Concessions and Agreements, the same body of articles "con-
tayning the man^r of Government wth several Imunities and priviledges,"[3] that Berkeley and Carteret were to adopt for New Jersey
six weeks later. This document, in the effort to harmonize proprietary requirements with certain current popular demands concerning
liberty of conscience and the right of representation in assembly,
must have cost some one a great deal of time and trouble, but it
never played the part in Carolina affairs that the same concessions
played in East New Jersey. When it was drafted there were very
few people in Carolina below the Albemarle and there is nothing to
show that any attention was paid to it in that region. Though it was
undoubtedly intended for Governor Drummond and his successor

---

1. *Ibid.*, I, 571, 677, 710, Henderson Walker wrote in 1703 "we have been settled
near fifty years in this place, and in 1707 one Lawrence said that about 47 years
before he had seated a plantation on the southwest side of the Chowan River."

2. *Ibid.*, I, 55.   3. *Ibid.*, 75–92.

Governor Stephens, as well as for any other governors that might be serving within the grant, it was never proclaimed as a whole. Many of its terms were, however, incorporated into the governor's instructions. Primarily the Concessions were designed for the use of John Yeamans who, through the influence of Peter Colleton, was now ordered to go from Barbados as the governor of the new county of Clarendon to be erected below the Cape Fear River. That his dignity and influence might be increased and he be encouraged to promote "viggorously" the new colony there, the proprietors prevailed with Charles II to confer upon him and his heirs the honor of a knight baronet, assuring the king that Yeamans fully deserved the title.[1] Also, in order to enlarge the territory of the patent, perhaps with the idea of enforcing the Concessions in Albemarle and certainly of bringing that section under their jurisdiction, they obtained a second charter, June 30, 1665, carrying the northern line to the upper end of Currituck Inlet.[2]

Yeamans left Barbados in October, 1665, in a flyboat of one hundred and fifty tons, accompanied by a small frigate and a sloop, with a large number of colonists. After a stormy voyage all were landed at the mouth of the Cape Fear, where they founded the first settlement of "Charles Town." But trouble followed trouble and from the beginning misfortune dogged their path. Fierce gales damaged two of the vessels and though the passengers were saved, all their equipment, arms, and ammunition which had been furnished by the proprietors were lost in the waters. The sloop sent to Virginia for help was driven ashore in the night and only with difficulty was it brought into Albemarle Sound, where the crew was cared for by the English planters. Yeamans returned to Barbados in January, 1666, but the vessel that he sent back to the Cape Fear with men and provisions encountered storms and contrary winds; its captain, Edward Stanyans, went mad and leapt overboard; and only after many weeks of buffeting, "assisted by a miraculous providence," was the vessel brought safely to her desired haven. Then it was, June 16, 1666, that Lieutenant Colonel Robert Sandford, a military man and not a mariner, with seventeen other members of this, the first and oldest settlement of Charles Town, started in two vessels, a sloop and a shallop, on a voyage of discovery to the southward. In obedi-

1. *Ibid.*, 93–98.
2. Map in Boyd's edition of Byrd, *The Dividing Line,* p. xvi.

ence to orders from the proprietors—given him while in London in 1664—Sandford entered on his mission to prepare the way for a second plantation within a new county to be called Craven. He coursed as far south as Port Royal, where he landed and by turf and twig took possession of the country in the name of the king. He had many experiences and adventures with the Indian caciques and their subjects, of which he has left a graphic account. Greatly impressed with the suitability of the region for settlement, yet unwilling to prolong the voyage because it was costing the proprietors twenty-five pounds a month for the hire of the sloop, he and his company returned to the Cape Fear, and reached there July 12.[1]

Though the settlement of "Charles Town" on the Cape Fear was fairly well started, with houses built, fields cultivated, and corn, tobacco, indigo, and potatoes planted, and though there were enough people there to warrant the calling of a general assembly, composed of governor, council, and deputies, the place did not prosper. Differences arose between Henry Vassall, the agent in England, and Yeamans and his company in Barbados regarding the influence of each with the proprietors and the nature of the privileges each desired should be granted the Cape Fear people. There was dissatisfaction in the colony over the way the quit-rents were imposed and the lands seated. Restlessness and discontent increased and the desire grew to remove to some other locality more salubrious and fertile. Despite all the proprietors could do they were never quite able to rid the place of the stigma the New Englanders had cast upon it, as a locality not fit for a Christian habitation,[2] and at this juncture Colleton, Modyford, and Yeamans united in urging the merits of the Port Royal region. In the summer of 1667 the end came. John Vassall, another of the ubiquitous Vassalls and the only proprietary appointee in the colony, writing, October 6, 1667, about "the unhappy loss of our Plantation," spoke of "the rude Rable of our Inhabitants [which] were dayly ready to mutany against me for keeping them there so long"; and said that after many had made their way overland to

1. *North Carolina Colonial Records*, I, 118–139; *Shaftesbury Papers*, pp. 57–62; *Early Carolina*, pp. 77–108.

2. The proprietors, as late as the spring or summer of 1667, made an effort to bolster up the dying colony, by issuing an appeal, perhaps drawn up by John Locke (Brown, *The First Earl*, pp. 154–155), to "all ingenious and industrious persons," extolling the advantages of the place and offering the privileges outlined in the Concessions (*North Carolina Colonial Records*, I, 153–155).

Virginia, he had been obliged to stop the first ship that came and to arrange also for the use of other ships to carry the remainder of the colonists wherever they wished to go. Samuel Maverick, at that time residing in Boston, wrote Lord Arlington, October 16, that "the plantations at Cape Fear are deserted, the inhabitants have since come thither, some to Virginia";[1] and we know that in addition many went to the Albemarle and others back to Barbados. Thus, once again, save for those in the plantations along Albemarle Sound, for the settling of which the proprietors had been in no way responsible, Carolina was empty of English inhabitants and the true and absolute lords in England had spent their money—and a great deal of it—very largely in vain.

The proprietors may well have been disheartened by the futility of their efforts. Colleton had died and been succeeded in the proprietorship by his son Peter. Clarendon had fallen from power and was in exile. The others were no longer at the height of their physical and mental strength. The Duke of Albemarle was worn out and died in 1670. In all his personal rights and titles he was followed by his son Christopher, a lad of seventeen, later to be governor of Jamaica, who during his minority was represented by his uncle, Sir Thomas Clarges. Carteret was over seventy and the Berkeleys and Craven had passed their sixtieth milestones. Of them all Ashley was the youngest, only forty-six in 1667, in the prime of life and competent to carry the heavy burden of continuing the work and of saving, if possible, some profit from the wreck of their hopes. He took up the task with enthusiasm and alacrity, having as his associate the young John Locke, whom he had met at Oxford in 1666 and had taken into his family at his house, Little Exeter House near Exeter House in the Strand. There the two men labored to save the situation and there it was that in 1667 Locke wrote the appeal designed to check the exodus from the Cape Fear. That appeal having proved

1. *Ibid.*, I, 159–160, 161; *Shaftesbury Papers*, p. 89. Most of those who returned to Boston must have been New Englanders. In May, 1667, John Vassall wrote to Major General Leverett, "desiring that the people with him at Cape Fear have some releife in their distresse." The governor and magistrates encouraged contributions on their behalf, enabling a committee in charge to send out a ship to bring them home (*Massachusetts Colonial Records*, IV, pt. ii, 337). Vassall himself went to Virginia, where he became involved in several law suits in connection with the estates of Samuel and Henry Vassall, deceased, for defamation and libel. In each case he was able to collect damages (*Virginia Council Minutes*, I, index).

ineffective, Ashley and Locke prepared for a new start.[1] At one time they thought that, after the return of Surinam to the Dutch by the treaty of Breda, they might induce English planters from that colony to migrate to Carolina; but they finally came to the conclusion that it would be better to make men and women from England only the spearhead of a new expedition and to draft a new scheme of government to take the place of the useless Concessions. Each proprietor promised to contribute five hundred pounds to be laid out in ships, arms, and implements for the settlement, which this time was to be located at Port Royal and nowhere else.[2] At the start three ships, the *Carolina,* the *Port Royal,* and the *Albemarle,* with Joseph West in charge of the expedition, carried nineteen heads of families, sixty servants, and thirteen passengers without servants, all of whom with West and his family, the proprietors' servants, and the masters and seamen brought the total to about one hundred and forty persons.[3] Not all of those mentioned reached Carolina and a few not mentioned joined the company at Ireland, Barbados, and Bermuda, for the vessels stopped at one or other of these places on their way to their destination.

The vessels sailed from the Downs shortly after August 17, 1669, bearing not only their cargo and passengers but also various instructions for the settling of the government. Among the documents was

1. Ashley's plans seem to have been conceived on a large scale, in the hope of obtaining profitable returns not only from land sales and quit-rents but from commerce and the fur trade. Acting on suggestions from two Bermudians, Hugh Wentworth and John Dovel, he with others—Albemarle, Craven, Lord Berkeley, Carteret, and Peter Colleton—obtained in 1670 a grant of the Bahamas (*Shaftesbury Papers,* pp. 160–161, 207–208, 440–445; *Calendar State Papers, Colonial,* 1669–1674, §311), thus bringing under proprietary control three centers of future commercial activity, Albemarle, Charles Town, and New Providence, the last named of which was to be under Wentworth as governor, though, as it happened he never served. A more personal venture was Ashley's seignory at Edisto, with his kinsman Andrew Percival as its head and trading agent. There he hoped to raise cattle and crops, engage in trade with the Indians, and promote a commerce with Bermuda, Barbados, and other colonies. But nothing came of the venture, possibly because he found his seignory up the Ashley River (St. Giles Cussoo) and Sir Peter Colleton's barony on the Cooper River more conveniently located for the purpose. Furthermore, the Edisto attempt to set up a fur trade independently of Charles Town and the monopolists there was handicapped at the start, because the region was in a dangerous quarter within the bounds of "the debatable land," to which Spain had a legitimate claim.

2. *Calendar State Papers, Colonial,* 1669–1674, §§41, 54, 55; *Shaftesbury Papers,* pp. 91–93.

3. *Ibid.,* p. 174.

a commission in blank, which Sir John Yeamans was to fill in with his own name or with that of any one else he might select as governor.[1] Arriving at Barbados in October, the vessels picked up Yeamans, but soon after leaving the island they were scattered by a storm and the *Carolina,* putting in at Bermuda to refit, was so long delayed that Yeamans, becoming impatient, refused to wait. He filled in the commission with the name of William Sayle, former governor of Bermuda, a man, as Yeamans himself said, "of no great sufficiency" but the best he could get. Yeamans returned to Barbados and the *Carolina,* with Sayle and an enlarged body of emigrants on board, reached Port Royal River about March 31, 1670. There they remained but two days, going thence to St. Helena Sound. But because of its nearness to St. Augustine, "in the very chops of the Spaniards" as they said, that place did not satisfy them, and despite the orders of the lords proprietors, they set out again to find a permanent lodgement elsewhere. Urged on by the local Indians they despatched a shallop (bought in Bermuda) on a tour of inspection, some thirty leagues to the northward, to a region known to the natives as Kiawah. Impressed with the favorable reports brought back by the shallop they removed from St. Helena and established their settlement "on a point defended by the main river [the Ashley] with a brooke on the one side and inaccessible Marsh on the other wch all at high tides is ever overflowne: joyning itself to the mainland in a small neck not exceeding fiftie yards." This location, first known as Albemarle Point and later as Old Town or Old Charles Town, lay on the south bank of the Kiawah or Ashley River, about twenty-five miles from the sea. There these colonists remained until in 1680, finding that Oyster Point at the junction of the Ashley and Cooper rivers was better adapted as a port town and more healthful and better capable of defense—a conclusion to which they had come as early as 1672—they removed thither by order of the proprietors, who instructed them to call the place Charles Town and to make it the seat of their government. With the erection of twenty or more houses in 1681, supplementing the buildings already there, they began the

1. Unusually complete details are preserved among the Shaftesbury Papers of the personnel, equipment, and cost of this expedition. The total charges came to £3200, and the amount contributed by the proprietors was £2645. Of the eight, five gave £500 each. Lord Berkeley's contribution, if any, is not recorded, Clarendon was in exile and Sir William Berkeley in Virginia, so that neither would have been expected to share in the costs (*ibid.,* pp. 117–152).

founding of the most important town in colonial times that existed in the region south of Pennsylvania.[1]

Thus were started on their way to maturity two small settlements, the last but one of those established in the seventeenth century and for many years the weakest of all that were founded on the American mainland. In the northernmost of the two the people, numbering in 1700 between four and five thousand souls, lived widely scattered on plantations, large and small, along the rivers and shores of Albemarle Sound. Nowhere were they gathered into any form of nucleated life that had the semblance of a town. In the other, with its center at Charles Town there were in the same year about the same number of whites and a much larger increment of Indian slaves and negro slaves. Already many of the white settlers had laid out large plantations, under the conditions offered by the lords proprietors, namely, along the Ashley, southward toward the Edisto and in the Port Royal section, while a few ventured westward into the back country and northward along the Santee. Not for many years, however, did they go many miles from Charles Town, on account of the danger always threatening from the Spaniards on the south and the Indians beyond the borders. For this and other reasons, South Carolina developed a form of social and economic life in which Charles Town was the only port and directing center, the objective of trader and planter alike, and the seat of business, where warehouse and office handled the raw material from the country and the frontier and shipped it to England in exchange for the manufactured goods needed in the colony and the woolens, duffels, and trinkets that were used in the Indian trade. The merchant had his estate in the country as the planter had his house in the town, so that to a greater extent than in any other colony town and country were bound together in a common interest. Charles Town became the social, as well as the business, heart of the colony and

---

1. *Calendar State Papers, Colonial,* 1677–1680, §1223; 1681–1685, §37. The location of Old Charles Town and its relation to the new settlement can be seen in Smith's maps, *South Carolina Magazine,* IX, 12; XVI, 49; XIX, no. 1. Light has been thrown on the early settlement by documents from the General Archives of the Indies at Seville, printed in the *South Carolina Magazine,* XXXVII, April and July. Though the accuracy of the information possessed by the Spaniards, which was obtained from the Indians, may be questioned, nevertheless certain statements, such as that in 1672 there were thirty small houses on the west bank of the Ashley and four on the east bank at Oyster Point (Charles Town); that there was no fort only a palisade; and that the main defense was four pieces of artillery covering the river are interesting.

though other towns came into existence, its preëminence in colonial times was never even challenged.

The two colonies thus founded within the territory of the lords proprietors were in many ways unique among the English settlements of the continental seaboard and vitally different from each other. They were alike in that they were the most southerly of all the settlements, each an outpost of English expansion, isolated and remote, far removed from the older centers of colonial life. One was separated from Virginia by difficult and dangerous forests and almost impassable swamps; the other, two hundred and fifty miles further south, was accessible only by water and lay on the edge of a frontier facing hostile peoples resentful of the English advance. Charles Town was in close proximity to territory claimed by Spain and to a chain of missions extending from St. Helena—or Port Royal as the French had called it—to St. Augustine and westward through northern Florida to the Apalachicola River, in the three provinces or mission districts of Guale (called "Wallie" by the English), Timucua, and Apalache. Ever since the time when Menéndez de Aviléz, Spanish governor of Florida and founder of St. Augustine,[1] had destroyed the French Huguenot settlement at Fort Caroline on the St. John's River in 1565, the work of extending the missions, north and west, had gone steadily on. First under the Jesuit priests and then under the Franciscan friars,[2] mission posts had been established to the northward along the coast, until at the time of granting the proprietary charter in 1663, they numbered eight or ten, each protected, as a rule, by a presidio or garrisoned fort. The stretch of coast from St. Augustine to St. Helena, containing San Mateo (Fort Caroline), Santa Catalina (near the mouth of the Savannah River), and St. Helena (Santa Elena, later Parris Island) was known as the province of Guale, from the Guale Indians near another mission at Santa Caterina. This territory formed "the debatable land," destined to be the scene of persistent warfare between the English colonists and the Spaniards, until it was finally abandoned by the missionaries in 1702. By 1705 Timucua and Apalache, extending westward to the Apalachicola River, were in ruins. The strength of the Spanish re-

1. *Pedro Menéndez de Aviléz, Adelantado, Governor, and Captain General of Florida: Memorial by Gonzalo Solis de Meras* (1923).

2. On the early Franciscans in Florida, see Geiger in *Colonial Spanish America* (1926), pp. 538–550, and on the Florida coast in 1696–1697, Dickenson, *God's Protecting Providence* (1699, and many later editions).

sistance ebbed and flowed according to the energy, enthusiasm, and self-sacrificing spirit of those who sought to convert the Indians, for the missions were more than religious centers, they were pioneering agencies whereby alone the Indian could be converted, civilized, and also exploited. These devoted, courageous, and long-suffering priests and friars served both church and state. As the friars saw it, their missions were outposts and training schools for the uplift of the Indian, and they themselves were both exploring and diplomatic frontiersmen, often more effective than the presidial soldier in holding the frontier and colonizing it with Christian converts.[1]

Originally Spain had asserted her title to the territories as far north as Virginia, but by the treaty of 1670, signed in the very year when Ashley's colonists were getting located on Albemarle Point, the Spanish and English crowns mutually agreed to recognize, at least temporarily, the principle of effective occupation, and thus placed the Carolina settlement on the Ashley beyond the border of the debatable land.[2] Unfortunately this treaty was not published by the Spanish governor until two years later and even then was pretty much ignored. In spite of the fact that during the reign of Charles II (1665–1700) the power of Spain was weakening, that her administration was becoming demoralized, and that the vice-regal government of New Spain was practically helpless in the presence of the aggressive policy of both the English and the French, the frontier missionary and the presidial soldier were sufficiently determined

1. Bolton, "The Mission in the Spanish American Colonies," *American Historical Review*, XXIII, 42–61.

2. Bolton and Ross, *The Debatable Land*, being a reprint of Bolton's introduction to "Arredondo's Historical Proof of Spain's Title to Georgia," issued as *Spain's Title to Georgia* (1925). The text of the treaty of 1670 is in Davenport, *Treaties*, II, 194 (§7). The northern line, as accepted by Spain, ran through St. Helena Sound, but we are told that Spain never accepted the theory of "effective occupation" as a working principle for all time, considering the agreement reached in 1670 as ending with the death of Charles II, which came in 1700 (Lanning in *Colonial Historic America*, p. 383). Other articles bearing on the subject are Bolton, "Spanish Resistance to the Carolina Traders," *Georgia Historical Quarterly*, IX, 115; Ross, "The Spanish Settlement of Santa Elena, *ibid.*, 352, 379; Ross, "Restoration of the Spanish Missions in Georgia, 1598–1606," *ibid.*, X, 171–199, with a map (this restoration, after the massacre by the Gualean caciques in 1597 was the dawn of the golden era of the Spanish missions in Guale, Timucua, and Apalache, which lasted until the intrusion of the Carolina traders, 1702–1706, which destroyed the Spanish influence throughout the three mission districts). Dunn, *Spanish and French Rivalry, 1678–1702* (1917), pp. 205–206, deals with the weakness of Spain, a weakness that is well brought out in the "Report of the War Board of the Indies to the Queen," February 12, 1674, *South Carolina Magazine*, XXXVII, 59–64.

and tenacious to prolong the contest for many years. The claims of Spain to the coast lands below St. Helena and her refusal to recognize the right of the proprietors to their southern boundary line—the twenty-ninth parallel of latitude—involved the Carolina settlers for nearly half a century in many bitter experiences and in much exhausting and extensive warfare.[1]

The Charles Town settlement was more than an outpost against the Spaniard, it was also the center of the fur and slave trade with the Indians, a form of frontier enterprise that took no account of boundaries and depended for its success on the boldness, powers of endurance, and diplomatic skill of explorer and trader in their haz-

1. Sandford found no Spaniards at St. Helena in 1666. By an exchange with a local Indian cacique, he left there Dr. Henry Woodward, the first white man in South Carolina, who wanted to study the country and learn the native language. Later Woodward was carried to St. Augustine, where he lived with the parish priest. He escaped in 1668 and started for England to report to Ashley, whose agent he was. He was wrecked off Nevis, and eventually joined the fleet under West, when one of the vessels touched at Nevis on its way to Carolina in 1669. There he played a very important part in opening and promoting the fur trade.

Two further incidents should be recorded. (1) In 1670 the *Three Brothers,* a sloop obtained at Barbados to take the place of the *Albemarle,* lost in the storm, put in at Santa Caterina thinking it was St. Helena. Incautiously the captain, mate, and others, including William Carr, "a person of good worth and a good linguist," and John Rivers, a kinsman of Ashley's and his agent, went ashore and were seized by the Spanish friars there and sent to St. Augustine. When the report of this outrage came to the knowledge of Governor Sayle at Albemarle Point, he despatched Captain Joseph Baily and a body of colonists and Indians in three vessels and fourteen periauguas, with letters for the governor at St. Augustine, demanding the release of the prisoners. Going ashore at Santa Caterina to deliver the letters for transmission to St. Augustine, Baily was seized and imprisoned on the ground that he and his companions were pirates and without the proper ships' papers. The Spaniards refused to surrender Baily, holding him in captivity for at least two years and a half. The incident caused a great deal of excitement at Charles Town and led to some diplomatic correspondence. The eventual outcome is not known. In retaliation for what was deemed an act of piracy, three Spanish vessels, with infantry on board were sent against Charles Town, but unable to cross the harbor bar and overcome by a storm they were forced out to sea and withdrew without attempting an attack (*Shaftesbury Papers,* pp. 169–170, 173–174, 175, 205–206, 228, 239, 249, 264; Baily's letter of December 12, 1672, is in *South Carolina Magazine,* XVIII, 54–56). (2) In 1686 came the attack on the Scots under Lord Cardross at Port Royal and the destruction of Stuart Town, which had been established in 1684 (*South Carolina Magazine,* XXX, 69–89; Insh, *Scottish Colonial Schemes,* ch. VI; Crane, *The Southern Frontier,* pp. 26–33).

From the opening of the eighteenth century to the Yamassee War of 1715 a renewed interest was aroused in the Florida country and the trans-Appalachian west, as the result of which the South Carolina colony was heavily involved in conflicts with the Spanish until the destruction of the mission districts, 1702–1706, and the burning of Pensacola in 1707 transferred to the English the hegemony of northern Florida, but at a heavy cost (Crane, *The Southern Frontier,* ch. X).

ardous and exciting pursuit of profit. In the southern, southwestern, and western frontier, from the Carolina border to the Gulf and the Mississippi River, were groups of Indian tribes, whose influence and importance in that quarter were paralleled only by the prominence of the Five Nations in the north. Among these tribes were the near-by Catawba, whose five towns lay north of the Santee (or Wateree) River and whose trade was a bone of contention between Carolina and Virginia; the powerful Cherokee on the upper Santee along the watershed between the Mississippi and the Atlantic coast, who by 1705 had become entirely subject to the English and whose villages ranged along the Blue Ridge southward to the last foothills of the Appalachian Mountains; the great Creek federation of Upper Creeks (Alabamas, Talaposas, and Coosa) and Lower Creeks (the Creeks proper), called the "shrewdest politicians of the south," lying north of the present boundary of Florida, in western Georgia, and in northern Alabama;[1] the energetic Chickasaw on the upper waters of the Tombigbee below Muscle Shoals on the Tennessee, who though comparatively few in numbers were believed to be the most warlike of all; the distant Choctaw, largest of the tribal groups—generally friendly to the French and sometimes in alliance with them—between whom and the Chickasaw was a perpetual feud, representing intrigues of the French on one side and counterplots of the English on the other; and finally, certain other tribes, few in numbers as were the Apalache, or numerous as were the Yamassee and the Tuscarora, the uprisings of whom were among the most frightful experiences of the South and North Carolina colonists, and comparable only with King Philip's War in New England.

For the mastery of these various tribes English, French, and Spanish competed fiercely, not so much from a desire for their territory as from greed for the skins of beaver, bear, buffalo, and especially deer—the slaughter of which almost transcends belief—and for Indian slaves obtained as a result of tribal wars, a form of traffic roundly condemned by the proprietors, but in the early years never suppressed. While Charles Town was the social and business center of the colony, Savannah Town (Augusta) was the focal center of the Indian trade, the starting point of all trails to the west. There the traders gathered, there the goods brought up the river were transferred from periauguas to packhorses and Indian carriers for

1. Swanton, *Early History of the Creek Indians and their Neighbors* (1922).

transportation into the Indian country, and there the great bundles of deerskins and the smaller bundles of other skins were distributed preparatory to their carriage, either by water or by caravans of horses and Indian slaves along the land routes, to Charles Town, where they were combined with other merchandise for transmission to England.[1]

Gradually the English traders widened the field of their operations, moving southward through the province of Apalache along the Apalachicola, where they met the Spanish traders coming north from the Gulf, competing for the trade of the Lower Creeks; northwesterly toward the Cherokee, trade with whom was always a minor factor; and, most important of all, westward toward the Mississippi, which they had reached before the end of the century. There they found the French already pushing eastward. The latter had come down from the Illinois country and, owing to the efforts of La Salle (1678–1687) and Tonty (1682–1704)—both of whom had reached the mouth of the Mississippi as early as 1682 and had taken possession of the country in the name of the king of France—were opening to their compatriots the lower reaches of the river. Through the activities of Pontchartrain, minister of marine in Paris, and of Iberville, the intrepid explorer of New France, the great task was undertaken of founding a French dominion in Louisiana. Iberville, having harried the English in the Hudson Bay region, having taken part in the sack of Schenectady in 1690, and having seriously menaced England's control in Maine and New York, now turned his attention to the south. In 1699 he began the work so ably carried on by his younger brother, Bienville, who early in 1702 left Biloxi, where Iberville had located a colony, and removed first to Mobile Bay and then in 1710 to the present site of Mobile. Later in 1718 he founded New Orleans. Thus after 1700 the French were in possession of the lower Mississippi valley, and prepared to dispute with the Carolina traders their westward advance.

As far as the trade itself was concerned, the Spaniards were never a serious menace, except as they allied themselves with the French

1. Dr. Woodward had established friendly relations with the Westo Indians, above Savannah Town, as early as 1674, but it was not until after 1682, when in the war of 1681–1682 the Westos were driven from their villages, that the southwestward trade was laid open. The Carolina traders worked first toward the south, and then toward the west and northwest. In their northwest advance they accomplished little, but in the southern and westward movements they were entirely successful, until the Indian war of 1715–1716 destroyed all hope of controlling the Mississippi valley.

to instigate Indian attacks or disputed with the English the alliances which the latter made with the Indians, particularly with the Lower Creeks. On the other hand, the French in Louisiana were to the English officials and traders an ever present source of concern, potentially dangerous rivals and competitors. Iberville and Bienville, on their side, were equally fearful lest the Carolinians draw away the Indian trade from the Mississippi and in so doing divert a highly profitable traffic from New France to the English settlements on the Atlantic seaboard. They fought the issue with all the powers at their command, and in so doing inaugurated the same conflict in the south that others from New France were carrying on in the north. They were handicapped always by governmental indifference at home, where before the War of the Spanish Succession King Louis XIV and the officials at Versailles were unimpressed by the possibilities of the fur trade, and even after the war was begun were so straitened financially as to have very little money to spend on military undertakings in the New World. They were thwarted also by positive opposition, as when on May 21, 1696, the French king issued an edict, which put a complete ban on all western expeditions for furs and ordered all Frenchmen out of the interior of America. They were hampered by the infrequency of ships from home, by a great lack of traders and merchandise, by the long distances over which their goods had to be carried, and by the inferiority and costliness of the goods when received. They wasted their own energies in local quarrels and personal disputes, which sapped their strength and prevented active coöperation in the one great task of outwitting English diplomacy. On the other hand, the French were favored by the easier transits eastward into the Indian territory, because they were able to follow river routes and so to avoid the burdensome land carriages such as confronted the English. Also, they got on better with the Indians than did their rivals, because they displayed greater sagacity in negotiating agreements and alliances and avoided the brutal and tyrannous methods that the English often employed.[1] But even so they were never·able to supply the tribes with merchan-

1. The Yamassee and Tuscarora wars were both brought on by the iniquitous conduct of the white men. In the journal of the commons house of assembly for 1700 (p. 32) we read, "Several of the Nations now in amity with us have been by the Ensolence and unjust actions of the Traders much abused, and by the Lewdness and wickedness of them have been a Scandall to the Religion wee Profess." Again, "Our Indians are in Love with [the Frenchmen's] liberality and conversation" (*ibid.*, 1701, 2d part, p. 4). See William Byrd's comment, *Board of Trade Journal*, 1714–1718, p. 62.

dise, arms, and ammunition of as good a quality, or at as reasonable prices as could their competitors.

Against the aggressions of the French England's strongest bulwark in the south was Carolina, for whereas the Carolinians had laborious overland journeys to contend with, they had no Appalachian barrier to surmount, as for instance had the Virginians, and in most of their expeditions could follow fairly level trails. Carolina, therefore, was the colony best qualified to meet the French along the southern frontier, just as New York was similarly qualified to meet the French in the north. The southern rivalry began early, for the trade once started grew with great rapidity, absorbing the time and energy of the merchants and officials in Charles Town, constituting for many years the most lucrative branch of the colony's commerce and making of those engaged in it monopolists of the business, much as the Dutch in Albany were becoming the middlemen and monopolists of the trade in that quarter.[1]

But important as is a knowledge of the Indian trade to an understanding of the course of events in South Carolina under the proprietors, even more important is it that we should pursue the wider implications of the story, because the rivalry between England and France for the mastery in the world-wide field of commerce and the colonies was just entering on its century long career. To many an observer among the English, both at home and in America, France by her colonizing activities on the Mississippi was drawing a circle around the English settlements and in so doing was threatening not only to cut them off from all the profits of the fur trade but also to check permanently their pioneering efforts to establish homes in the world beyond the mountains. Men of the stamp of Randolph, Quary, Bellomont, Basse, Nicholson, Spotswood, Keith, and Coxe in the colonies generally, and Joseph Blake, James Moore, and Thomas Nairne in South Carolina voiced their fears in many a noteworthy protest and appeal.[2] As far as the policy and purpose of the

1. Crane, "The Tennessee River as the Road to Carolina: the Beginning of Exploration and Trade," *Mississippi Valley Historical Review*, III, 3–18; "The Southern Frontier in Queen Anne's War," *American Historical Review*, XXIV, 379–395; and especially the same writer's exceedingly important work, *The Southern Frontier* (1929). One should read in this connection Professor McIlwain's introduction to *Wraxall's Abridgment of the New York Indian Records, 1678–1751*.

2. Crane, *The Southern Frontier*, chs. III and IV. Writers on our colonial history, particularly those dealing with the history of individual colonies (McCrady, *South Carolina under the Proprietary Government, 1670–1719*, for example) have usually

French leaders in Louisiana were concerned these Englishmen were justified in their fears, for Iberville and Bienville, when they set about creating a French colonial dominion in the south, undoubtedly had it in their minds to balance the French dominion of Canada in the north. But fortunately for England these Frenchmen did not have the support of the higher authorities in the homeland. Louis XIV was interested not in the fur trade but in mines of lead and copper and of silver and gold; and it was not until the death of Charles II in 1700 and the accession of a Bourbon to the throne of Spain that the idea of colonization took possession of the French official mind. Even then the French policy, as has been said, was "both faltering and hazy and lacked any clear perception of the possibilities inherent in the situation." France never sent into the region agricultural laborers, peaceful, hard-working farmers with their families; she sent only *coureurs de bois,* who cared nothing for settled life. To the officials at Versailles fears of an English advance westward to be checked by a clear-cut and aggressive programme were too remote and relatively too unimportant to demand governmental attention. With so little support from headquarters at this early pe-

ignored Anglo-Colonial, Anglo-French, and inter-colonial relations and in consequence have severely condemned the men in the colonies who showed themselves in any way in sympathy with England's policy. They have, as a rule, construed the recommendations of these men as of sinister import, designed for the purpose of overthrowing colonial "liberties." Professor McIlwain says truly that there is no phase of our early history in which there is a greater discrepancy "between the importance of the subject to contemporaries and the indifference to it of modern historians." The letters of these men are full of references to the importance of this southwestern trade and territory and to the necessity of more united action. But however much the Privy Council and the Board of Trade may have advocated this policy, parliament was not interested and in successive years ignored the bills for uniting the private colonies to the crown. It was only after a quarter of a century and the persistent efforts of Egmont and Oglethorpe, in an age of great insensibility to philanthropic enterprise, that Georgia was finally established as a buffer colony against Spain.

Randolph's letters can be found in his correspondence; a letter of Basse is in *North Carolina Colonial Records,* I, 889–890; and the letters of Quary, Bellomont, Nicholson, Spotswood, and Keith are in *Calendar State Papers, Colonial.* Coxe, *Description of Carolana* is one long argument against the French peril of encirclement (Crane, *The Southern Frontier,* pp. 48–60, "Origins of Georgia," *Georgia Historical Quarterly,* XIV, 93–102; Melvin, "Dr. Coxe and Carolana," *Mississippi Valley Historical Review,* I, 257–262; Ettinger, *Life of Oglethorpe,* 1936). Thomas Nairne, agent of South Carolina and itinerant justice among the Indians, sent, soon after his appointment in 1708, a noteworthy communication to Secretary Sunderland (in office December 15, 1706–June 15, 1710) urging war against both the Spanish and the French (*Calendar State Papers, Colonial,* 1708–1709, §632). Nairne sent over a map, "A Compleat Description of Carolina." The date of letter and map is uncertain, probably 1708 or 1709.

riod such men as Iberville and Bienville were bound to find themselves thwarted in the execution of their more ambitious projects.[1]

On the other hand, whatever may have been the facts in the case, both the Board of Trade and the Privy Council of England were alive to the danger of possible French encroachment and envisaged clearly the dangers of a French encircling movement.[2] But the Carolina proprietors were not so wise or farsighted, for they were not the guardians of England's colonial policy. They were more concerned for their profits from the soil than they were for England's future. Though vitally interested in the fur trade, which they hoped would balance the heavy financial outlays already incurred, they, like the majority of the colonists in general, seem never to have grasped fully the significance of the conflict with France either in the lower Mississippi or along the frontiers of New York and New England. They did, on one occasion in 1709, persuade the Board of Trade to bring a petition from the colony to the attention of the Privy Council, but they destroyed any good effects this petition might have had, by approving a law passed by the assembly in South Carolina to prevent Virginia traders from dealing with the Indians below the Santee. Thus they overlooked the larger issue in favor of a purely local advantage. But even if they had realized the menace of the French situation they could have done nothing to ward off the danger, because the obligation lay rather with the English government and not with a group of private persons, possessed of limited powers and resources.[3]

1. Parkman, "French Policy in the Lower Mississippi Valley, 1697–1712, *Publications*, Colonial Society of Massachusetts, XXVIII, 225–238.

2. *Calendar State Papers, Colonial*, 1708–1709, p. 328.

3. From 1699 to 1701 the proprietors did nothing more than express their desire for peace with the Indians and approve the assembly's law of 1701 forbidding Virginians from trading within the province (*ibid.*, 1702, §615; *Journals Commons House of Assembly*, 1701, p. 15). But in 1709, roused by addresses from governor and council (*Commissions and Instructions*, ed. Salley, p. 147; *Journals*, 1698, p. 32; 1700, p. 22; 1701, 2d part, pp. 3–4) they wrote the Board of Trade (*Calendar State Papers, Colonial*, 1708–1709, §544; *Journal Board of Trade*, 1709–1715, p. 39) urging that in the forthcoming peace councils with France, effort be made to remove the French from the lower Mississippi. This letter, together with a large number of communications from other parts of the colonial world and protests from Virginia against the Carolina law led the Board of Trade to draw up two representations to the Privy Council, June 2 and September 6, 1709 (*Calendar State Papers, Colonial*, 1708–1709, pp. 327–328, §716). On August 22 and September 26, the Privy Council, taking these representations into consideration, recommended that the proprietors disallow the Carolina law and that the information received be made a subject for discussion in the negotiations for peace (*Acts Privy Council, Colonial*, II, §1106). These

In point of fact nothing shows better the impotency of the proprietary system at this juncture in England's colonial advancement than the rise to prominence of the problems of trade and defense. Those persons, both in England and the colonies, to whom these problems were of paramount concern, were convinced that it was incumbent on the mother country, because of her rapidly expanding interests and her recently formulated declarations of policy, to shoulder new responsibilities. They wanted her to broaden the field of her governmental control, to consolidate and centralize her methods of colonial management, and by taking into her own hands the private colonies to present a united front against her enemies, with a view to checking the French advance at an early stage in its progress. They believed that in the contest for the Indian trade, South Carolina was no longer merely the landed possession of a board of proprietors but had become a pawn in a great game of colonial expansion, played by two growing powers, whose aims in the New World were the same, namely, to control the fisheries and the fur trade, to procure new areas of supply for the raw materials needed by their people at home, and to widen the markets available for those engaged in foreign commerce who were striving to enlarge the country's mercantile marine.

Under the proprietors the system of management was always weak structurally because of its indefiniteness and lack of precision. No one could be quite sure of the rules governing organization and procedure and no one knew just what was meant by the proprietors' will and pleasure. The Concessions and Agreements of 1665, which were to play an important part in the life of East New Jersey, proved to be useless in Carolina after the settlement on the Cape Fear came to an untimely end in 1667. As a substitute, Ashley and Locke (so it is supposed) prepared a new set of regulations covering government, landholding, the judiciary, and social relations, which was issued in 1669, just before the Ashley expedition started for Carolina. This body of law, known as the Fundamental Constitutions, is believed to have been prepared by John Locke, at that time but thirty-seven years old, with the assistance, perhaps, of Ashley himself, though the authorship is by no means certain. The document elaborated the powers granted the proprietors in 1663 and gave them a

circumstances brought out anew the weakness of the proprietors and cost them, in some measure, the good will of the crown.

free hand to reproduce all the institutions, privileges, and customs enforced, enjoyed, and maintained at any time by the bishops of Durham, in the county palatine of that name. These powers, authorized either by the proprietary charters or by the commissions and instructions issued to proprietary governors, were granted, as we know, to other proprietors also and to a greater or lesser extent were exercised elsewhere in America, particularly in Maryland.

There is very little that is strictly new in the Fundamental Constitutions of 1669 or in any of the later abridgments, the most important of which is that of 1698.[1] The various provisions are an adaptation of English institutions and law to a great frontier palatinate, supplemented by certain concessions taken from Harrington's *Oceana*.[2] Others were based on ideas current at the time, such as those that concerned religious toleration—"Noe person whatever shall disturbe, molest or persecute another for his Speculative opinions in Religion or his way of Worship";[3] that called for a popular instead of a standing army, for a balance of property, and for the use of the ballot instead of the lot or the holding up of hands, a form which Penn also was to introduce into Pennsylvania. The system was essentially aristocratic in that it was based on the possession of landed property and made land ownership the foundation of the whole political and social structure. This fundamental idea as stated in the Constitutions—"since all power and dominion is most naturally founded on property"—is closely akin to Harrington's utterance, "As is the proportion or balance of Dominion or Property in Land, such is the nature of the Empire."[4] In the distribution of the land two-fifths were granted to the hereditary nobility and three-fifths to the

1. One should compare the original text with the later variations and abridgments, particularly with the version of 1698, which contains only forty-one paragraphs as over against the one hundred and twenty of the original (*North Carolina Colonial Records,* II, 852–858).

2. Russell Smith, *Harrington and his Oceana,* pp. 157–161, followed by Professor Ewing, *Cambridge History of the British Empire,* I, 609. Harrington's work, either in the folio editions of 1700 or in the quarto edition of 1747, should be carefully studied by anyone who wishes to understand the various concessions and constitutions issued by the proprietors of this period from Shaftesbury to Penn.

3. *North Carolina Colonial Records,* II, 857 (§39).

4. Harrington, *Oceana* (ed. 1700), p. 39. In regard to the balance of property, a subject that runs through all Harrington's works, the following quotation is to the point, "A nobility of gentry overbalancing a popular Government is the utter bane and destruction of it; as a nobility or gentry in a popular Government not overbalancing it, is the very life and soul of it." Similar statements can be found in Harrington, *The Prerogative of Popular Government* and *Political Aphorisms,* in the edition of

manorial lords and the common freeholders, and in this way a distinct effort was made to prevent the creation of an overweighted aristocracy on one side and a numerous democracy on the other. In the setting out and planting of the land grants pains were taken to obtain a proper proportioning of powers, whereby representation should be determined more or less in accordance with the charges borne and the money paid in in the general assessment of property.[1]

The possession of land was required of all holding social rank or taking part in government. The unmarried landless man was practically unrecognized, because as Harrington wrote, "The peasant partaking not of the balance can in relation to government be of no account."[2] At the top of the pyramid were the proprietors, each with a right to a seignory of twelve thousand acres in each county, and next to them the landgraves, with four baronies each, amounting to forty-eight thousand acres in all, each barony to be "in one body" or "one entire piece."[3] Then came the caciques with twenty-four thousand acres, and finally the "commoners," lords of manors and freeholders or yeomen, the lords to have not less than three thousand acres or more than twelve and the freeholders at least fifty in order to cast a ballot, according to the accepted idea that "every man who is Impowered to dispose of the Property and Estate of others, should have a Property of his owne."

The higher dignities were to be hereditary and the estates attached to them were to be indivisible and inalienable. No estate was to be a barony unless its owner was a landgrave, formally appointed to that rank by the proprietors, and no land was to be deemed a manor unless patented as such by the proprietors. Any man who lost his rank lost his land and, vice-versa, if he lost his land he lost his rank. Except in certain details, names, and proportions, the arrangement

1700, pp. 238, 243, 273, 391. Mr. Smith points out the many instances in which the Fundamental Constitutions depart from and distort the Harrington model.

1. The two-fifths and three-fifths rule is very clearly applied in the conditions laid down by the proprietors in 1691 for the distribution of lands in a county. The land was to be divided into forty squares, of which sixteen were to go to the hereditary nobility and twenty-four to the "people" (*Commissions and Instructions*, pp. 52–53).

2. *Oceana*, p. 271.

3. In 1698 the commons house of assembly objected strongly to the size of the baronies and wanted each barony to be reduced to 1000 acres in one piece (*Journals*, 1698, pp. 30, 35). There had been for some time opposition to the granting of "such great tracts of land."

was in accord with English law and practice, the most novel features being the terms "landgrave" and "cacique," the first, a word well known in the border counties of northern England, and the second one borrowed from the Spanish name for an Indian chief. Even the complicated rules governing inheritance and alienation were in conformity with the usages at home. There was nothing new to an Englishman in the setting off of land outside the lord's demesne for the use of freeholders, who were to hold their lands by grant and pay a quit-rent to the proprietors, or in the introduction into the scheme of courts leet and leet men, the latter of whom were merely copyholders, as essential and accustomed parts of the demesne of every lord, whether proprietor, landgrave, cacique, or commoner.

The system of government was somewhat more artificially contrived than were the tenurial arrangements, and by just so much the more unworkable. In England were to be eight proprietors, each holding a dignified office. The eldest was to be the lord palatine and the others were to bear the grandiose and empty titles of admiral, chamberlain, chancellor, constable, chief justice, and lord steward, titles familiar to everyone connected with the English government. Occasionally some of them, such as the lord steward, who had the right to appoint the surveyor general, had duties to perform. The eight taken together were to constitute the palatine court, which could function if the palatine and three members were present, with reserved rights of appointment, of disallowing laws, and of hearing appeals from the colony. Each proprietor was to have his deputy in the colony, who supposedly was to look after his seignory and act for him in the local assembly or parliament. The governor in the colony, who had to be at least a landgrave, was to be appointed by the palatine court, and was to hold his office at the pleasure of the proprietors. If at any time one of the latter should go to the colony he was to become governor at once by virtue of his proprietorship. According to the first version of the Constitutions the local assembly was to sit as a single house consisting of governor, proprietary deputies, landgraves and caciques, and the deputies—the last of whom, elected by the freeholders, were to possess each at least five hundred acres of freehold. Later, as the system was worked out, the assembly sat as two houses, one consisting of the proprietary deputies, landgraves, and caciques, and the other of the representatives of the freeholders.[1] Provision was made also for a grand council in the colony, an institution borrowed from Venice via Harrington, which was to consist of fifty members, whose function it was to propose the laws to the assembly for the latter's acceptance, on the principle that laws should be initiated by the best and resolved by the most.[2] This useless contrivance was abandoned even on paper in 1691 and ceased to appear at all in the abridgment of 1698.

Provision was made also for local courts, for grand and petty juries, the verdicts of which did not have to be unanimous, as a majority vote would serve.[3] The somewhat remarkable stipulation that no man should plead before the courts for money or any other reward is thought to have been taken from the *Oceana,* but its inclusion is not surprising in view of the strong prejudice in the colonies against the legal fraternity, which in Virginia (1658) took the form of an act forbidding men within the colony to give counsel in any cause or controversy for any kind of reward or profit whatsoever.[4] No freeman was to be tried except by a jury of his peers and no one was to be accounted a freeman or to have any estate or habitation in the colony who did not "acknowledge a God." As would be expected from men who had approved the Concessions of 1665, freedom of conscience was guaranteed,[5] though officially the Church of England, "the only true and orthodox church and the national religion of the king's dominions" was to be the established church of the colony. Other churches and "professions" were recognized if supported by at least seven members and properly and publicly registered, and no one could hold office unless he were identified with

1. *North Carolina Colonial Records,* II, 853 (§6).

2. *Oceana,* pp. 242, 243. The governor's council in the colony, erected under a provision of the temporary laws or instructions, was called "the grand council," but it was a very different body from that provided for in the Constitutions (*Journal of the Grand Council, 1671–1680,* ed. Salley, *passim*).

3. This clause in the original text would seem to be contradicted by a proprietary emendation of 1694, which reads, "Our meaning is that the Jury consisting of twelve men so impartially chosen should always unanimously agree in the verdict" (*Commissions and Instructions,* p. 76 note).

4. Hening, *Statutes,* I, 482. The similarity between the language of the Virginia law and that of the Constitutions would seem to preclude a Harrington origin and to show that the text was borrowed almost word for word from the Virginia law.

5. On liberty of conscience in the *Oceana,* see pp. 58, 515–523, and aphorisms, nos. 22–25, 41–42.

one of these groups. Slaves could be members of a church as well as freemen, but in becoming so they would gain no advantage in respect of their masters. Every freeman and naturalized foreigner had to swear allegiance to the king and take an oath of fidelity to the proprietors. In the abridgment of 1698 the oath required that "I be faithful to the Palatine and Lords Proprietors of Carolina their heirs and successors and with my utmost power will defend them and maintain the Government according to this Establishment in these Fundamental Constitutions." The proprietors in their turn promised loyally to preserve to the freemen their rights and privileges as Englishmen.[1]

Needless to say this strongly aristocratic constitution, compact of convention and novelty and overstocked with many ingenious contrivances of an impracticable sort never became, in its entirety, a working system for the colony. In all probability it could not have been enforced even in an established and mature community, much less in a sparsely populated frontier, but it has to be reckoned with in the history of the colony for two reasons. In the first place, certain portions of it were actually put into operation. The palatine court became a reality and played an important and interfering part in Carolina's life. Each proprietor regularly named his deputy and some of the later proprietors resided in the colony and there exercised proprietary rights. Many landgraves and caciques were created, forming an hereditary nobility, with a right to sit in the governor's council, a right to which the assembly took sharp objection later, listing it as a grievance.[2] There were created at least twenty-six landgraves, beginning with 1671, and thirteen caciques, beginning with 1678, and some of the former retained their titles, as did Landgrave Thomas Smith, to the end of their lives. In a few instances, as in the case of the Bellingers, the title descended to the second and third generation, but, as a rule, the dignity expired with the original holder. Some of those so honored never visited the colony, as was the case with Abel Ketelby, James Griffith, John Colleton, and John Wick, landgraves, and John Ashby, cacique; but others crossed

1. *North Carolina Colonial Records,* I, 228, 231.
2. When Thomas Smith, a member of the commons house of assembly, was made a landgrave he ought to have removed automatically to the upper house or council. But the lower house so strongly objected to the change that he refused to go (*Journals,* 1696, pp. 6–7; 1697, p. 5; 1698, pp. 11, 17).

the water and for good or evil identified themselves with the colony's affairs.[1]

By order of the palatine court in England seignories, baronies, and manors were provided for, though apparently no seignory or barony ever contained more than twelve thousand acres. The earliest seignory, though not so called in the land records, was that of Shaftesbury himself on the upper Ashley River. In 1678 Governor West was instructed to locate, on the Wando River—the western branch of the T in Cooper River—twelve thousand acres, "as a Signorie" for Sir Peter Colleton. This estate became the family seat of the Colleton family, the only family of an original proprietor to reside in Carolina and the only one to acquire during this early period as many as half a dozen properties, constituting probably the largest amount of land held by anyone in the colony. The third and last of the seignories was that of the notorious Seth Sothell, who in 1690, while governor, received twelve thousand acres in Colleton County on the Edisto, but the grant seems never to have got beyond the paper upon which the warrant was written.[2] John Archdale, on becoming a proprietor, thought of taking up a seignory, but there is nothing to show that he ever did so.[3] The seignories of both Shaftesbury and Colleton are usually classed as baronies. In addition, Edmund Bellinger had two baronies, Tomotley and Ashepoo; Thomas Smith, two, Winyah and Wiskinboo; and the Colletons three besides their seignory, Okalee, Cypress, and Wadboo. Three other individuals had one barony each. There were a few plantations called "baronies," granted to landgraves or caciques, but they contained less than twelve thousand acres in one piece and so were not baronies rightly so called. In one case, that of Malling, dubbed a barony, the

1. Lists of the landgraves and caciques are given in McCrady, *South Carolina under the Proprietary Government*, pp. 718, 719, but in neither case is the list complete. Of the landgraves McCrady omits James Griffith, Edward Jukes, and Edward Willmot who obtained by fraud a patent which was afterward cancelled. Of the caciques he omits John Foster. Samuel Wilson wanted to be a landgrave but could not bring it about. The proprietors seem to have voted patents, in blank, that were never executed and to have received requests that were never granted. Whether a patent could be bought I do not know, but in 1703 Monck wanted to sell both his caciqueship and his barony (*Journals*, 1703, p. 79). Copies of landgrave patents, in Latin, are to be found in *Commissions and Instructions*, pp. 140–142, 174–175, 222–224, 257–258. There is a list of the hereditary nobility, 1671–1686, in *Calendar State Papers, Colonial*, 1669–1674, §721. John Price is mentioned, 1685–1688, §646.

2. *Warrants for Land* (ed. Salley), I, 103–104; II, 139, 140, 214–215.

3. *Collections*, South Carolina Historical Society, I, 106.

grant was very small and the grantee was neither proprietor, land-grave, nor cacique.[1] In 1718, after the Yamassee War had opened up the country to the southward, the proprietors ordered that four baronies be surveyed in lower Granville County, at that time called Port Royal County, which with six others, planned but never per-fected, were to aggregate 119,000 acres. Lots were drawn for the four, one of which—Oketee or Devil's Elbow—fell to the Colletons and another—Hobcaw—to John Lord Carteret, the later Lord Granville, which he sold twelve years afterward, without ever having attempted to settle or improve it.

Besides the seignories and baronies there were "manors," so called, which in all probability were never laid out.[2] In none of these estates —seignories, baronies, and manors—was there any exercise of ma-norial jurisdiction or anything to indicate that the possessors were other than the heads of large agricultural plantations, similar in every respect to the other plantations obtained under the land con-ditions issued by the proprietors in 1683, 1685, and 1693. Except perhaps socially and to some extent politically also, these titles and titled estates affected in no way the routine of life in the colony. The baronies were plantations upon which the South Carolinian, using Indian and negro slaves and white indentured servants, raised dairy products, corn, and domestic livestock. They reared cattle on their outlying ranches, made use of the forests for pipe-staves and headings, obtained from the pine-lands and lightwood lands mate-rial for the making of naval stores, and as early as 1690 and perhaps earlier,[3] turned the lower levels of marsh and swamp into rice fields, particularly along the tidal streams, where the irrigation and drain-age effected by the tide rendered the marshes along the rivers supe-rior to those farther inland.

1. H. A. M. Smith, *Baronies of South Carolina* (1931), made up of articles from the *South Carolina Magazine*.

2. *Warrants for Land*, II, 29, 209; *Commissions and Instructions*, pp. 3–4, 40, 61, 110. Grants of manors seem to have been limited chiefly to the Huguenots of Craven County, and then only if they or he "shall so desire." There is, however, one grant of 12,000 acres made to Thomas Amy, one of the proprietors, in 1694, "in two Manners if he shall desire it." I can find no evidence to show that any manors were ever erected.

3. Salley, "Introduction of Rice Culture of South Carolina," *Bulletin*, Historical Commission of South Carolina, no. 6. In 1700 the governor and council wrote, "Your Lordships Country hath made more rice the last Crop than we have ships to Transport" (*Commissions and Instructions*, p. 131). Nairne, in his *Letter from South Carolina* (London, 1710), gives an account of the rice culture, pp. 10, 11.

In the second place, the proprietors for more than thirty years attempted to persuade the colonists to adopt the Fundamental Constitutions by act of assembly. They began with the original version, "our excellent modell," as Shaftesbury called it, and later substituted a modified and shortened form, meeting each rebuff with instructions to the governors to come as nigh to the Constitutions as they could. Apparently they realized very early that the scheme was too ponderous for an infant colony and were willing temporarily to go along under much simpler working arrangements, until the population should have sufficiently increased to provide material for landgraves and caciques and for the very cumbrous system of council and courts. On January 12, 1682, out of deference to the Scots who were planning a settlement under Lord Cardross,[1] they issued the Constitutions in revised form, which they declared to be the "onely constitutions agreed to or signed by all the eight proprietors," and which they intended should be, as those of 1669 were supposed to be, "the sacred and unalterable forme and rule of Government of Carolina for ever."[2] When, however, it became evident that the assembly was entirely unwilling to give formal approval of the Constitutions or to make them the law of the province, the proprietors again gave way, declaring in 1693 that the Constitutions "are now ceased" and instructing Governors Ludwell, Smith, and Archdale to approach "as neer as possible" to the "sacred and unalterable" formulae. When they heard that the assembly was appointing a committee "to draw up a system of government for the future" they could only reply "but of what use this can be we know not, since they have so disrespectfully refused our Excellent Constitutions."[3]

But the proprietors had no intention of giving up the original plan. In 1698, reduced to only six efficient members, they reissued the

1. *Calendar State Papers, Colonial,* 1681–1685, §§807, 1780, p. 510; Rivers, *Sketch,* pp. 413, 421.

2. *North Carolina Colonial Records,* I, 368; II, 842.

3. *Calendar State Papers, Colonial,* 1693–1696, p. 84; *Commissions and Instructions,* pp. 34, 60, 67, 76. In their instructions to Archdale, August 23, 1695, they say, "You are with the assistance of the Grand Council to Inspect all our Constitutions and what of them you shall think most Expedient for the better Establishment of our Governm[t]: for the good and welfare of our People you are to present to the Gener[ll] assembly for their concurrance and what shall be by you: and our said Grand Council and assembly soe agreed on: You are to Transmitt to us for our Concurrance therein and to wayte our Determination in the mater" (*Journals,* 1696, p. 12). In *Commissions and Instructions,* p. 95, mention is made of a similar but later instruction, given by the proprietors, October 21, 1696, to James Colleton, ordering him to employ one John Stuart to compare and reconcile the various texts.

text in shortened form.[1] The reasons for doing so are not entirely clear, but the date is suggestive as showing the influence of the inquiry which the home government was making into the activities of the private colonies, in an effort to decide whether it were best or not to take them all into the hands of the crown.[2] By omitting some parts and modifying others, the proprietors reduced the paragraphs from one hundred and twenty to forty-one, but, strangely enough, without altering substantially their character. All that concerned the leetmen, manors, and the complicated system of courts was left out, but the rest was retained. It is not surprising, therefore, that the assembly, as it had consistently done before, refused to accept the shortened form, unless it were allowed to amend or add to the text.[3] So persistently did it adhere to this refusal[4] that, finally, the proprietors in sending instructions to Governor Sir Nathaniel Johnson in 1702 fell back on the familiar phrase, which they had used so often before, "to follow such rules as we have given in our Fundamental Constitutions, Temporary Lawes and Instructions to our Former Governors" and be guided by such of them as seemed "most fitt to be put in practice."[5] This is the last appearance of this phrase in the documents of the period and the last reference in the governors' instructions to the Fundamental Constitutions.[6] Yet it must always be remembered that scores of individuals signed the Constitutions from the beginning, promising allegiance to the king,

1. Reference is made in 1693 to a text "comonly called the *ffourth Constitutions*" (*Collections,* South Carolina Historical Society, I, 132; the full letter is in C.O., 5:288, p. 236). In that case the Constitutions of 1698 would be the fifth of the series.

2. *House of Lords Manuscripts* (new series), II, §§1047, 1115, pp. 412, 440–441; *Calendar State Papers, Colonial,* 1697–1698, §451.

3. *North Carolina Colonial Records,* II, 905; *Journals,* 1698, pp. 12, 21, 22, 28, 29–30. "We offered [the Constitutions] to the Lower House for their assent to, by a Bill of this House to be Pass'd into a Law; they Liked them not, so modestly laid them aside, and appointed a Committee to add to those or draw new ones" (letter from Blake, May 13, 1699, *Commissions and Instructions,* p. 115).

4. In a letter from Blake and council, September, 1699, appears this entry: "Our Assembly have Sate and will not medle anything in the matter of the Constitutions" (*ibid.,* p. 127). In 1700, "the Constitutions the Commons would not accept of" (*ibid.,* p. 131). In March, 1702, Governor Moore, in his message, recommended that the assembly take into consideration "the Last Constitution sent by the proprietors" and asked that a committee be appointed "to make such amendments and Additions as may be thought for the good and safety of the Province." The assembly debated the Constitutions paragraph by paragraph, but on the first reading defeated the bill to adopt them, September, 1702. *Journals,* 1702, pp. 48, 70–71, 88–89, 91.

5. *North Carolina Colonial Records,* I, 555; *Commissions and Instructions,* p. 168.

6. That the proprietors continued to enforce some parts of the Constitutions after 1702 seems likely from a phrase in one of Burrington's letters (1725), referring to

submission and fidelity to the lords proprietors, and obedience to "the forms of Government established by the Fundamental Constitutions." Only thus were such individuals able to hold land, to take part in the affairs of the province, to become members of the council and the commons house of assembly, and to obtain legal recognition as naturalized members of the community.[1] Thus for more than thirty years these Constitutions were a disturbing factor in the life of the colonists, and the determination of the proprietors to enforce them and the unwillingness of the assembly to accept them made it difficult for anyone, either in or out of office, to know just what were the laws they were expected to obey.[2]

To one unfamiliar with the tenacity of the English legal mind and the sanctity to an Englishman of a vested property interest, the persistence of the proprietors in clinging to this archaic and cumbersome form of colonial management would seem almost incomprehensible. It was a time when the whole colonial situation was under debate; when the Spanish and Gallic perils were looming up in new and menacing forms on the none too distant horizon; when the colonies were gradually winning recognition as potential assets contributing to England's prosperity; and when trade and defense were

the members of the assembly "which must be chosen and meet according to the Fundamental Constitutions" (*North Carolina Colonial Records*, III, 527). Similar words continued to be used whenever one of the proprietors appointed a deputy (*Commissions and Instructions*, p. 202). Probably the Constitutions were considered legally in being as long as the proprietary rule lasted.

1. Hirsch, *Huguenots of Colonial South Carolina*, pp. 114, 116, gives facsimiles of two loose leaves containing thirty names of those who signed, among them the names of Morton, Godfrey, Quary, Grimball, Bull, How, and others. The dates are from October 6, 1685, to April, 1689. The Constitutions referred to as signed by Governor Morton and his council on October 6 are those of January 12, 1682. On the second leaf are the signatures of four men who subscribe the Constitutions of July 21, 1669. The reason for this separate subscription is given in an unsigned address to Sothell, probably of date 1688 or 1689, from some one or more in the colony, who wrote that when Governor Morton called on the members of the general assembly, November 9, 1685, to subscribe the Constitutions of 1682, twelve of the nineteen members of the lower house refused, because they had already sworn to the Constitutions of 1669. Rivers, *Sketch*, p. 422; *Calendar State Papers, Colonial*, 1685–1688, p. 624 (compare §1162); *North Carolina Colonial Records*, II, 843.

2. *Journals*, 1692, p. 25; 1693, p. 8; 1696, pp. 16–17. Governor Ludwell, October 14, 1692, declared in his message that "as Yett there is no Established foundation of Governm[t]." In 1693 he said, "Since all the Constitutions Grants etc sent by the Lords have proved unusefull." In 1696 the lower house petitioned Archdale, saying "their Lordshipps allso Left the Governm[t] of this Settlement uncertain and were pleased frequently to alter the same, these mutations, hapning one on the neck of another, occasioned heart burnings and Discontents amongst the Inhabitants and Kept Many in Doubt whether they would Settle here or not."

becoming leading objectives in the policy of England's king and his advisers. Then it was that these eight men, possessed of a legal right to the soil[1] and government of Carolina, were declaring themselves entirely independent of the royal authority. Most of them cared but little for their property beyond the returns that might accrue from it and many of them were quite incapable of taking an intelligent interest in it; but because they had inherited, purchased, or received by assignment certain of the proprietary shares, as of a joint-stock, they maintained that they had a right to do what they liked with their own. Such was an Englishman's idea of a property franchise in the seventeenth and eighteenth centuries.

Who were these men? Of those whose names appear attached to the Constitutions of 1698—Bath, A. Ashley, Craven, Carteret, Colleton, Amy, Thornborough—only three, Ashley, Carteret (eight years old), and Colleton were direct descendants of the original grantees. Craven was a grandnephew. No one of these four took any interest in Carolina or were even cognizant of its affairs, the first three leaving the business to be looked after by trustees or guardians. Shaftesbury's share, for example, was administered after his death in 1683 by his second grandson, Maurice Ashley, who until 1725 acted for the incompetent son and the indifferent first grandson in the capacity of trustee. He was during the later part of the period a proprietor himself. William Thornborough, the secretary, a merchant of London and a proprietor in his own right, at one time served as trustee for four shares, those of the infant Colleton and three others. Clarendon's share was sold to Seth Sothell and after the latter's death became the subject of prolonged litigation, owing to a doubt as to whether or not Sothell, who died intestate, left any heirs. The two litigants, John Archdale and Thomas Amy, sat together at the palatine court for thirteen years, it being seemingly impossible to reconcile their conflicting claims.[2] Two other shares, those of the Duke of Albemarle and Sir William Berkeley, became involved also in long and costly suits at law. In the first suit the plaintiff was the Earl of Bath, who laid claim to all the Albemarle estate. He won his suit.[3] In the second, which got strangely mixed up with the

1. "The land is ours and we shall not part with it, but on our owne terms." *Commissions and Instructions*, p. 71.

2. McCrady, *South Carolina*, 1670–1719, p. 272.

3. "By a verdict in the King's Bench a decree in Chancery and that confirmed by the House of Lords," *Commissions and Instructions*, p. 76.

Clarendon case, the claimant was John Danson, a Quaker and a London and Carolina merchant, who held the Berkeley share by deed from his father-in-law John Archdale, also a Quaker. Both the Clarendon and Berkeley cases went into chancery, were eventually dismissed as insolvable, and the shares were put up to the highest bidder.[1]

Thus a right to the soil and government of Carolina was acquired by a group of men in England, of no great importance, only one or two of whom were at any time in public life or had had any experience in administration. Some of them were still minors served by guardians, and the rest were inactive and indifferent, content to leave their Carolina affairs to be looked after by trustees, who acted somewhat in the capacity of stewards of country estates. Three only were related by blood to the original patentees: John Lord Carteret born in 1690 and not of age until 1711, who was represented by Lord Granville, his uncle; William Lord Craven, born in 1697 and under the guardianship of Sir Fulwar Skipwith; and the infant, Sir John Colleton, bart., who as a minor had several substitutes at the board. Three others, Sothell (Clarendon), Blake (Lord Berkeley), and Archdale (Sir William Berkeley) were at one time or another governors in the colony, receiving their instructions from the palatine court, enjoying commendations when deserved and incurring criti-

1. Nicholas Trott, a merchant of London, who was at one time governor of the Bahamas, married the daughter of Thomas Amy and was assigned the Clarendon share by his father-in-law as a marriage portion for his wife. This share had been conveyed to Amy by the proprietors after Sothell's death, on the supposition that Sothell had left no heirs. Trott called himself "one of the true and absolute lords" and he seems to have been recognized in a way by the other proprietors, for I find his name once listed as a proprietor (*Calendar State Papers, Colonial*, 1706–1708, §372). In 1702 he appointed as his deputy in Carolina his cousin Nicholas Trott, Jr., formerly of Bermuda, a deputyship which the latter refused to accept, though he afterward served as deputy for the infant Colleton.

Nicholas Trott, Jr., went to Bermuda in 1690 from London, returned to London in 1691, but came back to Bermuda the same year. In 1693 he was appointed secretary and in 1696 attorney general, and became a member of the assembly. He took a prominent part against Governor Richier, and though falling into disfavor in the colony was upheld at Whitehall. He remained in Bermuda until about 1699, when he went to South Carolina, leaving several unfinished suits in Bermuda, which dragged along for many years. In Bermuda he married Jane Willis and there he had his early training and experience (I owe these facts to Dr. Henry Wilkinson, who writes me that he has unpublished documentary evidence for all the statements made). In South Carolina Trott was, at one time or another, attorney general and naval officer (suspended, 1702, but restored), speaker of the house (after the house once in 1700 refused to elect him), secretary and register of the colony and compiler of its laws, chief justice, and judge of vice-admiralty.

cism when things went wrong, as would any other governors. It is difficult to imagine a more unfit body for the administration of a colony than were these proprietors, particularly after 1700. Invested with supreme authority as rulers and landlords,[1] they were chiefly interested in the profits of their proprietorship, and when they found that they could not protect the colony by means of the revenues arising out of their quit-rents and were faced with the necessity of advancing money from the revenues of their estates in England, they were willing to give up their rights and surrender their charter to the crown.

One may not wonder that pressure was brought to bear upon the proprietors by many men of influence both in England and in Carolina to effect this surrender. The members of the Board of Trade at Whitehall and such English representatives in America as Nicholson and Randolph desired to get rid of the proprietary system altogether and to obtain for the proprietary colonies a more efficient order of government, to the greater peace and contentment of the colonists and the advantage of the mother country. In South Carolina were merchants and planters, who complained of the manifest inability of the palatine court to govern the colony wisely and to aid the people in their distress. They wrote of the constant fear of the Spaniards; of the heavy financial burden involved in meeting the cost of offense and defense in a war which lasted off and on almost continuously for a quarter of a century; of the necessity of

1. Under the proprietary regulations of November 20, 1682, September 21, 1683, August 30, 1685, and February 6, 1693 (the first contained in Morton's instructions, §10, and the last printed in *Commissions and Instructions*, pp. 47–59), lands were granted to any freeman or free person, under the headright or "arrival" rule, at the rate of seventy or seventy-five acres for a free settler and fifty acres for a servant or a negro. Though this rule continued to remain operative after 1695–1696, it was generally replaced at that time by the "purchase" rule, which allowed land to be bought at the rate of £20 for a thousand acres near the settlement and £10 for lands two hundred miles away "near the mountains" (*Journals*, 1696, p. 12). All grants carried a quit-rent: an ear of Indian corn (the colonial equivalent of a pepper corn) for a seignory; £20 more or less for a barony; twelve pence a hundred acres for purchased lands; and one penny an acre for lands granted under the "arrival" rule. Outside the seignories and baronies allotments ran as high as three, four, and six thousand acres in a single piece and as low as ten or twenty acres. Charges of excessive grants, which were deemed ruinous to settlement, led after 1700 to limiting the amount to 640 acres, for it was realized that large areas could not be rapidly improved and to the colonist land without stock had little value. Land upon which the quit-rent remained unpaid for sixty days was liable to action on the part of the proprietors' receiver general and many were the petitions sent in and acts passed for the remission of arrearages. For the system as operating after 1700, Nairne, *Letter*, pp. 47–49.

issuing paper money to meet the charges, a form of currency which depreciated so rapidly as to reduce the credit of the colony to a point from which it never recovered in colonial times; and of the local factional disputes, some of which owed their origin to the impact of the Anglo-Spanish-French rivalry, and others to political and religious discords arising within the colonies themselves. These disputes and discords, which in the Albemarle section took the form of armed uprisings, must now engage our interest, for they concern the domestic current of events in the colonies which we can now begin to call North and South Carolina.

NOTE: The formation of the Hudson's Bay Company was one outcome of the activities of the French explorers, Radisson and his brother-in-law, Groseilleirs, who with the royal commissioner of 1664, Colonel George Cartwright, sailed for England in 1665, in a vessel captained by Benjamin Gillam, elder brother of a Boston merchant, Zachariah Gillam (for whom see below, p. 254, note 3). The vessel was captured by a Dutch privateer after a fight of two hours. Cartwright and the Frenchmen were landed in Spain, and from there made their way to England, reaching London before the end of the year. Acting in conjunction with Zachariah, whom the Frenchmen had known in Boston and now met in England, they placed before the merchants in London and the courtier promoters at Whitehall—especially Sir George Carteret, whom they interviewed at Oxford—the advantages of the Hudson Bay region, of which they knew, probably, only from Indian reports. At the head of those concerned in the venture was Prince Rupert, the king's first cousin, and among the courtier promoters were the Duke of York, the Earl of Arlington, Sir Peter Colleton, Sir George Carteret, the Duke of Albemarle, Anthony Lord Ashley, and Prince Rupert's secretary, James Hayes, many of whom were already deeply involved in the affairs of the Royal African Company and the Royal Fishery Company, and in the settlement of New York, the Jerseys, and the Carolinas, and were soon to be applicants for a grant of the Bahamas. Allied with them were such London merchants as Sir Robert Vyner, John Kirke (whose daughter Radisson married), Francis Millington, William Prettyman, and others, mentioned in the preliminary grants and in the company's final charter of May 2, 1670, who, influenced by Radisson and Groseilleirs, were in all likelihood the first to support the undertaking.

An expedition was soon started. The king lent to Prince Rupert the *Eaglet,* William Stannard, master. The adventurers engaged Zachariah Gillam, supplying him with a vessel, the *Nonsuch,* putting up money and furnishing goods, trusting in his seamanship and experience. The two vessels got underway June 3, 1668, but Stannard with Radisson on board, finding his vessel unseaworthy, turned back and Gillam with Groseilleirs went on alone. They skirted the coast of Greenland and penetrated Hudson Bay as far as an inflowing stream, later called Rupert's River, at the southern end. There Gillam and Groseilleirs spent the winter, in a log house with a cave eight or ten feet deep, keeping their health "reasonably well." This occupation became the basis of England's claim to the Hudson Bay territory, which her authorities were to maintain against France for more than three-quarters of a century. The men returned in the autumn of 1669 and immediately, October 21 of that year, steps were taken for the erection of a regularly incorporated company. Preliminary grants were made in 1669 to Sir Edward Hungerford (for whom see the *D.N.B.*) and others, and the charter was issued on May 2, 1670, in the same year with the grant of the Bahamas and the permanent settlement of Carolina, at a time when the profits of trade were uppermost in men's minds. Zachariah had returned with a large cargo of furs and pelts, having traded, according to his own account, with 300 Indians. The outlook was full of promise. The company was given a monopoly of the trade of the entire northern part of America, a monopoly that was the more important because in 1638 Charles I had issued a proclamation forbidding the use of any material in the manufacture of hats except beaver stuff or beaver wool.

Gillam remained in the service of the company at least until September, 1675 (*Calendar State Papers, Domestic*, Charles II, 373, no. 4), when he seems to have resumed his former business of transatlantic and coastwise trafficking. When his father died in the year 1674 Gillam's share of the estate was administered by his brother-in-law, Richard Sharpe, because he was away from Boston in the service of the company (*Publications*, Colonial Society of Massachusetts, 29, p. 525). The record of his first appearance in North Carolina in December, 1677, shows that he came there directly from London, with goods on board, to sell or exchange for tobacco, that were manifestly of English manufacture. In certain legal transactions of the year 1678 he is mentioned as a "merchant of the city of London" and the owner of a ship, the *Caroline* (Proceedings in the General Court of Albemarle, 1679–1712, Raleigh), and he may well have had a counting-house there. From 1677 to 1680 he was mixed up with North Carolina affairs and the Culpeper rebellion and it was not until February, 1680, that he was discharged from custody in England, where he had been confined awaiting trial.

Sometime in 1680 or 1681 he was requested by the company to undertake another voyage to Hudson Bay, in order to carry out a new governor. But in the years since 1676 conditions there had changed. Radisson was once more in the service of France and interlopers were trespassing on the company's territory. When Zachariah, in the *Prince Rupert*, arrived at the Bay he found himself opposed by his old friend. He also found there his son, Benjamin III, in the *Bachelor's Delight*. Just what happened is not quite clear, but the company later claimed that there was collusion between father and son, the latter of whom was eventually seized by Radisson and sent off a prisoner to Quebec. But before this happened the father (called "Old Zach," though he was but 46 years old) had come to an untimely end. His ship, caught in the ice of Nelson River, was crushed and sank and Zachariah was drowned. (Radisson, *Voyages*, p. 281.)

Radisson, *Voyages*, deals with Gillam's experiences of 1682–1683. In the Royal Society Guard Book 19, nos. 19 and 29, are "Queries" proposed to "Captain Guillaume," one of which concerns the voyage of 1668–1669, the answers containing information about the voyage, the life in "Nova Brittania," as Gillam called the place, the people, and the country. These "Queries" appear in several different forms in the archives, some relating to the first voyage and some to the second, the earliest of which was contemporaneously printed. The original manuscript of a diary kept in 1682 by Benjamin III was, in 1753, in the possession of a Mr. Taylor, a merchant of Boston, but has since disappeared (Huntington Library, Loudoun Papers, 46, p. 459). Oldmixon's account (*British Empire*, I, 544, 557, reprinted by Tyrrell, Champlain Society, vol. 18) is almost negligible. Two important contributions are in *Minnesota History*, Vol. 16, by Fulmer Mood and Miss Grace Lee Nute, to the latter of whom I am indebted for assistance in the preparation of this note. Miss Nute is writing a biography of Radisson, but no one has ever dealt at length with Zachariah Gillam.

CHAPTER VI

THE TWO CAROLINAS: LATER YEARS

THUS the people of South Carolina stood, as it were, between two fires: on one side were the French, Spanish, and Indians; and on the other was a loose-jointed and inefficient board of proprietors in London, able legally to interfere in the affairs of the colonists and often to thwart them in their efforts at self-management. The colony was growing in size and increasing in extent. In 1708 the number of its people had reached nine or ten thousand, free, bond, and slave; the area of occupied territory was widening out in all directions toward the boundaries;[1] and owing to the profits of the Indian trade the colony was acquiring abroad a reputation for wealth and prosperity.

But in their choice of governors the proprietors were not always happy. At the beginning Sayle held the office and he was followed

1. The gradual expansion of the settled portions of the colony can be roughly estimated from the increase in the number of warrants issued from 1672 to 1711; 560 from 1672 to 1679; 603 from 1680 to 1692; and 2367 from 1692 to 1711. The test is not a certain one, as lands were granted that were never taken up and other lands were re-granted, that had been forfeited or escheated for felony, death intestate and without heirs, failure to seat in the country or to build in Charles Town, desertion, and non-payment of quit-rent. As far as the warrants go to show lands were set off in all the counties before 1711. In Craven, which ran twenty-three miles northeast along the coast between the Sewee and the Santee, where the settlers were almost entirely French Huguenots and Swiss Protestants from the Vaud (Lawson, *A New Voyage*, pp. 12–15, describes his visit and says that in 1708 about 70 families were there). In Berkeley, the most populous of all, which lay between the Sewee and the Stono rivers, and included Charles Town. In Colleton, which covered the region between the Stono and the Cambahee (land south of the Cambahee was at first reserved for the Scots). All the counties ran back thirty-five miles from the coast. Grants are mentioned as having been made in "Port Royal County," which included St. Helena and other islands south of Colleton County, where still lived remnants of the Presbyterian Scots, who in 1694 were reported as having made little progress in planting the region. No such county as "Port Royal" was ever officially so called, and it was not until about 1710, when the proprietors, urged on by merchants of London, planned to erect Beaufort Town as a seaport for the shipping of naval stores (which they did in 1711) that the name Granville County was selected (*Calendar State Papers, Colonial*, 1710–1711, §605). Lands in large quantities were laid out up the Ashley and Cooper rivers (Smith, *South Carolina Magazine*, XX), up and beyond the Santee, southwesterly toward Savannah Town, and, lavishly, in the Edisto region, including the many islands there.

by Joseph West, the man who contributed most to the foundation of the colony. He had commanded the first expedition in 1669 and after Sayle's death served as governor from 1671 to 1672. Yeamans, returning at this time, claimed the governorship on the ground that he was the only landgrave in the province and was upheld in his claim by the proprietors. On his death in August, 1674, West was chosen by the council, having been commissioned by the proprietors the preceding April, and but for a brief intermission, from the autumn of 1682 to the autumn of 1684—a period of little importance in the history of the colony—he served until June or July, 1685. At first he did not do any too well. Locke, relying on reports from the colonists characterized him as "faithful and stout," but unsuccessful as a governor, because of his pride and peevishness. There was some doubt regarding his right to the office, because in 1671 he had been named by Sayle on the latter's deathbed and during his first period of office he aroused discontent and almost mutiny by refusing to call a "parliament," because, as he said, there were not enough freeholders in the province to elect one. According to others, however, among whom were such important colonists as Yeamans, Scrivener, Owen, Gray, and Matthews—all of whom had a claim to membership in the council—his refusal was due to the fear that his election and actions would be called into question.[1] But as he settled down to his responsibilities he improved and "seems to have preserved the esteem and confidence both of the proprietors and the people and to have administered the trusts confided in him, honestly, skilfully, and successfully."[2] The records of his government, as well as the testimony

1. This was the origin of the so-called "Owen's parliament." William Owen came over with West in 1669 as Sir Peter Colleton's deputy, and when West refused to call an assembly, Owen questioned his title to the governorship and declared that no orders could be issued or laws passed without a representation of the freeholders. He brought about the election of fifteen members for "the establishment of laws for the present and better government of the people." These fifteen added to the five members of the council completed the number of twenty "as is by the Lords Proprietors institutions warrented and directed." As Owen was one of the fifteen and likewise had a right to sit as a member of the council by virtue of his deputyship, he would seem to have committed an irregularity himself. His associate, Scrivener, was immediately suspended from the council and he and Owen were debarred from holding office. The incident passed. Owen did not lose the good will of Ashley, and when the records of the council begin, August 28, 1671, he appears as one of its members, sitting until 1675 (*Calendar State Papers, Colonial,* 1669–1674, §§213, 471, iii, 473; *Shaftesbury Papers,* pp. 170–174, 203–204, 290–295, 311–312, 313–332, 471–475).

2. Smith, "Joseph West, Landgrave and Governor," *South Carolina Magazine,*

of his contemporaries show that he and his council, aroused by the depressed condition of the colony, did their best to set it on its feet. They protected it from the attacks of neighboring Indian tribes—Cussoos and Westos, prepared for and frustrated the threatened incursions of the Spanish from St. Augustine, and calmed the people within by settling quarrels and preserving the peace. Thus they made ready the way for the transfer of the settlement from the old Charles Town to the new, a transfer that had been under consideration since 1672.[1]

But the peace was not long maintained. On August 17, 1686, in the very year when West retired and went to New York, the Spanish appeared before Port Royal and completely destroyed Stuart Town (a short distance below the later town of Beaufort), a settlement begun in 1684 by Lord Cardross and his fellow Scots as a refuge for Covenanters. This settlement, but thinly populated because of troubles in Scotland which checked migration, had never really prospered. Quarrels with the merchants of Charles Town over the fur trade with the Yamassee, which these Scots wished to monopolize, had kept the settlement embroiled, and an attack which they had made on the mission station of Santa Catalina had provoked, so the Charles Town people declared, the Spanish raid, which ended with the invaders' pushing northward toward Edisto and plundering within the confines of the province itself. All this damage was made the more complete by "a Hurricane wonderfully horrid and destructive . . . attended," so runs the account, "with such dismall dreadfull and fatall consequences that the hand of Almighty God seemes to concurr with the Malice of our Enemies to hasten on Ruin and desolation."[2]

XIX, 189–193; "Governor West's Terms as Governor," XX, 147–149. West was governor from September, 1670, to April 19, 1672, when he was superseded by Yeamans, who remained in office until the end of July, 1674, dying in Charles Town sometime between August 3 and 13 of that year (for the reasons why he was removed from office, *Calendar State Papers, Colonial,* 1669–1674, §1277). West then became governor for the second time and served until May, 1684, when he was followed by Richard Kyrle, Joseph Morton or Moreton, and Robert Quary, all within a year. On the removal of Quary, West was again commissioned, but tiring of the office he retired, sometime between July 30 and September 9, 1685, going to New York, where he died. Morton then came in again and remained until the appearance of James Colleton in 1686.

1. *Journal of the Grand Council,* pp. 27, 31, 45, 79–80.
2. Insh, *Scottish Colonial Schemes,* pp. 209–211; Crane, *The Southern Frontier,* pp. 26–31; "Arrival of the Cardross Settlers" and "Spanish Depredations," *South*

Nor was the situation improved by the policy and activities of the next two governors, James Colleton and Seth Sothell. Colleton, brother of Sir Peter, was living in Barbados, but on being made a landgrave in 1686 he removed with his family to Carolina, built a house on Cooper River, and by virtue of his dignity assumed the office of governor. From the first he was opposed by a powerful group in the commons house of assembly, which was hostile to the proprietors, to their methods of granting land, and to the payment of quit-rents. Unable to obtain from the commons house the passage of a militia act, which he said was necessary in order to protect the colony against foreign invasion and to suppress domestic tumult, he placed the colony under martial law and enforced it against sundry of the inhabitants "to [the] apparent breach of their Libertys propertys and priviledges and to the dread and terror of their Maj^{ties} Subjects." While martial law was still in force Seth Sothell, turbulent, hotheaded, and a trouble-maker, arrived in the province and, on October 6, 1690, because a proprietor was superior to a landgrave, displaced Colleton and assumed the governorship. Under his aggressive leadership an assembly was called—irregularly the proprietors claimed—which on December 20 passed an act debarring Colleton, forbidding him ever to hold office again in the colony, and threatening him with a fine of five thousand pounds if he did not depart within two months for England. Though the palatine court disallowed the act, Sothell, the ringleader, retained his post and continued in office for nearly a year.[1]

The substitution of Sothell for Colleton was merely a shift from the frying pan into the fire. In 1689, after six years of arbitrary and disorderly conduct, Sothell had been driven out of the Albemarle province, having incurred both the hatred of the colonists there and the ill will of the proprietors. Scarcely had he reached Charles Town than he suspended Paul Grimball, the secretary, for refusing to deliver up the records and seal of the province, seized his papers,

Carolina Magazine, XXX, 69–89; *Calendar State Papers, Colonial*, 1685–1688, §§92, 174, 286, 1163; Rivers, *Sketch*, pp. 142–144.

1. *Commissions and Instructions*, pp. 19–22; Archdale's "Description," *Early Carolina*, pp. 295–296. The debarment of Colleton seems to have been in some way bound up with the conflict, which had been going on for a number of years, to obtain control of the Indian trade. Governor Ludwell in 1692 caused an inquiry to be made into the matter, but the outcome is not recorded (*Journal of the Grand Council*, 1692, pp. 33–34; *Warrants for Land*, III, 201). James Colleton was in the colony in 1692, but soon afterward left for Barbados and never returned.

and imprisoned him.[1] Similarly, in disregard of their private rights and of public law and in much the same manner as he had done over and over again in Albemarle, he confiscated the property of others, illegally and by force. He then followed up these acts of aggression by obtaining from the assembly (the "two late pretended parliaments") the act banishing Colleton and, supported by one James Moore and the Goose Creek men, continued his defiance of the proprietors. He intercepted letters from England, extorted money, and committed other acts which the palatine court called "arbitrary, oppressive, irregular, illegal, and dangerous." Convinced that he was planning to renounce all subjection to king and proprietors, the court, November, 1691, suspended him ("who is or pretends to be one of the lords proprietors"), charging him with "high treason,"[2] and in his place appointed Philip Ludwell, instructing the colonists to yield obedience to the latter as their new head. They ordered the removal of the deputies who had supported Sothell, the release of the imprisoned secretary and the restoration of his papers, and, in general, instructed Ludwell to bring peace to the distracted colony. Sothell, refusing to be dismissed, continued his efforts to seduce the inhabitants by "pretensions and inveiglings," until a second order disowning him was sent over in 1693. Any further mischief that he might have done was ended by his death in 1694.[3]

1. Petition of the secretary, Paul Grimball, whose house on Edisto Island had been sacked and destroyed by the Spaniards in August, 1686 (*South Carolina Magazine,* XXIX, 231; *Warrants for Land,* III, 199–201; *Commissions and Instructions,* pp. 24–33, 64, 65, 67). The charges against Sothell are contained in a letter to him from the proprietors, May 12, 1691. They number thirteen in all (*ibid.,* 29–33, 64–65).

2. *Calendar State Papers, Colonial,* 1689–1692, §1488; 1693–1696, §344.

3. *Ibid.,* 1689–1692, §§1496–1499, 1886, 1887. The order suspending Sothell was read publicly at Charles Town, April 9, 1692. He remained in the province, denying the legality of his suspension and of the provincial court to hear his case on the ground that he was a proprietor and hence above the local law. When called upon to answer, he refused for the same reason, asking the council how it "Dared to sit theire without him theire head." In the trial that followed, the jury found for Grimball and charged Sothell with the payment of £100 stg. and costs. Sothell refused to return the papers he had seized and there is nothing to show that he ever paid the fine. He was, however, heavily mulcted for his seditious speeches "highly tending to the Dishonor of the Lords Prop.rs." At the trial "Both by words and gestures [he outraged] the court in a mutinous manner," which if repeated, the court said, would end in his imprisonment and eventual banishment. He maintained his defiant attitude to the end and continued to stir up his followers to the utterance of seditious and mutinous speeches. These speeches gave rise to the laws passed to prevent false and scandalous reports (*Journal of the Grand Council,* 1692, pp. 10, 12–13, 18, 19, 20, 22, 24, 26, 27, 39, 40, 47, 48, 52 (court scenes), 51, 55, 56 (outbreak of speeches); *Commissions and Instructions,* p. 71, *Journals,* 1696, p. 15).

His predatory career in two colonies was not inappropriately followed by an acrimonious quarrel over his proprietary rights, revealing that there might have been irregularities in his private as well as his public life.

The efforts of the next three governors, Ludwell, Smith, and Archdale (1691–1693, 1693–1694, 1694–1696),[1] were largely devoted to the one great task of restoring harmony and peace and of bringing the inhabitants once more to their former state of affluence and prosperity. The task was not an easy one. Large numbers of the people, particularly in the Goose Creek region, had supported Sothell because of their dissatisfaction with the way the proprietors were managing the land grants, with the amounts of land that were falling into the hands of a few influential patentees, and with the pressure the palatine court was bringing to secure the arrears of quitrents. Conditions were complicated still more by the deadlock in the assembly resulting from an attempt to pass an act of indemnity and oblivion, with the upper house, composed of the governor and his council, for the measure, and the commons house, made up of the elected deputies, against it. The latter did not approve of the exceptions favored by the upper house and proposed to pass a bill that should declare an amnesty full and complete, maintaining that to do otherwise would make a "Sereene heaven seeme to Prognosticate a Storme" because such a measure was insufficient "to Settle the Country in pease and Quietnesse."[2] But by such reasoning the governor and council refused to be convinced. Finally in 1693 the issue was referred to the proprietors and they wrote Ludwell that the colony had no right to pass such a bill at all, at the same time chiding him for his quarrel with the deputies and bidding him effect a reconciliation on the ground that they would "gladly see people forgive each other."[3] As the only ones who had a right to decide the question, they issued a letters patent granting a general amnesty and pardons for all offenses against themselves and their Fundamental Constitutions, except in cases of treason, piracy, arrears of rent, and

1. Joseph Blake came in as governor between Smith and Archdale, but as he was in office only a few months his tenure is not significant. Smith's instructions, which are in C.O. 5:289, are word for word the same as those of Ludwell, with a slight addition to §27. Archdale, though given his own instructions, was ordered to follow those of Ludwell and Smith.

2. *Journals*, 1692, pp. 10–11, 12–14, 19–20, 21–22, 24–25; 1693, pp. 10, 11, 13–14, 16, 18.

3. *Calendar State Papers, Colonial*, 1693–1696, §269.

in the persons of James Moore and Robert Daniel,[1] who after Sothell were the chief offenders.

The result of all these transactions was largely negative. Ludwell was replaced by Thomas Smith, "a wise and sober, moderate and well living man," who did his best in an almost impossible situation. But the discontent continued and the fears and jealousies of the people seemed as deeply rooted as ever. New controversies arose. The deputies insisted that the Fundamental Constitutions were of no use to the colony and, to the wrath of the proprietors, proposed to draw up a constitution of their own, preparing at the same time a list of grievances that contained all the complaints they could think of. Among the more conspicuous items was that demanding the assent of the deputies to all laws and an increase in the number of elected representatives in the council.[2] One concession they obtained. The governor agreed that the right to initiate legislation, which had hitherto rested with the council, should henceforth be shared by both houses. Smith did not long remain in office. His health was poor and his sense of public duty, always acute, was weakened by seeming failure. He wrote the proprietors that they would better send over one of themselves, as there was no hope of peace in the colony unless some one came as governor with full power to redress all grievances. Acting on this advice the court sent over John Archdale, who arrived in the colony, August, 1694, to find matters in great confusion, with every faction ready to present its statement of wrongs.

Archdale was a Quaker, conciliatory and well meaning, but even good intentions could not surmount all obstacles. The deputies were determined to break down, as far as they could, certain of the proprietary prerogatives and to bring about such changes in local conditions as would conduce to the greater ease and comfort of life. Despite the fact that the proprietors would admit of no law that diminished or altered the powers granted them by their charter, a majority of the deputies maintained a steady pressure to overthrow some of their regulations, such as concerned the distribution of lands, representation in the council, fines and forfeitures, the oath of fidelity, and payments in sterling rather than commodities. The governor dissolved the commons house of 1695 by proclamation, on

1. *Ibid.*, §266; C.O. 5:288, pp. 222-283.
2. *Journals*, 1693, pp. 16-18, 35-37.

the ground that it was frustrating all his attempts at peace. The next house proved more amenable and coöperated with Archdale in his desire to put an end to the dispute. Many excellent bills were passed: arrears of rent were compromised or abated, and the burdens of escheat, distraint, registration of patented lands, the cost and methods of conveyancing, the raising and appropriation of money were made so much easier that when Archdale returned to England in 1696 the commons house, with considerable justification, could thank him for his "discretion, patience and labour."[1]

Though Archdale, in all matters that came to him for decision, acted wisely and well and left the country "settled," as he himself said, he could hardly have anticipated the troubles that soon were to harass the colony and disturb the state of serenity that he thought had been reached. Encroachments upon the prerogatives of the proprietors did not end with Archdale's successful administration, and the struggle of the deputies to obtain for the freeholders the full rights and opportunities of Englishmen, to vindicate their "liberties," and to resist any infringement upon what they considered their legitimate freedom of action continued to the end of the proprietary period.[2] In the larger field of English colonial policy, new issues were arising, creating new problems in the colony and bringing to the surface deep-seated differences of opinion that were equally to affect the course of events in the years immediately following.

For a long time the Indian trade, controlled privately by the leading men of the colony, had been a source of profit to the monopolists, a state of affairs that had given rise to complaints among those of the people who had no share in it. For twenty years it had been kept within the colony's borders, but the aggressive activities of the traders had gradually widened the area of operations and vastly increased the total value of the product. With Joseph Blake who

1. *Ibid.*, 1696, *passim*. Archdale's own account of his governorship is in *Early Carolina*, pp. 296–302.

2. *Journals*, 1702, pp. 76–78. For grievances in 1698, *ibid.*, 1698, pp. 34–36; for those in 1703, Rivers, *Sketch*, pp. 453–460. Notice the language used in June, 1703, "Very foundation of our Lawful Rights," "the duty we owe to ourselves as Englishmen," "liege and freeborn subjects of the crown of England," infringement of our Laws and Liberties," "the foundation of our English rights and liberties undermined." These phrases and others, all of which partake somewhat of the character of campaign oratory, were directed not against the proprietors but against Governor Moore and his tampering with the elections, his planning to attack St. Augustine, and his enforcing and obstructing the Indian trade.

succeeded Archdale as governor and with James Moore who followed next there began the great western push which, for the ensuing five years, carried the Carolinians to the Mississippi and increased the export of deerskins to fifty-four thousand annually.[1] The
abuses of the trade were such that in December, 1697, the proprietors wrote to Blake bidding him obtain a law to regulate the trade,
and in consequence there began the next year the long-drawn out
battle in the commons house of assembly over the passage of a bill
which should permit management by a public stock for the benefit
of the people at large, instead of by private capital in the interests of
the monopolists. The main contention was that the trade as it stood
was "a grievance to this Settlement and Prejudicall to the Safety
thereof."[2] Proposals to farm the trade were voted down and in 1703
an agreement was reached that the trade should "be brought into a
Publick Stock" and that those who managed it should be "Impowered to Trade by England if they see Convenient." But the bill, thus
framed, failed to pass, largely because the governor, James Moore, a
Church of England man, who had obtained his office by a shrewd
maneuver (by "fraud and flattery" said his opponents) at the expense of Moreton, a Dissenter, was suspected of fostering the bill to
his own advantage.[3] In the long run, however, the failure was due,
not to any cause that lay within the orbit of the bill itself, but to
antagonisms that had arisen in the larger political sphere. Factional
dissensions, based on fundamental differences of opinion as to the
policy the colony should pursue in its external relations was disrupting the peace of the assembly.

The presence of the Spanish to the southward in the mission districts of Guale, Timucua, and Apalache and the recent appearance
of the French at Mobile Bay and on the lower Mississippi were the
more ominous because of the declaration of war by England against
France in May, 1701. Preparations long under way to fortify Charles
Town and place the colony in a position to resist attack were pushed
forward with renewed vigor.[4] Friendly advances were made to the

1. Crane, *The Southern Frontier*, ch. XI.

2. *Journals*, 1698, pp. 18, 22, 31, 32, 34; 1700, pp. 17, 22–23; 1701, part one,
pp. 3, 15, 16; 1701, part two, p. 21; 1702, pp. 13, 23, 24, 25; 1703, pp. 7, 8, 11,
15, 26, 32, 35, 38, 41, 51, 95, 99, 101.

3. Ash, "Affairs in Carolina," *Early Carolina*, pp. 269–270, and editor's note; "Address of several members of the Assembly to the Proprietors," Rivers, *Sketch*, pp. 455–
456 (iv); *Calendar State Papers, Colonial*, 1702, §314.

4. *Journals*, 1701, second part, pp. 6–7, 8, 13, 14, 15, 32.

Yamassee, who occupied the country from Port Royal to the Savannah River, and to other neighboring Indian tribes, and agents were sent out with presents and soothing words, to win their confidence and prevent them from going over to the enemy. But the most spectacular events of the time were the outcome of Governor Moore's decision to take the offensive and by carrying the war into the enemy's country to forestall an attack on Carolina, which Moore and others suspected was the plan of the Spanish and French as their part in the European war. On August 20, 1702, Moore recommended to the assembly the taking of St. Augustine, "before it be strengthened with french forces," hoping thereby to relieve the colony of a dangerous enemy and to win the approbation of the queen in thus protecting "the fronteere Colony of all her Maj[ties] Plantations on the Maine in america."[1] His recommendation was bitterly opposed by those who were more interested in their "liberties" than in an aggressive campaign beyond their borders and who saw in Moore's plan only a buccaneering expedition for booty and slaves. They feared that the cost would bring into greater debt than before a colony that was none too prosperous and had already been brought low by two devastating fires in Charles Town and by epidemics of yellow fever and small pox. They disliked being browbeaten by the governor, whenever in the assembly any one of them plucked up courage to speak against the expedition. Moore was opposed, too, by the proprietors, who saw no reason why they should be involved in a war of expansion that ought to be carried on not by private persons at their own costs but by her Majesty's forces on land and sea.[2]

But Moore was of the stuff from which expansionists always have been molded. He was courageous and resourceful, though easily aroused, inclined to be quarrelsome, and resentful of opposition when once his mind was made up. He had, as he said, "the most Numerous

1. *Ibid.*, 1702, p. 64.

2. In November, 1703, the proprietors wrote to the Board of Trade, "Having received an Address from Carolina, wee have thought fitt to lay a copy of it before your Lordships, wherein your Lordships may perceive the due care we have taken for the welfare of the said Colony, nor have we omitted anything on our part for the protection thereof. But [in doing what we have] we are obliged to a greater charge than any profitts we receive from our Colony is able to support; therefore we hope [to obtain] H. M. most gracious protection and assistance in the defence of our Colony at this time of Eminent danger" (*Calendar State Papers, Colonial,* 1702–1703, §1268). This letter was prompted by an address from the commons house of assembly, which is referred to in the minutes of April 22 and 23 (*Journals,* 1703, pp. 66, 67).

Family of Relations and children in the Collony,"[1] and undoubtedly hoped for plunder in the form of Spanish plate and Indian slaves that would relieve some of his domestic needs. On August 22, 1702, the house, unconvinced, refused to advise the governor "to proclaim war against the French and Spanyards," but authorized the raising of two thousand pounds "for carrying on an Expedition agt St. Augustine."[2]

In the accomplishment of its main object the expedition was a failure. The six or eight small ships with eight periauguas, manned by a force of fifty Carolinians and thirteen hundred Yamassee Indians[3] and led by Moore in person, sailed along the coast and devastated and ruined the district of Guale, thus carrying one step further forward the terrorizing of Florida, which had begun a few months before when a force of traders and Creek Indians had penetrated the upper part of Apalache and defeated the Spaniards and their Indian allies on the Pedernales or Flint River. But against the bastioned castle of St. Augustine, to which the inhabitants of the town fled for refuge, the eight hastily equipped vessels were helpless. Without mortars or scaling ladders Moore and his followers could do nothing to penetrate the fortified walls, and, after an eight weeks' investment, a retreat was ordered. Having burned his vessels and the houses of the town, Moore escaped overland to join his periauguas, which had been left at St. Johns.[4] The losses were not serious but the expedition cost the colony £6000 more than the amount appropriated and led to the issue of paper money and the imposition of additional customs dues to make up the deficit. The colony, now in danger of a retaliatory attack, planned to renew the attempt, hoping for aid from England. Moore, though discredited by his failure and displaced by Sir Nathaniel Johnson in March, 1703, never lost the confidence of the proprietors and in December, 1704, at his own expense, completed the ravaging of Apalache, which had been begun by the traders in 1702. Marching across country from the Ocmulgee,

---

1. *Ibid.*, 1702, p. 48. Miss Webber in "The First Governor Moore," *South Carolina Magazine*, XXXVII, 1–5, gives Moore ten children.

2. *Journals*, 1702, p. 102.

3. The figures given in the various accounts differ considerably.

4. A good account is by Rivers, *Sketch*, pp. 197–202. Criticism of the expedition is in *ibid.*, pp. 455–457 and *Early Carolina*, pp. 272–274, both written by Moore's opponents. See also *Calendar State Papers, Colonial*, 1702, §1193; 1702–1703, §303, pp. 13–14; Carroll, *Collections*, II, 351–352. For a description of St. Augustine in 1696, see Dickenson, *God's Protecting Providence* (1790 ed.), pp. 109–112.

with fifty Englishmen and a thousand Indian allies, he fell upon the Spanish and Indians at Ayabale (Concepción), in the heart of southern Apalache and effectively routed them. With the despoiling of Guale, Timucua, and Apalache the danger to Carolina seemed to have been removed and the way opened to Pensacola and Mobile.[1]

But the glory was short-lived. The danger was not removed, and the road to Pensacola and Mobile was never traversed by any English force marching to victory over France. In April, 1715, the Yamassee, who had been Carolina's chief allies in the despoiling of Guale, infuriated by the callous and inhuman practices of the traders whose policy was to sell goods on credit and keep the Indians always in debt,[2] rose in a war of revenge and began a slaughter along the line of settlements from the Stono north to the Santee and westward to the trading factories among the Chickasaw. Roused by the Creeks, the real authors of the revolt, aided by the Spaniards from St. Augustine, and spurred on by the French from Mobile, the Indians with terrifying suddenness fell on the traders in Pocotaligo Town, the chief trading center among the Yamassee, and massacred the agent and others residing there. Other Indian tribes joined the conspiracy and soon the country around Charles Town and back from the coast was aflame with fire and destruction. That the colony was not ruined was due to the energy of Governor Craven (1711–1717), to assistance rendered by other colonies—particularly Virginia and to some extent New England—and to the fact that the Cherokee refused to coöperate and responded to the call from Charles Town for a treaty of neutrality and peace. At one time it was thought that the uprising presaged a general movement among the Indians at large to wipe out all the English settlements, but united action among the tribes was generally short-lived and the boldness and tenacity of the hardened English frontier fighters finally won the day. By the end of the year the war was practically over, though sporadic forays continued and peace with the Creeks was long delayed. South Carolina was saved from ruin, but her Indian trade

1. Carroll, *Collections,* II, 574–576. Accounts are given by both Bolton (pp. 60–62) and Crane (pp. 78–81) with full bibliographical details. Moore wrote that by this campaign ("I never see or hear of a stouter or braver thing done, than the storming of the fort") his forces had "made Carolina as safe as the conquest of Apalatchia can make it."

2. For the causes of the Yamassee War, Crane, *The Southern Frontier,* pp. 165–167 and for the war itself and its results, pp. 168–186. Also Carroll, *Collections,* II, 570–572; *South Carolina Magazine,* XXXII, 251–269.

and the prosperity which had accrued therefrom received a set-back from which her traders did not recover for six years.

This war with the Indians demonstrated many things, among them the invincibility of the colonists, which discouraged further tribal combinations among the Indians and started that migration from old hunting grounds to new which was to be so important a feature of later Indian history. It also made evident the significance of Carolina, not only as a frontier colony but also as the pivotal center of the southern Indian trade and as one of the rallying points for the English against the French in that great triangular contest for the control of a continent, which from this time on was to engage more and more the attention of the government in England. Lastly, it demonstrated the recklessness, if not the criminal absurdity, of a policy that left the care of such a colony in the hands of a group of private persons, unfit to carry so important a responsibility and inadequately supplied with funds to meet the emergencies that inevitably would arise. The Yamassee War brought one step nearer the end of proprietary rule, already foreshadowed by other events to which we must now turn our attention.

While thus an important issue, continental and almost imperial in nature, was in the balance along the southern frontier, there were presenting themselves for solution domestic problems that were almost as much a menace to the peace and unity of the colony as were the disordered conditions of the Indian trade and the terror of Spanish and French invasion. There had always existed a certain amount of friction between the upper and lower houses of assembly, because the upper house was composed of the proprietors' deputies, the hereditary nobility, and a few elected freeholders the number of whom, as well as the number of its own members, the lower house thought ought to be increased. This friction was especially noticeable in 1695 and again in 1700, when the deputies, proving unusually obstinate, went so far as to declare that the governor and council "were no house" at all, and in the deadlock that ensued they almost revolted against proprietary authority. Even after the deputies backed down on one point and "owned us a house," as the council put it, frequent conferences were necessary to iron out differences and to reach a common understanding in matters concerning proprietary privilege and the Fundamental Constitutions. The deputies were the more determined to increase their own powers at the expense of the proprietors, because of the uncertainties that existed as to the form of government and because of the doubts that prevailed as to just what laws were in force in the province. On one occasion they proved so belligerent that the council dissolved them, hoping that a new election would bring together a body "better tempered than the last."[1] The general situation was still further congested by the sensitiveness of the commoners who felt that the proprietors were too far away to know much about the domestic needs of the province and therefore were inclined to ignore local legislation whenever it was to their advantage to do so.

Political differences were intensified by differences based on religious and racial beliefs, for South Carolina was not homogeneous either racially or religiously. From the beginning the settlers were predominantly English and, until the turn of the century, Anglican; and these Anglican English were not only the wealthiest members of the community, but they also controlled the offices and set the pace in social life. Huguenots began to arrive as early as 1680 and in considerable numbers after the Revocation of the Edict of Nantes, locating on the Santee at French Jamestown and its neighborhood, in Charles Town, at the head of Goose Creek, and along the eastern branch of the Cooper River.[2] In actual numbers they formed about ten per cent of the population, perhaps five hundred in five or six thousand, but many of them early intermarried with the English, became absorbed into the Anglican Church, and in political controversies generally sided with the Anglicans. In matters political they wielded an influence out of all proportions to their numbers, for in the assembly they held the balance of power between the Anglicans and the Dissenters. The latter were Congregationalists (at Dorchester)[3] Presbyterians,[4] Baptists, and Quakers, the last named constituting in 1710 about two and a half per cent of the whole. They had arrived first in 1675 and were numerous enough to hold a monthly meeting at Charles Town in 1683. Governor Archdale was a Quaker, "convinced and separated from his father's house by the preaching of George Fox."[5]

1. *Commissions and Instructions,* pp. 136–139, 144, 147, 152.
2. On the first French settlers in South Carolina, *South Carolina Magazine,* XXIII, 101–123.
3. On the Puritan settlement at Dorchester, 1695, *Early Carolina,* pp. 191–200; *South Carolina Magazine,* VI, 62–95.
4. How, *History of the Presbyterian Church* (1870).
5. *South Carolina Magazine,* XXVII, 22, and for Mary Cross, XII, 106.

Trouble arose as early as 1692, when the members of the assembly, objecting to the presence of Huguenots on the ground that they were not Englishmen and in some cases could not speak the English language, insisted that they were aliens and should be governed by alien law. Though the proprietors ruled that any foreigner who had subscribed the oaths of allegiance and fidelity could be naturalized by act of assembly, the members refused to pass such an act, insisting that though the Huguenots might hold land they ought not to vote, sit in assembly, or serve on juries. They demanded that the members of the house be English, elected by Englishmen, and they called on the proprietors to issue writs for Englishmen only, because only Englishmen should be allowed to make the laws. On their part, the Huguenots, dissatisfied and discontented, claimed that they had been naturalized in England and at first refused to petition for a naturalization law, because it was unnecessary for them to do so. For four or five years the controversy raged, until in March, 1696, after several private cases had been dealt with favorably by admitting here and there a single elected Huguenot to the house, the assembly passed an act making aliens free, provided they could speak English, and granting liberty of conscience for all except Roman Catholics. Though occasionally hitherto a few Huguenots had sat in the assembly, all who could speak English now came into the full enjoyment of the rights of Englishmen.[1]

But of even greater importance in the life of the colony was the struggle for dominance between the Anglicans and the Dissenters. They were pretty evenly matched in both assembly and province, each making up about forty per cent of the population. Thus success on one side or the other depended to no small extent on the personnel of those in office and on the attitude of the Huguenot members of assembly. A test came in 1698 when the Anglicans presented the draft of a bill to settle a maintenance (£150) on a minister of the Church of England (St. Philip's) in Charles Town. This bill with some amendments was passed, sent up to the governor and council, and ratified on October 8 of that year.[2] Then in 1704 under

1. *Commissions and Instructions*, pp. 60, 63–64, 80–81, 84–85, 88, 92, 96–97, 99–101; *Journals*, 1692, p. 6; 1696, pp. 24, 27; 1697, pp. 6, 7, 11, 13; 1702, pp. 51–53 *et seq.*; 1703, p. 30; Hirsch, *Huguenots of Colonial South Carolina*, ch. IV.

2. *Journals*, 1698, pp. 18, 20, 21, 27–28, 33; Dalcho, *An Historical Account of the Protestant Episcopal Church in South Carolina* (1820), pp. 32–35.

circumstances that are not entirely clear, two additional acts were passed, one, on May 8, a test act for all members of the assembly, and the other, on November 4, establishing religious worship according to the Book of Common Prayer.[1] Some writers have ascribed the passage of these two acts to the influence of the palatine in England, Lord Granville, an overzealous high churchman, who, with enough votes to control the palatine court,[2] was determined to have the English Church the legally adopted church in the colony. In any case it is certain that he was responsible for the appointment of certain Anglicans to office, Sir Nathaniel Johnson as governor, 1703, Nicholas Trott, Jr., James Moore, and Job How, and that these men took advantage of the distractions of the Spanish War, the Indian trade, and the quarrels in assembly to establish their control over the colony. The Dissenters claimed that the majority, made up of Anglicans and Huguenots of Charles Town and Berkeley County, had been irregularly elected, and, with the hope of preventing the passage of the acts, certain of them withdrew from the assembly.

1. *Ibid.*, pp. 58–62; Cooper, *Statutes at Large,* II, 232. (1) "An Act for the more effectual preservation of the government of this Province, by requiring all persons that shall be hereafter chosen members of the Commons House of Assembly and sit in the same, to take the oath and subscribe the declaration appointed by this Act, and to conform to the religious worship in this Province, according to the Church of England, and to receive the Sacrament of the Lords Supper according to the rites and usages of the said Church." It is said that the majority for the passage of this act was only one.

(2) "An Act for the Establishment of Religious Worship in this Province according to the Church of England, and for the erecting of Churches for the Public Worship of God, and also for the maintenance of Ministers and the building of convenient Houses for them."

We do not discuss here the Church Act of 1706 which marked the victory of the Anglicans and the establishment of the Church of England as the official church of the colony. Dalcho, as above, chapter III, and appendix i; *North Carolina Colonial Records,* II, 863–867.

2. Lord Granville had two votes in the court, one for himself and one for the youthful Lord Carteret, his nephew. The others were William Lord Craven, whose guardian defended the acts, and Sir John Colleton, an infant. Four votes were sufficient for ratification. We are told that others among the proprietors refused to support Granville (House of Lords address, *Report,* American Historical Association, 1892, p. 31). In a letter from William Killigrew to Sir Charles Hedges, July, 1706, the statement is made that two of the proprietors were minors, two were in opposition, and one was a prisoner in the Fleet (*Calendar State Papers, Colonial, 1706–1708,* §499, i). As in that year the proprietors were Granville, Craven, Carteret, Maurice Ashley, Colleton, and Archdale, it is evident that the two in opposition were Ashley and Archdale, but the one in the Fleet I cannot identify, perhaps it was Danson, who if in prison would not be listed. Governor Joseph Blake was a proprietor but lived in the colony, and Ashley generally voted for him.

They maintained that the elections had not been free and ascribed the whole trouble to the fact that the new governor and his council had refused to ratify a new election law in order to manipulate the voting.

At this time, these Dissenters had four churches to the Anglicans one in the colony, and, outraged by these acts which they said had been passed illegally and also had destroyed the liberty of conscience guaranteed by the eighteenth article of the charter, they sent two of their number, Joseph Boone and John Ash, to England to expostulate with the proprietors.[1] Unable at first to make headway in that direction because of Granville's opposition,[2] they appealed to the House of Lords, which gave them a hearing in February and March, 1706. The house objected at once to that part of the act which provided for an ecclesiastical commission of twenty members, as an encroachment on the rights of the Bishop of London, in whose diocese South Carolina was. Even before the House of Lords took action, the proprietors, with nothing to say in their own defense, declared the second act null and void and instructed Johnson not to put it in execution.[3] Therefore the House of Lords went further in its condemnation. In its decision it said that the acts were founded on falsity in matters of fact, were repugnant to the laws of England, were contrary to the charter, offered encouragement to atheism and irreligion, were destructive to trade, and were likely to lead to the depopulating and ruin of the province.[4] On March 12, 1706, it drew

1. "Representation from Colleton County and Petition of Joseph Boone and sixteen merchants of London to the House of Lords," Rivers, *Sketch*, pp. 453–454. The "Petition" is also printed in *House of Lords Manuscripts*, new series, VI, 406–408; Stock, *Debates*, III, 115–118; *North Carolina Colonial Records*, I, 637–640; *Report*, American Historical Association, 1892, pp. 32–35. See also John Ash, "Affairs in Carolina," *Early Carolina*, pp. 270–271, and the editor's note. The pamphlet by Daniel Defoe, "Party Tyranny," *Early Carolina*, pp. 224–264, and John Oldmixon's narrative, *ibid.*, pp. 339–342, 344–347, are largely based on the accounts of the Colleton petitioners and of Boone and Ash. Mr. Salley goes too far, I think, in saying that Oldmixon's description of Carolina is "valueless" and "a mass of errors from title to colophon" (*Bulletin*, Historical Manuscripts Commission of South Carolina, no. 8, pp. 18, 22) and one wonders why, believing that to be the case, he printed it in the Original Narratives Series. Oldmixon, who lived as a boy with the Blake family in England, of which the Dissenter Joseph Blake of South Carolina was a member, may well have got information from this source.

2. *House of Lords Manuscripts*, new series, VI, 408.

3. *Calendar State Papers, Colonial*, 1706–1708, §158 (March 6, 1706); *Commissions and Instructions*, pp. 192–194 (February 27, 1707).

4. *Report*, American Historical Association, 1892, p. 30; Stock, *Debates*, III, 120–121.

up an address to Queen Anne, begging her to take action.[1] The queen in council referred the address to the Board of Trade and the board sent all the documents in the case to the law officers of the crown for an opinion. On May 17, Northey and Harcourt replied that the two acts in question were all that the House of Lords said they were, and rather covertly suggested that such an abuse of power ought to bring upon the proprietors the loss of their charter.[2] The board, acting on this advice, drew up a representation to the Privy Council, recommending that the acts be disallowed by the crown and that steps be taken for the resumption of the Carolinas into her Majesty's hands.[3] The Privy Council, approving of the representation, issued an order declaring the acts null and void, an exercise of royal authority that must have been very disquieting to Granville and the other proprietors. At the same time the council took into consideration the proper procedure to follow in obtaining an annulment of the Carolina charter by writ of quo warranto.[4]

From this time to the final surrender of the charter in 1729 the issue was not for a moment in doubt. The only difficulty to be surmounted was how tactfully and legally to bring about the desired end. Various moves were made, but accomplished nothing. The attempt to pass a bill through parliament in 1706 failed; a forfeiture by suit at law was estopped by the parliamentary privilege of peers; and a voluntary surrender of the charter was not likely to be effected until the situation in the colony had become tense enough to frighten the proprietors, and the state of the finances in England favorable enough to make it possible for the crown to offer a considerable compensation in cash.

The final and determining factor was the question of defense. A French and Spanish attack by sea in November, 1706, two years after the passage of the acts,[5] and the Yamassee War, of which an account has already been given, brought home to the proprietors their helplessness in the face of any dangers to the province requiring heavy financial outlay. During the years from 1706 to 1715 petitions from the colony poured in upon the English authorities, calling for

1. The full address is printed in *Report*, pp. 28–31, and in *North Carolina Colonial Records*, I, 635–637.
2. *Ibid.*, 642–643; *Calendar State Papers, Colonial*, 1706–1708, §328.
3. *Ibid.*, §336, i.
4. *Acts Privy Council, Colonial*, II, §1002.
5. *Calendar State Papers, Colonial*, 1706–1708, §517, i.

aid and demanding in unequivocal terms the substitution of the crown for the palatine court. When England hesitated, not knowing certainly how the change could be made, the colonists took matters into their own hands and in November, 1719, formed a revolutionary government and informed the last proprietary governor, Robert Johnson, that they would no longer recognize the proprietary authority. Johnson, unwilling to accept a commission from a revolutionary body, withdrew, and on December 21 a convention met at Charles Town, proclaimed the new status of the colony, chose James Moore temporary governor, and invited the English government to take immediate possession. This the English government did and in 1720, with the appointment of Francis Nicholson by the crown, South Carolina became a royal colony. Nicholson arrived and was proclaimed May 29, 1721. He named his own council and was welcomed with an address signed by over five hundred of the leading men, in which the subscribers expressed their joy that the king had at last taken them under his protection.[1] The end of the proprietary control of the government in South Carolina had come and from this time the palatine court ceased to exercise in that colony any of the governing powers granted by the charter. It only remained for the English authorities to settle the business side of the transaction, which concerned the ownership of the soil, but it was not until 1729 that the negotiations were finally completed and the charter was actually surrendered. Seven of the proprietors managed to squeeze from the English exchequer £2500 apiece for their proprietary land rights. The only one to hold out was Lord Carteret—the former youthful Sir John Carteret—and he refused—as we have already seen—to give up whatever possible returns might accrue from his eighth share of the quit-rents. It is much to be doubted whether, during the forty years of his possession, he ever received anything like a net profit of £2500.[2]

The end of proprietary rule in the southern province did not necessarily mean the end of proprietary rule in the northern province

1. *Journal of His Majesty's Council of South Carolina*, May 29–June 20, 1721. Printed for the Historical Commission of South Carolina, 1930.

2. For the history of the surrender in 1729, which in its details lies beyond the scope of this narrative, see Crittenden, "The Surrender of the Charter of Carolina," *North Carolina Historical Magazine*, I, 383–401. The text of the surrender is among the Close Rolls, Chancery 54:5386, no. 19. It follows the wording of the act, 2 George II, c. 34.

also. The province of Albemarle, known after 1691 as North Carolina, was far removed from its southern partner and in its history was pursuing an entirely different course. Geographically its lands were but an extension of those of Virginia. It was an isolated settlement, singularly out of touch with the outside world. During the first ten years of its existence its northern neighbor, Virginia, had looked upon it as in a sense belonging to herself, and in 1675, before the outbreak of Bacon's Rebellion, had made some effort to persuade the proprietors to part with it. But the latter, in order to quiet rumors that had got abroad among the people, assured the governor and assembly that they were fully determined to preserve their province of Albemarle "entire" and to maintain all the inhabitants in their rights as Englishmen, using Virginia only as a means for populating their territory the more rapidly.[1] Despite these excellent intentions, the proprietors paid very little attention to North Carolina, during the entire period of their control from 1666 to 1729. The settlement lay beyond their ken, and even a study of maps, such as the proprietors possessed, enlarged but little their knowledge of the location or its peculiarities. Communication by land was almost impossible except with Virginia, and even with Virginia, as the Quakers found to their distress,[2] the routes were difficult of passage, for they were heavily encumbered with woods, swamps, and rivers that made travel a jungle experience. Entrance and exit by water was blocked by sandbars, through which were passageways or inlets that admitted vessels of only light draft. South Carolina was so far away as to be almost completely out of the picture, and it is a commentary on the proprietors' knowledge of the wilderness they had acquired that at one time they instructed the people of Albemarle to send delegates to the assembly at Charles Town and only gave up the idea in 1691 when assured that such representation was impossible.

The northern province was expected to obey the Fundamental Constitutions exactly as were the people of the south and these Con-

1. *North Carolina Colonial Records,* I, 228. The proprietors wanted to break off all associations with Virginia on the legal and jurisdictional sides, to free the province from commercial dependence on New England, and to keep the Indian trade entirely in the hands of their own freeholders (*ibid.,* 231, 232, 235, 243–246, 253, 269, 286). Shaftesbury had aspired from the beginning to open up a direct trade with England, and for that purpose had obtained the grant of the Bahamas, had set up trading centers on the Edisto and on the Ashley, and had encouraged Dr. Henry Woodward to enlarge the Indian traffic.

2. *Ibid.,* 215, 226, 260.

stitutions were enforced in respect of the governor, the proprietary deputies, and the election of freeholders to both council and assembly. The people were ordered to take the oath of fidelity, to swear submission to the proprietors, and to conform to the requirements laid down for the distribution of lands. Their attention was frequently called to certain clauses which the proprietors wanted them to obey. There were, as far as I know, only two landgraves in the colony, Graffenried and Eden, and though one man was appointed a cacique he never came over. Sothell had a seignory on the Pasquotank River; John Bland had a "manor" fronting on Albemarle Sound; and there are a number of "manor plantations" recorded in the wills. In general it may be said that proprietary control rested very lightly on the colony, though it is equally true that such authority as the proprietors exercised, especially that of appointing the governor, was very unwelcome to the inhabitants. In the actual management of affairs the colonists were thrown back very largely on their own resources and left pretty much to fend for themselves. Robert Quary, who for a short time had been governor of the southern province and knew as well as anyone how matters stood, wrote in 1702 that the people in Albemarle were very uneasy and discontented, because for seven years the proprietors had taken no notice of them.[1] It was only when factional differences arose and reached the stage of armed conflict that the proprietors, always dissatisfied with the slow progress of the colony, felt called upon to interfere.

The problems that North Carolina had to solve were, therefore, wholly unlike those which troubled the southern province. There were no Spanish or French in their neighborhood. The Indian trade, such as it was, and controlled by the governor and his friends, made little appeal to the people at large, who living an easy life on their farms and plantations were satisfied with agriculture and its advantages. Traffic with the outside world was limited to Virginia, New England, and in some measure with Bermuda, though as a market the first named was cut off in 1679 by a Virginia law which provided that no tobacco should be brought into that colony from Carolina or elsewhere outside the capes.[2] Even in the case of New England and Bermuda the business was, in fact, largely in the hands of

1. *Calendar State Papers, Colonial,* 1702-1703, p. 14. Compare also *North Carolina Colonial Records,* I, 247, 303.
2. Hening, *Statutes,* II, 445-446.

New England and Bermudan sea-captains and merchants, whose vessels were small enough to slip through the inlets and thus enable their masters to bargain with the planters for their surplus stock. Tobacco and corn were the chief staples, with cattle, swine, and other domestic animals an essential part of the agricultural life. The population was relatively small, though figures in the case are widely at variance and unreliable. Randolph in 1696 reported only sixty or seventy scattered families, while in 1679 an unknown correspondent (governor and council?) put the number of tithables at fourteen hundred, a third of whom were Indians.[1] The inhabitants lived on their farms and plantations, of which some were owned by a few men of considerable wealth, but many more by those who were hardly able to make a living. With the aid of indentured servants, negroes, and Indian slaves, the owners cultivated these farms to the best of their ability, but, because of poverty and an almost entire absence of religious institutions and the restraining influences of a settled life, they and the people generally got a reputation for restlessness, quarrels, disputes, and factional feuds. The passage of a law intended to encourage the settlement of the country gave the colony a bad name, because runaway servants, insolvent debtors, and fugitives from justice were believed to take advantage of it; but reliable sources give little warrant for thinking that a very much worse state of things prevailed there than elsewhere.

Nevertheless conditions in North Carolina were bad. Captain Henderson Walker, president of the council, could say in 1703 that the colony had been settled for fifty years and for the most part of twenty years had been "without priest or altar" and before that time "much worse." The letters of the Anglican clergy are pathetic in their accounts of hardships, anxieties, ill treatment, inadequate stipends, and hostility from those whom they served, though it must be acknowledged that complaints came easily from those who either by reason of natural disposition or ill-requited efforts were often abusive and morose.[2] In 1704 Thomas Blair divided the people into four groups and characterized them thus: Quakers, who were numerous and "powerful enemies" of the Anglican Church; the irreligious who would be Quakers if they did not have to lead the moral life demanded by the Quakers; a third group "something like Pres-

1. *North Carolina Colonial Records,* I, 260, 467.
2. *Ibid.,* 571–572, 601–603, 689, 765–772.

byterians," evidently Anabaptists, led by "some idle fellows, who preach and baptize through the country"; and a fourth sort, fewest in number but the best sort, who were Anglicans and who might accomplish something for the "settlement of the Church government," if they were not opposed by all three of the others, who feared an established church that would levy tithes and other charges.[1] There can be no doubt whatever that under the proprietors North Carolina, irreligious, unrestrained, and resentful, was a poor and neglected colony, without a sound and settled government, and without a system of land holding that was either assured or permanent. Governor Hyde, who had reasons for his dislike, may or may not have gone beyond the truth when he said that the people were "naturally loose and wicked, obstinate and rebellious, crafty and deceitful and study to invent slander on one another and sow such seeds of sedition that they have generally reaped them in the plentiful crops of Rebellion."[2]

The population, dispersed over four precincts on the northern side of Albemarle Sound and the three precincts of Bath on the southern side, fell easily into sectional groups that became centers of disaffection and even revolt, while the governor at Roanoke was helpless in his efforts to reduce recalcitrant insurgents to submission. The very manner of settlement made centralization either in state or church practically impossible, and to those living in Currituck or Perquimans the proprietors in England must have seemed in another world, so far away as to be almost non-existent, except when their orders were to be enforced. To the planters of eastern North Carolina England was a very distant land, and one does not wonder that the people there and elsewhere were easily aroused by shifting policies that interfered with their well-being. The very system laid down by the proprietors only served to confuse and to irritate the colonists, because it was hopelessly intricate and wholly at variance with the simplicities of their plantation life. The grumbling among the poorer

1. *Ibid.*, 601–602. Also 571–572, 689, 765–772; *Early Carolina,* p. 216.

2. *North Carolina Colonial Records,* I, 850. Such wills and inventories as have been preserved for the period before 1700, show a life simple and unadorned—a little silver, much pewter, a few books, occasionally a gold ring. Anne Durant wore a gold ring on her thumb. Valentine Byrd's inventory mentions pewter, brass, tin, and bell metal, lignum vitae, and brass mortars. Plantation houses are valued at £40 to £80. As for education, we read of an order given in a will that the son should be provided with "schooling," that is, "to read, rite and cipher as far as the rule of three" (Early Wills, North Carolina Historical Commission; Grimes, *Wills,* I, 358).

planters was the louder because of the uncertain tenure of their lands, for which no patents had been granted; because of the demand for quit-rents, which they feared might be increased at any time; because of the occasional escheats and lapses that were enforced for failure to pay or to seat in due time; and especially because of the prosperity of those who reaped special advantages from office holding. As in New Jersey and South Carolina the very existence of the proprietary system made for popular unrest.

As for the proprietors themselves, they were as little able in the north as in the south to select good men for governors. They always had trouble in finding anyone willing to serve and those finally chosen were far from being properly equipped with the ability and discretion necessary to meet the many emergencies incident to their positions. One has only to follow the early career of Henry Wilkinson, who never came over,[1] and the later career of Seth Sothell, who did, to see how ill prepared these men were to govern a people, rude and quarrelsome, undisciplined, quick to resent injustice, and alive to the imperfections of executive rule. Popular opposition to proprietary demands was always latent and once, in 1691, when the palatine court gave the chief command to Ludwell at Charles Town, with authority to name a deputy for Albemarle, the effect in that section was to diminish rather than to enhance the influence and

1. For Captain Henry Wilkinson see my article in the *South Atlantic Quarterly,* XV, 216–222. So obscure has been and still is the early history of North Carolina that belief in Wilkinson as an actual resident governor has been widely prevalent among the historians of the state. My article, proving the contrary, was based on the following pamphlets: (1) *The Information of Captain Henry Wilkinson of what hath passed betwixt him and some other Persons, who have attempted to Prevail with him to Swear High Treason against the Earl of Shaftesbury* (folio, 11 pages, 1681); (2) [The same] *with the Information of Major Jarvis and Mrs. Sussanah Wilkinson* (1681); (3) *Animadversions on Capt. Wilkinson's Information, being Highly Conducive to the Better Improving and Disabusing the Minds of Men and tending to the Publick Peace and Safety* (folio, 18 pages, 1682). See also *Calendar State Papers, Domestic,* 1682, pp. 37, 41, 106, 539; State Papers Domestic, George II, 137, pp. 389–391; *Calendar Treasury Books,* VII, pt. I, 127. The *Animadversions* was probably written by John Booth, a pretended friend of Wilkinson's, who declared that all Wilkinson said was untrue and that in his desire to serve Shaftesbury he was carried away from the facts in the case. The account implies also .that the conspirators, of whom Shaftesbury was the head, were intending to sail for South Carolina. Booth was one of the "king's witnesses," who received £10 a week for the maintenance of himself and his wife (*Calendar Treasury Books,* VII, part I, 573). Some have thought that the *Animadversions* was the work of one Heather or Hater, who in 1682 prepared a "Relation" stating that the Wilkinson narrative was to his knowledge "all false" (*Calendar State Papers, Domestic,* 1682, p. 539). Neither Booth nor Heather is to be believed any more than Wilkinson himself.

prestige of the higher authority both in England and at Charles Town and to increase the power and self-importance of the popular assembly on the Roanoke.[1] When, finally, in 1712, the policy was again changed and instead of a deputy a separate governor was given to North Carolina, the position attained by the popular assembly was sufficiently well established to make infinite trouble for Edward Hyde, the first incumbent of the office. Hyde was a man whose chief qualification was his connection with the Clarendon family and his distant relationship to Queen Anne. He had been sent over as deputy governor in 1710 and on May 9, 1712, became the first governor of North Carolina. As was the case with his cousin, Cornbury of New York, he proved a lamentable failure, and his tenure only served to define more sharply than before the differences between the warring factions that had been destroying the peace and harmony of the colony for a quarter of a century. North Carolina entered on her career as an independent proprietary province in the midst of the bitter struggle of hostile parties, within and without the assembly, for the control of the government.

This struggle had begun very early, before 1676. In a sense it had been latent from the beginning. The settlers who had come to the colony before the authority of the proprietors was established had never taken kindly to interference by this outside group. Besides, the situation was complicated by the intrusion of another outside factor, the English government, which was trying, not very successfully, to enforce the navigation acts, particularly the act of 1673, which was designed to regulate the trade with England and to prevent the carrying of colonial commodities elsewhere than to English ports. The two factors had much in common. The proprietors favored this navigation act, both because they wanted to promote trade directly with England and because they feared that if they did not obey the law, they might endanger their charter. The question at issue was not so much the payment of the penny a pound duty on tobacco imposed by the law, as the stopping of trade with New England and turning it into English channels. For some time a half-dozen Massachusetts and Rhode Island sea-captains and traders—John Liscomb, Josias Winslow, and Zachariah Gillam of Boston, Joshua and Caleb Lamb of Roxbury, and Mordecai Bowdoin of East Greenwich, Rhode Island, and their associates had been controlling the tobacco

1. Connor, *History of North Carolina,* p. 42.

trade with the Albemarle, and it was strongly suspected that after carrying the tobacco to New England they reshipped it to Ireland, Scotland, Holland, France, and Spain, thus distinctly evading the purpose of the law.[1] This evasion the English authorities, particularly the lords of the treasury and the commissioners of the customs, were determined to prevent.

In November, 1673, warrants under the king's sign manual were sent to the governors of all the colonies, instructing them to swear officers into their places as collectors of the penny a pound or "plantation duty," as it was called, to be collected in the colonies from all who did not take out a bond to ship directly to England. In November, 1675, these warrants were followed up by additional instructions, ordering the governors to do all in their power to carry out the law. A collector and a surveyor for Albemarle were named by the Treasury,[2] but as they were not in the colony the governor at the time, Jenkins, made his own appointments, namely, Timothy Biggs, surveyor, and Valentine Byrd, collector. Jenkins was backed by George Durant, one of the oldest pre-proprietary settlers, but was opposed by those who favored the proprietors, among them one Eastchurch and a Thomas Miller, the latter of whom had been appointed in 1677 secretary of Albemarle and a proprietor's deputy. Thus the quarrel was the familiar one between the proprietary and the antiproprietary parties. The proprietors charged Durant and Jenkins with attempts to subvert their government. Jenkins turned out of the council the proprietor's deputies, dissolved the assembly, and had Miller arrested and imprisoned for having made treasonable remarks at a time when he was living in Virginia.[3] In its turn, the assembly refused to be dissolved and voted Jenkins out of office. Miller, at that time about thirty years old, broke jail, escaped with Eastchurch to England and there the two men laid their grievances before the palatine court. The latter, favorably impressed with the personality of the complainants, considering Eastchurch especially a discreet and worthy gentleman of excellent family, appointed the latter governor of the province and obtained for Miller, November 16, 1676, a com-

1. *North Carolina Colonial Records*, I, 244–245. For the New England traders, *ibid.*, 265, 273, 274, 298 and for New England vessels in Albemarle, 319, 325.

2. *Calendar Treasury Books*, IV, 498, 522, 852.

3. For Miller's "treason," *North Carolina Colonial Records*, I, 284, 290, 299, 313–317, 326–327.

mission as collector.[1] The two appointees, thus encouraged, prepared to return to the province, with every expectation of completely recovering their leadership.

But events turned out otherwise. On the way over Eastchurch dallied in the West Indies in the pursuit of a wife, leaving Miller to come on alone. Claiming that he was authorized by Eastchurch to exercise the functions of a governor, he turned out Valentine Byrd and, in his capacity as collector, despite a great deal of local opposition, gathered in, according to his own account, many thousand pounds of goods and "specialties."[2] He might not have been seriously interfered with had he not attempted to be governor as well as collector, and in that rôle to take vengeance on his enemies. With ill-judged vindictiveness and assuming an authority that he did not possess, he arrested Durant and the Boston trader, Gillam,[3] who shortly before had arrived from England with Durant as his passenger and with a much needed cargo of goods to be exchanged for tobacco.

Then the storm broke. From all parts of Albemarle people flocked to the aid of Durant. A revolutionary government was set up and an assembly and council were chosen, before which Miller, apprehended, was brought to trial. Proceedings were stopped for the moment by the receipt of a proclamation from Eastchurch—who with his bride had reached Virginia—ordering the insurgents to disperse.[4] Instead of obeying the order the rebellious colonists, before they separated, clapped Miller in irons and in his place as collector put John Culpeper, a former South Carolinian and a leader of the revolt. When four or five weeks later, news came of the death of Eastchurch in Virginia, the leaders of the anti-proprietary party organ-

1. *Calendar Treasury Books,* V, part I, 372.

2. *North Carolina Colonial Records,* I, 266–267, also 292; *Calendar Treasury Books,* VI, 404, 806–807.

3. Captain Zachariah Gillam, "old Zack," as he was called, lends picturesqueness to the story of the revolt. He was the second son of Benjamin Gillam, who with his partner, Thomas Savage, and his eldest son Benjamin constituted the mercantile and shipbuilding firm of Gillam and Company, with houses, sheds, warehouses, and a shipyard near the waterside at the south end of Boston. The elder Gillam and his son Benjamin engaged chiefly in coastwise business, contenting themselves with only an occasional voyage to England, but Zachariah and his son Benjamin III, were of more venturesome and roving dispositions. We first hear of Zachariah about 1666, when he was thirty years old. Probably he had crossed the water many times even before that date. For his connections with the formation of the Hudson's Bay Company, see above, pp. 226–227.

4. *North Carolina Colonial Records,* I, 282.

ized a government, called an assembly, and proceeded to conduct business in an orderly manner but "after their own fashion." They lodged Miller in a log house in the woods in lieu of a jail and in private houses confined others, among them Timothy Biggs. Miller and Biggs escaped and fled to England, there to recount the activities of the "siditious ffactions and Rebelious Rable" and to lay their side of the case before the Privy Council.

The scene of action was thus transferred to Whitehall. The insurgents sent over John Culpeper, who with Zachariah Gillam, also in England, defended their cause before the proprietors, the Lords of Trade, and the Privy Council. Testimony was taken, depositions were read, and the proprietors sent in a statement signed by Shaftesbury, Craven, and Peter Colleton.[1] They found in the conduct of the insurgents no especial affront to themselves or denial of their authority or that of the king, and they charged Miller with acting without legal authority, committing many arbitrary acts, drinking to excess, and putting the people of the province in fear of their lives and estates. They made it quite clear that they had no intention of giving him further employment or of recommending him to the crown for a renewal of his collectorship.[2] To prevent further trouble, which they believed to have been occasioned in large part by factions and animosities, "in which most or all the Inhabitants have been engaged,"[3] they proposed to send over as governor of the Albemarle province some one competent to inquire into the disorders, who was not concerned in the local feuds. They selected first Captain

1. *Calendar Treasury Books*, VI, 412, 415, 421, 569.
2. Miller says that he was confined in irons for two years in Albemarle; that all his plantations were seized by the rebels; and that on his return to England he obtained an order of restitution, the execution of which was prevented by the Earl of Shaftesbury. In the months of 1680 while the trial of Culpeper was going on in England, he and other sufferers received allowances from the Treasury in considerable amounts, with witness fees of 10s a week as long as the trial lasted. He resigned his collectorship in December, 1680, and the Treasury promised to find him another place, giving him at the same time £59 to recompense him for his losses. In further compensation he was given in 1682 the collectorship of Poole and Weymouth, but because of his impoverishment he fell into arrears to the king, was arrested, and died in prison in 1685. His bondsman died the same year and the latter's wife was sued by the crown for £1000, the amount of the bond. She reported that Miller's accounts were so "embezzled" they could not be made up and that there was no expectation of the recovery of the Carolina lands, though she planned to make an effort to obtain them. She was eventually released from the bond. (Information from the *Calendar Treasury Books, passim.*)
3. *North Carolina Colonial Records*, I, 327-328.

Henry Wilkinson, but as he got mixed up in the Shaftesbury plot and ended in prison, they chose of all persons Seth Sothell, whom they considered, strangely enough in view of his later career, a sober, moderate man. On his way over Sothell was captured by the Algerines. Then they selected John Harvey, who had been president of the council in Albemarle. Harvey died and the council chose Jenkins, while the commissioners of the customs commissioned as Sothell's deputy collector, Robert Holden, who seems to have held on to his office until 1685.[1] Victory clearly lay with the Durant party; peace for the moment descended upon the colony; and the proprietors, who in their dislike of troublesome incidents that caused them worry and anxiety and in their willingness to do almost anything to preserve order, saw with some complacency that at last "all things were in quyet and his Maj^{tyes} Customs quyetly paid by the people."

In the last analysis one is led to believe that it was neither the dislike of the "plantation duty" that brought about the rebellion nor any deep-seated objection to the proprietary rule as such, for after all that rule rested very lightly on the colony, but rather the conviction that the Durant party was the most representative group of the planters in Albemarle and the only one that could be trusted with

1. In January, 1680, Miller is spoken of as "late customs officer in Carolina," but he appears to have been reappointed and to have held the office, though remaining in England, until December of that year. He was then advised to resign and did so, one Henry Tale or Taile being appointed in his place, January 20, 1681. Tale did not accept because "he found that the office would not answer his expectations" and the next appointee, Robert Wilkinson, eldest son of Henry Wilkinson, who was planning to go out with his father, refused it for the same reason. The Treasury desired to do something for those who had suffered in Albemarle, but had great difficulty in finding men willing to take the collector's office. Miller had been collector in 1676, Sothell followed, August 17, 1678, but when the Treasury learned that he had been taken by the Algerines, it appointed temporarily Robert Holden as his deputy, March 13, 1679 (*North Carolina Colonial Records*, I, 244, 288). In 1680 Miller came in again as principal, followed by Tale, Wilkinson, Henry Hudson (July 19, 1681, who the February before had petitioned for relief, but died the next year). Then Timothy Biggs (called "Edmond" and "Edward" and "Mr. Gibbs" in the records), who had been comptroller and surveyor in 1676 (*ibid.*, I, 295–296, 318, 350) and died in 1684 or 1685. Then Edward Wade, who had lived in North Carolina and had a plantation, given him by Sothell, on Little River (Grimes, *Wills*, I, 352). Finally, George Muschamp, August 17, 1685. In view of the fact that until Muschamp came over, none of these, except Holden (who lived in the colony, served on the council, and later was appointed governor of the Bahamas, though he probably never went out, *Calendar State Papers, Colonial*, 1706–1708, §§939, 940, 1128; *Narratives of the Insurrections*, pp. 160–161, note), actually held office in the colony, it is not easy to understand who collected the "plantation duty" between 1677 and 1685. Perhaps it was not collected at all. Muschamp remained in office until 1694.

the colony's well being. Probably Shaftesbury sensed this fact in reaching his decision, knowing that the return of Miller and the restoration of his party to power would be, as far as the satisfaction of the colonists was concerned, the worst thing that could happen. Therefore, he was influential in bringing about the release of Gillam without trial and the acquittal of Culpeper, who had been brought before the court of king's bench at Westminster on the charge of treason.[1]

But if the proprietors thought that the colonists of the Albemarle section were at last united in the bonds of concord and good understanding they had reckoned without due appreciation of the ability of Seth Sothell to make trouble wherever he went. Arriving in Albemarle with the proprietors' commission Sothell succeeded, during the ensuing six years, in undoing much that the proprietors had hoped to accomplish in the way of bringing peace to the province. He was charged by them with disregarding the Fundamental Constitutions, particularly in the matter of the proprietors' deputies, and by the colonists with arbitrary conduct toward individuals; with imprisoning unjustly men of the standing of George Durant and Thomas Pollock—perhaps the wealthiest men in the colony; with laying violent hands on the plantations of lesser men without process of law; with committing other acts that were willful and capricious.[2] After six years of this sort of thing, a body of insurgents, led by Thomas Pollock, aroused possibly by news of the uprisings in England, Massachusetts, and Maryland, surprised Sothell at his plantation on the Pasquotank, shut him up in a log house, and kept him there until he renounced the government and took an oath, the nature of which is not given but which is described by the narrator as "a strange oath too long to be here incerted." When the news of the revolt came to the ears of the proprietors, they immediately suspended Sothell from his office until matters should be cleared up. Sothell remained in Albemarle for a few months and then departed for Charles Town, there to assume the government in entire disregard of the fact that the proprietors did not want him and had

1. *North Carolina Colonial Records*, I, 303–304, 332–333.

2. The charges are summed up in *ibid.*, 367–371. The circumstances of the imprisonment are in the same, III, 618–619. The date of the uprising is probably after May, 1689, and not as usually given in 1688. Wills were proven before Sothell as governor up to that time, which would not have been the case had he been deposed in 1688.

already appointed Philip Ludwell as the governor of both provinces, with power to name a deputy for the northern colony. Sothell remained in South Carolina but a year, with what results we have already seen. With his expulsion, with the entering of Ludwell upon his duties in 1691, and with the latter's appointment of a deputy governor for Albemarle, the history of North Carolina as distinct from the province of Albemarle, may be said to begin.

North Carolina entered upon its career as an independent proprietary province under auspices that were none too favorable. Its population at this time was little more than four thousand all told, and the territory, except in certain parts, was very thinly occupied.[1] The planted portions ran northward toward the "backside of Virginia" and southward across the sound toward the Pamlico River, where on a low bluff was soon to be built, by French Protestants from Manakin Town, Virginia, a small village, Bath Town. This village in 1709 had only a dozen houses and the whole of Bath County, except along the Pamlico and its branches, was settled hardly at all. South of the Pamlico toward the Santee there were as yet no white inhabitants. The northern boundary of the colony was in dispute and the planters living in that section were cultivating debatable lands and for many years did not know whether they resided in North Carolina or Virginia. Of the precincts bordering on the sound Chowan was the westernmost and largest and the least inhabited. In its religious affiliations it was largely Anglican, with an Anglican church, St. Paul's, already there, dating in its origin from as early as 1701.[2] Perquimans, the next, was occupied by both Angli-

1. Accounts of North Carolina at a slightly later date (1709) are in *ibid.*, I, 711-715 (letter from William Gordon) and in Lawson, *A New Voyage to Carolina* (London, 1709, with maps). The latter work deals almost entirely with the natural history of the country and with the Indians, with brief remarks on the government and the life of the colonists (74-88, 255-256). The *New Voyage* was reprinted in 1718 without change as *The History of Carolina*. On it was based Brickell, *The Natural History of North Carolina*, though by no means a slavish reproduction. A modern edition of Lawson's work was issued in 1860 at Raleigh. A number of Lawson letters are among the Sloane Manuscripts in the British Museum. It is a lamentable fact that the two men who have given us such admirable accounts of their respective regions, Thomas Nairne and John Lawson, should have been tortured and killed by the Indians.

2. The St. Paul's vestry records (Historical Commission of North Carolina) cover the period from 1715 to 1800. Those of date earlier than January 3, 1715, can be found in *North Carolina Colonial Records*, I, II. The present brick edifice was built from funds provided partly by the proprietors and partly by the colony, 1723 (*ibid.*, XXV, 193). In 1715 one of the vestry declared himself a Dissenter and was dis-

cans and Dissenters, among the latter of whom were the Quakers, described as "very numerous, extremely ignorant, insufferably proud and ambitious, and consequently ungovernable," a remark which, coming, as it does, from an Anglican missionary whose ministrations the Quakers bitterly opposed, must be accepted with caution.[1] Pasquotank adjoined Perquimans on the east, with a larger number of Quakers in its population, and more compactly seated, representing on the whole the most industrious, decent, and orderly seat of North Carolina life. One of the Anglican missionaries there joined "with the Quakers' interest" and lost caste with his Anglican brethren, whose work in the precinct was none too successful, leading the Rev. Mr. Urmstone to say that the people were "factious, mutinous and disorderly." Currituck, the last and easternmost of the precincts, was still a wild country, "a very incommodious place for damp colds in winter and mosquitoes in summer," in part made up of swamps and sandbanks and much uncultivable land. The inhabitants there, comparatively few in number, by virtue of their remote location and malarial surroundings, were less tractable and submissive to authority than elsewhere. It was there that Henry Hudson, deputy collector, stationed to watch the ships coming in through the inlets—Currituck, Roanoke, and Ocracock—was seized in 1677 and imprisoned with Miller up the Pasquotank.

The roads everywhere, growing worse as one went eastward, were in a wretched condition, so that transportation was difficult and slow and life was sequestered and dissocialized. At this early period the people in general, despite a good deal of poverty, managed to live simply, fed by the bounty of nature, and showed no ambition to improve their agricultural methods or to engage in industry or trade. Of course, dangers from the Indians were always present, but as Albemarle was not a frontier land or in the path of Indian marauders, the colonists were comparatively free from attack. Only from the Meherrin Indians up the Chowan, whose allegiance was claimed by both Virginia and North Carolina, and from some of the lesser tribes adjoining the southern Currituck and Bath precincts, who

missed, and in 1726 another turned Anabaptist and was likewise ejected. The church had several chapels of ease, one in Indian Town, kept strict watch over morals, and was the custodian of the standard weights and measures. The vestrymen, as public officials, had to take the Test and swear to the Declaration.

1. On the Quakers, *ibid.*, I, 711, 712, 713, 714, 720, 722. They formed, according to one authority, one-seventh of the population, according to another one-tenth.

committed many depredations, was serious trouble experienced. There were incursions in 1666 and again in 1677, when Zachariah Gillam and his stock of weapons were friends in need; but in the main the peace was kept. Indians lived near and among the white settlers, some as servants and some as slaves, and were less a menace than they were a nuisance. No serious troubles with the Indians occurred until 1711 and the outbreak of the Tuscarora War.

The appointment of Ludwell by the proprietors in 1691 and the appointment by him of his deputies in Albemarle, Thomas Jarvis and Thomas Harvey (1691–1694), insured a well-administered, peaceful and quiet colony,[1] but with 1699 and the promotion of Captain Henderson Walker, president of the council, to the governorship, there was introduced into North Carolina the same troublesome and disrupting issue—that of an established church—which, as we have seen, was such a disturbing element in South Carolina. Walker, an Anglican, distressed by the absence of a Church of England organization and aroused by the growing influence of the Quakers in a colony where the Anglicans were in the majority, obtained from the assembly in 1701 an act (the first Vestry Act) making the Church of England the established church.[2] This act aroused intense feeling among the Quakers and other Dissenters, who objected to the requirement that they should pay taxes for the support of another form of religious discipline than their own. The proprietors disallowed the act, but in 1705, when Captain Robert Daniel, who was thoroughly disliked and feared in South Carolina, was serving as Sir Nathaniel Johnson's deputy in the north, another act was forced through the assembly, which seems to have been a replica

1. The only troublesome happening of the period was the attempt of John Gibbs to oust Ludwell from the governorship in 1690, claiming that he had been elected by the council after the withdrawal of Sothell and that Ludwell was an imposter and a usurper. Gibbs was a planter of Currituck and he issued a proclamation denouncing Ludwell and commanding all persons to render obedience to himself. But he was supported by only a few followers and on the intervention of Nicholson of Virginia was persuaded to go to England with Ludwell and lay the case before the proprietors. One would like to know more about Gibbs, who was something of a fire eater. His daughter Mary married as his first wife Martin Bladen of the Board of Trade.

2. *North Carolina Colonial Records*, I, 709–710; Weeks, "The Religious Development of the Province of North Carolina," *Johns Hopkins University Studies*, X, nos. v, vi. Regarding the Vestry Act, the editor of the *North Carolina Colonial Records* refuses to consider it anything more than a re-issue of the act of 1701, but Mr. Weeks is nearer right when he says that "the evidence seems to indicate that [by it] men were required to conform to the English Church," p. 49.

of the South Carolina act of 1704. The passage of the act was due, in the first instance, probably to the influence of Lord Granville and afterward to the activities of the Rev. John Blair, the first missionary of the Society for the Propagation of the Gospel in Foreign Parts, who reached the province in January, 1704. Immediate impulse was given for the passage of the act by Daniel's expulsion of the Quakers from the assembly because they would not take the oath of allegiance to Queen Anne required by a statute of parliament of 1702.[1] The North Carolina act is known as the second Vestry Act, and though its terms are nowhere given it seems to have taken the form of an act of conformity, fastening the Church of England by law upon the colony and requiring the Dissenters to contribute to its support. A further act of assembly imposed an oath of office, thus debarring the Quakers from a return to power.[2] The Dissenters, joining forces with the Quakers against the new establishment, appealed to Governor Johnson at Charles Town, who having his own troubles of a like nature was in no mood to take on anything more. He removed Daniel, however, and appointed in his place Thomas Cary, a merchant of Charles Town, of none too good a repute down there, a tempestuous character, given to disturbances. Why Johnson should have selected as deputies for North Carolina two such men as Daniel and Cary is difficult to understand. The one was brutal and bigoted and a fiery Anglican; the other, supposedly favorable to Dissenters, was an unscrupulous politician, always seeking his own advancement without much regard to consequences.

Cary failed completely in the eyes of the Quakers, for he aligned himself with the Anglican party, following Daniel's course in demanding that the Quakers take an oath of allegiance, and on their refusing to comply, dismissing them from office. Still not satisfied he persuaded the assembly to impose a fine of five pounds upon anyone who, without taking the oath, should presume to stand for election, or having been elected, should sit in the house and take part in its proceedings. The Quakers, in exasperation, sent one John Porter to England, who with the help of the Quaker members of the palatine board, Archdale and Danson, obtained from the proprietors an order removing Cary, on the ground of neglect of duty

1. The parliamentary act may or may not have been intended to extend beyond the seas, but whether so intended or not Daniel's purge was clearly a political move without justification.

2. *North Carolina Colonial Records*, I, 622, "Oath appointed by law," July, 1705.

in failing to transmit copies of the journals and acts of assembly or, in fact, copies of any accounts giving the conditions of the colony and the state of its revenues. They entrusted the administration of the colony to the council until such time as it might appoint another governor.[1] The council elected as its president and acting governor, William Glover, a resident of Perquimans and an office holder in the colony, who formerly at a time when Cary was temporarily absent had been placed in charge of affairs.

Cary asserting that Glover had been illegally chosen turned against him and when Glover demanded, as Daniel had done before him, that the Quakers take the oaths according to law, formed a party of his own, with Porter as his ally and Edward Moseley a sympathizer. By that party he was elected president. Thus two presidents existed, each denying the validity of the other's election. Glover, upheld by Thomas Pollock,[2] a devout churchman and anti-Quaker, spoke scornfully of Cary's "pretended presidentship" and "pretended council," while Cary and his followers charged the Gloverites with failure to maintain law and order and with acting as if the days of Oliver Cromwell had come again. Glover and his party stood for the proprietors and their appointees as against what they called a "Plebeian Route," whereas Cary and his supporters, chiefly from the Dissenter groups, opposed the foisting of an established church upon the colony and the consequent encroachment upon the proprietors' promise of complete freedom of worship. So entangled in this quarrel are personal, political, and religious motives that it is difficult to consider either Cary or the members of his party as leaders in a great cause or as the stuff out of which heroes are made.

Into the details of the events that follow during the years from 1708 to 1710, with civil war imminent and rebellion a fact, it is impossible and unnecessary to go.[3] During the first part of the period Glover was using every effort to retain his position and Cary every effort to oust him from it. This phase was brought to an end by the intervention of the proprietors, who in 1710 selected Edward Tynte

1. *Commissions and Instructions*, p. 189.
2. On Thomas Pollock, Connor, *History of North Carolina*, pp. 103–104.
3. The details of this domestic tempest, the worst since the uprising of 1677 against Miller, can be followed in the *North Carolina Colonial Records*, I, 669–679, 709–710, 723–728, 731, 758–763, 768, 773–807, 911–921; *Calendar State Papers, Colonial*, 1711–1712, §§42, iv, 60, 78, i.

as governor of South Carolina and Edward Hyde as governor of North Carolina, thus for the first time putting the colonies on an equal footing each with the other. Hyde's commission, then in Tynte's keeping, was held up by Tynte's early death and in consequence the approval by the crown did not arrive until 1712. At first Hyde was accepted by both parties, but so unsatisfactory was his administration, and so manifestly was it in the interest of the Gloverites—for he selected both Glover and Pollock as his chief allies and members of his council—that Cary, disillusioned, rebelled and endeavored to overthrow the government by force. In March, 1711, the general assembly impeached Cary, as guilty of high crimes and misdemeanors, and committed him to the care of the provost marshal. But he escaped and continued to fight. Thereupon Hyde and his council appealed for aid to Spotswood, governor of Virginia, who, in his capacity as admiral, sent a vessel with marines, and, as captain general, assembled militia troops along the border. This prompt action overawed the insurgents and broke their morale. The leaders fled to Virginia where they were seized and sent to England for trial. There Cary and four others, at the office of Secretary Dartmouth, entered into recognizances to appear before the palatine court, when summoned, to answer the accusations which Governor Hyde sent over. They did so appear on several occasions, but the proprietors were unimpressed by Hyde's statement of charges and by the entire absence of evidence to support them. Unwilling to stir up more trouble where there had already been trouble enough, they listened favorably to the petition of the accused that they had been fourteen months away from their families and their farms, and allowed them to return home.[1] Cary reached Carolina in 1713, and there died sometime within the next five years.

The rebellion, though bloodless, had brought great distress to the colony, creating disorder and confusion, drawing men from their plantations to the neglect of their crops, and, in general, adding to the impoverishment of the people and their lands. For three years the unhappy country had been kept in a state of commotion and the people in a state of fear, uncertain whether peace and tranquillity ever would return. While thus suffering from trouble within, the

1. *Calendar State Papers, Colonial*, 1711–1712, §220; 1712–1714, §§25, 135; *Acts Privy Council, Colonial*, II, §1155; *North Carolina Colonial Records*, I, 806, 818, 819; II, 53. The proprietors were Carteret, M. Ashley, J. Colleton, and Danson. Lord Granville had died the year before, May 17, 1711.

colony was confronted with the most diabolical Indian onslaught the people of the Albemarle had ever known, comparable with the Yamassee War in the south and arising from much the same causes, the chief of which was the injury the Indians had suffered at the hands of the whites. Though Cary's enemies charged him with having invited the Tuscaroras to come to his assistance and though Porter was accused of having gone among them for the purpose of inciting them against the inhabitants of that part of the country which adhered to Governor Hyde—the western side of the Chowan[1] —there is no good reason for believing that even if this were in some measure true it was more than a minor factor in the case. For years, though less frequently than in the south, the traders had abused and cheated the Indians, and the surveyors—notably John Lawson in the north corresponding to Thomas Nairne in the south—had encroached upon their lands. They had kidnapped men, women, and children to be sold as slaves, and had committed brutalities against the men, outraged their women, destroyed their crops, and burned their cabins. It was frequently noted at the time that no murders or acts of hostility were ever committed by the Indians except in cases where the English had given the first provocation.

The Tuscaroras lived along the Roanoke and Pamlico rivers, with their chief towns on the Neuse and its tributaries and their hunting grounds extending southward toward the Cape Fear. Between them and Pamlico Sound was the small Huguenot settlement at Bath Town and a settlement of Palatines on the point of land at the junction of the Neuse and the Trent. The latter hamlet—the later New Bern—had been founded in 1710, through the efforts of Christoph von Graffenried, member of a Swiss patrician family, a man of ability with a love of adventure, who desired to better his fortunes in America.[2] Upon this hamlet, September 22, 1711, a body of Tuscaroras and other Indians fell with devastating effect. The war thus begun lasted for a year and a half, and the destruction was appalling. Stretches of country along the rivers were desolated, plantations destroyed, and individuals massacred. Along the Neuse and the Pamlico the people saw most of their houses and household goods burned and their cattle, horses, hogs, and other livestock either killed

1. *Ibid.*, I, 782, 796–797, 802, 811, 911.

2. *Christoph von Graffenried's Account of the Founding of New Bern*, edited with an introduction by Vincent H. Todd (North Carolina Historical Commission, 1920).

or carried away. The trade of the colony was ruined, "there being no grain, nor little or no pork this two or three years to send out, so that what few vessels comes in can have little or nothing except a little pitch or tar, so that many have not wherewith to pay their debts. Then the public is several thousand pounds in debt for men's wages employed in the country's service, ammunition, provisions, vessels hire, agents, messenger charges to our neighboring governments."[1] South Carolina sent help under the command of Colonel John Barnwell, who attacked the Indians near New Bern and forced the Tuscaroras to negotiate a treaty. But unfortunately for the continuance of amicable relations between the two colonies, he withdrew before completing the defeat of the enemy. In the exchange of asperities Barnwell's great feat of marching three hundred miles and fighting two pitched battles was lost to sight by the North Carolinians, the results were disparaged, and the generosity and promptness of South Carolina underrated. North Carolina complained because Barnwell left with his task unfinished; South Carolina was angered because her northern neighbor had so little appreciation of her sacrifice as to refuse Barnwell a grant of land south of the Neuse. Nevertheless, despite the heat engendered by the Barnwell controversy, South Carolina the next year sent Colonel Moore, and he, cooperating with Thomas Pollock won a "glorious victory," in which as Pollock wrote, Moore "hath bravely and gallantly discharged the trust put in him."[2] This success ended both the controversy and the war. The remaining Tuscaroras migrated to New York and joining the Iroquois federation made six nations where there had been only five before.

The Tuscarora War following the Cary rebellion and accompanied by outbreaks of fever, which brought added distress in their train, destroyed whatever lingering enthusiasm the proprietors may have had for their northern colony. Long since they had given it up as a paying investment, not only because of its domestic troubles but also because the growth of the colony failed wholly to meet their expectations. They were confronted with an unenterprising people, from whom they collected their quit-rents with difficulty, and were disquieted by the fear lest they might have to draw at any time upon their own resources in England to meet the colony's debts. The

1. *North Carolina Colonial Records*, I, 873–874.
2. *Ibid.*, II, 44–45.

affairs of North Carolina as well as those of South Carolina were getting very much out of hand and the problems raised by the domestic disturbances and external wars were rapidly passing beyond the power of the proprietors to solve. Furthermore, the latter were perplexed and annoyed by the long drawn out controversy with Virginia over the boundary question, a matter which fell within the field of royal rather than proprietary administration, but nevertheless affected their purses because it concerned the obtaining of quit-rents from the lands in dispute.[1]

With the return of peace after the Tuscarora War North Carolina entered upon her career as a normal colony, freed from the factional strife that had kept government and people alike in a state of turmoil, uncertainty, and mistrust. It did not become a royal colony at the same time with South Carolina, partly because there was no popular demand for the change and partly because the English authorities saw no legal incongruity in annulling one part of the proprietors' rights and not the other, even though these rights had been granted in a single charter. They justified their action by the power of the crown to appoint in times of "extraordinary exigency," a provisional governor, even though the charter had not been given up—a temporary expedient preliminary to a return of the province to the proprietor or to the crown. Thus in 1720 Nicholson of South Carolina received his commission and instructions from the king, whereas in 1723 Burrington of North Carolina received his from the proprietors. When in 1725 Everard wanted to succeed Burrington, he made his application to the proprietors and not to the Board of Trade or the Privy Council. Until 1729 all the laws passed by the assembly bore the enacting clause, "By his Excellency the Palatine and the rest of the True and Absolute Lords Proprietors of Carolina, by and with the Advice and Consent of the Members of the

1. This particular issue lies beyond the scope of our treatment. Virginia from the beginning had looked upon Albemarle as but an extension of her own territory, because it was the same country geographically and had been settled by her people. She resented the issue of the charter of 1665, which gave the territory to the proprietors, and she continued to lay claim on the east to lands about the head of Currituck Inlet and the Blackwater River, and on the west to the region along the upper Chowan where lived the Meherrin Indians. An irritating exchange of accusations and arguments went on for half a century until the line was finally drawn in 1728. On the subject see Boyd, *William Byrd's Histories of the Dividing Line* (1929), an admirable and definitive edition of one of the classics of colonial literature.

General Assembly, now met for the North East part of the said Province."

Even so one feels that during those years from 1719 to 1729 North Carolina was in process of becoming royal: the English authorities were keeping a watchful eye upon its affairs; the king had to give his approval before a governor could hold office; the commissioners of the customs were regularly drawing up the trade instruction which the king sent to the governors; and the Board of Trade was urging, as it had urged many times before, that the colony be brought into the king's hand.[1] To all intents and purposes, therefore, the last years of the colony's history as a proprietary province, witnessed the gradual passing away of the proprietary influence. The final surrender of the charter in 1729 was but a minor episode in the relationship of the colony to the mother country.

1. *North Carolina Colonial Records*, I, 359, 371, 630–633; II, 420.

CHAPTER VII

THE PROPRIETARY PROVINCE OF PENNSYLVANIA

WILLIAM PENN, the founder of the proprietary province of Pennsylvania, was born in 1644 on Tower Hill, during the excitement created by the first civil war in England. In 1648 his father, Admiral Penn of Cromwell's Western Expedition, moved to Chigwell in Essex, about eleven miles from London, where for eight years the boy enjoyed the advantages of an excellent private school. Then his father, suffering from Cromwell's displeasure after his return from Jamaica without the Protector's license, retired temporarily from the navy and withdrew to Ireland, where estates had been granted him under the Cromwellian Settlement of 1652. In Ireland the youthful Penn, always religiously minded, had his first contact with the Quaker missionary, Thomas Loe, who made a profound impression on the young man and later exercised a determining influence upon his life. Experiences then followed that strengthened his character and gave him a knowledge of worldly affairs. At the age of sixteen he matriculated at Christ Church, Oxford, remaining there but two years, perplexed by the entire absence of piety and learning and by the "useless and injurious pedantry" and the "empty shows and formalities that masqueraded as the religion of Christ." Expelled for refusing to conform to the regulations, he was sent by a troubled father on a European tour, during which he visited Paris and eventually Italy, and spent two years at the Huguenot college of Saumur in Anjou. There he studied theology, and not only became proficient in French but acquired also a working knowledge of Latin, Greek, and the writings of the early fathers of the church. After his return he lived for a while with his father in London and later, during the second Dutch war, accompanied him on one of his naval expeditions. Indifferent to the forms and ceremonies of social life, he took up the study of law at Lincoln's Inn and obtained thereby an acquaintance with legal forms and procedure that proved to be of great value in later years. When but twenty-two he was sent by his father to take charge of his estates in Ireland and the experience that he gained at this time gave him an insight into the business of a land agent. During the five years of this varied life he became intimate, in different degrees, with John Locke, Algernon Sidney, Benjamin Furly, Whitelocke, Stillingfleet (the chaplain of Charles II), William Coventry, Sir William Petty, and a number of the English lords in Ireland, notably Lord Arran, Ormonde's second son. Above all, he profited from the affection which Charles II and the Duke of York had for his father, the admiral, who had returned to the navy when the duke became lord high admiral in 1660. Young Penn had been presented by the father to the king on the day of his coronation and an intimacy sprang up between his sovereign and himself that deepened as the years passed. Circumstances were conspiring to prepare the way for the great work of his later life.

Penn became part of the Quaker movement after it had passed its first phase of extreme fervor. He became a real and fully converted Friend, but he did not follow the visionary beliefs of Fox or lend himself to the fantastic forms of dress and conduct adopted by Nayler and Eccles. In certain of his first pamphlets he attacked the existing forms of faith and was almost blasphemous in his denial of the Trinity, but in the most famous of all his religious treatises, *No Cross, No Crown,* an apologia issued from the Tower in 1669, he refrained from the denunciations of his earlier writings and dealt with the nature and discipline of the cross of Christ. From this time forward his attitude was marked by a sane and practical outlook on religion, a business-like way of handling controversial problems, and a realization of the fact that the world could not be reformed all at once or reformed entirely at any time. He was convinced that the principles according to which the Quakers shaped their lives were the truest and purest that could be conceived and superior to those according to which other religious communities of the day carried on their ministrations. Therefore, he began, more vigorously than he had done before, to lay stress upon certain major tenets, such as liberty of conscience, pacifism, and direct relations with God without the intermediation of ministers and priests. He deprecated the use of the "tempting visibles," as he called them, by which he meant the ritual and ceremonies of the churches, the churches themselves, the keeping of saints' days and holy days, and the customary terms of the calendar. He emphasized stability, good government, and the rights of Englishmen, and was able, especially in the defense which he made, when under the Conventicle Act of 1664 (repassed in 1670) he and William Mead were brought to trial, to confute his enemies by his knowledge of the law of England.

In this famous case, of great significance in the history of trial by jury, he succeeded, despite the bullying of the bench, Sir Samuel Starling presiding, in obtaining from the jury a favorable verdict. Though Starling refused to accept the verdict and sent Penn off to Newgate, the issue was revived when the jury, led by the foreman, Bushell, brought an action against Starling. After a delay of two years it obtained from the court of king's bench a decision upholding the fundamental rights of an English jury to bring in a verdict, even though the bench disagreed, and affirming that the jury could not be abused or fined for doing so. The incident defined an Englishman's rights in one very important particular and furnished a striking manifestation of the value of Penn's year of study at the Inns of Court. Certainly in this case Penn's knowledge of the law and his vigorous method of carrying the war into the enemy's country was of great and permanent importance, greater even than was the nonconformist policy of passive resistance—endurance of persecution, punishment, and even death, refusal to pay tithes, bear arms, and other negative attitudes—such as many of the earlier Quakers had adopted. Penn may have looked upon the world as corrupt and, like the Puritan before him, have seen doom impending and the day of the Lord drawing nigh; he may have denounced, as he did, all priests and sacraments; and he may have been convinced of the "vanity of the world and the irreligiousness of the religions in it," but he performed a lasting service for his country when, in his defense at the Old Bailey and in the pamphlets he wrote during the decade that followed, he endeavored to arouse his own brethren as well as others to a sense of their responsibilities as citizens of England.[1]

1. This brief account of Penn's early life is based largely on Miss Brailsford's *The Making of William Penn* (1930), which though pro-Cromwellian is excellent for all that happened before 1670. After that date it is less satisfactory. Miss Brailsford leans heavily on "the strutting Pepys," as she calls the diarist, and is inclined to take his remarks too seriously. In common with all Penn's biographers she shows little knowledge of the reign of Charles II and takes the conventional view of the king himself. The oldest biographies are those of Sewel (English translation, 1722), Clarkson (1813), and Janney (1852), which are standard works. Others, more recent, are by Dixon (1872) and Buell (1904), the former eloquent but not wholly to be trusted, the latter distinctly unreliable. Lives by Stoughton (1882), Fisher (1900), Grant (1907), Graham (1912), Dobrée (1932), Pound (1932), and Vulliamy (1934)—all

Penn's father died in 1670, reconciled at the last with his son, whom almost with his dying breath he commended to Charles II and the Duke of York, that they might continue toward the son the loyalty and affection they had always shown for the father.[1] The year after his father's death Penn, at the age of twenty-six, set out for the Continent on a missionary tour for the purpose of converting whom he could, much as he had been doing on a smaller scale in Ireland during the months when he was looking after his father's interests at Shangarry. Every convert to Quakerism was potentially a missionary and to the limit of his or her capacity was expected to spread the doctrine of the inner light among all ranks, from the highest to the lowest. Fox had begun his missionary journeys as early as 1647 and continued them year by year until his death. He visited England, Wales, Scotland, Ireland, North America, and the West Indies before 1673, and now Penn took up the task of carrying the Quaker message to Holland largely with the hope of winning over certain of the mystical and pietistic groups, which, because of superficial resemblances of life and doctrine, seemed open to persuasion. One effort made in 1671 and another in 1677 failed in their main objects, but they had one result, quite apart from Penn's ease of mind in a duty performed, for a number of Labadists followed Penn to America, and others, after a preliminary survey had been made in 1679 by their brethren Danckaerts and Sluyter, came over as a colony and settled in Maryland in 1683.[2]

Of Penn's journey to the Continent in 1671 very little is known, beyond the fact that with Thomas Rudyard as companion he

have the value of compilations, reflecting the point of view of the author, and the reader may take his choice. The writings of Dobrée and Pound are good, but the work of Vulliamy is full of the author's likes and dislikes and is written in such a highly seasoned style as to set one's teeth on edge. A bibliography of writings on Penn was issued by the Department of Public Instruction of Pennsylvania, *Bulletin*, no. 1, in 1932, and Hull's *Eight First Biographies* in 1936. The latter's *William Penn, A Topical Biography*, appeared in June, 1937, too late for use in this volume.

1. Admiral Penn was at the head of the navy office and the superior of Samuel Pepys for a part of the time when the Duke of York was lord high admiral, so that the two men for five years were in frequent contact officially as well as personally. Information on this point can be obtained from Granville Penn, *Memorials of Admiral Penn* (1833). In the Duke of York's *Memoirs*, pp. 113–114, will be found "Instructions for Sir William Penn," given under the duke's hand, November 11, 1664.

2. James, "The Labadist Colony in Maryland," *Johns Hopkins University Studies*, XVII, 277–312; *Journal of Jasper Danckaerts* (Original Narratives); Hull, *William Penn and the Dutch Migration to Pennsylvania* (1935), pp. 15–19.

joined Benjamin Furly at Rotterdam and spent most of his time in the effort to win over the Labadists and to convert Princess Elizabeth of the Palatinate, granddaughter of James I and cousin of Charles and James. But of the tour in 1677 he kept a journal[1] and we know that he visited the Netherlands and the Rhineland, and that by means of speaking, writing, printing, meetings, debates, and personal interviews, he recruited for the Quaker faith. In these missionary excursions he was accompanied by a number of Dutch and English companions and when at Rotterdam lodged for a time in the house of Arent Sonnemans or Sonmans, the father of Peter Sonmans one of the East New Jersey proprietors. From his association with Rudyard, Barclay, and the Sonmans family in Holland probably sprang the plan which brought the Quakers into control in East New Jersey after 1680. Penn made a third journey to the Netherlands in 1686, the principal object of which was to influence William of Orange to support the establishment of religious toleration in England. As the prince was the son-in-law of Penn's intimate friend, James II, after 1685 king of England, he was kindly received and had considerable success in his mission. From the interviews then held the prince may have been confirmed in his opinion that toleration of faith and worship was the right policy for England. Penn had written to the Princess Elizabeth "how can any man's Conscience be at another's dispose" and William of Orange believed (according to Bishop Burnet) "that conscience was subject only to God," naturally, therefore, the two men must have found themselves in accord on the subject, even though William would not listen to any proposal looking to the repeal of the Test Act.[2]

During the years when Penn was visiting the Netherlands and western Germany and during the intervals between these visits when he was keeping up a frequent correspondence with friends he had long known or had recently made, he was working out plans of a far-reaching nature for a refuge in America, where might be gathered the persecuted of any people, whether of England, Ireland, Scotland, Wales, the Netherlands, or the Rhineland.

The circumstances attending Penn's interest in America follow a natural sequence. As the son of his father, he must have known early of the lands beyond the seas and this knowledge could easily

1. *Penn's Select Works*, II, 398–503, and separately printed.
2. Hull, as above, *passim*.

have been expanded from his studies at Oxford[1] and Lincoln's Inn. But it was not until after his conversion in 1668 that the importance of the region impressed itself upon his mind. From conversations with Josiah Coale, who had made three missionary journeys overseas, and from his association with George Fox, who had returned in 1673 after many adventures and sufferings, he learned at first hand of the possibilities of the region. The knowledge thus obtained was supplemented by a personal experience when in 1674 he was invited to settle the quarrel, to which our attention has already been called, between John Fenwick and Edward Byllinge. As a result he became one of the three trustees of Byllinge's property, in association with Gawan Lawrie and Nicholas Lucas.[2] From this time on he found himself intimately interested in the affairs of West New Jersey, as trustee-broker for the disposal of Byllinge's shares. These shares he and his fellow trustees in part transferred to Byllinge's creditors and in part sold to two groups of Quakers, one from Yorkshire and the other from London, who in 1677 founded the town of Burlington in West New Jersey. But he did more than act as business negotiator. He himself drew up or supervised the work of others in drawing up the constitution or fundamental agreement— the "Concessions" of 1677—under which the infant colony was expected to function.

Penn at the time was but thirty-three years old, and if he himself enunciated the principles upon which this fundamental agreement rested, he was possessed of a maturity of mind and an idealistic conception of society that is remarkable for one of his years. That others as well as he had a part in the formulation of these principles can hardly be questioned, but that his was the master mind admits of little doubt. With this opportunity of framing a constitution that would represent the freedom of England and the rights of Englishmen, as he conceived them, he poured into his version all the ideas he had been gradually accumulating as the result partly of *a priori* conviction, partly of his study of More and Harrington, and partly of his conversations with the republican, Algernon Sidney, whom he had met in Holland and with whom he was on terms of intimate friendship. Also he was influenced by the treatment accorded his

1. Penn speaks of having had "an opening of joy as to these parts, in the year 1661 at Oxford." *Memoirs,* Pennsylvania Historical Society, I, 210.

2. Above, pp. 151–152.

fellow Quakers and by his own experience at the Old Bailey trial.[1] In this fundamental agreement are to be found such concepts as liberty of conscience; no taxation without the consent of the taxed; the compulsory use of the ballot whereby the purity of elections, so often demanded by Penn in his insistence on a free parliament,[2] might be maintained; the preservation of the rights of the individual to prevent such illegal arrests as had sent him to the Tower and Newgate; trial by jury, the verdicts of which were to be binding on the judges; and, finally, the right of the people in assembly to make the laws. Throughout this fundamental agreement there runs one great purpose, to preserve unimpaired such liberties as were guaranteed by law for the good government of a people, in accord with, as near as conveniently might be, "the primitive, antient and fundamental laws of the people of England." That Penn should have been so familiar with the laws of England as to make his strong defense

1. A study of the printed account of the trial will show that in 1670 many of the basic ideas embodied in the "Concessions" of 1677 were already well shaped in Penn's mind. These ideas are elaborated in the foreword and appendices to the printed account, additions which we may believe were prepared by Penn himself in his own defense, and which should be studied in the light of Penn's essay of 1675, *England's Present Interest Considered*, where many of the same questions are taken up. These ideas comprise liberty of conscience, civil and religious freedom; jury trial with the jurors final judges of law and fact; no man a freeman and privileged to enjoy his rights under the fundamental law of England if his freedom and freehold were made subservient to the will and interest of his judges; references to Magna Carta with exceptions against the indictment, to the confirmation of the charters and the sentence of the clergy against breakers of its articles, and to the case of Judge Keeling, 1667, taken from the journal of parliament. These citations sum up in Penn's mind the fundamental law of England (*The Peoples* $\begin{cases} ancient \\ and\ just \end{cases}$ *Liberties Asssrted in the Tryal of William Penn, and William Mead, At the Sessions held at the Old Baily in London, the first, third, fourth and fifth of Sept. 70, against the most Arbitary procedure of that court,* 1670, reprinted, 1825, in *Penn's Select Works,* I, 179–223, and again in 1908, not from the original state, as the editor thinks, but from the second state, in which the "Asssrted" of the original has been corrected to "Asserted." The pamphlet was reprinted also in 1707, in a book entitled *The Phenix,* which contains as well, "The Second Part of the Peoples Antient and Just Liberties Asserted, in the Proceedings against and Tryals of Thomas Rudyard, Francis Moor, Richard Mew, Richard Mayfield, Richard Knowlman, Gilbert Hulton, Job Boulton and William Bayley . . . against the arbitrary Procedure of that court, and Justice there, September 30–October 7, 1670, when the prisoners were discharged").

2. "England's Great Interest in the Choice of this New Parliament" and "One Project for the Good of England, that is, Our Civil Union is Our Civil Safety," *Penn's Select Works,* III, 181–188, 189–205. These addresses were prepared in 1679, when Penn campaigned in the interest of his friend Sidney, who was standing for election to parliament.

before the court and to expound so expertly the rights of Englishmen in the fundamental agreement or "Concessions" of West New
Jersey, is a witness to the thoroughness of his work at Lincoln's Inn
and to the skill which he had displayed in defending his fellow
Quakers against the attacks of the government. In none of his later
essays did he present this broad and comprehensive statement that
placed the liberties of the people above prerogative. As far as one
can judge, he did not, before he received his charter for Pennsylvania, think it either right or fitting that such great power should
rest in either proprietor or crown. He believed that government
existed for something more than the enforcement of law and order,
an agency rather for social service and the betterment of the masses,
if we are to form an opinion from the few sentences found here and
there in his writings on government and the magistracy, as in his
England's Present Interest Considered, written in 1675, where he
discusses fundamental laws.

But Penn did not believe that the West New Jersey settlement
could meet his needs or those of his fellow Quakers. He wanted a
colony of his own, large enough to become a sanctuary for all persecuted Protestants, a place where under his own immediate gov-
ernance he might put into application, as in a "holy experiment,"[1]
the principles and practices of life and conduct, which, he felt, had
been lost sight of in the corrupt world of England. The times
weighed heavily upon him. Beginning with 1680 a reaction in the
king's favor was taking place. The country party, led by Shaftesbury,
which in 1682 was reported as "down in the mouth and without
confidence" was losing its influence, and the government was free to
enforce the Conventicle Act and to suppress the Quaker movement.
At no time since the restoration of 1660 were the sufferings of the
Quakers so acute as during the years from 1679 to 1683, when the
administration was adopting, as never before, a coercive policy, determined to suppress conventicles as unlawful and to arrest and imprison those who took part in them. The Quakers suffered more
than the other non-conformist groups, because they refused to meet
in secret or to end their meetings even after their buildings were
barred or destroyed. They and the other Dissenters were charged

---

1. The words "holy experiment" are to be found in Penn's letter to James Harrison, August 26, 1681, "there may be room there [in Pennsylvania], though not here
[in England], for such a holy experiment," Janney, *Life of Penn,* p. 166.

with perverting the religion of the king's subjects and debauching the people with their doctrines. They were called "dangerous fanatics," "poor deluded Quakers," and "insolent violators of order and uniformity." They were dubbed "zealots," "vipers," and "the vermin which swarm in the land," a "schismatical factious people," who ought to be suppressed as enemies of the king and his government. The Quakers, in their turn, construed the Conventicle Act and earlier and similar acts as contrary to the law of God, and they declared that no magistrate had a right to rob them of their goods, imprison them, or bring them to ruin for errors about religion.[1]

There is no doubt that many of the town mayors and others of the civil magistrates were loth to put the laws into effect and we know that Secretary Leoline Jenkins bade the officers observe the laws of humanity as well as the laws of the kingdom. A good deal of the hounding was the work of malicious informers and overzealous Anglican clergymen, the latter of whom were angry, because their tithes, which with fees and offerings were the source of their living, and the attendance at their parish churches were being seriously reduced. Penn, though not himself molested, was prosecuted as a popish recusant, as early as 1678, and rendered liable, under an old act of Elizabeth (1585), to the payment of heavy fines. It has sometimes been said, that confusion in the pronunciation of "Saumur," where he studied, with "St. Omer," the Roman Catholic seminary on the Continent, and his close association with the Duke of York and his confessor Father Petre[2] explains the treatment to

1. Harrowing accounts of the treatment of the Quakers during these years can be obtained from the *Calendar of State Papers, Domestic,* 1679 to 1683. It is said that at one time 1400 were in prison, and the suppression of the meetings as seditious gatherings reached its height in 1683, when Quakers were charged with participation in the plots of 1681–1682, with affronts to the government and to religion as by law established, with refusing to take the oath of allegiance, and with holding unlawful conventicles.

2. Bishop Burnet is usually held responsible for the rumor (*History of My Own Times,* ed. 1840, I, 441), but other evidence exists to show that the report was current before 1679 and that it was more than a rumor. In that year a list was drawn up of over a hundred names, including the name of "William Penne, of Worminghurst, Esq," of those who had been prosecuted "as Popish Recusants but in reality [were] true Protestants" (*Calendar Treasury Books,* V, pt. II, 1256–1257), which shows that the charge must have been made at least one or two years earlier. On April 30, 1681, a warrant was issued "to stay all further process against William Penn of Worminghurst Place, co. Sussex, for 20*l*, supposed to be by him forfeited for one month as a Popish Recusant . . . the Treasury Lords being well satisfied that said Penn is not or ever was a Popish Recusant (*ibid.,* VII, 131). But the accusation was brought again

which he was subjected, but too many other Quakers were included in the accusation for such an explanation to be even plausible. That the charge was a general one is shown by the fact that many Quakers made the written declaration against transubstantiation, required by statute (30 Charles II, c. 2), in the hope that they might not suffer from the law against popish recusants.[1]

What Penn saw or thought he saw as he looked out over the political and religious world of England and the Continent[2] was his poor country, distractedly substituting man-made law for the law of God, persecuting the poor and the helpless, and bringing untold misery upon those whose only crime was obedience to conscience. He saw plots and conspiracies, charges and counter-charges, perjury and subornation, indulgence and hypocrisy in high places, a government unjust, intolerant, and without mercy and a people beggared, destitute of subsistence, and often homeless. He saw a widespread violation of liberty and property and a disregard for that freedom which he believed rested on the fundamental rules of "venerable antiquity."[3] What further lay in store for the unhappy land he knew not, for in that year 1680 he saw the governmental authorities planning to take new measures of oppression rather than to lighten those already in force. We know that in Penn's case, as in that of Winthrop half a century before, the fears were worse than the reality and that conditions were far less hopeless than he thought them; that persecution though widespread was nowhere vindictive or cruel or near the extermination point that some predicted; that the instincts of humanity were not entirely gone from those in authority; and that at bottom England was sound, solvent, and sober-minded.[4]

and again during the years from 1685 to 1689, and is discussed in a pamphlet entitled *A Letter to Mr. Penn, with his Answer* (1688). The subject is dealt with by Hull, in his *William Penn and the Dutch Quakers*, pp. 303–305, and in his *William Sewel of Amsterdam*, pp. 88–92. Mention of it will be found in Sewel, *History of the Quakers* (1844), II, 305–319.

1. *Calendar State Papers, Domestic*, 1680–1681, p. 595.

2. In his letter to the council and senate of the city of Embden, issued in 1674, he speaks bitterly of the persecution of the Quakers there. *Works*, II, 198–202.

3. For Penn's description of the state of England in 1675, see *England's Present Interest Considered* (*Works*, II, 268–320), particularly chapter two and "A Corollary."

4. *Calamy Revised* (Matthews ed., 1934), p. lix. Mr. Matthews points out that the persecution under Charles II was intermittent; that "all the penal legislation was never enforced everywhere at one time nor anywhere continuously through the reign"; that the Cavalier Parliament, in adopting the Clarendon Code was but following "the theory and practice of every previous English government"; and that "while the enlightened few, chief among whom was the king, advocated liberty of worship, the

But Penn, unable to take the view of a detached observer, turned his thoughts to the New World, where from Rhode Island to the Carolinas were hundreds of his Quaker brethren, living often scattered and remote, but in the main free from the malevolence that pursued the nonconformist at home. He must have obtained already a fairly accurate idea of the lay of the land there and of the parts still vacant, for maps, such as they were, abounded. His New Jersey responsibilities had necessitated some knowledge of the region, and the Duke of York and Sir John Werden were a source of information upon which he could easily have drawn. He must have known that there was a stretch of unoccupied territory, lying west of the Delaware, between New York and Maryland, though just how its boundaries ran he was as little informed as were others. There is some reason to think that at the time he was having money troubles in connection with his estates, either in England or Ireland, but just what they were it is impossible to determine.[1] In any case he had a claim against the exchequer for £16,000, which covered money his father had advanced for the subsistence of the navy plus the pay due his father for many years of service and the interest on the capital sum. In drafting his petition for a grant of land in America he took occasion to remind the king that the debt was among those repudiated by the Stop of the Exchequer in 1672, and that for want of the money he and his mother were seriously embarrassed. Evidently, he did not expect the grant to extinguish the debt, but hoped that by means of it he might obtain a revenue large enough to restore his fortunes and enable him to carry on a profitable commercial enterprise as well as an exemplary holy experiment. Therefore on June 1, 1680, he sent in his petition to the king.

Penn's petition revived an issue that was already troubling the king's advisers, that of England's present and future colonial policy.

governing class as a whole held to the long established theory of religious nonconformity being tantamount to civil disobedience." A careful study of the Domestic Papers of the period bears out this conclusion. The persecution of the nonconformists under Charles II did not compare in intensity and harshness with persecutions in England and elsewhere in earlier centuries.

1. There are several intriguing references in the Treasury Books and elsewhere to petitions for relief and hints of a mortgage from one "William Pen" or "Penn" (Calendar Treasury Books, IV, 327, 353; V, pt. I, 45, 489; VI, 659, August 20, 1680. The references V, pt. I, 45, 489 are now P.R.O., Gifts and Deposits, 32: 33, p. 175; 34, p. 16). The entries are obscure, even in the originals, and would not arouse suspicion were it not for the fact that there is a suggestion of financial trouble in Penn's petition for a charter drawn up in the same year (Hazard, Annals, p. 474).

As the seventeenth century wore on those in charge of colonial affairs—the Privy Council and the Lords of Trade—began to realize the difficulties involved in creating so many private colonies independent of the control of the crown. The peoples of Massachusetts, New York, the Jerseys, and the Carolinas were evidently not enjoying the rights of their fellow Englishmen at home, and the prevailing system of decentralization was menacing the efforts of the government to enforce its laws of trade and to provide adequate defense against the French. After 1675 and the setting up of the Lords of Trade as a royal commission, the members showed unmistakeably their unwillingness to increase the number of colonies of this type. They turned down petitions of private persons for proprietary grants; they removed New Hampshire from under the jurisdiction of Massachusetts and made it a royal colony; they rejected the claims of Stirling and Hamilton on the ground, as afterward stated, that to revive dormant claims would lead to unspeakable disturbance and confusion; and they brought about the annulment of the charters of the Massachusetts Bay and Bermuda companies. In September, 1682, they issued this pronouncement, "We think it not convenient to constitute any new propriety in America nor to grant any further powers that may render the plantations less dependent on the crown."[1] This policy took more definite form after 1696 and accounts for the many attempts made in the early eighteenth century to transform the proprietary and corporate governments into royal colonies administered directly from Whitehall by the crown.

But fortunately for Penn this plan of control in 1680 had not become a fixed rule applicable in all cases; so that when in the summer of that year he sent in his petition to Charles II for a grant of land in America, the request received careful attention by the king's advisers. Although it was well known that the king favored the petition and would like to see the grant made, it cannot be shown that he brought pressure to bear upon those to whom he turned for a decision.[2] The question of the grant was under advise-

1. *Calendar State Papers, Colonial,* 1681–1685, §696. This policy was adopted by the Lords of Trade after Penn's charter had been issued, when they refused in 1682 to grant the petition of the Earl of Doncaster for a propriety in Florida, but it was certainly in their minds before that date.

2. In an article printed in the *Journal* of the Friends Historical Society, XXXII, 1–19, entitled "William Penn and English Politics in 1680–81," Mr. Fulmer Mood argues on behalf of a closer connection than has usually been seen between the grant of Penn's charter and the political rivalries of the period. He advances the opinion

ment for nine months. Secretary Sutherland referred the petition to the Lords of Trade, with the request that they report what it seemed best to do. The lords examined the petition carefully. They sent copies of it to Sir John Werden, the Duke of York's secretary, and to the agents of Lord Baltimore in England in order to find out if they had any objections to offer. They sent Penn's draft of a patent to the attorney general and to the chief justice of the court of common pleas, each of whom made important modifications and additions. They discussed at length the troublesome question of boundaries, of how so large a grant could be fitted in between the claims of the Duke of York on the north and those of Lord Baltimore on the south and of how they could meet Penn's wishes as to a frontage on the Delaware and Susquehannah rivers. After a number of amendments had been made and after nearly every one had taken a hand in determining just how the boundaries should run—with the inevitable result of producing interminable controversies afterward—the patent was started on its way through the seals. On March 4, 1681, it received the great seal at the hands of the lord chancellor. The draft, before it was finally engrossed, was written by William Blathwayt, who cannot greatly have relished the content of it, for he was an outstanding opponent of the whole proprie-

that Charles II deliberately brought about the grant for party purposes and that affection for Penn and a desire to compensate him for the debt due his father were reasons put forward to conceal the real truth. This truth he finds in the king's determination to get Penn, the Quakers, and other Whiggishly inclined Dissenters out of England at a time when the balance between Tories and Whigs was fairly even and the political outlook uncertain. To remove from England "These humble folk [who] supplied the real voting strength of the Whig party," Mr. Mood thinks, would have been distinctly a Tory advantage at a critical time. He thinks further that Penn fell in with the plan because he saw in migration the only way to guarantee the "republican ideals" of toleration, peace, and opportunity for success in life that he and his Whiggish friends favored.

The argument is interesting but it requires that we believe in a collusion between Penn and Charles II that is not, as far as I know, even hinted at in the records of the period. To start with the assumption that Charles II played such a leading part in the transaction as intentionally to use it for party ends, while not beyond the bounds of possibility, is purely conjectural and must be treated as such. Mr. Mood has probably overstated the voting influence of the "humble folk," who were, with some noteworthy exceptions, simple people with no vote at all. I doubt if anyone can say how many of them were freeholders or voting burgesses. I think, too, that his terms "countless hundreds" and "thousands" suggest more than the four or five thousand English Quakers and other Dissenters that actually went over before 1685. None of these were of the landed nobility or landed gentry and few of the city merchants and rich Dissenters, the ones whom the Tories chiefly feared. Nevertheless Mr. Mood's thesis deserves consideration.

tary system and an upholder of the policy of greater centralization.[1] But to Penn it was a matter for rejoicing. On that day he wrote in exultation to his friend Robert Turner in Dublin—who was afterward to play a very important part in the life and government of the colony—"know that after many waitings, watchings, solicitings and disputes in council, this day my country was confirmed to me under the Great Seal of England, with large powers and privileges, by the name of *Pennsylvania,* a name the king would have given it in honor of my father."[2]

This charter to Penn was no Stuart contrivance designed for the purpose of curtailing "liberty." It was issued unwillingly by the king's advisers to one who was known to be a close and intimate friend of the Duke of York—himself a proprietor of land in America—and it was couched in the only form known to the lawyers and officials of the day, that of a proprietary possession. The lords could not prevent its issue but they could and did add such clauses as would make the charter conform somewhat to the conditions of the time. They made it a compromise text, partly medieval and partly modern, a curious co-mingling of the past and the present, representing on one side the precedents of the lawyers and on the other the ideas which gradually were becoming a part of England's colonial programme. It was Penn's misfortune that there was no other form except the proprietary known to the chancery officials for making such a grant as he desired. From the first, it contained discordant factors: the prerogatives of a medieval proprietor; the regulations made necessary by England's new policy of centralized control; and the idealistic purposes of a man who wished to found a state based on the most honorable principles of toleration, morals, justice, and brotherly love. In these discordances lay the seeds of troubles to come.

1. *Ibid.,* 1677–1680, §§1373, 1390, 1404, 1544, 1565, 1574, 1580, 1592–1595, 1603, 1609, 1619; 1681–1685, §§6, 8, 29, 32; Hazard's *Register,* I, 269–271, 273–274; Jacobsen, *William Blathwayt,* pp. 118–119, 304. Blathwayt belonged to the group which has always been anathema to American writers on colonial history, because the latter have construed England's attempt to organize her colonies as a blow at "liberty." Penn's biographers, unfamiliar with the history of England's colonial policy, have always been troubled to understand the long delay which took place before the charter was granted and have ascribed this delay to the fact that Penn was a commoner and a Quaker. There is nothing to show that Penn's rank or religion were ever considered as factors in the case.

2. *Memoirs,* Historical Society of Pennsylvania, I, 208–209.

By the charter Penn became the proprietor of a vast but loosely bounded domain, extending from New York to Maryland and back toward the interior through five degrees of longitude. The northern line was the forty-third degree of latitude and the southern a twelve mile circumference around New Castle, which was supposed to connect with the fortieth parallel marking the southern line. The ambiguity of this description and its geographical inaccuracy left the question of the lower Delaware undecided and opened up a century-long conflict with Maryland and New York as to just what the words of the charter meant. Of this vast area Penn was made the true and absolute proprietor, to hold the land in free and common socage, as of the royal castle of Windsor, paying therefor fealty and allegiance and two beaver skins on the first of January in each year. Though all reference to the palatinate of Durham was carefully omitted, Penn was given almost equivalent authority in the complete control he could exercise over the soil, in his right to determine the form of government, in his extensive privileges of local appointment, and in his ability to issue ordinances of his own in time of need. He could initiate and promulgate laws, but only with the advice, assent, and approbation of the freemen in assembly, that is, as later shown, by the freeholders. In all its main features the charter followed the standard type, differing, however, from charters of the earlier period in that it reduced considerably the proprietary prerogatives, toned down the strictly feudal aspects so as to render them as innocuous as possible, and reserved to the king all his sovereign powers. In this respect Penn's charter, compared with that of Lord Baltimore, issued fifty years before, or even with that of the Duke of York, issued in 1664, represents the changes which had come over the mind of the English government since the king had been restored to his throne. Whether this minimizing of the proprietary features was the work of Penn himself, who in his earlier writings defended the liberties of the people as against the prerogative of proprietor or crown, or the work of the Lords of Trade and other of the king's advisers it is impossible to say. The latter may well have desired to reduce to the lowest possible terms the feudal terms of the patent.

However this may be, the lords were certainly responsible for many important limitations upon Penn's proprietary independence. As guardians of England's colonial interests it was their business to see that the new province should be brought, as far as possible, within the orbit of the king's control. Therefore, they caused to be introduced into the charter a number of requirements that went far to neutralize Penn's authority and to subject him to the new rules and regulations that England had been fashioning since the capture of Jamaica in 1655. These requirements, seven in all, were written in by the Lords of Trade, assisted by the attorney general and the lord chief justice of the court of common pleas, to whom the lords referred the text of the document, with requests for emendation and enlargement.[1] In the first place, the new province of Pennsylvania was to observe with the utmost strictness the various navigation acts which had been passed by parliament in the years 1660, 1663, and 1673. That this requirement was no idle one appears from the fact that in 1684, only two years after the settlement, Penn was called to book by the Treasury for allowing a Scottish-built ship from Inverness to trade contrary to the acts and compelled to pay a fine of £53.[2] Secondly, Penn and his successors were to keep an agent, resident in London or its neighborhood, to answer in the courts of law for any offenses committed against the navigation acts or for any wilful default or neglect of the same. The stress thus laid on obedience to the acts of trade is easily understood, not only because they lay at the very heart of England's policy but also because up to this time they had been very loosely enforced and the government was obliged to make strenuous efforts to tighten up the whole system.[3] To the same effect was the third point, that Penn must admit into his ports all royal officers or their deputies appointed by the commissioners of the customs for the collecting of the plantation duty levied under the act of 1673.

In the fourth place, the province was to send to the Privy Council, within five years of their passage, a transcript or duplicate of all laws for the king's confirmation or disallowance, and if these laws were not acted on in England within six months they were to stand in the colony as of full force. Though certain of the royal colonies had been sending their laws to England for some time, no such clause as this had ever before been introduced into a proprietary charter, where the right of disallowance had been carefully reserved to the proprietor himself.[4] Fifthly, the king retained the full right of

1. *Calendar State Papers, Colonial*, 1681–1685, §8.
2. *Calendar Treasury Books*, VII, 1455; VIII, 212–213, 1009; *Colonial Records*, I, 90–91.
3. This point will be discussed at length in the next volume.
4. This clause, as also that regarding the agent, was introduced on the insistence of

receiving, hearing, and determining all appeals from the courts of the province and of reversing at will any judgment of these courts. The right of appeal was allowed in the royal colonies, but it had not been allowed in the proprietary colonies, and in New England under the corporate system appeals to the Privy Council from the local courts had been repeatedly denied. Such denial was enforced in Massachusetts before 1684 and in Connecticut and Rhode Island before 1699, when the Privy Council made the rule that it was the king's inherent right to hear appeals from his subjects anywhere. That settled the matter.[1] Sixthly, the lord bishop of London, Henry Compton, who was one of the Lords of Trade and especially concerned for the spiritual welfare of the colonial members of his diocese, demanded that the Anglican church have a footing in the province, and that if twenty people petitioned for an Anglican preacher he should be sent. The lords agreed to this request and asked the bishop to prepare a clause for insertion in the charter. This the bishop did, thus starting the growth of a powerful Anglican community destined to play an important part in the religious and political history of the province.

Most remarkable of all these provisions, the seventh and last, concerned the question of the parliamentary right of taxation, expressed in a clause of considerable ambiguity. In the charter the king promised never to impose a tax on the inhabitants of the province or on their property, "unless the same be with the consent of the proprietary, or chiefe governor, or assembly, or by act of parliament." Did that mean that parliament in 1680 believed it had the right to impose taxes on the people of Pennsylvania without their consent? The issue remained a purely academic one till 1765 and the passage of the Stamp Act, and it may be doubted if the inclusion of these words in

Chief Justice North of the court of common pleas, to whom Blathwayt sent the first draft of the charter for inspection (*Calendar State Papers, Colonial,* 1677–1680, §§1580, 1592). Scores of Pennsylvania laws were disallowed in the eighteenth century, as can be seen by examining the notes to the *Statutes at Large,* vols. II–XII, which begin with the year 1700. The first volume has never been issued. The laws from 1682 to 1700 are printed without comment in *Laws of the Province of Pennsylvania* (1879). Laws were transmitted to England as early as 1693 (*Votes of Assembly,* I, 100; *Minutes of the Provincial Council,* I, 418–422, hereafter cited as *Colonial Records*) but what happened to them does not appear. In 1697 the Board of Trade ordered Penn to send over the laws, which Penn did, but there is nothing to show that any of these laws or those of 1692, if received, were acted on. As far as I can discover the first law disallowed was in 1699.

1. *Acts Privy Council, Colonial,* II, §732.

the charter ever disturbed the mind of Penn and his successors until the question became vital after the Seven Years' War. But that is not the essential point. Why was the statement inserted and what did its sponsors think it meant? Who was responsible for it and what was the particular situation in England in 1680 that made its insertion seem necessary? A difficult question this, but one worth answering, if possible, though no attempt will be made to answer it here.[1]

We do not know that Penn objected to any of these restrictions upon his freedom of action, although they bound him hand and foot in obedience to the colonial policy that England had been shaping for twenty years. As compared with Baltimore's charter, which was wholly proprietary, that of Penn was in a sense half royal, though in a manner wholly different from the half royal provisions of the Massachusetts charter of 1691. If the proprietary features look to the past, the recognition of the king's sovereignty looks toward the eighteenth century and the future, and the Lords of Trade were able to bring about indirectly what they could not accomplish by direct action, that is, the dependence of the new province upon the mother country in all that concerned the king's sovereign rights. In this respect Penn's charter was different from all the other proprietary charters issued for provinces in America.

Penn had obtained what he wanted, a wide territory within which to apply his ideas regarding government and the way the social and moral order should be maintained. He was given full and uncontrolled possession of the soil, which he could sell to purchasers and allot as he pleased. Naturally he was satisfied, and in his assurance that other things did not matter, he wrote on April 18, 1681, a month after the charter had passed the great seal, a letter "for the inhabit-

1. Neither Shepherd, *Proprietary Government in Pennsylvania*, p. 174, nor Osgood, *The American Colonies in the Seventeenth Century*, II, 12, discusses the matter. Osgood merely remarks, "Thus the possibility that parliament might tax the colonies was clearly recognized." But was it? In 1670 during a debate in parliament upon England's relations with Ireland, the report from the committee of supply contained this sentence, "We do not yet offer to tax our plantations" (Stock, *Debates*, I, 318), and there is no evidence to show that before 1680 anything had happened to alter the mind of parliament in this particular. In the "Restrictions" proposed by Chief Justice North in 1680 appears this phrase, "The power of making laws . . . to raise money is in Mr. Penn and the Assembly," and nothing is said about the power of parliament. Were the date 1689 or later the answer might be easier, but in 1680 parliament was in no position to demand the right of taxing the colonies. I have a word or two on the subject in my *Colonial Background*, p. 51, and there is something about it in *Cambridge Modern History*, VII, 199–200, though no explanation is there proffered.

ants of Pennsylvania," in which he told all prospective settlers that they would be at the mercy of no governor "who was come to make his fortune great," but would be allowed to shape their own laws and to live a free and, if they could, a sober and industrious people."[1] Having sent over commissioners in the autumn of that year, as we shall see later, with ample instructions to lay out plantations and start a town, and having drawn up a body of concessions determining the conditions under which he would distribute his lands, he settled down to the most difficult of all his tasks, the framing of a government and the drafting of a series of laws for his province that would enable him to make his experiment holy.

Penn's series of laws is elaborate, a compendium of moral precepts and convictions, placing every phase of human life, civil and social, on the highest level of righteousness, sobriety, and honorable conduct. These laws are a witness to Penn's purity of soul and almost childlike faith in the goodness of his fellow men when once removed from the corrupting influence of the debased world of England. They constitute a code of Quaker principles applied to actual government and to the realities of human existence in a new colonial enterprise. They concern civil administration, elections, court procedure, the exercise of justice, fines, penalties, and prisons, frauds, falsifications, and perjury, defamation and the spreading of scandalous rumors, the duties and obligations of office-holders, the registration of land and vital statistics, marriage and the bringing up of children, and the observance of the Sabbath. Above all else they lay stress on the liberty of worship, on toleration for all who believed in God, and on the punishment of offenses against God and society—a long list.

But his scheme of government is very simple. Provision was made for a proprietor, who was also the governor—with a deputy in the province during his absence—whose only peculiar prerogative was the possession of a treble vote in council. Then there was to be a council, an unwieldy body of seventy-two members, later reduced to eighteen, one-third of whom was to be elected each year and after seven years to be ineligible for re-election until a year had elapsed. Governor and council were to originate all legislation and see to its execution, to exercise oversight over all judicial business and choice of officers, to try all persons impeached by the popular assembly, to

1. Hazard, *Annals,* pp. 502–503.

sit on their own adjournment, and to appoint committees concerned with the safety of the province, the location of plantations, markets, towns, and highways, to watch over trade and the treasury, to erect schools and encourage inventions, and to concern themselves with morals, virtues, and manners. In action, two-thirds of the council were to constitute a quorum and two-thirds of the quorum were to decide all matters of importance. In lesser matters one-third was to be a quorum and a majority was to decide.

The members of the assembly or house of representatives—two hundred in number and never to exceed five hundred—were to be elected by the freemen, a term defined in the laws as meaning, in Pennsylvania as everywhere else, a freeholder,[1] who, as first defined, was to have one hundred acres of land if a free person or fifty acres if a free servant. If landless, a man might vote if he paid scot and lot, equivalent to a borough or municipal tax. Later this qualification was reduced to fifty acres or fifty pounds a year. The assembly was to meet yearly and its chief function was to "resolve" what the governor and council "proposed," that is, to accept or reject bills, but not necessarily to alter or amend them. The right to initiate legislation did not come until 1696, and the right to amend and alter, never authorized by formal law, was the subject of controversy for many years, the assembly exercising the privilege whether it had a right to or not. The assembly could impeach and in all its business was required to make use of the ballot. When in 1683 Penn issued a new frame a few alterations were made. He reduced the number of the councillors to eighteen and of the assemblymen to thirty-two; he dealt with the problem of aliens at the suggestion of Benjamin Furly, and granted to each freeholder full liberty of hunting and fishing on his own land.[2]

1. Since the days of Cromwell, the opinion expressed later by Locke in his essays on government was "that only the freeholders really constituted the body politic and that they could use their property as they pleased, uncontrolled by obligations to any superior, or by the need of consulting the mass of men, who were mere tenants at will, with no fixed interest or share in the lands of the kingdom." Tawney, *Religion and the Rise of Capitalism*, p. 258. Above, p. 115, note 1.

2. The "Concessions," the "Frame of Government," and the "Laws agreed on in England" are printed in *Votes of Assembly*, I, xxiv–xxxv, and reprinted in Thorpe, *Charters*, V, 3044–3069. Among the Penn Papers in the Pennsylvania Historical Society is a draft prepared by Penn, preliminary to his final draft of the "Frame," representing his earliest attempt to write a constitution. He sent what he had prepared to many friends and advisers, among them Benjamin Furly in Rotterdam, who took

From this brief analysis it will be seen that the representatives of the freeholders in assembly were not expected to concern themselves with the government of the province and that as far as the freeholders at large were concerned their share in the management of affairs was exercised by their representatives in council, an elected body unlike that in any of the other proprieties. Penn's interpretation of "popular liberties" was thus distinctly circumscribed. He believed not in the divine right of kings but in the divine right of government. He gave power into the hands of the governor and council and refused it to the popular assembly, and he confined the right to vote to those only who possessed land and property. He was not a believer in democracy any more than were the other idealists of the century, but he never went to the other extreme of believing in the strict interpretation of his proprietary rights, as did Lord Baltimore.[1] Though he was the true and absolute proprietor and the representative of the king in the province, he took no advantage of the fact, as far as government was concerned, other than to refuse to allow the constitution to be changed without his consent or that of his heirs. He required the members of both council and assembly to make a declaration of allegiance to the king and

Penn to task for depriving the assembly of the right of initiating laws (*Pennsylvania Magazine*, XIX, 304).

The main features of Pennsylvania's government are to be found in the first "Frame"; another issued in the same year reads like one of Penn's pamphlets, in that it contains chiefly moral axioms, the only one of importance being that which exhibits Penn's belief in the divine right of government, and his conviction that frames and models were of little worth, "there being nothing the wits of men are more busy and divided upon"; none of which are likely to serve all places alike. He expresses his preference for that form of government "where the laws rule and the people are a party to those laws." Governments, he says further, are like clocks which go from the motions men give them, for they depend on men rather than men on them. "Liberty without obedience is confusion and obedience without liberty is slavery."

1. Penn's reputation for courage, initiative, and vision rests upon other things than his constitution for his province. His relations with the Indians, his plans for a general European federation (written while he was confined in the Fleet, 1693), his views regarding the value of colonies as a source of strength to the mother country (1680, printed but never sold, so that copies are exceedingly scarce), and his scheme for a colonial union are phases of his thought that manifest an idealistic spirit ("Essay toward the Present and Future Peace of Europe by the Establishment of a European Dyet, Parliament or Estates," *Works*, II, 838–848; "Plan of Union for the Colonies," February 8, 1697, *Pennsylvania Magazine*, XI, 495–496; *Benefit of Plantations*, London, 1680. See Vol. IV, Index. Also *Memoirs*, Historical Society of Pennsylvania, VI, 264–265, 265–281). Penn's greatness lies also in his advocacy of religious toleration, his championship of peace, and his unswerving faith in the reign of law and justice.

of fidelity to himself,[1] but he never looked on the declaration of fidelity as anything peculiarly personal to himself. He was confident that others were as benevolent as he was and that he could guide his people by paternal oversight and control them by personal persuasion. He never forgot that he was the father of his province and that for it he was spending his private fortune, and he confidently believed that those for whom he was making sacrifices would respond in like manner out of gratitude for what he was doing. Never among all the proprietors was anyone more grievously mistaken or more painfully disillusioned.

Before Penn had completed his plans for government and the distribution of lands, he prepared two pamphlets, *A Brief Account* and *Some Account of the Province of Pennsylvania,* which he had printed in London in 1681 and circulated in England, Wales, and Ireland. Translated into Dutch by his old friend at Rotterdam, Benjamin Furly, and into German by Jan Claus, Penn's Quaker printer friend of Amsterdam, the *Some Account* and other writings, sometimes in print and sometimes in manuscript, were circulated widely in the Netherlands and western Germany. In this way, as Professor Hull says, Pennsylvania was probably the best advertised of all the American colonies.[2] It is not surprising, therefore, that from the beginning the province contained the most variegated assortment of people, both racially and religiously, of any settlement along the Atlantic seaboard or elsewhere. Finns, Swedes, Dutch, Germans, Irish, Welsh, and English made up this polychrome and polyglot community.

Eager as he was to go to his colony in person and to make it his permanent home, Penn was obliged to wait until his preparations in

1. For the oath of fidelity, *Votes of Assembly,* I, 8, 43, 57; *Colonial Records,* I, 322–323, and elsewhere.

2. *William Penn and the Dutch Quakers,* p. 308. Professor Hull speaks of Penn's "correspondence bureau," at the head of which was Benjamin Furly. Five of Penn's pamphlets were translated into Dutch and German and issued from Rotterdam and Amsterdam presses. We have mention of a pamphlet by one Robert Wood, which was part of this extensive propaganda organized by Penn not only in the Netherlands but in the British Isles also for the purpose of obtaining settlers. Thomas Rudyard was at George-Yard, Lombard Street, London; Robert Turner was in Dublin, and other correspondents were in Edinburgh, Hamilton and Aberdeen, each of which places became a center of information and action. There is an elaborate account of Furly, Penn's right hand man in the Netherlands, who turned the Dutch and German migrations toward Pennsylvania, in *Pennsylvania Magazine,* XIX, 277–306. Furly was from Colchester, England, whence he went to Rotterdam, where he married a Dutch wife and settled down in the mercantile and shipping business.

England had been completed. That he might not seem to be failing in his promises, he sent over in April, 1681—only a month after receiving his charter—his cousin, William Markham, with instructions to call a council from among the people there, to read his letter and the king's declaration of subjection, and to get into communication with Lord Baltimore. All this Markham did. Later in the year he despatched four commissioners, Captain William Crispin, chief,[1] John Bezar, William Haig, and Nathaniel Allen, with a number of settlers, to make provision for all newcomers and to pick out a site for a town where the river was navigable, the land high and dry, the region healthful, and where satisfactory conditions existed for docking and the promotion of trade. Crispin having died on the way over, Penn sent Thomas Holme as his chief commissioner, with a letter to the Indians and with instructions to aid the other commissioners and Markham in forwarding the settlement. The site had not been selected when Holme arrived, and the task of finding one was rendered difficult by the size of the place Penn demanded. Holme performed his part of the work admirably. He drafted the plan of a town after Penn's specifications and adapted it to the site finally chosen between the Delaware and Schuylkill rivers —a plan which Penn published in 1683 as part of his advertising programme for promoting the sale of his lands. Holme continued his survey of the country about, the results of which he embodied in a second map finally published in 1687.[2] Many copies of these maps, both in their original drafts and printed forms, were circu-

1. Captain William Crispin had been a friend and cousin of Admiral Penn's and had accompanied him to the West Indies in 1654, in command of one of the vessels. Markham was Crispin's first cousin by marriage, so that Penn, Markham, and Crispin were closely connected. Crispin does not appear to have been a Quaker, but Bezar, Allen, and Haig were, as was also Holme (on Holme, *Pennsylvania Magazine*, XIX, 413–427; XX, 128–131, 248–256). Haig was of a Scottish family one of whose descendants was General Haig of the World War. Crispin died on his way to America at the early age of 54, so that he was only 27 when he accompanied Admiral Penn. There is a life of him in the *Pennsylvania Magazine*, LIII. The instructions to the commissioners are in Hazard, *Annals*, pp. 527–531, dated September 30, 1681. Penn's letter to the Indians, *ibid.*, pp. 532–533.

2. It has been usually thought that Holme's maps of 1682 and 1687 were the earliest prepared for circulation purposes, but there is another probably earlier, as it is referred to in Penn's *Brief Account* (issued by Benjamin Clark, George-Yard, Lombard Street, 1681). This map bears the title "A Map of some of the South and East Bounds of Pennsylvania," and was apparently based on Herrman's map of Maryland of 1673. It is reproduced by Mr. Albert Cook Myers in *Pennsylvania Magazine*, XLVIII.

lated alike in England and Pennsylvania and used to illustrate and emphasize the advantages which Penn offered to all who were willing to accept his conditions of land purchase and distribution. These conditions, already planned with great care and embodied in the "Conditions and Concessions" of 1681, constituted a kind of contract between himself and all who bought or adventured in Pennsylvania.

Before Penn left England he disposed of large tracts of land to those known later as "first purchasers," a part of whose land was to lie in the "country" and a part in the city that he was planning to build. But when he found that in order to carry out the terms of such sales—the allotment of ten acres in the city for every five hundred in the country—he would have to enlarge his city beyond the capacity of any available site, he ordered an area to be set off adjoining the city proper to be known as the "liberties," for the purpose of taking up the excess. Thus the lands of the province fell into three disproportionate parts: the common land in city and country— the largest portion of the territory—from which allotments could be made by grants of one kind or another; the proprietary reserves of a certain number of acres out of every one thousand assigned, selected by lot and all in one piece; and the proprietary manors, of which there must have been over a hundred, some of them indistinguishable from the reserves and others in the form of sub-manors within the proprietary manors, none of which were manors in the legal acceptance of the word.[1] Though there is no doubt that Penn expected courts leet and baron to be erected, there is nothing to show that manorial jurisdiction, properly so called, was ever introduced into Pennsylvania. During the earlier years land conditions were in great confusion. Grants were made very carelessly. Quarrels arose between the "first purchasers" and later arrivals, and claims were bandied about that were difficult of settlement because the original deeds were rarely recorded and the loose management of the land office gave ample opportunities for fraud. Not until the arrival of Penn's son Thomas in 1732 was the land system adequately organized and the tangle of claims straightened out.[2]

1. There is a volume of maps among the *Pennsylvania Archives,* 3d ser. IV, showing seventy-six proprietary manors. The list does not include the manors granted to private individuals. In his elaborate discussion of the land system Shepherd has very little to say about the manors.

2. However much Penn might minimize his proprietary prerogatives on the gov-

The stress which Penn laid, in his instructions to the commissioners, on a river frontage with ample docking facilities and waterside abutments for all "first purchasers," shows that he was more interested in commerce than in agriculture, and that ready access to the ocean and to large bodies of inland water was a prime requisite in the successful carrying out of his plans. One cause of his long dispute with Lord Baltimore was his desire to have an outlet on Chesapeake Bay and to control the Delaware exit to the sea. His controversy with New York shows that he was trying to extend his boundary far enough to the north to tap the Indian trade with the five nations, and this effort, though unsuccessful, became the starting point in a compromise which later gave to the state of Pennsylvania the opening on Lake Erie that it has today.

As Penn scanned the map for the purpose of determining his boundaries, he realized that his command of the Delaware stopped at a point twelve miles north of New Castle and a long way from the capes which marked the entrance of the bay into the ocean. He saw that he was in danger of being shut out from the Atlantic by whomsoever might possess the territory to the southward along the western shore of river and bay. In the year 1682 this territory was occupied by a conglomerate of Dutch, Swedes, Finns, and English, living at New Castle in the north, at Whorekill[1] (also known as

---

ernmental side, he made no concessions in all that related to the ownership of the soil. According to the charter he was the sole lord of a feudal seignory and from that lordship, as well as from trade and commerce, he expected to reap a sufficient profit to recoup himself in some measure for his expenditures. He could sell, enfeoff, and otherwise alienate his lands to such persons, in such amounts, and under such tenures as he pleased. He could erect manors privileged to hold courts baron and leet with view of frankpledge. He could reserve lands and manors for himself and his heirs, constituting estates which he could cultivate and improve on his own behalf; and he could add to the occupied area new lands by purchase from the Indians, toward whom, from the beginning, he displayed a spirit of friendliness and a desire for honorable treatment worthy of his idealism. He had instructed Markham to confirm all the Swedish and Finnish holdings, possession of which rested on grants from the governor of New York, and to guarantee all rights of ownership, even though, as it happened, these holdings embraced some of the best lands along the Delaware River. He had no intention of disputing the New York titles in Pennsylvania as Philip Carteret had done in East New Jersey. He saw that it would be distinctly to his advantage not to make the Swedes discontented, particularly as he was greatly in need of settlers. He called them "a plain strong and industrious people" (*Pennsylvania Magazine*, XVII, 86–87). For a legal estimate of Penn's seignorial powers under the charter, see *ibid.*, XXIII, 61–63, XXXVIII, 427, 430–431, and the "Breviate," XXIII, XXIV, prepared in connection with the claims of the later Penns to be free from all taxation of their reserved lands and manors.

1. Originally Hoornkill and named by De Vries after his Dutch home at Hoorn.

Swaanendael, Deale, and now as Lewes) in the south, and in the center by an offshoot of settlers from Whorekill, who separated later under the name St. Jones (Creek) County. Whorekill was started by De Vries in 1631, with twenty-eight settlers, who busied themselves with whaling and farming until they were wiped out by the Indians. An attempt made the next year to re-occupy the place was not sustained from New Amsterdam, and Samuel Godyn, the patroon who fathered the project, sold out in July, 1634. This locality was the nucleus of Sussex County and today is considered by Delawareans as the cradle of their state. Because the land had been occupied by the Dutch in 1631—the year before Baltimore obtained his charter—the Duke of York's governors of New York, and later Penn himself, denied Maryland's right to grant lands there, as Baltimore had been doing during the years from 1670 to 1682—some 19,000 acres to forty-five persons, within what Baltimore called the "County of Durham."[1] In 1676 Andros introduced there the Duke's Laws, established courts of justice for New Castle and Whorekill, and made various other rules for the government of the Delaware region. In 1680, at the request of the people themselves, he separated St. Jones from Whorekill and gave it a court of its own. Thus he created three judicial districts or counties, which were known, when Penn's first council met in 1683, as New Castle, Kent, and Sussex.[2] At Whorekill and St. Jones were Dutch, who had returned thither after 1660, and a number of Englishmen, probably from the eastern shores of Maryland and Virginia and possibly from West New Jersey and New York. At New Castle—founded by Stuyvesant as Fort Casimir in 1651 and named New Amstel in 1657—were Swedes, Finns, and a few Dutch, engaged in farming and the fur trade. We hear of Scots and Frenchmen coming in later. The number and social origin of these people changed at different periods as families came and went, attracted by the advantages of the local-

1. For a discussion of the whole question see Powell (author of *A History of Delaware*), "The Fight between the Penns and the Calverts," *Maryland Magazine*, XXIX, 83–101. The list of grantees is given in the same, XXX, 161–164.

2. *New York Colonial Documents*, XII, 664–665; *Pennsylvania Colonial Records*, I, 57; Turner, *Some Records of Sussex County, Delaware* (1909), pp. 1–40. The relative size of the counties of province and territories can be ascertained from the 1694 penny per pound assessment: Philadelphia, £314; New Castle, £143; Sussex, £101; Kent, £88; Chester, £65; Bucks, £48. In 1700 the order is Philadelphia, £1025; Chester, £325; Bucks, £225; New Castle, £180; Kent, £139; Sussex, £100. *Votes of Assembly*, I, 85, 139; *Colonial Records*, I, 462.

ity or frightened away by the Indians or the threats of the Marylanders as the case might be. No accurate estimate of the population
there is possible for this early period, but taking the country as a
whole, from New Castle to Whorekill, there may have been between
seven hundred and a thousand altogether.[1]

This was the territory that Penn wished to add to his province and
for which in the summer of 1681 he made a personal application to
the Duke of York. At first the duke demurring refused to give up
his right of possession, although he must have known that it rested
on nothing more substantial than the fact of conquest, for his charter
from the king said nothing about the lands west of the Delaware.
However, from the beginning it seems to have been assumed that
the duke was to become the proprietor of all the territory that the
Dutch had hitherto controlled and that had been seized in the conquest of 1664. Sir Robert Carr had taken New Amstel in the autumn
of that year, and as the fort and town had been the heart and center
of the Dutch administration on the Delaware, its capture was construed as bringing into the hands of the English the remaining
region to the southward, or as the phrase went "the county of New
Castle and the tracts of land depending thereon in America." The
duke's title had been tacitly recognized when in the charter to Penn
the eastern end of the southern boundary of his province had been
placed twelve miles north of New Castle; and it was recognized
again when Penn made his request of the duke and not of the king.
After a month's hesitation, the duke gave in, because of the regard
which he had for the memory and faithful services of Penn's father,
the admiral, and on August 24, 1682, executed the necessary leases.
These were two, one covering the towns of New Castle and the land
within the twelve mile radius, and the other the land to the southward as far as Cape Henlopen. Though these leases carried no

---

1. Johnson, *The Swedes in America* (1914), p. 370, puts the population in 1658
at "about 600 souls," but says that it is impossible to determine how many of these
were Swedes and how many Finns. Louhi, *The Delaware Finns* (1925) believes that
"a large and vital part of the population of the states of Delaware, Pennsylvania, and
New Jersey" came from Finland or from that portion of Sweden which was occupied
by Finns, a statement that must be accepted as a patriotic gesture. Louhi's book has
neither references, bibliography, nor index and must be used with caution. The author
seems to think that every Swede was a Finn; that when contemporaries spoke of
Swedes they meant Finns; that New Castle was a "Finnish colony"; and that Upland
was a "Finnish country." He minimizes at every opportunity the place and importance of the Swedes, and discloses his purpose in writing the book when he calls his
people "the first real Americans," p. 327.

rights of government, as far as their language is concerned, Penn always claimed that "by virtue of these deeds he had the power of making a governor there, for the duke had so before and he has now, he conceives, [for] he has the grant the Duke of York had from the crown."[1] In making this statement in 1697 Penn was hardly honest, for when these deeds were executed the Duke of York had no grant from the king, and after such grant had been made, as was done March 22, 1683, the duke executed no further deeds in Penn's behalf. Therefore Penn's sole title to the government and soil of the Delaware counties rested on two land leases of doubtful legality, because in 1682 the duke himself had no certain title to the region.[2] The very fact that the duke, undoubtedly urged on by Penn himself, tried to obtain a royal confirmation seven months after the leases had been signed, shows that both Penn and the duke had

---

1. *House of Lords Manuscripts,* new series, II, 412; Stock, *Debates,* II, 195; *Calendar State Papers, Colonial,* 1701, p. 92.

2. The leases are printed in Hazard, *Annals,* pp. 586–593; *Votes of Assembly,* I, xxxv–xxxviii. The king's charter to the Duke of York, March 22, 1683, is among the Penn Papers ("Charters and Frames of Government," p. 1). It has never been printed, as far as I know, except in a newspaper. The territory granted is given as follows: "All that the Towne of Newcastle otherwise called Delaware and fort therein or thereunto belonging scituate lying and being between Maryland and New Jersey in America. And all that Tract of land lying and being upon the River of Delaware and all islands in the said River of Delaware and the said River and Soyle thereof lying North of the Southermost part of the said circle of twelve miles about the said Towne. And all that Tract of Land upon Delaware River and Bay beginning twelve miles south from the said Towne of Newcastle otherwise called Delaware and extending south to Cape Lopen."

The Earl of Sutherland, in commenting on this charter, says that it was never completed. We know that it passed the privy seal for it is recorded on the patent rolls (Car. II, pt. I, no. 24), but for some reason or other in passing from the privy seal to the great seal it seems to have been held up. We know that Baltimore petitioned against it at this point and that his petition was referred to the Lords of Trade, who decided against it (*Calendar State Papers, Colonial,* 1686–1688, §456). There appears to be an entry or docket of the grant in the Hanaper Office books, which ordinarily would mean that the great seal had been attached, but in this case the Hanaper entry may have been made before the sealing, though why I cannot say, unless it be the delay which would carry the business to the death of Charles II, thus putting an end to the process. Then it was that the crown lawyers advised James II to go to the chancery court and have his title legally established (*Calendar State Papers, Colonial,* 1717–1718, §177, i, p. 93).

Quite apart from the question of whether or not the king's grant of March 22, 1683, to the Duke of York ever passed the great seal, the document itself is interesting, when compared with the king's grant to the duke of 1664, because of the absence in both of all references to an assembly of the freeholders. Except for certain additions and slight changes of wording the two charters are alike, twin sisters in fact.

doubts as to the soundness of the title.[1] This doubt is further emphasized by the desire of the duke, when king, to give Penn a royal
charter, placing the latter's title beyond dispute, a desire that was
frustrated by his flight from England in 1688. Penn refers to this
intention in one of his "answers." We are told that in 1688, James
instructed Sir William Williams, the solicitor general, to draft a
letters patent for the king's sign manual, but that the attempt, having been obstructed "by the disorder the Court was in a little before
the Revolution," the patent got no farther in its progress through
the seals. In 1702 Penn hoped the charter would be issued by Queen
Anne, but nothing was done. Though his claim, as against that of
Lord Baltimore, was confirmed by chancery in 1750, that of the
crown was never given up. So well understood was this flaw in
Penn's title that in 1717 the Earl of Sutherland sent in a petition to
the Board of Trade asking that the counties be granted to him, saying that he was ready to prove that they belonged to the crown and
that the king had a perfect right to dispose of them. Joshua Gee, the
mercantilist, who was Penn's agent in England at the time, had
little to say in answer to this petition, except that everybody in

1. The best that Sir John Werden could say in defense of the duke's claim was
that the territory had been for fifteen years "an appendix and part of the Government
of New York" and he supposed "the duke's right would be preferable to all others,
even though it should not prove to be strictly within his patent" (*Calendar State
Papers, Colonial*, 1677–1680, §1403). Dongan said much the same thing in 1687 and
could not believe that the king intended to annex the lower counties to Pennsylvania
(*Documentary History of New York*, I, 153).

2. *Calendar State Papers, Colonial*, 1702, §1207. A copy of this letters patent is to
be found among the Penn Papers ("Charters and Frames of Government, 1685–
1696," pp. 11–19, twenty-one folios) and is printed by Mr. Burton Alva Konkle in
his article, *Delaware: A Grant yet Not a Grant*, pp. 37–46. There is in one of James
Logan's letters a reference to another charter for Delaware offered Penn by James II
in 1686–1687, which Penn refused because it gave him the right to raise money
without an assembly, a right that was contrary to the law of England (*ibid.*, p. 35).
I have had the privilege of reading in manuscript Mr. Konkle's "David Lloyd and the
First Half-Century of Pennsylvania," and am indebted to him for other favors also.
    Judge Rodney in "Early Relations of Delaware and Pennsylvania" (*Papers*, His-
torical Society of Delaware, new series, XI, and reprinted in the *Pennsylvania Magazine*, with Mr. Konkle's article mentioned above) thinks that if only the king had
had a little more time before running away and could have "signed the charter," the
whole history of Delaware would have been changed. But charters do not "happen"
as easily as all that. The king's sign manual was not necessary to the validity of a
charter but the great seal was, and to obtain the attachment of the great seal was
often a long process. The king's "signing the charter" would not have made a whit
of difference with the history of Delaware. But had the charter, giving the lower
counties to Penn, actually passed the seals, then Delaware might have been "Lower
Pennsylvania," and the course of its history been entirely changed.

Pennsylvania was contented with things as they were and that he hoped the noble earl, who had undoubtedly been egged on by greedy ones in America, would not "lend an ear to those who for private ends endeavour to scrape a hole in the title of a Gentleman's estate in America." The earl's petition was pigeon-holed but it had one important effect.[1] It caused Penn's family to renew the negotiations, begun some years before by Penn himself, to sell the province to the crown for a price. The matter was not settled until 1727—nine years after Penn's death—when the government finally refused to pay the sum asked. It is quite possible that the buying off of the Carolina proprietors at the same time had something to do with the reluctance of the Treasury to spend any more money getting rid of the proprietary governments in America.[2]

But as far as Penn himself was concerned these causes for worry and anxiety lay in the future, and it must have been with a thankful heart that in September, 1682, he set out on his first voyage to his new province. Before departing he wrote a long letter, pathetic in its tenderness, to his wife and children[3] and sent many injunctions to his Quaker brethren in England to hold fast to that which was good. The voyage was slow and distressing, a third of the passengers died of small pox on the way over, and it was not until October 27 that the *Welcome,* passing up the Delaware River, cast anchor off New Castle. The next day Moll and Herrman, the duke's agents, acting under the terms of the indenture of August 24, delivered the territory into Penn's hands, according to the time-honored forms of conveyance by key of the fort and by turf and twig, with a porringer

1. *Calendar State Papers, Colonial,* 1716–1717, §§434, i, ii, 471, 505, 514; 1717–1718, §177, i; *Board of Trade Journal,* 1714–1718, pp. 209–210. Penn's answers were never considered satisfactory by the Board of Trade (for example *Calendar State Papers, Colonial,* 1717–1718, p. 89). When the argument based on the leases of 1682 proved unconvincing Penn fell back on title by conquest (*Maryland Archives,* XVII, 149, 150; *Calendar State Papers, Colonial,* 1717–1718, p. 87). The subject is referred to in *Calendar Treasury Papers,* 1708–1714, p. 360. It is reviewed at great length in the report of the attorney and solicitor general, October 21, 1717, and more briefly in the representation of the Board of Trade, September 8, 1721.

2. *Acts Privy Council, Colonial,* VI, §382; *Calendar State Papers, Colonial,* 1710–1711, §326, i (memorial, 1710); *Calendar Treasury Papers,* 1708–1714, pp. 360, 428, 574; 1720–1728, pp. 14, 393; *Penn-Logan Correspondence,* I, 226, 245. The amount agreed upon was £12,000, of which £1000 was paid in, only to be returned by the family when negotiations were discontinued.

3. Janney, *Life of Penn,* pp. 187–193. The passengers on the *Welcome* were mostly Friends from Sussex, Penn's neighbors, an incomplete list of whom is given in *Memoirs.* Pennsylvania Historical Society, I, 467–471.

containing water and soil of the river.[1] Penn received the submission of the inhabitants, commissioned justices of the peace, and instructed Markham to act for him in taking possession of the lower counties of Kent and Sussex. He called a court (November 2), over which he himself presided, and bade its members continue their administration under the Duke's Laws until they could be governed by laws of their own approval. He then passed on to Upland, the first town within his own province. There (November 8) he issued orders for the calling of an assembly to be composed of the elected members of a council and assembly from six counties—Philadelphia, Bucks (Buckingham),[2] and Chester in the province, and New Castle, Kent, and Sussex in the Territories, although he had no authority to summon members from the lower counties and no provision whatever had been made for their election. At this assembly which met December 4, 1682, rules and regulations based on those of the English parliament were adopted; and after long debate the "Great Law" in sixty-nine articles was passed as a temporary expedient to last only to the end of the next year. In the preamble and opening clause this "Great Law" contains a noteworthy declaration regarding liberty of conscience. At the same session was passed, on petition from nineteen of the deputies from the lower counties,[3] an Act of Union, binding together the freeholders of New Castle, Kent, and Sussex with those of the province under a common government; and on further request, the assembly naturalized the Swedes, Dutch, and Finns, placing them on an equal legal footing with the others.[4]

From Upland Penn went to West River on the Chesapeake and

1. Judge Rodney prints in his *Early Relations*, pp. 6–7, the report of John Moll, one of the attorneys in fact for the Duke of York, and a prominent inhabitant of New Castle, giving an account of this transaction.

2. The name "Buckingham" was at first given to the town of Bristol, *Statutes at Large*, II, 162.

3. Rodney, *Early Relations*, pp. 11–12.

4. *Votes of Assembly*, I, 1–6. The Act of Union, which Judge Rodney thinks "sprang from the brain of Penn himself" and not from any spontaneous or "express desire on the part of the people of the Lower Counties themselves" (*Early Relations*, pp. 13, 15), is in the same, I, appendix, ii–iv; in Hazard, *Annals*, pp. 615–619; and in *Laws of Pennsylvania* (1879), p. 104, where is also the Act for Naturalization, pp. 105–106. The "Great Law" is in Hazard, pp. 619–634, and in *Laws of Pennsylvania*, pp. 107–123. Because the "Great Law" was due to expire at the end of 1683, the next assembly, March, 1683, considered and debated another collection of 80 laws, which are given in *Laws of Pennsylvania, 1682–1700*, pp. 127–155. The collection of 1683 must not be confused with the "Great Law" of 1682.

there discoursed with Lord Baltimore in an unsatisfactory parley, to which reference has been made in a previous volume.[1] He also undertook by water a trip to New York to pay his respects to the duke's governor there and another across the Delaware to Burlington to see how the West New Jersey colony was getting on. During the time he was in his province he lived in the dwelling house of Thomas Fairman, surveyor, at Shackamaxon, now Kensington, where the first Quaker meeting had been held in 1682. From there he watched the building of his new city, located about four miles up the Delaware from the mouth of the Schuylkill, near the Swedish farms at Wicaco, adjoining the land of the old Swedish church, *Gloria Dei,* as it stands today. He saw arising along the river front a group of four score houses and cottages ("such as they were," he remarked), all built within a year, where merchants and handicraftsmen were already doing business, and the farmers nearby were engaged in ploughing, sowing, and watering, and garnering such crops as had been started the year before. He journeyed on horseback about the province, studying the soil, flora, and fauna, the creeks and the rivers, with keen interest in the possibility of cargoes, wherewith to supply the ships which, in his mind's eye, he saw frequenting the river and lying up at the docks. Because he wished to keep this trade in his own hands, he refused an offer while in England to sell a monopoly of it for £6000.[2] Best known of all his activities were his negotiations with the Indians, whose customs he investigated and whose language he tried to acquire. The results of his observations he presented at great length in a report which he made to a company formed in England known as the Free Society of Traders.[3]

This company or society, contemporaneously called the Pennsylvania Company, was a joint-stock concern composed of two hundred members from England, Wales, and Ireland, who subscribed £10,000 to a common stock, with the promise of trading facilities and an allotment of 20,000 acres. The company planned to send over servants to build houses, to set up "a glass house for Bottles, drinking glasses, and window glass, to plant and improve land and

1. *Calendar State Papers, Colonial,* 1681–1685, §1175; Penn's letter to the Lords of Trade, August 6, 1683. Vol. II, 360–361.

2. Penn to Robert Turner, *Memoirs,* Pennsylvania Historical Society, I, 212, 213; letter from James Claypoole, September 10, 1681, *Pennsylvania Magazine,* X, 189.

3. *Early Pennsylvania* (Original Narratives), pp. 224–244.

for cattle, to supply the Islands and continent of America and we hope to have wine and oyle for Merchandize, and some linon however hemp for cordage and for Iron, Lead and other Minerals we have no doubt off. so through the blessing of god wee may hope for a great increase. And it may come to be a famous Compy." These expectations remained sadly unfulfilled. Though the company set up its offices in the new city and entered upon its work, it never prospered, partly because of the scarcity of money in the province which obliged it to sell for credit, thereby involving it in heavy losses; partly because of the inefficiency and chicanery of some of the company's officials in Philadelphia;[1] and partly because of the opposition that the land grant received from those, particularly in the assembly, who saw monopoly written in the company's charter. The society struggled along for a few years but eventually gave up the trading side of its business and confined its energies to the improvement of its estate. Even in this endeavor it failed and its affairs were wound up in 1723.[2]

James Claypoole wrote in 1683 that "people were coming in fast" and Penn when he first came over estimated the number at 4000 souls.[3] These included Dutch, Swedes, and Finns—the Swedes largely in the majority—and the English who had begun to arrive after 1664, some of whom had settled up the Delaware, laying the foundations of Bucks County,[4] while others crossing from West New Jersey had established themselves at Upland, New Castle, and

1. Letter from James Claypoole, July 14, 1682, *Pennsylvania Magazine*, X, 195. Claypoole was the treasurer of the company and, as he had a brother in Barbados, he hoped to open up a profitable business with that island. But he early became tired of the whole affair and wrote in 1684, "we have neither credit nor money and now must sue people at law or be compelled to lose all . . . I am so weary of the society's business that I will get clear as soon as I can" (quoted by Baldwin). He had a separate and private grant of land of his own and wanted to develop it. The president of the company, Dr. Nicholas More, was found so difficult to get on with that he was dismissed in 1684. In 1685 he was impeached by the lower house for various misdemeanors and threatened with the loss of all his positions. *Colonial Records*, I, 135–137.

2. On the society, Baldwin, "American Business Corporations," *Report*, American Historical Association, 1902, II, 259–263; Davis, *Essays in the Early History of American Corporations*, pp. 41–45; *Pennsylvania Magazine*, V, 37–50; XI, 175–180; *Colonial Records*, I, 40 (§31); *Penn-Logan Correspondence*, I, 189, 252, 261.

3. An excellent chapter on "The People" is in Keith, *Chronicles of Pennsylvania*, ch. V.

4. *Colonial Records*, I, 513–514.

Whorekill.[1] The first people to come directly because of Penn's advertising campaign were the Welsh, who, influenced by the preaching of Fox and suffering from attacks on their conventicles, had begun to migrate as early as 1675. The "Apostle of Quakerism" in Wales, John ap John, obtained from Penn a large grant of land, known as the Welsh Tract, Cambria, or New Wales, containing at first 30,000 acres and later 50,000, which was controlled by a few leading men from six Welsh counties and was gradually parcelled out to purchasers. The Welsh emigrants, unlike those from England—who as a rule were plain people, small farmers, tradesmen, and artificers—were from the best social classes, and it is not surprising that they looked upon their grant as a barony, in which they could have wide jurisdiction, independent of the central administration.[2] They received their allotment in September, 1681, and arrived in various vessels during 1682. Though their numbers were never large, they left a deep impress upon the region of their occupancy, as the place names of Merion, Radnor, Haverford, and the like and the political contributions of such men as Thomas and David Lloyd amply testify. Their migration was short-lived, partly because persecution at home ceased and partly because the Welsh promoters charged Penn with failure to make their tract a county palatine. Soon they were lost in the cosmopolitan environment of the land into which they had come. Similarly few in number were the Irish Quakers, most of them either from Ulster or Englishmen who had been born in Ireland or had recently gone there, all of them migrating as individuals or in small groups, farmers, agriculturally minded. Among them were three outstanding men, of great influence in the history of the province, Thomas Holme, Robert Turner, and James Logan. In the migration of the Quakers from Ireland, one sees at work the same influences that were operating elsewhere, to which may be added the distress caused by the restrictions Eng-

1. Later in the seventeenth century the influx of the English directly from the mother country was rapid and on a considerable scale, the emigrants sailing from London and Bristol, among whom the Quakers were dominant. This flow continued, increased by settlers from other colonies, Bermuda, New England, and the West Indies, throughout the entire colonial period, though after 1720 the Scots-Irish and Germans became the more conspicuous elements.

2. Penn proposed later to add the Welsh Tract or parts of it to Chester County. This proposal was bitterly resented by the Welsh, particularly by Thomas Lloyd, who declared that such annexation threatened the independence of the Welsh Tract and was, therefore, a breach of the original agreement. *Ibid.*, 265, 266.

land placed upon Irish industry and trade. They too, like the Puritans before them and the Quakers from England, were in fear of the impending doom which they believed to be hanging over the European world.[1]

The first compact settlement after the founding of Philadelphia was Germantown, established in the autumn of 1683. The founders were people from Krefeld in the Rhineland and Krisheim in the lower Palatinate. They were partly financed by an organized society of Germans in Frankfurt-on-the-Main, whose agent for the purchase and administration of their land was Francis Daniel Pastorius. Pastorius was a gifted German writer and the only university trained and legally minded man among the immigrants and the only one of the German society actually to come to America. The Krefelders and Krisheimers were Quakers, who strictly speaking were not Germans but Rhinelanders, the subjects in one case of the Prince of Orange and in the other of the Elector of the Palatinate. Germantown was therefore a Quaker settlement, neither German nor Mennonite. The migration had begun in 1682, while Penn was still in England. The Krefelders bought of him 18,000 acres, not all in one piece, and the Frankfurt Company bought at first 15,000 acres, increased afterward to 25,000. Pastorius arrived on August 20, 1682, and the Krefelders the October following. Negotiations with Penn on the spot led to the setting apart of 6000 acres, the endorsement of which on Penn's warrant reads, "Warrant vor ein Downship von 6000 ackers." This land was obtained by Pastorius in the name of both the Krefelders and the Frankfurt Company, but it was settled solely by the former. Two years later, after the town was well begun, Pastorius, himself a Quaker, went there to live. There he died in 1719.[2] By 1690 the little town, in which were Quakers, Lutherans, and an occasional Mennonite,[3] had sixty houses and about three

---

1. Duniway, "The English Settlers in Colonial Pennsylvania," *Pennsylvania Magazine*, LII, 317–341; Glenn, *Merion in the Welsh Tract*; Browning, *Welsh Settlement of Pennsylvania*, pp. 18–42; Myers, *Immigration of the Irish Quakers into Pennsylvania*, pt. II, 41–109, 186–190. Mr. Myers estimates the number of Irish Quakers that came over between 1682 and 1750 as from 1500 to 2000. He gives excellent biographies of the three leading men from Ireland: Logan, pp. 234–247; Holme, pp. 247–256; Turner, pp. 257–262.

2. Of Pastorius Professor Hull writes, "A worthy Quaker 'Pilgrim' and pioneer he was indeed, and may well be called 'the Pioneer of German immigration into Pennsylvania,' but not 'the Founder of Germantown.'" That distinction Professor Hull reserves for the Quakers from Krefeld.

3. The Mennonite migration from the Palatinate did not get well under way be-

hundred people. It is an interesting fact that Pastorius, influenced by the same ideas that actuated the Free Society of Traders and the purchasers of the Welsh Tract, should have asked Penn for a separate jurisdiction for the Krefelders, that is, the equivalent of a manor, barony, or county palatine, with independent functions of their own.[1]

Such were the racial and religious characteristics of the province Penn was called upon to govern under a charter that endowed him with some of the attributes of a feudal lord. Dealing with inhabitants who differed in origin, experience, and intellectual and social status, he had not only to reconcile racial antipathies and calm religious prejudices, but also, and particularly in the lower counties, to counteract local tendencies toward decentralization. Also he had to square the legal rights of a true and absolute proprietor with the equally legal rights of the free subjects of an English king, for such was the standing of every free person in the province. And all this he had to do often at long range, for he lived in Pennsylvania less than four years altogether (1682–1684, 1699–1701). Two circumstances favored him: his charter was less proprietary than had been the earlier ones; and he himself was an idealist. On the other hand, two things were against him: first, aristocratic by instinct he was certain to be influenced by the power he exercised; secondly, neither practical nor sagacious, he had to learn by bitter experience that ideals are difficult of application. In critical emergencies, when he should have been firm, he gave way on point after point,[2] and in his choice of men to serve him he was frequently unwise. Distressed by

fore 1700 and the Mennonite influence in Germantown did not reach its zenith before 1712, so that for the first thirty years of its history Quakers, Dutch, English, and Welsh were the leading people of the community. On the Mennonites, Smith, *The Mennonites* (1920); *The Mennonite Migration* (Pennsylvania German Society, 1929, XXXV, ch. IV).

1. Learned, *Life of Pastorius*, pp. 132–133. In addition to Learned's life, which is a monument of accuracy and completeness, Professor Hull's reinterpretation of the story of the settlement of Germantown is the most reliable source of information that we have (*William Penn and the Dutch Quakers*, chs. IV, V). Pennypacker, "Settlement of Germantown" (*Pennsylvania Magazine*, IV, 1–41) and the same at greater length (*Papers*, Pennsylvania German Society, IX, 49–195, 177–199, declaration against slavery) constitute the best and perhaps the only adequate history of the latter community. Professor Hull prefers the spelling "Krefeld" for "Crefeld" and "Krisheim" for "Kriegsheim."

2. Note, for example, his relations with Pastorius, Learned, *Life*, pp. 127–129. Penn gave way on three important points in issuing warrants locating the land purchased by the Frankfurt Company.

increasing indebtedness, due in part to the thievery of the Fords,[1] torn by troubles with Baltimore on one side and the home government on the other; discouraged and disillusioned by the failure of those he trusted to live up to his own ideals, he was a pathetic and tragic figure. "I abhor," he wrote in 1693, "contention, nicetys, doubtful disputation, divisions, etc., and am for patience, forbearance, long suffering and all true moderation." But no peace was to be his. In 1705, he writes, "I am a crucified man between Injustice and Ingratitude there and Extortion and Oppression here."[2]

Penn returned to England August 16, 1684, mainly to defend the southern boundary of his province against the claims of Lord Baltimore. It is doubtful if his remaining in the colony would have altered the course of events, because the proprietary prerogatives were breaking down in Pennsylvania as well as in the other proprietary provinces. His continued presence might have slowed up the process but could never have checked it altogether. The popular assembly had always for its guidance the procedure, practice, and privilege of the House of Commons in England; the freeholders had before them the rights, franchises, and immunities of the king's subjects at home, to which they were equally entitled because the king had retained all powers of sovereignty over the province. Even though these rights and immunities were not expressly mentioned in the royal charter and even though it might have been difficult at this time to state exactly what they were even in England, nevertheless they were implied in the obligation under which each freeholder stood of giving allegiance not only to the proprietor but to the crown also.[3]

1. The rascality of Philip Ford is well brought out in Shepherd, *Propriety Government*, pp. 184–198. Shepherd, basing his conclusions on the "Breviate of Evidence" (*Pennsylvania Magazine*, XXIII, XXIV) estimates Penn's losses before 1688 at over £13,000, and during the first twenty-two years of his proprietorship at over £24,000. Markham said in 1690 that the experiment had not only brought in nothing but had cost Penn heavily from his own estate, *Colonial Records*, I, 328.

2. *Pennsylvania Magazine*, XXXIX, 216–217; *Penn-Logan Correspondence*, II, 71.

3. Some idea of what an Englishman before 1688 considered his legal rights can be obtained from Henry Care, *English Liberties or the Free-Born Subject's Inheritance* (London, without date, but compiled by Care before his death in 1688 and issued for Sarah Harris in 1691. A second edition was issued for Benjamin Harris, probably about 1700. A fifth and sixth, revised and enlarged by W. Nelson were issued in 1721 and 1774). The subject can be traced further during the eighteenth century in the following: G. J., *The Laws of Liberty and Property, or a Concise Treatise of all the Laws, Statutes and Ordinances made for the Benefit and Protection of the Subjects of England and the Preservation of their Lives, Estates, Land and Tenements,*

The struggle which took place in the colony during the years from 1682 to 1701 was a complex of warring forces. On one side was the authority that Penn possessed as true and absolute lord and proprietor, tempered at every point by his desire to do all that he could for the happiness and contentment of his people—a conflict between aristocratic leanings and Quaker ideals. On the other side was the determination of the popular assembly and its leaders to put into practice those principles of government that were finding application in other English colonies in America and represented the liberalizing trend that characterized the vigorous political life of Charles II's England. The settlers in Pennsylvania—the last colony to be founded in the seventeenth century—having but recently come from England, Wales, and Ireland, considered themselves part of the English scene, as it were. Having followed the events that brought about the revolution of 1689 and placed power in the hands of parliament, they were determined that the assembly in Pennsylvania

Goods, Chattels, Rights, Privileges, etc. (second edition, 1734); *A Guide to the Knowledge of the Rights and Privileges of England* (1757); *British Liberties: or The Free-Born Subject's Inheritance* (1766).

All of these writings lay stress on trial by jury, and Care (pp. 224–228) and *A Guide* (pp. 152–153) cite the facts in the Bushell case and refer to Sir John Vaughan's *Reports,* where the details are given. Care mentions also the Penn-Mead trial. *The Laws of Liberty and Property,* though having sections on "Judges" and "Jurors," furnishes no illustrations. There is an article on Henry Care in the *Dictionary of National Biography.* That there was some connection between Care and Penn would appear from a pamphlet issued in the year 1688, the year of Care's death, entitled, *Some Queries concerning Liberty of Conscience directed to William Penn and Henry Care* (London, 1688), containing 58 queries, among which are several relating to the colonies, such as "Regarding the Laws of Carolina toward Toleration" and "A French Government set up in New England," etc. The writer is manifestly sceptical regarding the existence of any real toleration in the colonies.

It is important to notice that Penn and other writers during the Restoration period based their demands for the rights of Englishmen, not upon any theory of the rights of man or upon any speculative political principles, but upon the fact that such rights were ancient and fundamental, dating back to the days of earlier kings and even to Alfred the Great. This is well brought out in a pamphlet issued in 1659, H. N., *Letter sent to General Monk, To St. Albans the 29 of January. Wherein The Antient Government of England, founded upon Magna Charta, and the Petition of Right is Vindicated and Proved to be a popular and Free Commonwealth; All the marks of Soveraignty being in the People.* Writers, in the eighteenth century, on the other hand, taking the ground that Cromwell and the Stuarts had "clipp'd the wings" of an Englishman's ancient rights and liberties and that the "great and happy Revolution" of 1689 had restored them, were coming to believe that every man had "a fixed fundamental Right born with him, as to Freedom of his Person and Property or his Estate, which he cannot be deprived of, but either by his own Consent or some Crime" (*A Guide,* p. 1). One reads little of "antient rights" in the eighteenth century, but a great deal about them in the seventeenth.

should follow the lead of its great exemplar over seas. There was nothing democratic or strictly popular in this determination. What Penn's antagonists were striving for was the ascendancy of the assembly and not of the people as such, for at this time no one suggested or wanted a widening of the popular franchise.

The first assembly met at Chester, as we have already seen, on December 4, 1682, but the first council was not brought together until the following March. The assembly immediately organized itself in parliamentary fashion with speaker, committees, a body of rules and regulations, and in the passing of laws followed the familiar routine of first and second reading, debate in committees of the whole house, and third reading, together with the use of the division in determining the vote and the ballot box in the election of the speaker.[1] It received from the proprietor the laws he wished to have adopted, and those the members debated, amended, and passed. To the extent that the Frame of Government allowed, the first assembly sprang into existence full grown, a fact that testifies to the familiarity of its leaders with English parliamentary procedure. The second assembly, meeting March 12, 1683, was even more constructive than the first. It passed an Act of Settlement, designed to meet conditions arising out of the fewness of the people, their insufficiency of estate, and their lack of skill in matters of government. It reduced temporarily the number of representatives in council and assembly, provided for yearly meetings on March 10—a provision strictly adhered to as regards the year but frequently departed from as regards the day and the month—and they affirmed the right of the proprietor to initiate laws and of the assembly to pass them.[2] On April 2 the proprietor presented the assembly with a new Frame of Government, drawn up by himself on the spot for the good and benefit of the freemen "with much earnestness," as Penn said, "in his spirit toward God at the time of its composure."[3] This frame was passed by the assembly and together with the laws and the Act

1. Until 1689 the ballot box was never used for the local elections of deputies or councillors (*Colonial Records*, I, 269, 282). On April 1, 1689, however, the council (Thomas Lloyd, president) ordered "that each County shall hence fforward Elect or give their Suffrages according to Charter, viz: by the ballot" (*ibid.*, 324).

2. *Votes of Assembly*, I, 11, 13, 21. The Act of Settlement is printed in *Laws of Pennsylvania*, pp. 123–126, and the laws made, *ibid.*, pp. 127–155; Hazard, *Annals*, pp. 615–619. Hazard wrongly conjectures that the Act of Settlement was adopted at the first assembly, on December 7, 1682.

3. *Votes of Assembly*, I, 21; *Colonial Records*, I, 72.

of Settlement constituted the great Charter of Liberties. It was not, however, much liked by the deputies, because on the whole it favored the prerogative rather than the freeholders, enlarging rather than diminishing the powers of governor and council and reminding the deputies—a point Penn frequently made in his controversies with the assembly—that they must be careful not to do anything to lead to the forfeiture of the royal charter.

In the five years that followed, the assembly strengthened its position and defined more exactly its privileges. It exercised the right of adjournment, though accepting without demur the right of the governor and council to prorogue and dissolve. The speaker, always appearing before the governor for his approval, "disabled" himself in parliamentary fashion as unworthy, and, on acceptance, asked for the customary privileges of access to the governor, freedom of speech and debate, and immunity from arrest. The assembly had several skirmishes with the local courts over the freedom of its members from summons, the giving of evidence, and the serving on juries, and each time won its point. Though it did not secure the right to initiate legislation until 1696, it did not confine its share in the making of laws to "yes" and "no," but early obtained the privilege of making proposals or sending in petitions to the council, of asking the latter to drop or alter certain bills before they were actually framed, and of requesting conferences in cases where bills needed explanation or were open to diversities of opinion or possible error. Over the question of its right to amend bills a heated controversy took place. For although the word "advice" in the charter seemed to imply amendment, the council for a long time opposed the right of the assembly to make any change after a bill had received the approval of all its own members.[1] But the assembly thought otherwise and, insisting on its right to amend "as it thought fit," was able to carry the day.[2] Though before 1688 it had exercised complete control over its members, reproving, silencing, fining, and even expelling sundry representatives who overstepped the bounds, it was at times obliged to deny, with considerable asperity, the right of governor and council to interfere with its membership in any respect whatever.[3]

1. *Votes of Assembly,* I, 31; *Colonial Records,* I, 184.
2. *Votes of Assembly,* I, 38; *Colonial Records,* I, 108, 109, 183–184.
3. In May, 1688, the assembly greatly resented the remark, reported to have been made by one of the five commissioners, who were acting in the place of a governor,

The council also was sensitive as regards its dignity. In the cases of Anthony Weston, arrested and whipped for contempt, of Samuel Atkins, who issued an almanac referring to Penn as "Lord Penn," and of William Bradford, who printed controversial books antagonistic to the government, it made it clear that in matters of self-importance one house was as tender as the other.[1] The council's frequent denials of the assembly's assumptions, which may have been due to orders from Penn to check the assembly's encroachments, came to something of a climax in 1688, when the assembly having become suspicious of the council's inquisitiveness locked the doors of its chamber and bound its members to secrecy. One gets the impression that the council, though composed of elected representatives, was becoming a little arrogant and, in its dealings with the assembly, was none too tactful. The assembly had its grievances also and did not hesitate to air them.[2] Such was the general situation when on December 17, 1688, Captain John Blackwell arrived in the colony, appointed by Penn as his deputy governor.

Blackwell was an old Cromwellian soldier, who had married the daughter of General John Lambert, treasurer of Cromwell's army, and had come to New England in 1685, and taken up land in northeastern Connecticut in the interest of certain English and Irish Dissenters. Failing in his immediate mission, he obtained patents of his own and was preparing to settle down in Windham County, Connecticut, when he was called upon by Penn to go to Pennsylvania as his representative there.[3] He was a relative of Penn's, as also of William Markham, Penn's cousin, and he may have been selected on that account. He was not a Quaker and was probably as unwise an appointment as Penn ever made, which is saying a good deal, particularly at this juncture when the relations between council and assembly were near the breaking point. Penn should have known that Blackwell, though a grave, sober, and wise man and identified with no party in the province, but yet a non-Quaker and a soldier, was not a happy choice as resident governor of a province in which

"That the power of judging the Qualifications of each member was invested in the Breast of the Governor and Council." It immediately sent to the council to find out if the report were true. But the council had adjourned. *Votes of Assembly*, I, 43.

1. *Colonial Records*, I, 92, 165, 366–377.
2. *Votes of Assembly*, I, 43, 44, 46, 47; *Council Records*, I, 226.
3. *Collections*, Massachusetts Historical Society, 3d ser., I, 61; VII, 155; Larned, *History of Windham County*, I, 183. For Penn's opinion of Blackwell, Janney, *Life of Penn*, pp. 341–345. Blackwell's commission and instructions are dated July 12, 1688.

a holy experiment was being tried. Blackwell's troubles were rather with the council than with the assembly, for the former, endeavoring to check the assembly's encroachments, resented the appointment of an outsider in any case and the more so because after Penn left the colony in 1684 the governorship had been for four years in the hands either of the president of the council or of five commissioners of state appointed for the purpose. Two members of the council who very early had denied Penn's right to send over a deputy at all refused to recognize Blackwell as governor; and when one of them carried his opposition so far that Blackwell ordered him to leave the chamber, he refused to go saying that he had been elected to the council by the freeholders and by them only could he be removed.[1]

More serious in many ways than these expressions of dissent, which constituted acts of insubordination to the will of the proprietor, was the conflict that arose between Blackwell and two leading men of the province, one, the most highly respected Quaker of his generation, and the other, in later years, Penn's great antagonist as the champion of the rights of the assembly. One of these men was Thomas Lloyd, intimate friend of Pastorius, a former president of the council and acting governor, and keeper of the great seal. The other was David Lloyd, possibly a distant kinsman of Thomas's, whose deputy in the chancery he was, clerk of the county court of Philadelphia, clerk of the assembly, and attorney general.[2] The cause of the controversy was the refusal of Thomas Lloyd, as keeper, to pass letters patent commissioning five provincial judges at the order of the council, because he considered the order in no wise proper and the commissions "more moulded by ffancy than fformed by law." Blackwell resented the use of the word "ffancy" as an unbecoming expression, and interpreted Lloyd's refusal as a contempt of the proprietor's authority. The controversy with David Lloyd arose from his declining, in scornful language construed as contemptuous, to deliver certain records of the provincial court for the inspection of the council.

As the council itself was not united in its opinion regarding the legality and justness of the governor's position, and as two of the

1. *Colonial Records*, I, 244.
2. On Thomas and David Lloyd, Sharpless, *Political Leaders of Pennsylvania*, pp. 55–113. Excellent accounts of these Welshmen are in the *Dictionary of American Biography*.

members not only registered their dissent but refused to continue
their attendance, the debates became very heated and on one occasion gave rise to so much noise and clamor that persons passing by
in the street stood still to hear.[1] The Lloyds were legally wrong in
the stand which they had taken, manifestly for the purpose of obstructing the proceedings of the council on the ground that governor and council had "a designe or intent to subvert and overturne
the frame of government and make voyd the Charter of Privileges."
And they were not upheld by the proprietor. Penn who was wres-
tling with heartbreaking problems at home was deeply distressed
by the unseemly treatment of his governor. Once before he had
written to Thomas Lloyd in reproof of his conduct, saying, "Do not
be so litigious and brutish . . . O, that some one would stand up for
our good beginnings and bring a savour of righteousness over that
ill savour." Now he wrote in like manner to James Harrison, "I am
sorry at heart for your animosities . . . for the love of God, me
and the poor country be not so governmentish, so noisy, and open
in your dissatisfactions."[2]

Penn had said when he appointed Blackwell that if the latter did
not give satisfaction he would lay him aside. Therefore, after fourteen months of almost continuous bickering with the council on one
count or another, he recalled Blackwell in February, 1690. Blackwell was more than willing to go, saying as his last word to the
council, "I doe with all heartiness declare my Rejoycing in the Opportunity and leave I have of Resigning and surrendering [my place
as governor] . . . as a man who sought to be discharged from it."
His last remark about the Philadelphia Quakers was to say that
"each prays for his neighbor on First Days and then preys upon him
the other six."[3] At the same time he begged the council to stop its
persecution of Thomas Lloyd, saying that he knew the man "both
in his weakness and accomplishment" and earnestly desired to end
the disputes between the two. The members of the council heeded
this request and when Penn empowered them to elect their own
governor, beseeching them to avoid "factions and parties, whisper-
ings and reportings, and all animosities, putting their common

1. *Colonial Records,* I, 245, 249–250, 253, 294, 297.
2. Penn to Lloyd, Worminghurst, November 17, 1686, *Historical Magazine,* 1st
ser., III, 105.
3. Quoted by Pound, *The Penns of Pennsylvania* (1932), pp. 215, 217.

shoulder to the public good," they, as "good men and patriots," elected Thomas Lloyd as their president.[1]

The period of Blackwell's governorship was in every way unfortunate for the peaceful course of Penn's experiment. Not only did the members of the council quarrel among themselves, with the governor, and with the Lloyds, but the assembly took advantage of the situation to charge the councillors with being "ill ministers," the chief authors of the arbitrariness in government, and unworthy to serve as chief magistrates. It said further that the frequent want of a quorum, the refusal of the members to attend, and their inactivity when present prevented the council from doing its proper work. It complained that even when the members did attend and acted harmoniously they frequently displayed an "unbecoming behaviour" toward the freeholders of the province or engaged in unlawful and rigid proceedings against the assembly.[2] It charged the council with failure to redress its own grievances and, when the council told it to mind its own business, it repeated its statements more vigorously than before and demanded that it should not be dissolved until its grievances had been considered and acted on. To this demand the council made answer that nothing could be done, as there were not enough councillors present to make a quorum.

However, with the recall of Blackwell, the situation soon improved, and with the surrender by Penn of the government of the province into the hands of the freeholders' representatives in both council and assembly, peace once more reigned. Members of both bodies subscribed anew their declarations of allegiance and fidelity and the two houses settled down to the usual legislative routine. The members were on their good behavior, hoping for Penn's early arrival, as his continued absence was regretted by all as "extremely to our prejudice."

But Penn was not yet ready to come. The revolution of 1688–1689 had driven from the throne his protector, James II, and for some years after that event he had the misfortune, as Benjamin

1. *Colonial Records*, I, 316, 321. Thomas Lloyd served as president and acting deputy governor until the arrival of Governor Fletcher in April, 1694. Though the proceedings of council are defective after September 11, 1690, Lloyd's continued service is shown by letters from him of August 21, 1691, and March 27, 1693 (*Calendar State Papers, Colonial*, 1689–1692, §1708; 1693–1696, §§218, 396.

2. See especially the proceedings of the assembly that met on May 10, 1689, *Votes of Assembly*, I, 48–56; *Colonial Records*, I, 261, 270–274.

Franklin later expressed it, "to lie under the Suspicions and Frowns of the Government,"[1] because suspected of plotting the restoration of the king. The declaration of war against France in 1689 brought home to him and his Quaker brethren in the colony the unwelcome question of military duty, the more perplexing because Penn by his charter was the captain general of the military forces of the province. Blackwell had urged his council to take some action regarding participation in the war, but partly on principle and partly on account of the expense involved, it had dismissed the issue as too difficult for it to cope with. As one of the members said, they preferred to remain passive. Though the non-Quaker element was willing to do military duty, both in offense and defense, the Quakers refused, thus bringing upon themselves the denunciations of Nicholson of Virginia and of Copley of Maryland, both of whom execrated Penn's "pernicious principles" and condemned the Pennsylvania assembly for its refusal to fight even if the province were invaded.[2]

Thus in England charges against Penn were accumulating. The quarrel with Baltimore; the reports of the unsettled state of the province, and the trouble Penn was having with the lower counties; rumors of connivance in matters of piracy and illegal trade; and above all the conviction that prevailed among the members of the Privy Council and the Lords of Trade that the grant of Penn's charter had been a mistake and that the time had come for the king to assume, temporarily at least, the powers of government in Pennsylvania—all these circumstances furnished ample justification, from the English point of view, for the appointment of Governor Fletcher of New York as the governor of Pennsylvania also, thus transforming the proprietary province for the time being into a royal colony.

Fletcher, though commissioned as early as March 18, 1692, did not reach Pennsylvania in person until April, 1693, Thomas Lloyd continuing as governor until that date. Fletcher offered Lloyd the first place on his council, but Lloyd refused the offer, perhaps on account of his health, for he died the next year. Markham, Robert Turner, Andrew Robeson, and Patrick Robinson—of whom Turner was a

1. Benjamin Franklin, *An Historical Review of Pennsylvania* (1812), p. 18. Regarding the authorship of this work, see Hull, *Eight First Biographies*, p. 111.

2. *Calendar State Papers, Colonial*, 1689–1692, §§1324, 1583, 1708. Thomas Lloyd wrote to Leisler in 1691, "While retaining a good regard for your difficulties we are unable to answer your requirements. We have no public fund or revenue, our infancy not yet being trusted with the very requisite expenses of government, which have so far been defrayed from our private purses." See the same, 1693–1696, §218.

Quaker and one of Penn's oldest co-workers in the Quaker cause—all accepted. Others were added later, some of them Quakers, so that it is difficult to accept Sharpless' statement that "Fletcher was opposed by the whole Quaker body in public life . . . [and that] Friends refused to sit in his council."[1] The significance of Fletcher's administration is that for nearly two years Pennsylvania was run as a royal province, with a governor, appointed by the crown, a lieutenant governor and a council appointed by the governor, and an assembly elected as before by the freeholders. Legally, the form of government established by Penn in his frames was abrogated and Fletcher was expressly instructed to introduce into the province of Pennsylvania, the county of New Castle, and all the lands thereon depending the rules and methods obtaining in New York. Because in several important respects the royal system of government was more favorable to the assembly than was that of Penn, it happened that during these two years the advantages rested with the lower house. Very early Fletcher said to the assembly, "The constitution of their Majesties government and that of Mr. Penn's are in direct opposition one to the other. If you will be tenacious in sticking for this, it is a plain demonstration that you decline,"[2] which was merely another way of saying that both systems could not prevail at the same time.

The first difficulty concerned the laws which had already been passed and which the assembly hoped Fletcher would confirm. On

1. *Political Leaders,* p. 88. The refusals were chiefly in the judicial field—that of the justices of the peace (*Colonial Records,* I, 370–375), but even there many Quakers accepted office, if those subscribing the declaration but not taking the oath can be assumed to be Quakers.

2. *Votes of Assembly,* I, 68; *Colonial Records,* I, 402–403. The addresses of the freemen and the replies of the governor are given more fully in the *Colonial Records* than in the *Votes of Assembly.* In May, 1693, just before Fletcher left for New York, a conference was held, made up of committees of council and assembly and presided over by Fletcher's lieutenant governor, William Markham. A very instructive debate took place upon the question of confirming the province laws. The committee from the assembly argued that the laws had all been taken to England by Penn and as they had not been acted upon within the required six months they had become law by default. The council committee, not being sure of this, argued that in any case the consent of governor, council, and assembly was all that was necessary to make a law and that "sealing" was only a ceremony that meant nothing. The strongest point made, however, was that to abrogate the laws already passed in the province would be to throw the people into great confusion. Fletcher knew that such would be the case, and he compromised, saving the king's prerogative. *Colonial Records,* I, 418–422.

this issue the debate was long and somewhat acrimonious, and it is not quite clear just what was the outcome. Apparently, Fletcher confirmed enough of the existing laws to keep the machinery of justice going and refused to confirm only measures distinctly contrary to the law of England, of which there seemed to be quite a number. On the whole his attitude was friendly. He promised to do all he could for the safety and satisfaction of the people, demanding in return nothing more than obedience to the king and queen and the avoidance of unnecessary debates. The Quaker was often as long-winded as the Puritan and Fletcher disliked discussion as much as did Andros. The assembly accepted the situation as gracefully as it could, though it took advantage of the opportunity to issue a remonstrance saving all its rights and privileges. What it considered these rights and privileges Fletcher was soon to learn. It demanded the right to initiate legislation, which was possessed by all assemblies in royal colonies; to pass on amendments made in council before a measure became law; and above all to obtain a redress of grievances before making a grant of supplies.[1] The committee that presented this remonstrance to Fletcher was headed by David Lloyd, who thus in the year 1693 began his career as defender of the privileges of the popular assembly, anticipating at this early date the leading issue of the colonies in the eighteenth century, namely, the encroachment of the assemblies on the royal prerogative in the person of the royal governor. Lloyd stepped into a strategic position the next year when he was elected speaker of the house.

The assembly profited by the two years of royal rule. The most troublesome question concerned the share that Pennsylvania should take in the war against the French, carried on from Albany as the concentration point. The assembly was willing to aid in clothing and feeding the Indian allies, but would have no part in military operations, and when the business of raising money was taken up demanded the right to say how the money should be spent. It wanted "to appropriate the money raised for public uses or for the utility of particular persons without first giving it to the king": that is, it did not want Fletcher to spend all the money on the war. In an address to him it cited the previous practice in the province, the practice in England, and the customary method employed in some of the neighboring colonies.[2] Fletcher seems to have com-

1. *Votes of Assembly*, I, 77.   2. *Ibid.*, 87–88.

promised this matter also, allowing the assembly to appropriate a portion, the rest to be used as the governor and council directed. But the assembly was not satisfied with this compromise, and when the governor issued an order dissolving the body, it refused to adjourn on the ground that all the grievances had not been redressed. Resuming its session under David Lloyd as speaker, it said that the assembly would not dissolve until it had dissolved itself. That Lloyd was demanding more than any royal governor could concede is evident from the fact that the members of the council, two at least of whom were Quakers, agreed that Fletcher had acted with great prudence and moderation.[1] Fletcher had already been deeply offended by the refusal of the assembly to grant supplies before grievances were redressed and at the time had threatened the colony with annexation to New York. Having charged the members with wasting their time by sitting for nineteen days searching for grievances, "without the least consideration of their Majesties service in the security of the province," he refused to pass certain bills, which he thought contrary to the law of England, or an encroachment on the king's prerogative.[2] How the matter would have ended is a question that can never be answered, for on August 9, 1694, Fletcher's commission was revoked and Penn was once more invested with all the rights of government in his province.

The experience with the royal government had certain definite results. The assembly discovered a new strength and David Lloyd a new and enlarged means of contumacy. Penn was brought face to face with the fact that Pennsylvania was not only the seat of a holy experiment but also a part of England's colonial world and that he owed a duty to the crown as well as to his people. The Lords of Trade were willing to grant his petition for restoration, after the crown lawyers had decided that he could no longer be kept out of his rights unless his charter were revoked. They recommended that his government be restored on certain definite conditions: that he promise to go over himself and take charge of his colony; that he would obey the royal order requiring the province to furnish eighty men for the Albany expedition; that he would personally declare his fidelity to their Majesties and obtain from the assembly an act of submission; and, lastly, that he would adjust satisfactorily the troublesome question of the laws in force in the province. Penn

1. *Colonial Records*, I, 445.   2. *Ibid.*, 466, 468, 470, 471.

promised everything, because if he did not, or if he failed to carry out his promises, the lords threatened to restore Fletcher, a plan that might lead to the loss of the charter and annexation to New York. As Penn could not leave immediately for Pennsylvania he obtained from the lords permission to appoint as his governor for the time being, William Markham, who had been Fletcher's lieutenant governor. All terms having been agreed to, an order in council was issued August 9, 1694, restoring the proprietary government.[1] Markham called the last meeting of Fletcher's council, March 26, 1695, and his first as Penn's governor, April 22. The assembly met the following September. It is perhaps worthy of note that David Lloyd was no longer speaker or even a member of the assembly for more than one year. He became a councillor in 1696 and again in 1698, 1699, and 1700, when he was removed by Penn for certain disrespectful remarks which he had once made about the king.[2]

Markham has been charged by Pennsylvania historians of the "democratic" school with subservience to the prerogative, much as David Lloyd has been charged by the older pro-Pennian writers with demagoguery. The facts must be faced. As Penn's governor it was Markham's duty to maintain as far as he could the charter rights of his superior. Lloyd, particularly after 1700, represents the anti-proprietary party and, encouraged by the results of the Fletcher administration, took up the cause of the assembly and carried it farther than ever it was carried in any English colony in America. Even in the council he opposed Markham and made it exceedingly difficult for him to bring the assembly to terms in regard to the prosecution of the war. Markham reproached the deputies for sitting and accomplishing nothing, with forming "a very silent and close" assembly, demanding a confirmation of privileges before appropriating money, and wanting to take from the proprietor many

1. *Calendar State Papers, Colonial,* 1693–1696, §§1144, 1166, 1181, 1186, 1187, 1188, 1213, 1238; *Acts Privy Council, Colonial,* II, §561; *Colonial Records,* I, 472–476; *Votes of Assembly,* I, 89; *New York Colonial Documents,* IV, 108–110.

2. In a vice-admiralty case, 1698, David Lloyd, then a member of the council, asked the marshal of the vice-admiralty court by what authority he acted, and when the marshal produced his commission, "Lloyd held it up in a scornful manner, saying 'this is a fine baby, a pretty baby, but we are not to be frightened by babies' " (*Calendar State Papers, Colonial,* 1697–1698, §907; *Colonial Records,* I, 603–604, where will be found Quary's representation to Penn and Penn's suspension of Lloyd, which marked the beginning of that life-long enmity of Lloyd for Penn and his secretary James Logan, which is one of the most striking features of Pennsylvania history in the early eighteenth century).

of his charter powers. The most lively controversy took place over the reëstablishment of the old Charter of Liberties, which the assembly said could be restored, not by the fiat of the proprietor but only by legislative action, a position that Markham vehemently opposed. Out of this discussion came the proposal to draft an act of settlement in what is known as "Markham's charter," which the governor presented to the joint council and assembly on November 3, 1696, calling it "a frame of government much the same with the charter, but with some emendations and alterations." This draft he asked the assembly to draw up in the form of a bill, after which he would consider whether to pass it or not.[1] The content of the new frame and the method of its adoption was a defeat for the proprietor, because in its final form it was an act of assembly and not a grant from above, and testified to the right of the assembly to initiate bills equally with the council. The frame allowed the assembly to sit on its own adjournment, to appoint committees, to present grievances, and to have its members paid for their attendance. It divided the functions of administration between council and assembly, to the advantage of the latter, and prohibited the governor from performing any public act without the advice and consent of the council. As both council and assembly were elected bodies, the new act distinctly circumscribed the independence of the proprietor and his deputy, though by placing a fairly high qualification on the right to vote, it equally circumscribed the share of the people in government. To the extent that it dealt a blow to proprietary rule in Pennsylvania it represented the influence of the Fletcher administration and foreshadowed the famous charter of liberties of 1701.[2]

The remaining years of the Markham rule were largely concerned with the difficulty of meeting the demand of the English government that Pennsylvania coöperate in the enforcement of the acts of

1. *Colonial Records*, I, 507–508.
2. The Markham Frame is printed in *Pennsylvania Archives*, 4th ser., I, 55–56; Thorpe, *Charters*, V, 3070–3076; *Laws of Pennsylvania*, pp. 245–253. A somewhat detailed analysis is given in Shepherd, *Proprietary Government*, pp. 280–284. In return for the Markham Frame the assembly passed a bill appropriating £300 "for the support of the government and for relieving the distressed Indians inhabiting above Albany" (*Votes of Assembly*, I, 97, 98, 99; *Laws of Pennsylvania*, pp. 253–256). But Fletcher had still to remind Markham that, according to the agreement with the Lords of Trade, the province owed eighty men for the war (*New York Colonial Documents*, IV, 101, 227, 706). To this the council and assembly replied that they were ready to observe the king's further commands "according to our religious Persuasions and Abilities."

trade.[1] The passage by parliament of the act of 1696, the stiffening of the customs service, the erection of the vice-admiralty courts, the peremptory orders sent to the colonial governors, and the issue of new and exacting instructions for the execution of the acts—all were beginning to play a very important part in the history of the colonies and in none was there more dissatisfaction than in those that were proprietary. In Pennsylvania Randolph and Quary were at hand to charge the province with neglect and to draw from the assembly replies to their "false accusations"; and cases in the vice-admiralty court, which was set up in 1697, provoked resistance to a jurisdiction which was disliked by the colonists because of its procedure under the civil not the common law. Complaints were made that Pennsylvania was harboring pirates,[2] was allowing tobacco to be shipped directly to Scotland, was trading illegally with the Dutch colony of Curaçao, was admitting vessels coming directly from the Continent with European goods, and otherwise interfering with the operation of measures that England deemed necessary to her prosperity. All these charges were agitating authorities both at home and in the colony and were distinctly undermining the influence and prestige of the proprietor.

When, therefore, in 1699, Penn found himself free to cross the water and take his place in the colony as resident governor, he was confronted with conditions fundamentally different from those which had existed when he was last in America from 1682 to 1684. The members of the assembly, dissatisfied with the Markham frame of 1696, were considering the drafting of another. They spent hours debating such questions as the reduction in the numbers of the elected representatives, which they wanted restored to those provided in the frame of 1683, that is, three from each county for the council and six for the assembly, a request that Penn granted at once.[3] Other issues also were debated and Penn on receiving the

1. What this policy was in its many ramifications will be taken up in the next volume.

2. *Votes of Assembly*, I, 107; *Colonial Records*, I, 550–551, 565, 575. One of those charged with piracy or at least with assisting pirates was James Brown, son-in-law of Markham, who in 1699 was expelled from the house "as unfitt to sit here." Brown had become involved in scandalous intrigue with Every, the pirate (*Colonial Records*, I, 580; *Votes of Assembly*, I, 114). The assembly passed a bill against pirates in 1700 (*Votes of Assembly*, I, 115; *Laws of Pennsylvania*, pp. 284–285).

3. The assembly of May 10, 1700, was made up of six members from each county, but that of October 14, 1700 of only four (*Votes of Assembly*, I, 118, 123).

measure noted above made a very conciliatory speech, at the same time recognizing the important fact that the assembly had taken the initiative in the matter and was really forcing his hand. He made a far-reaching concession when he agreed that control of affairs lay with the representatives, who were to see "what Laws are fitt to be Left out and what to be made and you with mee are to prepare and propose them." "I say this," he added, "the rather because of a false notion some have gott becaus you are my Council therfor you are not the people's representatives . . . if there be anything that jarrs, alter it; if you want a law for this or that, prepare itt."

The representatives took Penn at his word and a grand committee of council and assembly began the preparing of the new frame. On May 13, 1701, the draft was read at a general assembly. Additional meetings were held and in another grand committee and in committees of council and house, where debate was free and full, the work at last was completed. It is a pity that we do not know the pros and cons of the discussion, but the significant fact is that Penn was willing to accede to any form in which the representatives wanted the charter cast. It was only when the assembly began to demand changes in his land regulations and the rectifying of abuses in allotments that he showed his displeasure. He was willing to hand over the government to council and assembly, but he would not surrender any of his rights as the proprietor of the soil. Debate continued, the assembly preparing its draft, which was presented to Penn, while he in turn prepared "the draught of such a charter as he could grant them." This draft the assembly accepted and amended, saying very frankly that the only thing which stood in the way of an agreement was the controversy that had arisen between the province and the three lower counties regarding the number of representatives in assembly and the latters' determination to legislate for themselves. This matter having been settled, as we shall see, by the secession of the counties, the charter was adopted on October 28, 1701.[1]

For three-quarters of a century this charter of liberties remained the constitution of Pennsylvania. Even though Penn promised to grant another which should be better adapted to the circumstances of the inhabitants, he never did so, and the province continued dur-

1. The Charter of 1701 is printed in *Colonial Records*, II, 56–60, and in Thorpe's *Charters*, V, 3076–3081. The proceedings of assembly, as far as any details are given, can be followed in *Votes of Assembly*, I, 142, 143–144, 148, 163; *Colonial Records*, I, 613. There are no minutes from October 27, 1701, to April 12, 1702.

ing the colonial period under an instrument that contained one feature unique in colonial annals. As the charter represented the victory
of the assembly, so it might be expected that the assembly would
reap the fruits. This it did at one stroke by eliminating the council
as unnecessary to the passing of laws. The enacting clause introduced into the charter reads: "By the governor, with the consent
and approbation of the freemen in general assembly met." As by this
time very little was left of the proprietary prerogatives, such as the
issuing of ordinances, the control over justice and the courts, and
the enjoyment of perquisites other than those accruing from the soil,
this clause meant that in all important particulars the assembly was
supreme, with entire control over legislation, taxation, and its own
organization and membership—the only unicameral law-making
body in any of the colonies. It was limited in but one particular—
the obligation to send copies of its laws to England for the king's
approval or disapproval. Its members were given all the rights and
immunities of the freeborn subjects of England, as enjoyed in other
of the king's plantations in America, and so were placed on an equal
footing with the king's subjects everywhere, a position which the
inhabitants of all the proprietary provinces had for years been seeking to attain. Except in the appointment of the governor, proprietary rule in Pennsylvania, as far as administration was concerned,
virtually came to an end then and there. How Penn and his appointees later felt about it was expressed by Governor John Evans
when, addressing the assembly in 1707, he said, "My third reason is
you have told me that a certain Charter, prepared at the Proprie-
trs. Departure should have been executed, which Charter I find
upon enquiring to have been a project of the same Gentlemans to
Incorporate this Province, and take very near the whole power, both
in matters of property and Govmt., out of the hands of the Pro-
prietr. and Govr. and lodge it in the People, Leaving the Govmt.
very little besides the Title, with the power only of appointing
Judges of Life and Death, and a very few other small matters, by
which it plainly appears that the aim is to reverse the method of
Govmt. according to our English Constitution, and Establish one
more nearly resembling a republic in its stead."[1] Because the proprietors and their governors were not ready to yield on all points to
the demands of the assembly, there ensued during the first quarter

1. *Colonial Records,* II, 325.

of the eighteenth century a battle royal for control. On the part of the proprietors, shorn of many of their governmental prerogatives, the contest was not with "the people" but with an assembly elected on a limited franchise and controlled by an oligarchy of Quaker leaders, who dominated Pennsylvania politics until the outbreak of the Seven Years' War.[1] No democratic principle was at any time involved.[2]

While thus on the governmental side one provision of the charter took from the council all legislative authority and whittled down almost to nothingness the proprietory prerogative, another curtailed the proprietor's territorial control and brought about the separation of the lower counties from the province, that is, of Delaware from

1. Treatment of this subject belongs not here but to the story of the assembly in the eighteenth century. The controversy reached a climax when, in 1725 and 1726, the leading spokesmen on each side, James Logan for the proprietor and David Lloyd for the assembly, issued their manifestoes. Logan prepared a "Memorial," defending the proprietary prerogative under the king's letters patent, as expressed in the Widow Penn's private instructions to her governor, which was published by authority of the assembly. Lloyd replied in *A Vindication of the Legislative Power* (Philadelphia, March 19, 1725) in which he expressed the wish that the proprietary authority be eliminated in all but a few particulars. He charged Logan with "designs against the Constitution of this Government and disregard to the just Merit of the first Adventurers, who carried on the Administration of the Government and first settlement of this Country at their own charge, as also the Slights and Neglect of his Duty toward the present Inhabitants, which seem to be diffused all over his Paper, and so are the Imputations that he unfairly throws at former Assemblies," etc. Lloyd would have the house censure Logan. Logan replied in THE ANTIDOTE. *In some* Remarks *on a Paper* of David Lloyd's *called* A Vindication of the Legislative Power. *Submitted to the Representatives of the Freemen of Pennsylvania* (*Pennsylvania Magazine*, XXXVIII, 463–487), in which he offered an antidote to Lloyd's poison and tried to show that Lloyd's law was misapplied, his reasoning false, his reflections on the proprietor unmerited and unjust, and his whole performance instead of being "a Service to the Publick is truly a Dishonour to the Government." Lloyd came back with "A Further Vindication," dated March 4, 1726 (unprinted, among the Penn Papers, "Assembly and Provincial Council," in fifteen folios), the argument of which is too long and too complicated to be analyzed here. I am indebted to the Historical Society of Pennsylvania for photostats of Lloyd's papers.

At an earlier date Logan spoke of Lloyd as "a man very stiff in all his undertakings, of a sound judgment and a good lawyer, but extremely pertinacious and somewhat revengeful" (*Pennsylvania Magazine*, XLIII, 87; *Penn-Logan Correspondence*, I, 18). In 1709 Penn spoke of the activities of Lloyd and his followers as "The restless endeavours of a few malcontents to throw the government into confusion," and of Lloyd himself as "turbulent and ungrateful," a "base man" that would be rewarded "according to his villany."

2. Eshleman's essay, "Struggle and Rise of Popular Power" (*Pennsylvania Magazine*, XXXIV, 129–161), deals with this subject, but in its antagonism to Penn it exaggerates the importance of the so-called "popular forces" and frequently makes statements that are not warranted by the evidence cited.

Pennsylvania. The text reads, "If the Representatives of the Province and Territories shall not hereafter agree to Joyn together in Legislation . . . [then] at any time within three years . . . the Inhabitants of Each County in the Territories shall have as many persons to Represent them in a Distinct Assembly for the Territories as shall be by them Requested." This provision means that if, after three years' consideration of the question, the lower counties still wished to have a separate legislature and should make their wish known in the proper manner, they should have it, even though they remained, as before, under the governor of the province. This clause was the result of many years of controversy and ill will, during which political animosities, racial and religious differences, and discontent in the lower counties arising from narrow boundaries and social and economic handicaps widened the breach and hastened the eventual separation. There were but few Quakers among the inhabitants of the counties, the majority consisted of Anglicans and Calvinists, who disliked the Quaker rule.[1] The counties were much less advanced financially and agriculturally than the province and possessed no commercial opportunities comparable with those of Philadelphia. Their people foresaw with dismay and foreboding the inevitable expansion of the province and the increase in its wealth and population, and feared lest the counties should become in time merely a dependent and submerged part of a larger whole. They dreaded the legislative dominance of the province over them and knew that as new counties were added to the province and the membership in the assembly was consequently increased they would be outvoted and at the mercy of a majority that might have little consideration for their needs.[2]

Such were the reasons that underlay the determination of the people of the counties to break away from the province and to have a legislative body of their own. But however much this sort of rea-

1. What the Quakers thought of the people of New Castle can be judged from such remarks as these. Isaac Norris spoke of the town as "that Frenchified, Scotchified, Dutchified place," where he had been in attendance on the assembly for seven weeks. He thought the delegates from the lower counties vociferous in their demands and he was glad to be back from that wearisome place, where there was "much teasing" in assembly and where the various speakers were "almost off their hinges, for they would croak loudly" (*Penn-Logan Correspondence*, I, December 8, 1700). Other not dissimilar comments could be cited and doubtless, if we had them, similar ones from the other side. The dislike was mutual.

2. *Votes of Assembly*, I, 154, 155; Rodney, *Early Relations*, pp. 24–27.

soning might influence men's opinions, it could not be used for argument when the legal aspects of the case came up for consideration. Then was demanded concrete evidence that could be presented when required, and this evidence the counties found in the fact that not only was Penn's title uncertain but that his legal right to their government and soil was also open to legitimate doubt. Disbelief in the soundness of Penn's position was not new to the counties. It had been entertained years before when the planters of the region had refused to pay quit-rents, because they claimed that if paid to anyone these quit-rents should go to the Duke of York and not to Penn. It was revived again during the discussion over the charter at the session of September–October, 1701, held in Philadelphia, when the proposal was brought forward that the laws passed during the preceding session at New Castle in 1700 should be confirmed, lest some one construe these laws as illegal because passed outside the province. The deputies from the counties immediately became alarmed by this proposal, foreseeing that if laws passed at New Castle for the province were illegal, then laws passed at Philadelphia for the lower counties would be illegal also; and if, as was likely, new counties should be added to the province and future assemblies should meet only at Philadelphia, then would the lower counties be beyond the pale of all provincial legislation. When the assembly refused to withdraw the bill for confirming the New Castle laws, nine of the lower county members left the house; but as two others remained the assembly continued to function and both the bill and the charter were legally passed, October 28, 1701.

On October 25, even before the bill and the charter were adopted, the representatives of the three lower counties sent an address to England drawing attention to certain aspects of the situation and laying special stress upon the fact that Penn had answered all their requests for protection with silence or with "ineffectual discourse." Also, they sent two addresses directly to Penn himself, but without result. In their complaints they were supported by Robert Quary, the judge of vice-admiralty, who had his own quarrel with Penn over the vice-admiralty jurisdiction, and was only too eager to show that Penn's title to the territories was illegal and that for eighteen years Penn had exercised all powers of government there without any commission from the crown. Quary said further that the territories were exposed to pirates and that the Quakers would do nothing to protect them and he thought it most unfair that a region possessing so few Quakers should be subject to Quaker rule. This protest, upheld by letters from Randolph, brought the issue into the open at Whitehall, and the Board of Trade, notifying Penn, then in England, of Quary's letter, requested him to furnish proof of his title. As Penn could do no more than refer to the title deeds of enfeoffment from the Duke of York and the deliveries of seizin by Herrman and Moll in 1682, the board expressed itself as dissatisfied. It agreed to recognize Penn's right to appoint a governor for both the province and the territories, but only on condition that every such appointee receive the king's approval and that Penn and his successors should make formal declaration to the effect that such approval in no way diminished his Majesty's right and claim to the three lower counties. The board's recommendation was approved by the Privy Council, January 21, 1703.[1] The people of the counties, after a year of further argument, accepted the situation. On November 22, 1704, the first independent assembly met at New Castle, and except for the person of the governor, the separation from Pennsylvania was complete. The new colony, which had not even a name during colonial times, was unique in that its right to exist rested on no charter from the crown. It was never obliged to send its laws to England and its affairs very rarely came to the knowledge of the authorities there. Though in two other instances, those of Massachusetts–New Hampshire and New York–New Jer-

---

1. *Calendar State Papers, Colonial,* 1701, pp. 91, 93 (Randolph's letter), §§973, 975; 1702, §§270, 275, 277 (address from the representatives), 305 (Quary's letter), 463 (Popple to Penn), 638, ii, 1207 (Penn's reply), 649 (Popple to Penn), 1141 (board's decision), 1208; 1702–1703, §§207, 218, 219 (Penn's acceptance of the reservation and the order in council of January 21, 1703); 1708–1709, §§12, 12, i; *Board of Trade Journal,* 1714–1718, pp. 193, 194; 1717–1718, pp. 87–95 (legal review of the case); *Acts Privy Council, Colonial,* II, §885. The declaration continued to be made by Hannah Penn (*Board of Trade Journal,* 1722–1728, p. 226), and by all the succeeding proprietors (*ibid.,* 1759–1763, p. 370, for example). By an irony of fate the act confirming the New Castle laws, which had started the whole trouble, was disallowed by the crown (*Calendar State Papers, Colonial,* 1701, §975; *Statutes at Large,* II, 497–498).

There is no doubt that the circumstances attending the separation of Delaware from Pennsylvania and the actual separation itself were distressing events to the proprietor, who wrote in bitterness of soul, "I struggle for that poor country's preservation to the wasting of my time and purse," and again, "God forgive those wretched people that have misused me so, and preserve my spirit over it . . . Pennsylvania has been a dear Pennsylvania to me" (*Penn-Logan Correspondence,* I, 75, 305–306, 307–308, 314). In 1712 he said of himself that he was grown old and infirm (he was 68), but he hoped to see Pennsylvania once more before he died. In that year he made his will and died in 1718.

sey, there was for a time a single governor for two colonies, in each of these cases the governor was royal and had two separate commissions from the crown. In Pennsylvania–Delaware, however, but a single commission was issued for the governor and that by the proprietor. But as that commission was not valid until the appointee had received the king's approval and the proprietor had made his declaration, the Delawareans looked on themselves as in the king's hand, the governor being proprietary for the province and royal for themselves. If one accepts this interpretation, then Delaware, during the colonial years of the eighteenth century, is to be considered a royal province.

Yet the counties were never treated as royal by the authorities at home. No instructions were ever sent to the governor of Pennsylvania designed especially for them. No separate file of Delaware papers was ever set apart in the Plantation Office and no seal was ever prepared by the royal engraver in England for Delaware's exclusive use. Before 1696, when the first collector for New Castle was appointed,[1] the counties seem to have fallen, more or less by uncertainty of interpretation, outside the obligations imposed by the trade act of 1673 and during that time their merchants were not called upon to give bond or to pay the plantation duty.[2] But in the eighteenth century, in matters of trade, though never entered separately in the lists of the colonies, they were considered in all respects similar to other colonies civilly organized.[3] Legally, by a *salvo jure* clause, despite caveats entered with the Board of Trade by the Pennsylvania proprietors, they were declared, as of right, a possession of the crown and not of the proprietor, for only by sufferance was their governor, with the king's approval, allowed to be a proprietary appointee. For this reason the conclusion was reached, logically at least, that in law the deputy governor of Pennsylvania held without limitation of time, but that the same person as deputy governor of the three lower counties held only during the king's pleasure. Just how this view of the case could have been worked out in practice, had an attempt been made at any time to enforce it, is difficult to see, unless the king had seen fit to appoint a separate governor of his own for the

1. *Calendar Treasury Books*, XI, 313; *Colonial Records*, I, 534, 543.
2. *Calendar Treasury Books*, VIII, 517.
3. In 1696 the decision was reached that "the three lower counties and other plantations held in propriety by grants from the crown were subject to the acts of trade and other plantation laws, in like manner as are all the other of the English plantations." *House of Lords Manuscripts*, new series, II, 21.

colony, an appointment which was never even considered by either the Privy Council or the Board of Trade. The exact constitutional status of Delaware in colonial times is something of a problem in colonial history.[1]

In determining the factors that were influential in shaping English settlement in America, I have limited my field of observation to the period from the founding of Jamestown to the overthrow of the proprietary governments. Though in the case of the Carolinas, the Jerseys, and Pennsylvania pursuit of the subject has carried us into the early years of the eighteenth century, it has in the main confined our attention to the century before. Even in Maryland and Pennsylvania, which remained legally proprietary down to the Revolution,

1. In 1734 Charles Lord Baltimore revived Maryland's claim to the three lower counties in a petition to the king, asking for an explanatory charter confirming to him and his heirs the whole peninsula, contained within the circuit of the charter of 1632, notwithstanding the *hactenus inculta* clause. The Privy Council, August 8, 1734, referred the matter to the Board of Trade. In rebuttal Penn's sons wrote the board reasserting their title. The next year, January 9, 1735, Quakers of the counties, informing the board that there were several thousand Quaker families in the territory, likewise petitioned against Baltimore's attempt to recover the territory. The arguments can be followed in the *Board of Trade Journal*, 1728–1734, p. 409; *Acts Privy Council, Colonial*, III, §§241, 409; VI, §§439, 441; *Pennsylvania Archives*, XVI, which contains the Breviate (lawyer's brief or summary of the case); Matthews, *Resurvey*, pp. 169–175, 290–294. The controversy led to the famous chancery suit, which lasted from 1735 to 1750, and ended in the confirmation of a temporary line laid down in an agreement of 1732 (Matthews, pp. 163 to 166), which was destined to remain the accepted boundary until the final settlement in the years from 1763 to 1768, establishing the Mason and Dixon line.

For the final termination of Penn's claim to the three lower counties, see Judge Rodney's article, "End of Penn's Claim to Delaware," *Pennsylvania Magazine*, LXI, 182–203 (April, 1937). As early as 1788 the proprietors' agent, Edmund Physick, began the attempt to recover for the proprietors rights to all escheats and ungranted lands in Delaware and to such feudal dues as alienation fines and quit-rents due from the landholders there. Ejectment suits were begun, twenty-nine eventually, some of which were ended and new ones started between 1798 and 1812. In one case the Penns were nonsuited, but unfortunately on other grounds than the legal justness of their claim. The other cases were either abandoned or discontinued. Yet even as late as 1814 the heirs of Penn had not given up all hope of a settlement, but nothing further was ever done.

It is of great interest to follow the litigation that accompanied the final obliteration of the feudal claims of those proprietors who retained their titles to the soil down to the Revolution—the heirs of Fairfax, Granville, Penn, and Baltimore. For the Fairfax claim, see Groome, *Fauquier during the Proprietorship*, ch. X; for that of Granville, Connor, "The Granville Estate and North Carolina," *University of Pennsylvania Law Review*, 62, pp. 673–697; for that of the Penns in Delaware, Judge Rodney's article above. No satisfactory study has been made as yet of the claims in Maryland of the Baltimore family, as far as I know.

prerogative had little significance after 1689 and 1701, except as regards the ownership of the soil. It was during the seventeenth century, therefore, that the great work of settlement was brought to an end and a new period was ushered in of our colonial history. Other colonies were to come, on the mainland as well as in the West Indies, but none of them represent, as do those whose careers we have traced, the operation overseas of the major forces making for English expansion. The final settlement of Nova Scotia, the founding of Georgia, the bringing of peace and order to the Bahamas, the attempts to populate and administer the Floridas, and the occupation of additional islands in the Caribbean—all belong to a later and a different era, when England, in a new commercial and colonial mood, possessed of widening ambitions and confronted by dangerous continental rivals, was endeavoring to regiment her colonies and to bring them all within the bounds of a centralized control.

Even in writing about the seventeenth century I have made no attempt to render the colonial story entirely complete or to round it out either chronologically or geographically. I have wished to do no more than interpret the peculiarities and characteristics of the colonies with which I have dealt, to explain the divergencies of their beginnings, and to point out certain features indicative of their efforts to break down the religious and political conservatism that resulted inevitably from the circumstances of their settlement. One important object in so doing was to link up the colonies more closely with the land of their origin and to show how impossible it is to understand their history unless we understand that of England also. Anyone writing comprehensively of the colonies must know of the changes through which the English constitution was passing during the century and a half before the American Revolution, of the temper and outlook of those who sat in parliament and held political office, and of the policies of the government and the reasons why such policies were formed. Otherwise we have at command but half the evidence from which final conclusions are to be drawn and the treatment tends to become isolated and provincial, limited to the history of but thirteen colonies and concerned solely with those features that anticipated the formation of our great Republic. Such treatment ignores the place that our colonies occupied in the larger world of England and the Continent.

As in our presentation we approached the end of the seventeenth century we found ourselves confronted, every now and again, in the case of nearly all the colonies, with certain new conditions that disclosed the presence in England of a policy of commercial and colonial management, a clear-cut purpose in process of definition at Westminster, Whitehall, and the Plantation Office. It is for us to discover what that purpose was. Before we can go farther in our analysis of conditions in America, it is necessary that we study thoroughly England's efforts not only to administer the colonies in the interest of trade and the revenue but also to adjust her commercial and constitutional relations with them in the interest of greater simplicity, smoothness, and efficiency. A detailed study of the subject from these angles will show how inextricably England's colonial objectives were bound up with the activities of thousands of the colonists engaged in the regular business of making a living. It will also show the defects and weaknesses of the English system of administration and its inadequate machinery for enforcing the orders and laws prepared by king and parliament with a view to making the colonies dependent on the crown. In short, such a study will build up for us a vital and impressive picture of the Anglo-American scene in the seventeenth and eighteenth centuries.

With a knowledge of what the English authorities were trying to do and why they were doing it we shall be better prepared to grasp the significance of the first fifty years of the eighteenth century of our history, which have been called hitherto the "neglected period." We must know something of the acts of trade and navigation, of the royal customs service and the vice-admiralty courts in the colonies; and in England of the establishment and work of the Board of Trade, of the attempted enforcement of mercantilist ideas, of the gradual formulation of a centralizing programme, and of the failure of the executive authorities in England to obtain the adoption of such a programme by parliament in the eighteenth century. Eventually it will be necessary to trace the constitutional status of king and parliament and to follow the shifting relationship that existed between the executive and legislative branches of the British government, before we can justly appraise the importance of the colonial assemblies in their struggle against the exercise of the royal prerogative in America and their resistance to other phases of British control. The inner meaning of the "neglected period" and the causes of the American Revolution cannot be determined by one who confines his investigation to the American field only.

INDEX